GW00374689

ON INTIMACY

A Forgotten Art

Julia Robinson

THIS BOOK CONTAINS EXPLICIT SEXUAL MATERIAL

THAT MAY OFFEND SOME SENSITIVE READERS

On Intimacy

Copyright © 2017 Julia Robinson

All rights reserved.

ISBN: 9781521723647

Independently published

*To Pallas Athena, the Melissae
and John Caron*

Traditional story tellers know it is a brave thing to tell a story
and just as brave to read or listen to it.
If we open to let a story affect us with the life it contains
we will inevitably see ourselves in the story itself.

Deep thanks to all the soft souls I have shared intimacies with – strangers, friends and lovers – who have opened up their inner temples to commune with mine, without whose openness this book and any emotional richness in my life would have been impossible. Extra incredibly deep gratitude goes to John Caron who encourages me to be who I am. Gulp.

All the stories in this book are real experiences. Names and places have been changed.

Contents

By Way of Introduction

Eternal

Is this flame eternal?
Is this wood eternal?
No but fire is.

While living in Greece I was pulled into the embrace of the Aegean School of Fine Art. One night we watched a distressing documentary, Agelastos Petra (Mourning Stone) by Filippos Koutsaftis. It was presented to us with her characteristic, erudite grace by the genius Euphrosyne, a dear friend of the school and also Filippos' childhood friend. The film exhales a delicacy that breathes an awareness into each step of how the ancient pilgrimage to the Apollo temple at Eleusis (22 k (13½ m) west of Athens) has been destroyed physically, emotionally and spiritually. One stretch has become impossible to walk due to a McDonalds's built directly over the pilgrim route making through passage impossible. In other parts, mechanical diggers mindlessly dig out foundations for cheap housing, only to discover ancient burial sites, while high rise buildings mock from above on high anything ancient below.

Local people whose humble lives gyrate around preserving the remnants of this delicate power, have been left jobless, hopeless, lifeless. The route was a pilgrimage that thousands upon thousands of people took over hundreds of years: layers upon layers of humanity interwoven into one shared journey of infinite experiences. So many souls have been intimately transformed by walking along this same ground which now holds nothing more than mindless activity appearing to do little more than destroy anything that lingers of the sacred.

The film's magic sensitivity evoked in us all the Wonder and Awe of the Greek Gods and their magnificent power to craft humanity. Sat on our plastic seats in the white high ceiling art studio we were gently lifted into the delicate finery of the Gods' ability to create such Grace and Beauty in the lives of any human psyche humbly striving to connect to, and venerate, that which is more than us, to that which is wordless, indescribable. The film was so intricately crafted that while simultaneously allowing us to feel this empowerment it also created in all a deep well of utter Despair at people, humans like us, mindlessly destroying all memory, all recognition of anything other than ourselves, as if intent on destroying anything that gives life any true meaning.

Meanwhile in Greek literature class we were reading the epic tale of 'Odysseus'. Within its magic I glimmered an image in which, at least for me, the Greek gods appeared to be that which is eternal within us. Happiness, for example, is

6

experienced presumably across most if not all human psyches, across time and space. We die, but Happiness continues jumping from psyche to psyche, nestled eternally in the collective. We as individuals are finite; emotions are Eternal. I began to see nebulous clouds of 'that' which connects us all.

Two-thousand-eight-hundred years ago Odysseus' son, Telemachus, walks disconsolate along the beach and calls in Pallas Athena, the goddess of Wisdom, Courage and War Strategy, and he is filled with her – with Heroic Endeavour – and is spurred on to begin his own long hero journey. Who are these gods? Could they simply be the Beauty and Grace that allow us to feel what it is to be beautifully and gracefully alive? Are they the Angst and Sadness that allow us to rectify our paths into a deeper place of dwelling?

I cycled home from the documentary, to my white-washed house, tears washing down my white-washed face. I was disconsolate. I saw face after human face pass through my mind, blank faces, faces fueled by depression, faces filled with fear, with numbness, with anything but Grace and Beauty. The Greek economy was taking its toll on the people. As my bike and I snaked through the little narrow lanes a voice inside my head asked, *what are we doing to the gods? What are we doing to kill off emotions that allow us to feel elevated, kind, full of love? Full of ourselves?*

I began to see how we are cutting ourselves off, not only from ourselves and our gods and goddesses but also from others with their own connections to their gods and goddesses. The picture is bleak: the breaking down of connections throughout the fibre of humanity, as if intimacy were but a dream someone once had that wasn't even us.

But surely intimacy is a place where, for a time, we shed our defences to allow ourselves to commune with another in the emotions that together we share? I have felt that the more we express of ourselves at our very depths, the more universal we become and the more we talk to everyone's heart of the one song that springs from the birth of humanity. Surely as we get closer to our origin we find our origin-ality to turn back to the world and express the universal in our own unique way, to share it, and allow ourselves to come alive? 'Original', not to be different, nor to stand out; but 'to express Origin': to express the timeless in our unique way – to express the gods.

And suddenly it seemed so clear: we are not just killing the gods, we are also killing ourselves.

How can we truly live if we are too afraid to feel? As I look around, I feel we all have – wherever we are, whoever we are – a yearning for greater intimacy. Plato said, 'Know Thyself'; perhaps intimacy – with ourselves, with others, with life itself – is why we are alive? But how to soak into ourselves like morning dew into grateful ground?

That night, as the early hours turned the sea into a giant pool of ink, I found myself in a Greek Taverna down by the sea front. It was nearly closing and being winter everyone but a straggler at the bar had gone home. I sat at a little round table allowing myself to feel caressed by my on-going love for the black-and-white tiled floor and asked my friend, the barman, for a half measure of ouzo from the barrel. My face was a mess after the hours of sobbing at home. I needed the ouzo, I said, to recover. Angelos smiled and handed me over the little glass gently declaring that it was on the house. Sat there in my memories I vowed – while dipping, baptising, a long forgotten engagement ring in the glass of ouzo – to give myself two years to write a book to help bring back the gods.

The River of Being

We are born into
an eternal conversation
which continues
long after we pass away.

A New Old Story

In this story
she is air borne
able to sink sublimely
into smoothed clay
deep inside toes and fingers
and a sensuous tongue.

In this story
fear is held
behind rusty garage doors
in greying hairs
that aren't hers
by bony knuckles
cradling a stubbled chin
intent on catching
alarmingly loud
weather forecasts
and the vaguely understood
shipping news.

In this story
fear is not falling in love;
I like this she says
finding her air caressed
in the castle arms of his soil,
my dreams come true
I am love and I am loved.

She says, and she is
and I say, 'Yes, give me that.'

PART I

Outside Is Inside - Being Intimate With Oneself

Delving into personal intimacy
that weaves in and out of a poem
written in 250 BCE.

Before Knowing You

I yearn to write lines of love
of you adoring something
so simple
as how I clean my teeth:
beholding me through the mirror,
my back resting on your fortress chest
my spare hand stroking
the warm forest arm slanting up
through the valley
of my well explored breasts;
a funny smile,
obstructed by the drawbridge of my toothbrush,
becomes four
as we marvel at how
we both see reflected
in the other's eyes
the flecks of life
glistening in our own.
Beautiful thoughts
bringing empty, stony echoes
into this chasm of lonely wilderness.

THE FOOL.

I walk through the valley of death, poetically, internally. You did it for real, in California, with your ceremony in the desert, allowing your beautiful high, your deep connection. Sunrise sees you drinking in the red of the sky after taking medicine. You. All alone. Beautiful you, young you, walking, lithe like, through the desert. Slithering snake. I bet you were naked. I imagine you in a space where god becomes like man for the sake of man and man becomes like god for the sake of god. In my mind you are a moving Greek myth bending to become a flower, to dance your minute delicacy around its giant stem as it grows dancing light into your heart.

And then eventually the come down, back to the tent, the winds picking up. Zipping up, coming in from all that expanse, faced with the confines of canvas, forced to go within in a different way, alone now, disconnected from that other world.

I remember being startled when Prof. Amador Vega said that the pain of being a god for a moment of eternity is in the return and realising we are not god: the pain of our humanity. I can see you, through time and space, sat back in your flayed human skin, raw rubbed by sand and sun, feeling denser now, separated from humanity. Feeling small now after the ever expansiveness of space, feeling the terrifying immensity of the skies suddenly so far away, sensing the beating heart of the world that had been so tangible before, now dimmed, hiding back behind the flowers. Brutally forced out of power, out of the expansion of being everything, to return to small.

I feel you aching for people not present. You are left only with You. Nothing but you and your beating heart, getting faster, and your drained energy seeping into a hard desert floor under a flimsy, dog-eared camping mattress, accompanied by nothing but your breath; wondering how long it will continue. When will it stop? How long is a night? Where will you go? The desolate desert winds mirroring your soul. Whirlwinds of thoughts bringing ramshackle fears into your dream world.

The void slowly opens her devouring orifice.

Under the twilight skies you desperately pack up, wind whirling sand into the crevasses of your skin, your gear, your soul, and you hike back to your little, fragile car. To drive. To calm the mind. Drive. Looking for friends. Drive. Looking for company, looking for anything but this emptiness. Drive. Hours of long straight highways, the dotted lines on the dusty road coming into the windscreen like stars in a space ship.

Zip

Zip

Zip

Zip

Zip

Zip.

Hypnotising yourself out of that dark fear, running, running, running away.
Wanting to know what it is all about, too afraid to find out.

—

You tell me years later, two decades later, mid forties, that you understood
something more. Before going into the desert you'd asked to know direction,
you'd asked to be shown what to do, who to be. You'd asked for guidance and it
had been given to you, if only you could have heard it: allow yourself to be
vulnerable, allow yourself to sit in nothingness, to be alone in meaninglessness.
Be brave and walk through the valley of death, alone in the dark of the deepest
night, without even the stars to guide your way; to have the courage to be alone
within yourself, to sit in the confines of that tent, to sit in yourself, and face the
screams, face the gargoyles of your fears and walk through them to the other
side; to withstand aloneness and the fear of being alive, to know that you can, so
as to never have to run away – ever again - so as to not base a lifetime on running
from fears, running from the nothingness, from crazily grasping onto sands of
meaning as they slip through your fingers and you scream for time to stop
running through your being.

But you didn't.

—

You tell me all this as I cry down the phone. I have been alone for so long; so
long I have been forced to make company only with myself: years of
meaninglessness, of non-producing, of waking day by day with nothing to do,
with no reason, drowning in the fear of worthlessness. How many hour-long
moments have I gazed through the glazed over glass of my windowed eyes, blank
walls my mirror, the aspects of my mind my only companions, forced into
conversations with the within?

I have developed relationships with trees, taking me to a place where seconds
take years, yet I am invisible because I move a billion times too fast. I move at
the speed of human, where I cannot see the immense beauty of their dance, for a
step takes one of my lifetimes. I have been dragged down, kicking and
screaming, into the beauty of presence, into my own beauty that comes up from
the presence of the world.

I scream holding onto my name, which dislodges off its hook. I want it to fit; I want my name for myself. I scream, a child clinging to a broken toy. Irreparable, this distance cannot be returned. I have stepped too far and seen too much to claim ignorance. I must continue.

Into Nameless, without body, without form, into where this one Being gives all the power to exist. The flower is my cousin, the moon my mother, in this loneliness I become all of humanity, leaving behind all that I am not.

My presence becomes unwrapped from its covers of meaningless meaning; my presence is allowed to breathe.

I am in the first breath. Is this a second awakening?

A baby breathes her first breath and timed with the stars, with the moon's gravitational pull, with the energy of the sun, becomes unique. When did I first breathe a second time? Who have I left to become who I always was?

Dionysus was born a second time out of a thigh.

Outside in the far distance I still have my body. I recognise the hand, but not the sensations. They are constantly birthing. Eternally anew. I think about all those times I do not recognise the details of my face in the bathroom mirror, new lines, my eyes constantly changing their vision. They staring into me, asking me to open as I cling still, afraid of presence. Why afraid?

I remember bliss. How many people have experienced it? Do the flowers live in it? Are we unaware of it like fish cannot see water? Would the flowers be shocked to feel what we humans want to feel, as we endlessly repeat fears, anger, jealousy in some vain attempt to control life and keep everything still. We seem to do anything but allow ourselves to see presence in the void of our hearts. Why do we struggle so hard to push away from all this meaninglessness and so blind ourselves to our true beauty, our own true selves? Why are we so unable to let go even as we are dragged through life backwards, clinging desperately onto the monstrous shapes of ignorant fears?

—

'I should have stayed in the tent', you say.

He who obeys Nature returns through Form and Formless to the Living,
And in the Living
Joins the unbegun Beginning.

I awaken to my presence, sat in this nothingness of a day, beside these white painted walls, behind the pane of glass, watching rain pour, watching trees dance; too still for any thoughts, emotionally exhausted, unable to feel, to think. I lie, my body a stone, as if on medicine. Movement zero.
I shudder. Is this death?

—

I shudder, panic, feel strangled by the close confines of the meaninglessness of my life. My mind screams suicidal thoughts in silence. I have no place to go. Birds soar; I feel my inescapable heaviness.

I can no more. I unzip this tent of self constriction. I leave my room and go walk in the rain.

—

The woods find me. Their boughs are the embrace that keeps me from madness. These are my family. I slink to their feet, feel wrapped in the curves of their trunk. In the out-breath I feel their green soothing. I slow down again, back into the rhythm of life.

I gaze.

This is beauty. Far away from an art gallery, I am surrounded by true art. I think of fairies. Moss green curves in the interplay of trunks and earth, the intricate work in the strokes of branches, interweaving patterns of delicate vision. My head is supported by a loving trunk, my body by sub-stance, by the mother of all. Matter matters. It is meaninglessness that is meaningless.

The joining is Sameness. The sameness is Void. The Void is
infinitive.
The bird opens its beak and sings its note
And then the beat comes together again in Silence.

I hear my breath, a river of calm, caressing my body, allowing air that was not me, to come in, what was not mine, to be touched by me, to be changed, to be warmed by my presence, to become me. I cannot hold onto this gift, but return it, return myself, to the one breath that moves the patterns between the branches.

At the end of one breath, a slight pause: I hear silence.

The next is quieter. Each breath dying down into a deeper place, softer, harmonious.

Until it would seem my body is so relaxed it is not breathing. I hear it from a distance. A complete openness in my belly to all that is, digesting silently as my presence plays communion with Presence.

I realise I am:

alive.

My body is vibrating, the heavy solidity lifting away.

My breath circulating freely, silently, lovingly.

I am balancing on the edge, becoming fully alive. All that I was only moments ago is dead.

I tingle. I am Joy.

I feel the tree, breathing into me. It kisses me.

I would stay here forever.

Nature and the Living meet together in Void.
Like the closing of the bird's beak
After its song.

Imagine if every human felt this…how life would change…I feel myself slinking down, opening.

I fall into a womb. Above I feel my body taking on all responsibility. I surrender. Once I get out of the way, my muscles unspring returning to their natural state. In this deeper relaxation, Peace flows.

It knows.

The psyche knows to heal itself.

When 'I' am not.

—

My lips smile

down here all makes sense.

A still sense of a soft diffused light called Love.

Why would I ever block this out?

Is this my presence? The presence nourishes me, gives me strength to show myself, to grow into my own, to shed my bark and become a supple nymph in the river of breath.

Peace seeps into my body, bones relax.

—

I sink further,

on the edge of being able to stay awake as I awaken to this:

nameless.

Letting myself become one with it.

All is foolishness, all is unknown, all is like
The lights of an idiot, all is without mind!

Fears push on my bladder. I know that old trick. It is not real.

To obey is to close the beak and fall into Unbeginning.

I fall into myself. Soft velvet.

Time dissolves, meaningless.

This is all there is, this is all I am.

As I become smaller, going further and further within to who I am, I expand out into all that Is.

Blissful nothingness.

———

Jaw softens

I feel myself as one

Swimming in the see-through-ness between inside and out, I remember myself.

I sink in my own simplicity.

How could I ever have forgotten?

———

Gentle.

Open.

Empty.

Time slows into the Eternal.

I am filled.

———

Through the silences I hear car, wind, birds, the rustle of animals. There is another world.

I don't want to return.

I feel the father, my thoughts, coming to pick me up from school…coming to take me back to the land of the living dead, to the meaninglessness, to words and ideas and the projections of mind.

I feel the bark of the mother softly push me onwards, telling me that I am. I can deal with living in her, in her material, I can deal with the hard flakes of deathful unconsciousness gnawing on the edges of words, I can deal with demons that fling themselves at me, my own or others. I can deal with it all.

I can separate with my sword of discernment, I have the protection of the father now, of feeling my presence, of the Spirit. All I need do is return and allow myself to be met, allow myself to be seen, only my own dragons can be dominated by me, only my own world can be healed by me.

I cannot heal anywhere else but in myself.

Thoughts are coming in faster now. Are they insight or poison?

I think of the minute doses of poison that can heal. I think of my responsibility to experiment into the right dose that is healing for me, that will open me up within and without, and also know the dose that will bring me down, into a world of depression, of becoming closed down, lost in self-referencing mind-stuff, of being closed in the circle. In-firm.

I am coming out of this deep wellness of being, back up to the dreaded surface.

I open my eyes. Breathe out deeply. Am greeted by green beauty. A balm for this deep wound I have again come out of. Seeking the healing, far within.

I stand shakily. Head rush. Knees ache from inactivity, I take a tentative step and continue onwards.

Cocoon

Inside
there is a place
full of light.
It strokes me back
into comfort
heals me.
Embalmed
in trust
I float in hope.

Too soon the ephemeral eternity
turns to dust in my hands;
I am left only with me.

*An experience of going into
intimacy and connecting to
other versions of ourselves.*

Our birthright

Divinity;
we don't know how to be
and yet we are.

When I catch up with my friends I tell them about him. Everyone I tell seems to love hearing our romantic story that is softly sculpting chapters in my heart: *Chance Meeting in Paradise, Rough Start, Passing the Test, Wild Sex, Falling in Love, Moonrise, Hearts Connecting, Poetry on the Plane Back Home.*

He writes: 'It's snowing here in Boulder. Soft and cold. Full heart.'

Abandoning my comfort zone, love opens a slit, wet and warm, into a greater being.

—

Orpheus, my singing trainer, advises me, with a gay swipe of a bent wrist, to expect nothing from this. He's been hurt in the past and doesn't want me to be hurt in the same way. 'Keep your expectations low. Protect yourself,' he says in a fatherly assurance. Sure, I think, we had four wonderful days. Sure we did. Nothing lasts forever.

I meander in my memories. I am swimming again into the setting sun, reliving the feeling of floating for an instance in pure harmonious alignment, merged with the entire cosmos as my sea-cold but relaxed body immerses as one into wave after wave of wondrous beauty, astonishing in the fact that I am part of it all – included. I swim through the undulating waves marveling at the myriads of awe inspiring patterns and realise: I too am bathed in this same light of the sun, I too am part of the whole, part of this dazzling display of Life.

I see the orange flickers on the crest of waves as the wake from my own breast-stroke interplays in the voluptuousness of nature embracing all that is. I am part of it all. I am nature. I am in this cold spring sea. I am. I see again how the Spring sun sets, only to be quickly followed by a full blue moon, and how Paul stood there, recovering from shivers on that cliff path and with both his arms stretched out tells me how a full moon will always rise at the same time as the setting sun.

I mull over my mental photo album of us walking back and me asking him if he has fallen in love, not realising I am projecting onto him what I cannot accept about myself. He stands there and showers me with an invisible vulnerability that is too evident to pretend I have missed. On that crumbling sandy step, I see him floating out from an awkward smile, his darting eyes resting in mine, as he timidly nods a, 'Yes.' And we kissed for the millionth time. We stood right by the sea's rippling waves, only just keeping our trainers dry and did a little ceremony launching wild flowers we had picked into the rippling water and making up poetic words to throw into the wind. It seemed so perfectly obvious as we snooped around a little house right on the edge of the water to see if we would like to buy it and live together happily ever after.

Four nice days.

Over.

Time to get real.

I nod to Orpheus. Yes, I think, he's right.

—

He writes: 'I think we should see each other again, I'm very sure of that. I'm not sure yet what the circumstances should be, maybe you could come to Boulder after your school is done?'

Come across? Just like that?

I have a life here, I have the choir, the art school, my little flat where I can look over the bay to the sea, where I can watch the Blue Star Ferry come in and out at the prescribed times and feel the reassurance of nautical clockwork. I can watch the activities of life in Paroikia down below as if watching child gods play at Lego village. Here I have the warmth of the Greeks and the people living on the island, of the air, the bougainvillea, the blue sea. The sea!

If I go I will miss the summer and the sea. I don't know anything about Boulder, CO. It is in The United States of America, that landmass I swore I would never go to again, full of insecticides and chemicals and all things false: the birthplace of present day capitalism, imagery and greed. I miss him so. I am trying so hard not to love him. I am trying so hard to forget. *This is crazy. Should I go?*

A week later, my brain can take no more of my heart pulsing into chaos. I am distracted too much to read, I cannot concentrate on translation work. I cry in choir rehearsal over *Lullaby Song* – twice. I have to leave the studio to recover. I cry into the sea while swimming under the empty crescent moon. I cry on the seafront with my friends over ouzo and chicken sticks. *Why all this crying? Go to the states? I don't know him! Four days. I miss him. He is wonderful. Maybe he is not wonderful.* 'What if he is an axe murderer?' another friend asks. I laugh, but it is not impossible. 'I've slept with him,' I say, 'surely I would know?' She shrugs. Right then it was impossible for her to know that six months later in her rented out flat in France, her heavily depressed friend would argue passionately over music with his friend and end up killing him with a kitchen knife. 'It happens,' she says dully.

Back on my terrace, by my beautiful little white washed flat, bare feet caressing the marble floor, my mind continues whirling. I look out to the horizon: flat, no waves. They are all inside.

Yes. No. Yes. No. NO! Yes, No. Maybe.

'AAAAAAAAAAAAAAaaaaaaaaaaaaaaaaaaahhhhhhhhhhhhhhhhhhhhhhhhhhhhhhhh hhhhhhhhhhhhhhhhhhhhhhhhhhhhhhhhhhhhhhhh!! !!!!!!!!!!!!!!!!!!!!'

I am alone. I know it. So I can: I can go there, wherever this is taking me.

I hear a vehement scream surging up through my bulging throat shattering the peace across the bay.

It is as if the scream coming out from my mouth, pierces through the bay, through the clouds, sending out an SOS to another, invisible reality. My mind is blank, numbed with fear, all I can do is hear this surprisingly loud scream. I am falling into it, becoming it.

I want to collapse. I want to fall under the enormous weight I am carrying in my aching heart.

In the midst of the screaming I look to the sky and say, *'Heeeeeeelllllppppppppp!!!!!! Pllleeeeeeeeeasssssssseeeeeee hhhhhhhhhhhheeeeeeeeeeeelllllllp!!!!', I sob, 'Show mmmeee out of my feeeearsaaaaahhhhhhhhhhhhhhhhhhhhhhhhhhhhhhhhh!!!!!'*

Tears are streaming down my face.

I feel a presence; as if there were a something on the other end of a piece of spaghetti, slowly sucking in an umbilical cord between us. It shortens closer and closer until that between us is nothing but our lips. I feel a loving presence wordlessly connecting to my soul, filling me with the courage to continue, to get through this. To keep going. I go back into peace. I am screaming but my voice is far, far away: inside I hear me as echoes at the end of a long dark tunnel. Deep inside I feel presence to presence; so very familiar. *Which one is me?*

In a blast of intuition I realise the other IS me, myself, from the other side. It is me. I am it.

———

In the crowded little tavern Patty and I are in our zone. I lean over the table, as if sharing a secret, there is a question in the air. 'Sometimes I believe,' I say 'sometimes' to not sound like a complete airhead, 'that in between lives, our souls realise, from the perspective of residing in that one white light, what it is that we didn't get, what we didn't realise in the last life, the thing that we need to continue growing as an entity, and sort of pick out a perfect next life for us to learn that lesson, to get through the blockage…' I'm embarrassed – I sound so new-age, so unscientific – but I can't get away from facing that I really do believe it.

'Like everything that happens to us is a gift?' says Patty. It used to be our mantra. For a time she swam laps and to get it into her psyche repeated it in her mind on every stroke. I nod uncomfortably. This is a hard one, it's easy to say when it's a matter of whether to go to the States or not for love, but Patty has just had a miscarriage. She looks at me, I can see in her dark almond eyes that she's been there too in her mind. I can see the same distant disquietude around her eyes that stare off into space, in the side of her soft words as she says, 'I don't know.'

—

Do we choose our life? Can we mould it?

—

I am sat in the auditorium. My favourite professor is giving a lecture on Symbolism. 'Plato talks of the river of oblivion. We wade through it and as we are born, an angel touches our forehead and we forget.' I listen, shifting a little in the uncomfortable university seats. I love Professor Raimon Arola. How to explain the simple? The simple is where the truth hides, for no-one looks there.

That little seed of life, that swam through the river of oblivion to enter into time, forgot all else to become me. I feel miniaturised in Awe.

—

I hear a story of a little three year old, whose parents bring home their new born. She insists on spending time with her new baby sibling. The parents keen to let them bond say, 'Yes, of course!'
'Alone!' she demands and will not give in.
The parents, wanting these first steps to be as harmonious as possible, come to the solution that they will turn on the baby speakers and leave her with her little baby sister for a few minutes, alone. Totally alone.

Through the speakers they hear her say urgently, 'Tell me! Tell me about God! I'm beginning to forget!'

—

I am sat in the little room she's set up to receive clients for Akashic Registers. 'Before you were born, or were anyone, it's as if all of our souls are in a space filled with white light. Your soul is very enthusiastic! When they ask, 'Who wants to do this?' You put your hand up, so to speak, and say, 'I will! I will!' You take on things almost to your limit, so that you are almost completely overwhelmed, so that you have almost taken on too much…' I nod. I know that feeling, the mouth of my psyche jam packed, having bitten off almost more than my life can chew.

Fall from Eden

Mental idea.
Easy to sketch out in my mind.
Psychological reality.
Material reality.
Dense.
Overwhelm.

I have no idea what path to take… either to stay here in my Greece, where hearts are open, where I am sun kissed, where I am close to art, or to fly and leave behind all this, to an unknown heart in a foreign land with someone I do not know, who I am feeling overwhelming emotions for. I call out. Panic. I am

24

facing the dark void…

As the scream gets louder, I feel a presence, a presence that feels as if it is me in the Eternal, the one who from above is choosing what is best for me before I am born. It is the me at the other end of the string of spaghetti where neither time nor timelines exist. In this space of psychic weakness nakedly unprotected without any of my separating walls of ego, without any logic showing me the path, without any emotions in place, I feel its closeness. I feel close to me, myself.

I feel sparkling light. I feel this other on the other side sending me love.

Inside of me, I feel myself landing, everything is light, the heavy weight is lifting.

I feel myself being wrapped in a comforting sense of wellness: everything is going to be OK.

Back through the heart

Angst riding my body
I wonder how on Earth
I will get through this.
Stewed in despair
I am reduced
to pleading;
I call out to someone
somewhere, nowhere,
'Help! Guide me!
Quell my fears!'
I feel a comforting presence
as if a telephone line
were shortening to nothingness,
a golden cord being taken within
by two lovers sensually
sucking in a string of spaghetti.
Face to face we kiss
sensing the other is I, myself,
in a higher form:
a re-creator of idea into
the dense mundane matter
of this my life.
It is I myself
at the other end of eternity
giving me courage to keep continuing.
I myself
who has constellated all this,
with my own loving essence
to help me remember.

In the film Interstellar the main character, Cooper, goes into the fifth dimension. He floats in the immaterial, on the other side of the wormhole, on the other side of space. Trying to communicate with the physical on the other side, he sees himself, sees his daughter, sees all stages of time merged and unmerged.

I slowly float out of a meditation and remember *I am in a room.* To my dismay, I discover the legs on my body have gone to sleep. It probably happened a while back.

Cooper is floating, through all of the time combinations of his daughter in her room. He tries to communicate to her through the membrane of worlds colliding. She feels it, she feels his energy, she knows it is not a ghost. She knows it is love. She doesn't know it's her daddy, because her daddy is also in her time, right now, somewhere in the next room. Space and time are doing strange things. When she returns as an adult, decades later, to that same space, back to her childhood room, her father is not present in her perception of time but he is still there, behind the membrane, she can still feel it. No time has passed for him since she was a little girl. He is still there where time has become irrelevant.

From her perspective only anger fills the echo he left behind. To her he is well gone – years lost in space. But she feels that same presence she felt as a kid: the familiar feelings of someone who loves her. Now she knows it is her daddy communicating. The same ghost as her childhood, existing in a different time, existing out of time. She knows because she loves him. She knows because she still feels his love. The way he loves is tangible in the air. She knows because she trusts.

—

Sometimes in the midst of a vacuum, as I am being whirled into a wormhole and am losing touch with stability, when the world has become totally chaotic and I cannot cope and I feel like I'm going to die in too much psychic tempest, instead of screaming I hang on desperately to a memory of Trust. As I sink inwards feeling myself rushing into the eye of the storm the Lighthouse of Trust holds me from spinning out – and there, deep within I am delivered into a presence of calm. I feel love. It feels like me. A 'me' I can't be yet.

Feeling presence

I know about love
the way a field knows about light
the way a tree grows
through twists and turns of time.
I know about how I feel
when I hug a trunk tight
wishing it were you
yielding to
this presence
inside,
me, but not me.

On my way out to the movie, keys in hand, I see the oat biscuits and think, 'I'll pop those in my bag, maybe I'll want them later.' If we don't get going we'll miss the start of the film.

—

Mercè is a friend who is so dear to me that I have no idea where to place her in my family tree. She started the masters course and dropped out, too wise, too experienced to be able trust many of the professors' overextended egos. She is a woman who I can fly with – our minds so similar – that we go through territories that are at the same time familiar and strange, well trodden and virgin, and always with a sense of inspiration as if we had uncovered ancient mysteries to open into our brand new world.

Mercè

We wrap our hands around coffee mugs
and light up forbidden cigarettes
in cowboy imitations
of freedom and campfires,
our minds forming
smoke dances together
as we venture through the numinous
in joyous tandem flights
sharing so deeply of ourselves
that invisible bridges
recreate us from within.

Happily exhausted
surface logic kicks in:
we belly laugh
suddenly seeing ourselves
in such stark brightness
and abandon ourselves to
the exhilaration of
pressure release.
Feet on the ground
we marvel over our finds:
brand new truths
unearthed back from antiquity
that in the light of day
simply crumble in our hands:
eternity a wisp on the tip of our tongues
ephemeral once more;
so instead we talk about
what to have for lunch.

Once, up on the Costa Brava, Mercè and I made this massive theory that encompassed time and space and energy and matter. We were stoned. Fortunately we recorded the whole thing on her phone. We were talking for hours inside which, time stopped ticking. We floated through space, lying on the little grubby hotel room bed while the other Jungkies were having a siesta. We flew through space as we talked about how we contain all the versions of who we are.

'Because the me that is talking is not the me that was talking, right here, in this same space but five minutes ago.'
'Claro!' she says in Spanish, 'We're not the same ever, but we contain all that we are. Inside of me is the little girl Mercè, the little boy Mercè, the child within, the adolescent, the adult, the wise, the stupid, the aggressive, the peaceful Mercè,' she looks out, waves her arms around, 'the old Mercè who is about to die. In me are hundreds of me. All competing to be in the driver's seat.'

We laugh. I laugh dangling between worlds: it is absurd, it is real, it is maybe. She looks me in the eyes straight, unflinching, 'I hold conference,' she says, softly sharing a deep secret, 'It's a diplomatic democracy, everyone gets to vote.' I love her. She has natural blonde hair, looks like a Swede, but is Catalan through and through. She is vibrant, it shines through her light filled blue eyes, and through her goofy white teeth. I simply love her. True, true. 'Each Mercè has a different posture. Each conducts energy differently depending on how we sit, or stand or where I put my shoulders.'

We marvel together over the fact that we are changing every second. She says 'I've been working on how we can hold and channel different constellations of our different parts simply through our postures.' We start messing about, playing at postures. I love this feeling of being so free. We sit upright, slightly tense, hands on knees. 'What do you feel?'
'Nice little girl…'
'Yes, me too!'
'You do something!' I laugh.
She stands, chest out, taking up space. I copy. 'No one fucks with me.'
'I'm like, policewoman-in-control, got-a-gun-if-I-need-to!'
It's my turn again. She looks at me, 'What are you going to do?'
I sit on the bed, legs slightly open, one arm taking my weight behind me, the other hand holding my slightly cocked chin. I feel into it. She does the same. We feel inside of ourselves, what is this posture saying?
'Come-over-here-lover-boy!'
'¡Si señora!'

We are acting out postures and finding how amazing it is that we each feel such similar sensations in similar postures. We try the hysteric, 'I-need-attention-right-now,' and the standoffish, 'Executive-woman'. Shoulders change places, backs bend and straighten, legs are closed or open.

Soon we are laughing all over the place doing different sexual positions for different energies: the nun, the bitch, the go-getter, the-timid-but-don't-leave-me-behind posture. It is actually quite amazing how the feelings in each posture are completely different. It is equally amazing how our feelings seem to coincide over what postures our bodies are talking.

We lie on the bed laughing, panting slightly, staring at the ceiling. My head is on her arm. Why do we not laugh this hard more often? I feel like I am in a *Thelma and Louise* film. The freedom is intoxicating.

'Bueno, escucha a esta Nena,' she says besides my ear, 'whenever I get onto my moto I sit in the posture of driver-in-control. I sit back, right on my rump, shoulders back, arms out, hands firm on the handlebars and I know that I am in control. I am Mercè-the-safe-driver.' I imagine her getting on her bike on the corner of Vilamari and Sepulveda. It's where I also get onto my Vespa outside her house often exhausted but elated after talks just like this.

'One day,' she continues 'I'm sat back on my bike and a car comes along while I'm just coming up to a red light, the driver changes lane without looking and knocks me off my bike. I fall, roll over the road, and get up. I stand up, brush myself down, pick up the bike and sit back in my position. I'm not hurt, I turn around to him and say sternly, 'Be careful, you could have really hurt someone driving like that!' and drive off.' We laugh. I can feel the mattress underneath us like a trampoline. 'I'm convinced it's only because I was in Mercè-Moto posture that I didn't get hurt.'

—

I am jumping slightly, feet shim-shimmering over the ground, wanting to dance out my message, 'Guess what just happened!' I beam out, 'What?' he laughs, ready for the good news. 'I just sold two books in Innisfree!'

'Well done you Miss Poet of the year to be!' My chest comes out as I walk to him. I feel myself expanding into the possibilities of all that I am. I kamuzle into his outstretched arms and we kiss, hugging, dancing, nearly falling over. Mouth buzzing as laughter bubbles up again.

—

So in this time and space thing, Mercè and I continue with our theory as to where we can connect to our other-selves within ourselves through a sort of wormhole. If we make the same posture putting our bodies into the same shape as the original posture when we had the original idea or sensation it really helps. We can go into that place in our minds – into the fifth dimension if you want to sound pompous – and go to a situation and see the people involved in them, see the different perspectives of each person, and send them love, showering them with white light. Heal.

—

I come out of the film and glide into the toilets, holding myself through my tears. I can't cope any longer. Overwhelm. I close the door, lock. Sit on the toilet and feel myself as if suffocating, breathing out for air. Overwhelm. My breath is fast, it only gets to my chest. Steam train breath. Toilet cubicle. I cup my hands, blow into them as if trying to blow into a paper bag, or a balloon, just like my mum told me to do. I am eleven, in the school toilets. Overwhelm.

—

I speak to Mercè over Skype. She is sweating from the Spanish summer, I have my jumper on in the English summer.
'¿Sabes? I've always had this arthritis in my hand?'
'Yes, that's why you have plastic plates…'
'Si! So it got so bad that I couldn't bring my fingers together…'
She puts her hands up to the camera to show me how it was. I feel an upsurge of emotion, wanting to protect her, wanting her not to suffer. I stay still, listening to her; listening to my emotions too.

'So I go to the Filosomatica course in Italy and we are put in pairs. The facilitator says that we are going to be given the opportunity to investigate the source of a problem in the body. So, of course, I chose my hands.'
She has the blinds half way down, to keep out the sun. Her walls are painted orange. I associate so many good times with the colour of those walls.
'I go into a relaxed state,' she says, 'a sort of hypnosis, but it isn't, just deep, deep…you know?'
'…like total relaxation…?' I ask,
'Aha…and I brought up the situation, I already had an idea of what it could be.'
Me too. It's not a secret that Mercè started to remember only a few years back about family abuse that started when she was four. 'And I felt it, I felt into it, and saw with compassion. Compassion is such a big tool for me at the moment.'

I look through Skype to her and love her. I am empty letting her pour in. 'And I see myself and the other. And then I had to try and send white light, it was really hard. Really hard. But I did it…I managed it. I managed to send white light into the situation…' she pauses, swallows, she is ready in anticipation, 'and now look!' Her hands go to the camera, fingers touching thumb.
'Wooooow!!' I am genuinely amazed. I know how she couldn't close her fist. I lived through it. That was years ago.
'But you know my first response to a closed fist?'
'No.'
'I can protect myself now…'

I see how time folds, going backwards, going forwards. It looks lineal on a piece of paper, but when it folds it becomes the same point. Like C.G.Jung said about life being a line connecting two dots, but eventually we realise it is actually just one and the same dot.

—

I am on the sofa in the psychologist's office. This is what one does in America. Shirley is the bestest. I love her. She is just really, really brilliant. I have never met a human being like her. She can read me, and my energy, and she is showing me how to manage it better, how to start to feel myself in my energy space.

Shirley says, 'A great way of bringing the energy into your life is imagining the feelings you want to reside in. It's the feeling that we really want, so imagine yourself sometime in the future feeling gratitude. No image necessary. Feel yourself feeling Gratitude for everything that has happened, Gratitude for everything that has got you to where you have got to.'

We close our eyes.

It feels so good. Thank you so much. My body is brighter, lighter, more expansive. I feel it connecting with the earth on my seat, on the soles of my feet, the rest is floating in a soft intense light, feeling peace, feeling good, feeling full of gratitude for life. I am alive! Happy! Well!

The expansive feeling glides further through my relaxed muscles, into a greater space, smiling.

Thank you.

I feel as if I am nothing but a smile.

The tip of the leaf of a hologram of a rose holds all the information of the whole of the rose.

Expanding Outwards

When we laugh
I feel it in me:
a golden glow
hailing from
the cosmos.

I drag my existence to Bristol University to help my friend Marieke with her PhD study on Consciousness. I met her on a Vipassana day retreat. She needed people who had meditated for more than 5 years. It made me feel special: at last I'm well qualified for something that is important to me.

I turn up with suitcases. It is a bit embarrassing and I admit that things didn't work out at my brothers. I have no contacts here in England. I know no-one and I'm in culture shock. This is my homecoming after being away for fifteen years. I have managed to bag a bed at a kind soul's house who I have only met twice before. I am going for two nights, and after that I have no idea where I am going to go. I have one thread: in two days a Hakomi course starts in London that I have already paid for. How to get there? Where to sleep? My left eye keeps twitching, it feels like it is my whole body.

I feel proud to have got to this interview. We've had it planned for some time, had to change it a few times. It was now or never.

I wanted to do it. It seems crazy to do it right now, when I should be in absolute panic. But it is actually just what I need: it is grounding. Thank you Universe.

Thank you for giving me this hour or so of respite where I can pretend I am not homeless, but simply a person in an interview, nothing but a meditator.

I slip into this psychic warm bath and forget what it means to be Julia right now in the crazy scary world and simply be Julia in a PhD interview about meditation.

We meditate for half an hour together. Her telephone sounds Tibetan bells and we open our eyes.

As my eyes accustom to the light I remember we are in her office. I am feeling so good: peaceful and relaxed. I always go deeper when I meditate with another.

She asks me if there was anything of note to tell her about the meditation, any event that stood out.

There are many. I don't know what to choose from, so I just say the first one that comes into my head: 'I felt tension in my stomach.'

She asks me lots of questions. Lots.

Her words are impregnated with deep care and kindness. She is like a hen listening for chicks in her eggs. Sending warmth.

I describe my sensations in minute detail, and eventually I come to an image. 'And what kind of image?'
'It was those mice in, *Who Moved My Cheese.*' I wonder if that's the right translation. 'Have you read it?'
'No.'
'There are two rats, the two humans are dead because they didn't expect any change, they doggedly thought that everything was fixed and that they had cheese forever. The two mice are cleverer and noticed the change and go out looking for new sources. They find a lake of milk and get stuck in the middle of it…they can't get out…there is nothing but horizon. They fear drowning in it. One mouse gives up, stops moving, sinks to the bottom, dies; but the other, without any reason to believe, continues to trust, against all odds, and keeps treading milk, and finds it getting more and more solid. It turns into butter…the mouse has churned the milk into butter and can walk over the top of it back to a more solid reality.'

It takes a lot longer to explain than to see the flash.

I really would not have remembered this if it weren't for her questions. I would have jumped over it – just not thought about it – not given it any real meaning. But now suddenly I realise that it is a message from my deep unconscious, a place where there are no words, just symbols, images, 'Keep going,' it is saying, 'don't give up, you are fine. Right now it feels like there is no answer, nothing but unobtainable horizon, but there are other dimensions out there, other possibilities that you just cannot imagine from where you are. Just keep going.'

With Marieke I feel like I have just gone down a level of fractal awareness into a greater dimension of consciousness. As if a secret garden were opening up to me in front of my inner eye, full of wonderful green leaves and colourful fruits and flowers. I feel as if I am communicating with myself.

I feel somehow that I am being guided into a deeper meaning to all of this. I don't say so. I am too shy.

'And then? Did anything happen afterwards?'
'Yes!' I do remember something, 'I felt the knot in my stomach loosened a little.'
'How did it feel?'
'As if it were a knot that was not so knotty any longer, and an expansion, like an energy release.'
'How did you sense that?'

I am right in that space where imagery is more adept than the word. I am swimming in images. I am excited. This is the first time I have ever spoken about this level of experience that is, after so many years of meditating, becoming familiar to me. 'Well, it is well…erm….' I have no words. 'It was like an explosion of release of pent up energy.'
'And how did you experience that explosion of release of pent up energy?'
'Like, erm….well…it's…like concentric rings coming out from a point right here,' I point to my stomach, 'and expanding in waves…like those pictures of nuclear bombs exploding…I'm not sure how that fits in, it is the opposite of destruction…but like…' My hands are both on my stomach now as if they were holding a big tennis ball and then move out as if an explosion, 'like, erm,' I move my hands backwards and forwards rapidly…'it's not like this, but this is the nearest I can get.'

I realise, for the first time, that I have been observing my energy field for years. I hadn't realised. I hadn't realised that I could. I didn't know I had that talent, that gift.

'Thank you so very much!' I say to Marieke at the end. 'I am amazed how detailed it all is. I am amazed how much detail there is in such a small segment of a meditation. It's amazing. How long were we talking?'
She smiles, delighted, she is a deep introvert with quiet, kind, beautiful energy. She smiles sunshine. This was her first interview. I'm glad it was with me. I feel honoured to have helped her through this hurdle in her PhD. 'About an hour, I timed it.'
'Wow, we were talking for about an hour about something that took about 5 seconds to happen!'

She somehow showed me how if we stop going so fast through time, and mine down on just one incidental experience, we can uncover all the information that exists about ourselves, in that coordinate of time-space. We can access information about that particular posture that we are holding, the posture being either physical or mental, about that particular constellation of Julia(s) that existed in those five seconds.

If we go slow enough everything, everywhere, is a secret garden that leads to other worlds, smaller, subtler, simpler.

Sinking into Self

I find the strength
to harness my mind
to go into (just) one:
open to be awed
I deepen, seep, slow down
into more juice
into deeper nourishment
through one of
a million gates
down into...

I gaze out of my little room that overlooks the trees in the Dartington Estate, and fall into wonder. Sat still, mentally and psychically I swim in the peace of nothingness. I am so much happier here than in Bristol. I have space to wonder, space for non-doing, time to open up.

I meander around the idea that as we stop repressing our emotions with our minds, in the space opened up, a past situation arises, a situation that is ready to come out, like a splinter in the skin of a thumb. I begin to realise how much I believe that we hold memories inside of us, like a knot.

I also realise that I am beginning to seriously believe that when I remember a situation quite clearly, when I remember how it felt to be alive in it and send love and white light and compassion to all those involved, when I bring in a greater, more expansive perspective distanced by time to the Julia that is manifesting in that moment, then I am healing the past.

I am healing present patterns too. I believe, even though the cynical part of my brain scoffs a little, that this is time travel. I believe that we can send love to our past selves, to my past Julia's, and that we can send and receive love to and from our future selves, my future Julia's. I believe that there is no past or future. But my logical brain scoffs again, points out the wrinkles around my eyes.

But I do believe it. I just don't know it.

Deeper in, not further along

Find the Eternal
in the here, now
for there is nothing
outside time.

When I was little I loved Paddington Bear. I had the wall paper, I had the bedspread and the pillow case and I had the Paddington Bear pump bag. I hung it with pride outside the infant two class. I was five and a half and a bit.

I remember very, very clearly, a time when once my brother had gone to sleep, I felt my teddy bear being alive. I knew it. I remember KNOWING that there was life in Big Ted. I shook him, 'Wake up! Speak to me! I know you exist!'

Three decades later, I lie in the posture I lay as a little girl. I go into the image of me as a little girl. I lie flat with my arms in a cross across my chest so that if I die in my sleep Jesus will know that I am a Catholic and will let me into heaven. I breathe in peacefully and calmly. I calm my mind. I observe my breath calming. I see the teddy bear right beside her head. I send my little Julie love. Is that the life she felt in Big Ted?

Am I going bonkers? It doesn't feel like it, it feels as if I'm getting saner.

—

We are driving back from Interstellar. I am reconnecting back to being me, Julia, in a car, living on planet Earth. Simple. I am exhausted. I need sugar. 'God I could do with something sugary – that was really heavy! I need to ground.' I suddenly remember, a loving soul put oat biscuits with bits of raisins in my bag.

We get home. Joseph turns off the engine. We don't get out, not right now, because I've not quite finished getting to the point. We've driven the long way round just because we like being in the car together. 'So if there are a lot of Julia's in me, existing concurrently now, I can actually access them. The old Julia in the 'future', the adolescent Julia, the Julia who was screaming in Greece and felt like she was communing with a loving presence….et cetera, et cetera – and I can send her love. So I think all the emotion in the film WAS necessary, actually!' Which was his opening gambit, 'Too much emotion for me,' he'd said. 'If not,' I conclude, 'to me nothing else makes sense.'

We get out of the car and continue talking over the top of the car's roof, I say seeing only his shoulders and head, 'It's like when Anne Hathaway says that love is the only thing that we can understand that goes through time and space, apart from gravity and something else.' Joseph looks at me in the crisp night. I just have to get this out before we end our chat, 'Carl Gustav Jung said that Eros is the only thing that humans are conscious of that extends further out than human consciousness.'
'Really?' says Joseph into a sort of suspended silence.
We laugh. I think I gone and done a right old overkill.

I flop into bed. Lean over awkwardly and turn off the little light. The film has made me feel so alive, so full of excitement, so full of images of travelling through space, travelling through time, of black holes, of the power of love. Though part of me wants to jump up and down on the bed, I lie still, trying to ground, trying to relax.

I lie there and go into the memory, that re-cord[2], of me in Greece screaming mental chaos over the bay. I'm looking from a higher aspect of time, feeling how over the two years the relationship with Paul has grown so beautifully between us. 'It is OK,' I want to tell her, 'Paul is a wonderfully deep, sensitive being: kind, generous, loving. It is OK to go.'

It really was good for me to go to the United States, to follow my heart, to learn all that I have learnt with him over the last two years. It was so, so good for me. From this place – of higher understanding, of ad hoc wisdom, of seeing how the fibres of my life have spun deeper colours since the decision to say yes to Paul after only four days of loving him, of taking that risk and catching a plane to the other side of the world – I see that it really is a good decision for the Greek Julia to take, it really helped me on my path to knowing myself more. I am so full of love, for me now, for me then, for Paul.

I lie there, full of compassion for the Julia in Greece who is screaming in front of the dark hole of a wormhole. I send her my knowledge that going to the States is a good decision; I send her that deep feeling of peace that will give her the bravery to continue. I fill the image of her with soft sparkling light. I send her my love.

Forgetting

I don't remember
from before I forgot:
Plato's river obliverated[3]
by the angel's soft touch
on my new-born forehead.
I don't remember
being discarnate
and floating in amongst –
without this fear
without this angst
without being made from ribs,
and the conflicts
of this, my brain.
I don't remember.
But I believe I fell willingly
into this darker space
where time speeds
and experiences years
as they slowly carve lines
into the crumbling dust
around my eternal eyes.
I sense it,
but can't remember.

And then there is you
a portal to somewhere
somewhere that is
not here,
not now,
somewhere where we
are in our nature:
properly close.

The magic of changing our inner skies and
so creating a knock on effect for butterflies
on the other side of the world.

Changing underneath

Her presence shocks
I feel explosions of sensation,
transporting me into
her parallel world
where colours
dance in dimensions
unknown at home.

'A job has a vibration to it.'

Shirley looks across to me, eyes full of soft warmth, 'it is not necessarily anything to do with CVs, it is to do with the vibration that you emit.' She pauses. 'You will attract the job with the vibration that you hold.'

I believe her. I have paid her a lot of money to believe her. It is a silly trick, but it works. It hurts to pay her. But I do and I want it to work. I believe that I can write. I believe that I can make money from writing.

I leave Shirley's office and decide that I am worth spending money on for food. I go to a burger joint. Afterwards, while digesting, I write a poem. I want to know what it sounds like and whisper it into my closed hand. A woman, who has been sat opposite me the whole time, engrossed in conversation with her friend, is suddenly alone.

'Are you doing school work?' I am used to this. She means University. I left 20 years ago.

'No,' I say, pleased with the compliment, 'I am writing a poem.'

'Ohh that's lovely.'

'Here's…' I say, rooting around the rapidly expanding black hole in the universe of my bag all the while keeping eye contact with my new prey, 'a book that I've written.' I feel a familiar corner and yank, *'Paros Poems*, it's an island in Greece where I used to live.' I pull the said treasure and out of the void into the light shining off the metal table.

'Ohh' she says, 'but no thanks, I'm not interested.' Her friend comes out from the toilet.

'This girl,' she says to her relieved friend, 'is writing poetry.' I still have my book out on the table by the *Fancy* tomato ketchup.

'This is my book,' I say, embarrassed to feel my unscrupulous salesperson taking over.

'I'll have one,' she says reaching into her purse. And just like that she buys it. This is the first sale in months.

Half an hour later she comes back and in a hurried, secret tone says, 'I have a story that I need writing.' I look at her as if as if she were a messenger from the gods. 'And I will pay you for every word.'

———

I tell Shirley about the 250 dollars the woman gave me for writing her story. We sit buoyed on an air of congratulatory co-creation. Flying in this dizzy freedom of spirit I soon crash up against my fear of returning to England.

'You know,' I say, embarrassed to be so fearful after her magnificent lesson on attracting energy into our lives, 'I've been away for fifteen years…I don't know what to expect.'

'What is it that you are worried about?' she asks.

'Like where will I live? But more so, how will I pay for it? England is so expensive. It's not like Greece, or here staying in Paul's house. I don't know how I will survive. I have no support system. No friends who I can call on. I…' I don't have any imagines, just an overwhelming feeling of dread.

'Remember how we connected with gratitude a couple of weeks ago? It's the same principle. Imagine what it is that you would like, just go within and see it, attract it into your field.' I close my eyes. 'And when you do – feel gratitude and light and love being with that image.'

I try to do it, but I can't do it. I am too afraid. Too afraid that I cannot support the image of a little cottage with a garden and a river flowing at the end of the garden. The cottage on the corner of my imagination feels claustrophobic. I don't know how to make it feel bigger. I don't know how I could ever pay for even this small cottage. I don't know. I… 'I can't do it.' My chest collapses.

'?' Shirley asks with her kind eyes and honey silence.

'It's just that all these fears come up, and…' *Money? Human company? Water leaks? Jobs? Washing machines? Where will I buy food? How will I buy food? Car?* 'What if my imagination doesn't yet have the ideal solution that actually exists for me? What if I block what actually is, imagining something else that isn't actually good for me?'

'I get you. I go through similar things.' I breathe a sigh of relief. 'So, instead,' she says sat in her beautiful chair, surrounded by big pot plants, 'imagine yourself by a river of time, you are looking backwards from where you are, grateful for all that has transpired to get you to where you are. Bathe in white light, in gratitude for what has brought you to where you are. No need to imagine anything; just let the gratitude and the light fill up your body for living in a beautiful place, for finding peace.'

———

I am riding into town along the river path. I am now in a completely different country and a completely different time. This is England, nine months after being in Boulder. I live in a wonderful 'pad', it is perfect for one. It found me through one of my friends in the funk band that we both play in. It is one big space, with a split level for the bed. Its high ceiling and big windows give a wonderful space to feel free in.

White walls highlight the beautiful triangular wooden beams and I love the feel of it as the really big window at the end makes it look like a chapel. I often lie in bed looking out through the windows into the garden. If you walk along the adjacent farm field, over the Steam Railway tracks, you come across the River

Dart meandering down through the tree lined valley that four miles or so below will flow past the township of _____, Devon[4]. I could not have imagined it. I love it. And it is affordable.

This is a different me now. I am living in a part of the world that is hobbit country. The bike that I have manifested for free into my life is wonderfully old. The frame is a gorgeous sit-up-and-beg Mary Poppins style. It's super cool because it's original from years back – the style that trendy new bikes try to imitate. I love it, even though when I ride it, the clunks and clicks and whirring noises are more like a brass band warming up than a serious street vehicle.

I corner a beautiful spot on the river and as I am admiring the flow of the water down the river the peddles suddenly don't engage with the back wheel.

—

'Well,' he says in the middle of the industrial estate, 'the back [technical word that sounds familiar and reminds me of my dad] is broken.'
'Could I fix it?' I plead.
'You could, the part isn't expensive, but unfortunately you'll need a new chain, and you've also got the time worked on it. You're looking at 50 pounds.'
It has one front brake, the other is broken. 'Is it worth it?'
He looks uncomfortable, as if I've just asked him, 'Are you a human being?' and he doesn't know if it's a joke or if I'm slightly mentally deranged and could be dangerous.

—

'Sorry I'm late,' I say, panting – I've just run part way up the hill past the castle – 'my bike broke.'
'Oh that's horrible. Flat?'
'No, it's worse than that.' I say quickly, 'I think it's dead.'

I am in hyper-alert mind. I can only focus on minute detail. She asks me where I want to go. My mind and I have both got stuck on the broken cog. I am unable to come up out of my vortex of bikelessness. *How will I get home?* My brain cannot compute choice of local places to relax with tea accompaniment or anything at all other than the cog on the back wheel and how this is going to affect my life in every minute way. A normal conversation right now feels like a mountain away. And I don't have a bike to get there.

'I can't concentrate. I'm sorry, I'm not really here, suddenly with the bike broken everything's changed.' I stare at the medieval black beams on one of the buildings over the road. Everything is different. My internal map has to shift. My house is suddenly a long way away. I'm not sure how I'm going to get there. I'm not sure about tomorrow and timings. *How will I move about?* My plans are suddenly obsolete. I don't know how to get a new bike. *Where from? How? With what money?* It's like a tiny little cog that I didn't know was so integrally part of my life has suddenly changed absolutely everything within it.

—

Change a bit of the whole and the whole changes.

—

'Be the change you wish for the world,' says the Sticker of Gandhi around Paul's water bottle.

—

We are sat at in the Plaza de Gracia. It's a lovely autumn day, and I have my favourite Sherlock Holmes style hat on because it is just cold enough now. This is where Dubie and I first met; the day she handed me the keys to her flat so I could stay there. Just like that. She'd seen me for fifteen minutes. But she'd seen me more than anyone probably ever has, just in those glances across the table.

We know each other well now. Sometimes too well. I'm telling her what Osley told me fifteen years ago. 'Get a hologram of a rose. Cut it in half.' She twiddles with her sunglasses. 'You don't get a rose bud and a stem, but you get two half sized roses. Cut it in four, you get four roses. In eight, eight roses, in sixteen, sixteen roses, thirty-two, sixty-four, a hundred-and-twenty-eight.' I think of my ZX Spectrum from when I was nine as I look at the bell tower in the middle of the plaza.
'Cut it however you want and the number of pieces you have will each have a full rose in proportion.'
'What?'
'Like cut it into a million and you'll get a million tiny little roses.' I imagine the million little pieces floating independently in space. Dubie just looks at me. Waiting for me to continue.
'So,' I continue, 'put them all back together, all the million tiny little flowers and you get one big rose again: the original rose that we cut up.' Dubie nods just once.
'Which means…' it's hard to keep going, like I am at the bottom of the sea, moving all these images in my head – I'm connecting it to consciousness, which is where this conversation started, and to parts in people, to parts in the world, to universes, to the microscopic that we can't see, 'that if we put all the little bits back into a whole, into the original hologram we had before we cut it up, every part holds all the information of the whole.' I pause as the waitress brings me an agua con gas and her second cafe con leche, 'So then the tip of the leaf, is just a tip of the leaf, nothing more, nothing less, but,' I say, imagining myself to be like a magician, 'it also holds all the information about all of the rose.'

She looks at me, a sparkle in her eye. She knew it already. I smile back: we're of the same kind. Sisters somehow.

—

No matter how far down we go, part within part within part, each has all the information of what it is part of.

Ad infinitum.

I gasp.

———

We are each a cog in a system, a psyche, a family, a group, a community, a society, a world.

———

By changing a cog in the whole, we can change so much!

———

In the Transition Town Film Festival the electricity crashes and the film goes black. We cheer as the projector flickers on and groan as we are submersed back into darkness. In the dark a man stands up in front of the audience, many of whom are lit up by the flash lights on their mobile phones and in a very English accent says, 'Thank you for your patience,' as if he were personally responsible for the Town Electricity System, 'in the break our friend Daniel is offering a workshop on effecting and perceiving change.' We clap politely. A little too controlled. Being part of the audience I feel us on the edge, our inner children clamouring to go rampantly out of control. The projector flickers on again. We cheer, beginning to not care if it stays on or not.

After the film, that overran by twenty minutes, I trundle down into the cafe to where this Daniel guy, a grey pigeon of a man, is offering what I expect to be a typical conceptual idea that has no bearing on reality. I am annoyed to be piqued enough to not want to miss it. He is at the cafe bar with his laptop. A group of about fifteen of us huddle around. It was meant to be on a projector, but today appears to be disaster day and it isn't working.

'This is a simulation of two billiard tables,' he says, 'that are exactly the same.' Each has twenty-five balls spread out in a 5x5 grid. He presses a button for the two white balls to break simultaneously and the balls are bounced around the two tables, unsurprisingly in exactly the same way. He resets the screen. 'I'm just going to move this yellow ball at the front here on the left hand table a smidgen to the left.' And with his mouse he moves a ball on the left hand table almost imperceptibly.

He looks up, towards us, his audience, with eyes of, 'Are you ready?'

This better be good, I think, *I want to get back to the next film.* On the press of a button both white balls simultaneously break, moving up their respective tables, the computer tracks each of their paths again. Their paths are the same, just as before, until due to the slight juxtaposition of that ever so slightly moved yellow ball the white ball on the left hand table eventually bounces at a different angle off a red ball that has also had its course changed due to a slight knock on effect from an another ball. From here on in the path of the white ball on the left hand table is dramatically different: its destiny changed forever.

'Wow,' I say aloud, and cover over any fear of them seeing me as the weirdo-who-talks-to-herself by putting on my face of self-confidence. Daniel looks at me. I feel our eyes click as he sees that I've got it. I feel the glee of an idea falling on fertile ground, synapsing from one mind to another. The idea in his head has gone out and multiplied as an image in me. It feels like a magic transmission. I feel like Neo in *Matrix* being upgraded with knowledge.

Words Magicking Images

Such a tiny action
motioned by love:
a poem
marvelling at it all.

I send it out to the world
unable to go with it.

Time later
– days, years –
a reader!

A sigh escapes
at what the words create.
They marvel too.
Magick.

The Buddha twirls a flower. Mahākāśyapa suddenly receives the transmission. They smile into each other's eyes.

—

An initiate's world clicks into place in the 'wordless sermons' of Eleusis as a mown ear of grain is silently shown in the course of the mysteries, three-thousand-five-hundred years ago.

—

Daniel looks over at me as I gasp the 'Wow!' In my eyes he suddenly changes from being a grey pigeon - I begin to find him attractive. We smile. I have seen (some of) his idea. It is glorious: it takes time to effect a change in the world.

We will never know the result of our actions, because we will never know what would have happened if we hadn't done what we have done.

—

'Let's watch *'¡Qué bello es vivir!'* *It's a Wonderful Life* is Ricard's favourite film. He just loves the clumsy guardian angel Clarence saving George Bailey from jumping off a bridge and committing suicide. Bailey wants out, stuck in the vortex of feeling his life is a waste, he an abject failure, but Clarence shows him how by simply being in the world, with his good heart and his good actions, he has radically altered everything. How many lives he has touched! How different his community would have been if had he never been born! He just couldn't see

44

it because there was nothing to compare it to. He couldn't experience the world without him in it.

—

'I feel broken,' moans Chuck. This is not the first time we have been here. 'I can't…I just can't….' my heart goes out to him. How to help him with the monthly migraines? How to ease his depression? How to knock him out of OCD? 'Why all this?' he pleads, putting his shaky hands to his head, holding the pain.

'What was your first memory?' I ask. 'You know that already!' he says, as if I don't listen to him. But for me this is the root: he at four, hiding underneath the table, seeing his mother from under the fringe of the table cloth collapse onto the floor at the hand of his father. His grandfather beating his wife. His great-grandfather, a staunch, strict, punishing Christian, who felt he was protecting goodliness by beating the shit out of his family, protecting them from sin. From his own sin. No one allowed to mention, even know, why he and his family had to flee their homeland Germany after the Second World War. Instead, all were subject to the anger exploding within him.

I saw it boil up once in Chuck. We were in Nepal, falling in love, celebrating in a little secluded courtyard restaurant. There had been a dispute with the waiter. I personally hadn't seen much problem. Had it all happened behind my back maybe? Suddenly Chuck was pushing his chest up against the waiter. Arms back, ready to strike. The tension, like that before a thunderstorm, clenched around his muscles. Both men were eying each other like daggers. My heart was in my mouth. In amongst all of the tables of diners, there was my love, my soft, caring gentle man, gone berserk.

He managed to pull himself out before the energy devoured him, but even in my blinding fear of seeing who I was in love with, I recognised it was a heroic feat of his to simply step back.

In Barcelona, on our sofa, I say to him, 'It feels as if, deep within, you are changing the patterns that you have inherited. As if you have put a damn against the river of rage that is flowing through you, through the generations of men in your lineage.' Chuck whimpers. 'It's not easy,' I say, 'It's as if you are some melting pot, so that as the anger settles, it can start to become creative.'
'I'm lying on a sofa, doing nothing day in day out,' he slaps his thigh, angrily. More pain.
'You are an artist, you are a photographer, you are a meditator. You are, slowly, slowly, changing the energy that is within you…look at your work!'

He cannot get it. He is lost, swirling in the void of not reacting. Cannot see the woods for trees. Cannot see. Progress is too slow for him to see he is changing himself. I feel I can though – and though it's really not easy to live with – I admire him for it.

Mise en Abyme

Seven generations,
living inside,
affecting our actions
though they have died.
My parents' wounds
I know too well,
mingled and thrashed
within my own shell.

My grandparents too,
voice their fare share
of rebels who ran
too afraid not to dare,
butchers who danced,
and the arrogant rich,
humbled farm fingers
ploughing the ditch.

Now the great-grands
are all but stories
whose lives lived out
have forgotten glories
of butchers and farmers
and factory lives
Irish beatings
and runaway wives.

Their parents form
not even a blur
sixteen forgotten
their loves do not stir.

Double their parents
and double, double again,
what hides in those numbers
that rattle my reign?
Religious and crooked,
the generous and greedy,
murderers and saints,
the headstrong and needy;
the poor of the parish

the rich fallen daughters
adventurous sons
and men back from slaughters;
the priest's hidden bastard,
the honest branded liar,
the devout once-a-weekers
and women on hire;
wind whipped beggars,
and workers of trades
the spinners of yarns
and household maids;
drunkards and mystics,
writers and dancers
terrible cooks –
and all with no answers.

In a blink of an eye
Two hundred 'n fifty-four
births and deaths
that my ascendants bore.

They hang their woes
upon my head,
their unfinished work
my daily bread.

Their hard-won gifts
are my body and mind
to loosen the pain
for our hearts to unbind,

releasing the light
by removing each thorn
healing dark pasts
for those yet unborn;

for after my generation
there are seven more
waiting to receive
their destiny's chore.

How 'the curse' has been repressed
in our cultures and in so doing
destroyed many a relationship.

I: Between Moons

Pasted by layers
of university papers
I am a woman
emasculated by
blue cowboy jeans
striding me into the world:
a smoke screen
over the stranglehold of
an invisible, western burqa;
my femininity left
shivering out in the cold.

Laia, a woman I dated for three years, is shouting at me. Again.

I don't get what is happening. Suddenly all the rules have changed. Suddenly it appears that what was OK yesterday is not OK today. I can't fart without her erupting into a rage. It feels like she is making everything up. *What has got into her?* I shut down. She cries that I am not there for her. I mean what the fuck does she want from me? I'm there and she's screaming I'm not there and crying over it, when clearly I am right here. *What am I supposed to do? Why can't she just leave me alone?* My body has tensed up ready to flee, wanting nothing but to get out, to leave her. To leave her to abuse herself - not me.

Next day she comes to me, wants to be held in my arms. I open up stiffly, unsure. Unsure of how she will react, unsure if I want to comfort this uncontrolled demon of a woman. Her face is white, exhausted. Her eyes look softly into mine, tinged with cobwebs of sadness. 'I'm sorry,' she says. I don't say it's alright, because it isn't. 'I just started my period.' A window smashes through the tiny attic where I have been hiding in my mind. I can see the sky, there is a breeze that whips out the stale air. Claustrophobia floats out into a broader horizon, unshackled. *I get it!* Suddenly I get what was happening. She was PMTing[5]!! OK. In the opening space, I can give again.

'It's OK,' I say holding her, embracing her lovingly in my energy. 'It's OK petal.' I feel her soft cheek resting in my neck like a safe harbour. 'Are you OK? What do you need?' As I feel her soft body against mine I think, *if I didn't get it and it happens to me too every moon, how on earth are men ever going to even begin to understand?*

II: PMT (Pre-Menstruation Tension)
The Unwanted Guest

i
That bitch has come again,
without as much as an invite
squatting in my body for
an eternity of days.
She scares me and my loved ones
whipping us
into egg shell walkers
and with her barbed tongue
hijacks my voice
to rub salt with merry malice
into our unhealed wounds.

Her force of conviction weakens me -
on my knees I wonder
if actually she's the real one
who I imprison wickedly
throughout the rest of the month?
Is it only now,
debilitated,
guard down,
that I allow
my expression true?
Or,
am I nothing more than
a spineless sweet faker,
a silent twisted traitor
impotently observing her harsh rule;
a feeble coward, cowering
in the creviced corners of my caved in mind,
forced into becoming
nothing but a false smile
stretching over the stench
feebly faking serenity?

In the brass band I am wobbly. I can feel it. It is embarrassing. My tolerance levels are lying sharply on the dusty floor of frustration like a pair of open scissors. Les says, stepping without a blind bit of caution into the minefield, 'What's going on with the cornets? You were all over the shop.'

The scissors snap, 'Some of us are PMTing...' The words spit out like fire. I see no reason why this internal crashing of hormonal waves should be kept secret. I can barely see the music. I am finding it hard to even breathe properly. It's not easy to be where I am, and though it's invisible, it doesn't mean it doesn't exist. Marjory, turns her grey-capped head half around to me and into the air between us says with sharp demonstrative space between her words, 'Too-much-information.'

It's the old school protocol: the curse should be hidden. I feel as if I have been betrayed by a sister. But once my red subsides, underneath it all I get it: she's never been allowed to talk about it herself, for her it has always been an issue swept under the carpet. She probably couldn't talk about it even with her mother.

But even so, in this day and age, I don't see why I need pretend nothing is happening to me. I don't want to be in that under-carpet cage.

———

I explode. I've been holding it for too long now, days, months. 'Like what the fuck do you mean? *You* want? Can't you see, can't you see how this is all about *you* again?' In my eyes he drops into passive aggression. 'Can't you just

answer me?' my voice is rising.
The emotional wires within me are short-circuiting. Heat. Heat. Rage.

He keeps his eyes on Broadway, driving steadily to Sunday morning contact jam.
I am sat in a pressure cooker. His silence puts fire to the pot. I feel my breath like
dragon breath.

'Taaaalllllkkkkkk to me!!!!!' I imagine the front windscreen shattering with the
sharpness of my voice. He waits. Torturing.
'I was trying to.'
'Just try harder!'
'Not while you are like this.' And slows down to a red light.
'Fucccccckkkk you!!!!' I open the door and half step, half roll out. It is exciting,
like the Dukes of Hazard. I have no shoes on. I am on the other side of town. I
storm off in a random direction. He drives off. *Fuck him*. I begin to walk. *Am I in
danger?*

I hope I've ruined his dance. I hope he is worrying.

III: Another Bloody Surprise

Reduced to the rip of primeval pain
crusading up from where
our tail bones once grew
I crash into fertility's death.
Mourning sneered at
by vomity blood
curdling into thick, sickly, sticky
balsamic vinegar.
Body pulsating out into ripples
bigger than its physical
as I flail around borders
rapidly dissolving;
I attempt to straighten into
one last protest
to stay in the world.
My stomach splits in two
-too weak not to implode-
the pain knocks me heavily back within;
too far away now to reach
any safe shores of the receding outside,
I hang onto a threadbare hope
that the tiny blue pill
will hold out against this rush
of ghastly femininity.

I lie on the bed. A tear drips along my nose and gathers in the corner on my lip
joining a reservoir of runny mucus. I am but a stone, petrified. I cannot move,

pain is aching out through my womb. Inside the distant sensation of vomit is riding up through my body. I need the toilet: it is such a long, long way away. I am frozen in pain. I can't get there. I can't. Another convulsion of pain. Involuntarily I double up.

IV: The Relief of the Normal

Colours have returned!
I am back
feeling again.
I feel like me:
centred, happy, clean.
Left to my own hues
for ten glorious days.

It is like someone were turning on the colour in the world, as if a dial were being tuned to fuller potential. A vibrancy shimmers through colours. There are colours! Being forced inwards – into the dark, into the black within, the dull red fireworks of pain – is now but a distant memory. *Did it happen to me?* I am free again to go into this garden of life, into the world as a fully functioning being. I walk a light step. Indeed I can walk out the door without effort. The sun is shining. It seems like a miracle!

V: Wolf howls to the ovulating moon

Cry bitch, cry you fucking loser
sobbing over split milk
believing in the power of love!
How does it help you now,
you fucked up wall flower,
how does it help you now?

Break through your stinking innocence
meet the bitch you really are:
drunk on the power of your dark sting,
believing, so they will,
your own pretense
as you dance
all petal like and sickly sweet
snaring passing low-lives
with your vibrant colours
stealing their buzz
as you manipulate them
with cruel talent
into pollinating your desires.

So many years, I have been petrified of PMT and ovulation. I've gone through it now three-hundred and sixty times, crashing against the rocks of its shadow. So much fear around that bitch monster coming out and destroying all that I love.

Before I knew that ovulation, fifteen days before a period, sends a cocktail of hormones through my body - distorting the world, distorting others, distorting my own connection with my feelings, my thoughts - how many relationships did it destroy?

Fear of anger. Fear of losing control. Fear of opening the cage door. Fear of 'her' coming out. Fear of being a nasty bitch. Fear that I am nothing but.

—

We are in the hot tub at Paul's. We have taken medicine, which is what he and his community call it. We are tripping together with the aim of knowing ourselves better. This is a spiritual journey. It is also fun. The warm water is bubbling up around my neck. I am in an altered reality. My body decides to try going into foetal position in the middle of the hot tub. I submerge into a sublime state: time stops. I am in the womb. I am a tiny foetus, held, loved. The hot tub has become my mother's womb. I have done nothing now that anyone can ever blame me for – I have not burst into human life yet. I float in bliss. Bliss. I am bliss. I feel my cells relaxing, remembering.

I hear a voice coming from a well spring deep within my own waters, 'You are good. You are a good person.' I hear it. I wonder, *did I ever wonder if I was good?* Fears flash before me of being 'bad', of me screaming, sobbing, crying with uncontrolled emotions bursting my banks. 'You are good,' the voice repeats, 'you are a good person.' My body clicks, shifts, my mind readjusts to this new image of me. I am a good person. I am good. I am not bad. I am a good person. I am good. I float in that space of deep nourishment, feeding on the goodness.

I burst back into life, breathe in a rush of air. I feel I am taking my first breath. I am back in the hot tub, back in this other altered state of reality, back in the space ship from floating in the sublime. I am back and I am a good person.

Everything feels different.

—

When Aunty Barbara died it came mangled in a trough of guilt as I felt billowing relief. Now there will be no family tensions…not like before. *One should not speak badly of the dead.* I felt a knife edged fear of being damned by God mixed with the fear of her spirit not quite angelically looking down from the skies and putting a curse on me and my innocent, honest, uncontrollable feelings. I kept my trap shut, but still, once in a while I felt how free the world felt without her in it.

I trace through my family tree. On both sides there are women who have been suppressed. I ask my mum. She tells me that in our lineage there is a strain of women through the generations who were nasty. Nasty. I feel it in me. I feel this pressure cooker of being unheard, of being chained to the husband's image of what women should be. I feel the suppressed scream of pain of my Aunty Doreen who wanted to be a seamstress but wasn't allowed to travel to the other side of Manchester – according to Granddad it was too far. I feel my Mum's insecurities of not having finished school because she had to work in the fields picking peas and digging out potatoes. I know too well the sting in her tail. I feel my grandmother whose shrivelled face I remember as abject tiredness. Mum says, 'She had a sting in her tail. That's where your Aunty Barbara got it from.'

I feel my dad's side. The Irish lot. My Great Grandmother, who fell in love with an Orange, she was a Green. They eloped to England. He ran back. Left her with four children. Alone. I feel her rage of having sacrificed everything for a love that he couldn't hold. I feel her rage of him not upholding what is imprinted, now with dirty blood, on her heart. How could he forget how they felt when at that local dance they felt it for the first time, all cleaned up dressed in their glad rags, both fiery, dancing high, connecting as if through time? How could he ignore them falling so hard into each other's hearts so it felt impossible not to risk all for love?

I feel my Grandmother, her daughter, the party girl who got high on life, dating men who would never commit; I feel the cage wrap around her as she felt forced to get married, wings clipped because of the bump in her stomach. How after four years, she was left with the reality, as he, my Granddad, went back to where he came from, back to freedom and left her alone with my Dad.

—

Where does this psychic pain come from? Is it all mine? Is any of it mine? I think of all those people who are affecting me through the seven generations above. I do the sums: me, add two parents, add their four grandparents, add eight more of their parents, then sixteen, thirty-two, sixty-four, one-hundred-and-twenty-eight psyches running through me from seven generations. One-hundred-and-twenty-eight!

I feel the weight of the river - angst and fear and joy and pain: a thousand toxins and sweet perfumes - flowing through me, grinding me to the ground.

—

Walking through the Flatiron mountains by Boulder one fine summer day, between moons, hiking through thoughts, I see in my mind the movement of the waxing and waning moon: the feminine. Is it, I wonder to myself, that we as children want women, our mothers, to be a constant full moon, for her to deny herself anything but full breasted kindness? Do we carry this on through to our adulthood, so that women are not allowed to experience each of her aspects, not allowed change, suspended from connecting with our true sexuality, with our creativity, with our hag warriors, our nasty bitch sharpness that destroys the obsolete, with our Amazonian hunter hearts? The moon is constantly changing. I feel myself inside constantly changing. I feel embarrassed that I am not stable.

Walking down the hill back to the car, I wonder, *Are we all forced to stay stagnant, fixed smiles framing the appearance of being nothing but full moons?*

—

I am struggling under the weight of PMT. I have awoken the bitch…I am right on the edge of my period. For the first time in my life I suddenly think – what is wrong with bitch? She defends me! I realise what is wrong with 'bitch' is that men are afraid of her. I have repressed part of myself for the sake of men and now I decide not to. Everything is not spick and span. I am not nice right now and I don't have to be.

Rising above

Body vibrating higher
than it can sustain
I wobble dangerously
at the top of becoming.
The bitch is out!
Loving me
- in her own way -
protecting me
she rubs up against all
we ever learnt kneeling in the
white stenched church.
I don't need your
saints now:
don't need your 'cure',
I forbid you to rob me
once more of this moon power
you would demonise
only because
you can never experience it.

I don't need your manly protection now
I am better left alone
but if you have to,
say yes to all of me
– to all of my aspects –
or receive the wrath
of generations of women
arising from the confines
unable 'til now
to be themselves.

From: <julia.butterflypress@gmail.com>
To: <debramagik@gmail.com>

If we become all of ourselves, how would the world change? I don't know…I have a massage in an hour…god-send cos I can barely hold all this feminine energy, energy of repression becoming unrepressed...it has a destructive edge to it...but so beautifully creative if it is allowed to express...why not be 'bitches'...i.e. women in power? xxxJ

—

I feel the heat of the rage. I cannot work anymore on the computer, cannot concentrate. I storm down the high street, trying to pound this excess of energy out through the concrete. I am anger on fire. Down through me from generations past I feel red lines of rage of the feminine coursing, wanting to consume me, me wanting to consume the world. I feel high. I feel my eyes through filters. I do not know if I am living my own rage or the rage of my female ancestors. I do not feel like me.

It is irrelevant, the animal inside wants to rip men's limbs out and eat them live, just like Dionysus, the god of the orgiastic feminine. I want to dance myself into naked flames where I can shout out my pain, where I can attack and be held, where I can be transmuted, like a knife that burns red to white. I feel my veins burning.

Series of Poems: Channelling Rage

I

I feel the witches
through both sides of me
– what to do?
I can trap them no more
from ramping and raging
in moonlight destruction,
can't be sickly sweet all the time
depolarised, impotent,
just for the sake of men's fears.

I feel her rising through the flames.

II

I am
all womb
all vagina
– they are angry.
Part from my path!
Leave me my power!
Trying to drag me back
into the prison of the mind
will leave you with
more than just scars.

56

I see Christopher in the street. He sees me. I can barely carry this inner world around with me. I can tell in his gaze that he sees. He holds me tightly. I fall into him, wanting to stab him, to hurt him, to punch. I am held. He is far stronger than me, even with this raging within me. My breath is hard. I struggle against him pushing against this straitjacket. He holds me in his peaceful, firm kindness. My breath settles, I feel myself landing, coming into my body. I feel myself being held in my rage. It comes as a surprise to feel he is not afraid of me. I feel I can express all of this that is myself right now and he will not run. I feel myself healing a wound, right there, on the High Street outside the Methodist Church surrounded by the smell of the butchers. He is holding me and my rage and I am OK. I am not a whore, or a bitch. I am a good person, holding, processing all this raw angry energy that maybe is not even my own.

III

Solidly
kind, unafraid
of the heat of my female
power, his legs and arms firm,
steady heart. In the tight angry hug
I feel my panting recede with the flames.
My breath becomes the wind of a safe harbour.
He pulls me gently onto terra firma. Eternally grateful.

PART II

Making The Path By Walking It - Finding Our Own Way Through The Wilds Of Relating

Invisible lines between moving
psyches that are constantly setting,
changing, opening and closing.

Behind the Lines

In awe I burn
in this intimacy;
coloured flames
lick our bodies,
kaleidoscope swirling
rips me away
from who I was.
Now nothing between us
and the devouring fires of life.
I scream:
too much.
Vertigo high
the fall
churns my stomach.
Fear cools
the burning of this
bonfire of love.
Collapsing I fall,
content again
to be back on safe ground.

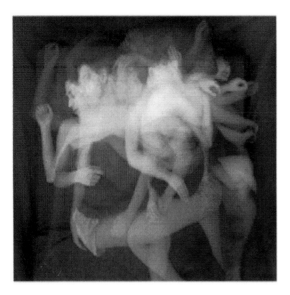

I've managed to sneak through the back door into Lora's T-group. They've stopped new-comers for a time – the dynamics were getting a bit out of hand. I've somehow been coerced into becoming a gate-crasher by her saying, 'I'll teach you the basics, you'll be fine.' We're in the car, travelling down Highway 7, to the bottom end of the city, where the big houses are. I'm in the passenger seat in more ways than one.

'So, there are hand signals,' she says staring through the windscreen, 'this one,' she wriggles her fingers, 'means, 'that resonates with me', then there is,' she puts her fingers and thumb together and points them to the sky, ''come back to the present moment,' and there is, there are more, erm, ok yea,' she takes both hands quickly off the wheel, and makes quotation marks with her two forefingers and two middle fingers, ''headliner', which means that you feel it necessary to give a bit of information about your present state, but you shouldn't go into detail. It's about the here now, nothing else, but if there is something that you feel is affecting the here now that you are bringing in with you then you can say,' she does the finger movement again, 'headline'.

'Right,' I say, only half understanding, feeling increasing overwhelmed by the prospect of getting there soon, '…and like, what do we do?'
'Well,' her voice slows into her elfish glee, '…you'll see.'
'No more clues?'
'You sort of sit in a little group, and say what you feel in that exact moment.'
'Anything?'
'Yeah, feelings and sensations.'
'Like what?' I feel panic rising, 'like what?'
'Well,' she says, without a lot of conviction, 'like 'I feel a tight constriction in my throat,' or 'I feel happy hearing what you just said,' or 'I feel a strange urge to …' I don't know, 'kiss you!''
'Really!?'
'Well, I guess, but that doesn't happen…but if they did the other could then say, 'I feel nervous that you want to kiss me,' and leave it at that. It's not that you can do whatever you want, but you can say want you feel and sense and *own* it. Honestly. Sometimes people say, 'I feel like I would like to put my hand on your shoulder, would you be OK with that?' Then the person being asked can say how they honestly feel, like, 'I feel panic as you say that,' or 'Yes, I would like that,' or just not respond. It's all about listening to ourselves and to others honestly without having to justify what is happening.'

I sit in the passenger seat, unable to control the car and get it to turn back. The Sunday morning Five Rhythms dance place whizzes past. I still know where I am. She seems merry, 'It's impossible to explain really…anything can happen.' I gulp. We are going so fast.

'But, like, any advice, tips?'

'Just keep it in the 'I', just own your feelings.'

'All of them?'

'Yeah, but again, you don't have to justify anything…you can just say, 'I feel sad,' and leave it at that.' I feel tightness in my chest and the urge to scream – but I don't say it. 'You'll see how it is,' she says calmly, eyes on the road, 'It's impossible to explain really…you'll be fine.'

—

I am sat, without Lora anywhere near, in this massive house, in one of the several enormous rooms. I feel like I am in a film. This house is what the Americans call a 'show home'. A show-off home. I'm about to do my first ever sensitivity training group, more commonly known as a T-group. We've split into little groups and I've managed as casually as I can to find the house's third lounge. There are three other people sat cross-legged on cushions on the floor. This is where I am to experience practising deep honesty. It feels safe because it doesn't feel very real. 'Shall we begin?' *Begin what?* I want to ask in a very loud voice, but I can't, because I'm meant to have already done this. No newcomers welcome. I nod. I am hoping to portray an air of laissez-faire.

We sit in the circle, all looking at each other. Nothing is happening. I have no idea if I should be doing something. Each person looks at the others. Quizzically; a smile in their eyes; tiredness under their eyes. No words. Just looking.

I don't do silence well.

After hours of seconds going by, a guy called Dave eventually says, 'I feel tired.' I look at his sagging face - he looks it. No answer.

A woman who I've already forgotten her name says, 'I feel calm, happy to be here.' We all smile at her. Pause. Silence. I am in myself, feeling all these strange sensations. No words for them. A guy called Tonka (*where do these Americans get their names?*) says, 'I feel expansion in my chest. I,' he pauses and does the quotation marks. I feel a little buzz in my forehead*: I know that! I've had Lora training!* I hold out, trying to look like I've seen this a million times. Tonka says, 'Headline: I just did a wonderful healing session and I'm still feeling the effects.'

'I feel tingles in my spine that you feel good,' says the woman.

More silence.

After a while of repressing my need to shout into the silence, I manage a, 'I feel a tight constriction in my throat.'

'I feel like I want to help you,' says Dave. I panic*, help me in what? What doesn't he see that I need help in? Why me?*

'I feel uncomfortable imagining you are uncomfortable,' says Tonka. The woman gazes at me. I realise they are all looking at me.

'I feel uncomfortable you all looking at me.'

The two men drop their eyes, but the woman says, 'I feel that it is OK to keep looking at you. I feel that I need to keep looking at you.'

'I feel like hiding,' I say looking into her eyes.

'I feel a constriction inside hearing you say that,' says the woman. The other two men look at me again.

This is full on.

I was hoping to just watch for the first session.

—

The T-group keeps digging, like 'spiritual' archaeologists until between us all we reach some nugget of socio-psycho gold. Someone breaks down in tears. Me. I can't take the tension of it all. All this attention is too much. I've been alone for so long, yearning to be with people, and then suddenly they are all staring at me. I burst out, 'I feel like I'm burning in the light of all this attention.' I sob. They sit, compassionate. Staring. This is the first time I've ever done this. It's wyrd to be sobbing in front of strangers who are comfortably holding my space; as if this is just fine. After a time the welling dies down, someone passes me a box of tissues.

'I feel embarrassed: I have no idea why I am crying…' I say dismayed. My head is down, but I can feel their presence, I feel them watching me. It is unsettling and comforting all at the same time. I feel like a drama queen. I start to feel shame. I sit red-faced, too embarrassed to say anything.

'I feel so grateful,' says the woman, 'through your tears, I can feel my own sadness.'

The other two men's fingers flutter: they 'resonate'.

'I feel honoured to experience your tears. I feel myself connecting at a deeper level.'

'I am grateful for you holding me like this,' I say, starting to use my voice again. It actually feels deeply moving to be able to break down in front of others and not be ostracised.

The woman bursts into tears, sobs, 'I just….' sobs again, 'I just…I feel…I'm so lonely!' The other two men sit and hold space. I do the same. Following suit. It's so nice not to be the centre of attention anymore.

'Headline,' she says, finger air quotation, 'I broke from my boyfriend last week.'

The alarm for forty-five minutes goes off.

We sit in companionable silence in the cleared, calm airs after a storm.

At the end is the closing. Everyone gets a timed minute to recap the session from their point of view. The others simply listen, give their attention, hold space. Simone Weil wrote, 'Attention is the rarest and purest form of generosity.' It feels like water to a desert.

It sounds corny, but actually it's not. Not always. It feels as if we are going closer to the source together, to that place where Jung says he dips in his hat and drinks for a while.

When it's my turn I am surprised at my honesty, 'I've been feeling so unnoticed. As much as America seems like England, it's so different. I'm a fish out of water. I felt a deep desire to be seen by someone, anyone, but when you all did give me your attention, it was awful. I felt like I was burning up. I felt myself being brought out into the light, and with it came a deep seated fear that maybe I am not as brilliant as I imagine myself.'

I pause, I've used an English word, 'Maybe I'm not,' what's an American word here? 'as awesome as I think I am.' I suddenly feel daft saying a word I'd never use, I grope around in clumsy-land, 'It's as if I'd prefer to be in the darkness of not being seen instead of having to actually see who I really am. I'd prefer to stay with my delusions of who I am rather than see the reality of me. It's much easier to cry about not being seen, rather than risk not making the grade I've set for myself.' I feel exposed, vulnerable, and yet safe. They are just listening, this is about me, not them. 'Yeah…' I say as a way to end…I look around sheepishly. They do not seem horrified. They seem used to sharing. I breathe in and sit back exhausted; that was a big upheaval.

Tonka, who I disliked from here on in, puts his hand on my knee. The tone is one of 'caring'. It feels ok at first.

It's the next person's minute to share. His hand feels too static, too unmoving. I give my attention to Dave who is talking. He's the last to do a personal share. The hand contact is starting to get sweaty. I imagine my cotton shorts being pressed into uneven creases underneath his damp heat.

I move my leg away. He removes his hand. Good.

My leg is now uncomfortable in this new, spontaneous leaning away position. I've said my piece, told him by body language. I listen to Dave, and then after a little while return to being cross legged. Tonka returns his hand. *Brrrrrrrrh…*

I move my leg again, just for him to get the (double) message this time, and I do it a little firmer. I feel the twist in my body, a sort of extra message to him: underlined and in bold. He removes his hand. A little air runs fresh over the sticky part. It feels better.

I sit back.
He puts back his hand.

I feel flashes of hot waves ride through my body and get caught in my throat. I feel my head and neck constricted, tongue hard on the top of the roof of my mouth.

When will the talking end? Must I just grit my teeth? Can I talk? It finishes at last. It's only been minutes, but it feels bad in my stomach. 'Can I just say something?' we are being honest here...I don't know the rules, not sure about format, don't know if this is a possible talking time...but this is about how we feel right now isn't it? Dave, who I'm starting to realise is the leader, says, 'Yes, of course...' Friendly, nice, safe.

'I feel really uncomfortable that,' I hear their ears pick up in interest, I turn around to look at Tonka, 'you had your hand on my knee the whole time without my consent.'
'What do you mean?' he says, as if astonished. *Maybe he actually IS astonished?*
'It was uncomfortable, and,' I say, *Is this ok? Am I breaking the rules? I'm definitely being open and honest,* '...it was sweaty.'
He surprises me by exploding, 'It's YOUR responsibility to maintain YOUR boundaries! How am I supposed to know if you don't say anything?' I wonder *did he really not get any of my body communication?* 'You've made me look like a creep, like I have been groping you.'

A thought flashes through my mind that that is exactly what he is and has done. My eyebrow rises, uncontrollably – hopefully imperceptibly. I feel my eyes open up wider, air hitting under the lids making my eyes dry. A sudden flash of more light. I feel myself on the edge of shock. I stick to my standard emergency defence strategy and pull out my I'm-spiritual-and-can-handle-this voice, 'It was uncomfortable,' low, slow, soft tone. I imagine I am talking to a scared animal, 'I didn't like it.'

He can't deal with this new image of himself. He wants to be admired, wants to be respected for being a healer, to be something more than a man who gropes. 'You have to set your own limits. I can't do that for you! Look what you've caused, look what you are creating!!!'

—

At home, Paul hears all about it, and hugs me through the floods of tears.

Later I wonder if Tonka was actually right, maybe I did need to be able to set stronger boundaries. It's not his fault that he can't see what he can't see. Wisely I hold back from saying, 'Moron.'

—

To watch Paul dance contact is like seeing a transformation in real life. I fell in love with him dancing, as we roly-polied down the big stone steps outside the Agios Konstantios church on Paros. *How old are those steps?* I remember watching a palm tree come in and out of my vision as I circled around, Paul holding me up like a star above his head. Once our dance was over, we lay, happily expressed, on the steps steeped in time. I floated across the millimetre void between my lips and his face and found myself kissing him on the cheek. Daring. Even though I was sure he was gay.

Turns out he's lesbian. Perfect.

Afterwards, in the States, I had to get used to the opposite him, the one that closes down and goes into a deep cave somewhere near the centre of the earth; the one who is only physically present. I had to get used to that enormous inner space, like being in a school sports hall alone. Echoes. Body tiny small in the immensity of the space where I can scream and no one will hear.

He dances like a divine being, flies with his weightless body into people's hearts. He's able to dance deep into the wild fire of curves and whishes, in whirls of delight while constantly contacted with the other somewhere, an elbow, a nose, or their whole body – that's the dance: to weave in and out of sensuality, sometimes wildly.

There are often older men in these experimental worlds such as Contact Improvisation. To be kind we could say they are sublimating their sexual energies: at least most of them. But there are a few who cross the line. I never danced with Bryan. I never wanted to. He had that invisible lick smack when he looked at women – younger women. He got thrown out. I don't know what he did, but I can imagine. Two or three women complained about him. Quite a few didn't – they just didn't come back. Eventually he ruffled enough feathers that a committee meeting was called. The community concluded, 'Go to a psychologist, and then come back and see us.'

He did.

A few months later he said he was ready. Paul had to hold counsel. I imagine there was a lot of shuffling. No-one wanted him back, but their word is their word. Good people.

'Bryan,' Paul says evenly, softly - not willing to judge, not right now. Byran nods, looking innocent, 'how do you see it now?' Under the joy of the spot light of attention Bryan blathers on about being a man, about how he respects the men for what they manage to resist, what they hold back from. And it goes without saying that he'll never, ever do that again. His words come out of his mouth for a long time. I know Bryan, he can intellectualise anything, he can turn the deepest emotions into a verbose essay and as he winds up into his eventual grand finale he looks up, out from his world, pleased with himself, glancing around at his 'audience' ready for compliments. Normally I can't remember anything that he has said. It's hard to escape from that kind of psychic mechanism.

'And how about the women, how do you feel now?' Paul asks, wanting to know if he understands about traumatising them. Is there empathy, a feeling of responsibility for the effect that he's had?
'Yes,' he nods solemnly, 'I hope they come back.'

So he was thrown out for good. He had not got it. Matthew, John's mate, laughed when he heard, 'You threw him out for doing what we all want to do, but don't?!'

Which, actually, is the key: they don't do it.

I – The Invisible

Once too often
he stepped over the line -
did what all the men want to do
but don't;
so was cast out.
'What line?' he pleads
blind to the invisible,
he listens to the answer
the grammar, the words,
but cannot hear:
'the ones the women create.'

II – Thin Lines

Thin lines
between
strong and weak
success and failure
kind and cruel
veils of invisible thinness
separated only by will.

—

'A good cuppa tea,' he said sitting down heavily as if he had ridden through several woods or put a roof on a house. Freecycle is wonderful. You can pick up other's trash without having to go to the tip. He had brought a mouse for me, and a USB that lets one hole become three. The tea was the exchange for him bringing it in his car to my house through the Devon rains.

'Erm soya?' I ask, 'or,' I am trying to bridge distant worlds in the silence of his confusion. I search on Joseph's shelves, does he ever use cow's milk? Relief. Green lid, 'or…' I say looking closely at the label, scrutinising.
'Semi,' he states. 'Yes, semi'll do.'
'How did you know it was semi?'
'The green lid,' he says politely, too politely because it carries an air of bewildered, 'where've you been all your life?' I don't go into details. I've only been in England a couple of months.
''Av you got saccharin? I'm tryin' to lose weight.'
'Err, no. Honey. I've got honey.'
'That'll do,' he says like a farmer, 'I've never 'ad honey in ma tea before.'

We talk. He was one of those normal people: had a business cleaning houses under the process of being constructed. He talked me through it all, in detail. Dust from drilling, clean up, next stage, mess from putting the bathrooms in, next stage, clean up. It was reasonably interesting. I didn't expect to have much more of a conversation. I am just whiling away the time until he finishes his tea. I glance, hopefully not too often, at the clock.

He is keen to show me that he's doing well. I have no idea why. It seems that he is actually doing well enough. His guilelessness strikes me. He seems both excited about being alive, full of the hope of finally making it, and a deep tiredness of never having had a break. He has an air of wanting to care, wanting to love, wanting to be safe. Somehow we get onto the subject of age. We both take an obviously familiar, Peter Pan delight in the other shaving off 10-15 years from our ages. 'Forty-five,' I say, but I'm really thinking fifty-two. It's embarrassing to go massively over the top – that panicked look is hard to back out from. 'Wow, you don't look 60!' and he doesn't, until I start looking. Actually yes, I can see it in the lines, in the chiselledness of his chin. But really he has such a baby air to him, the type who is trying so hard to do right that you want to squeeze their cheeks, to support them somehow like a mother watching their child on sport's day. He looks like he's sat how his mummy's told him to sit when in the company of a lady; his big hands making the cup look like a child's play set.

He tells me that he's on his fifth or sixth wife. I laugh, 'Surely you must remember, you haven't just forgotten about a wife?'
'I forget. I get muddled.' I glance at the clock again, but less desperately. 'I've always been afraid of growing old alone,' he admits. 'Actually I've always just been afraid of being alone, and I,' he pauses, doesn't really know where to go, he's letting out all his secrets like a little kid showing his box of treasures – sticks and bones and dead animals – he tries to lighten the load, '…listen to this, you'll laugh. My first wife, I met her when I were 22. I was living under my brother's bakery, sleeping there, with the rats scamperin' around the floorboards just above ma head…it were 'orrible. I met her in a dance. We got married two weeks later, with a special permit, 'cos you normally 'ave to 'ave more time before getting married, like two months 'n' after five weeks I left her. Seven weeks in total we knew each other.'

This is more interesting than how to clean cement off windows. *Who is this man?* I feel a slight unease but I cannot locate it; something, somewhere is wrong here. Something wrong inside. He looks and feels so caring, but can't hold a relationship. Going through the curtain of intimacy into those uncontrollable flames is not easy for anyone, but this is something else – *but what?* I can smell something…

Suddenly he says, quickly, quietly so that I nearly miss it, 'I was abused by my granddad.' He says it so casually, as if it was quite normal to be abused. I wonder if I've heard wrong. I don't say a word. I just hold the silence. 'I didn't know it was wrong, I didn't know it were any different. My dad beat me, but I thought that were just what families are. I've got two little kids, and I never beat them once in my life. Not once.' He's got good reason to be proud. Good reason, that's really not easy to do. It's massive to hold back family habits ingrained at an early age. It's the Hercules task of working through family karma. I've heard a similar story of a guy who my aunty spoke with volunteering in prisons. He was proud of not being physically violent to his woman, of not doing to others what had been done to him.

'Good on you. That's not easy,' I encourage, and I mean it.
'And if I shout, they'd be confused that I be shouting because I normally never raise my voice.'
I can imagine: he's like a big soft giant. I look into my teacup – still half full – and breathe in, wondering if we have come to the end of the conversation. Part of me wants to up and run.

'There have been a few things in my life that I'm not proud of,' he looks up and catches my eye. In the gaze I see, all that I can manage to describe as, a movement left to right around his eyes. I'm not sure if it was with his irises, but I sensed a shift? His…? I interpret it as a message that he is not sure whether to go on, he wants to confess to this stranger who has no impact on his life – but should he, is it safe?

I smile, stay solid, nod. If he wants to open the door I'll not lock it.

He meanders a little, and says, '…I paid for it though.' He fingers his tea cup.
After a long pause, I guess, 'You were in jail?'
His eyes drop, 'Four years.'
I want to shout out excitedly 'What for!?' like a little kid in a pantomime, but I stay quiet for a little time, and then ask, 'What is it like being in jail?'
'I was in an open wing.'
'What's an open wing?'
'You've got a wing, with a kitchen and a bathroom and corridors of rooms. You can go anywhere. Well, the door at the kitchen is locked, you can't go out of the wing.'
'Ohh right, so you weren't in a locked cell?'
'No. We were safer cos we was the VP wing.' He looks down, suddenly like a little boy afraid of bullies. I wonder what VP is? VIP? Did I hear wrong?
'What's VP?'
'Vulnerable Persons,' he says quietly, embarrassed. Needs his mum.
'What did you do?' I say softly, motherly.
Before launching in, he pauses. Looks at his hands around the teacup. 'I had sex with a minor.'

I feel a wave of shock go through me as I realise that I'm having a cup of tea with a paedophile.

I stay still, I stay open, deep down I know this man is a good man. I feel it. I want to feel it. I'm not sure if I feel safe.
'She was 13,' he says, telling his story, 'She told 'em afterwards.'
'Told them what?' I wonder if I should be delving down here, but it feels like he needs to tell someone… it feels like he really needs to offload. It's a big price for a USB thing and a mouse from freecycle, but it makes me feel alive that I'm allowed into his world and can help another human being; it helps me feel my own strength to give space to such claustrophobic places, to help by

accompanying someone in these murky realms…maybe this was always the point of this right now? I can cope with this, so far, I can cope.

'She lived with her parents and I used to pay her 50p to wash ma hair.' I imagine some horrible brown print wallpaper. 'Before anything happened she'd just wash ma hair. Nothing could happen could it? Her parents were in the next room. We weren't really together, not really, but we used to talk about when she,' he laughs nervously, suddenly realising the extent of what he's about to say, '…grows up,' he looks me in the eye, please be kind, his eyes say, please be kind, he swallows, '…we'd get married.' There is that air of innocence again. I can feel love in the air somehow; he actually believed in them as a couple.

'It happened when she was washing your hair?'
'It were gradual, at first she'd wash ma hair and she be holding me, and I'd be, like this,' his shoulders go up, squeezed together and I guess he's imitating holding himself below the table, he's moved out of the pose quickly. I don't really get it. I guess she, or he, was holding his penis? '…and her mother and father were in next room,' he repeats, and then his head goes under, as if into the earth, and he says quickly, joyfully, impishly, 'that were part of the excitement.'

I breathe in. Taking stock. I mean, we have all been there surely? Inappropriate sex: affairs with married people, bosses, same sex for the first time…it is exciting. It is. But thirteen is wrong - it just is. At the same time I can get that he felt excited, that he got turned on with that raw edge of being caught. Give him a bit of a break. Really. Just today. I nod. I can guess what he feels. I too am human. I've fantasised with minors. The difference being I would never want those fantasies to come true: I would be horrified.

'But I know now,' he says sat back in his good boy posture again, 'the police taught me in the prison workshops: I know that you can't be friends with children.' I sit still, expressionless. I feel myself gawping inside. It's so interesting being given the space to see into another person's existence, into their thoughts, their emotions. A *W-H-A-T ?* flashes through me. I suddenly mind-glance back over what he's just said. There it is*: he doesn't get it.* He cannot see any lines between people at all, no boundaries, even afterwards, even with police workshops. He has no idea what he did wrong, or why what he did was a crime that put him in jail. He is stumbling about in the dark. When he was little, abuse was the one constant of reality, it was drilled into him. No-one taught him about his own personal boundaries. He has none. No-one taught him about others' personal boundaries, he cannot see them. He is handicapped with respect to lines, limits, boundaries. Blind.

'So, now I know, you can't be friends with them.' He looks up towards me, not quite at me. Now he knows the rule. I can feel him looking for recognition that what he has just said is still correct. Like some little kid who has nearly got the alphabet down pat but isn't quite sure if he's reeled it off right. He has no idea what it means, he just knows that saying it in the right order gets smiles from adults around him. Saying it in the wrong order will get him into deep trouble. I'm looking into his world, over the table of now empty tea cups. I can tell he's totally unaware of why you can't have sexual relationships with children. It feels good, soft, exciting – so why not? If everyone is playing, why is that bad? If they smile…? He is really trying hard to do the right thing, with the scant tools that he's picked up from the workshops in the prison, following his sort of invisible guide through dark swamps of life. It is not OK to have sex with children. That's the rule. He knows to stick to their rules, blindly, else he'll be banged up again.

—

'It's all about the line: that strange thing that doesn't seem to exist unless you step over it,' I say to Joseph the next day, sat in the same chair, the same kitchen, feeling safe again. 'The line is a dragon lying in wait, almost non-existent…until you step on it. It's the cute little teddy bear that turns into a wild animal and goes berserk with a machine gun. Just because it feels good doesn't mean it is good.'

—

Gary tells me in the car that he has had no female friend, ever. A glimpse into another world. I'd had misgivings about him after the first Contact Improv class. My main prejudice was the tattoo down his left arm, homemade, prison style. A woman's name. Must be right handed. On his right wrist, three wobbly letters of a woman. *Second wife? Daughter? Mother?*

After class I avoid making any eye contact, trying not to connect in any way at all. I just don't like the look of him. He's got one of those rubber faces of having made a lot of bad decisions in life. I don't want to be part of the next one.

Joseph who has brought me to contact says, 'There is a Contact Improv jam coming up this Sunday in Eden Rise, I can't make it.' I have no car, Joseph would have been my lift.
'I'm not sure I'll be able to get there,' I moan.
'I can pick you up and take you if you want?' the words, in Gary's voice, are somewhere behind my back. I suddenly click into a new set of parameters. I need a lift. I'll take a lift. My ideas shift: he seems safe enough to take a little risk.

—

In the car to the Sunday jam I get into hyper-monologue, a defence strategy in which I put all my words together as fast as possible so that no-one can get close: walls of words. I realise, even through my panic, that I'm overdoing it. *Stop! Breathe! Remember you have a body!* I remember I am sat in a car. I am safe right now, right here. Breathing in quietly but deeply I remember that panic is not the only option. I sit for some seconds in silence and then I turn things around. 'How was your day?' I ask. It feels invasive, as if I'm asking too personal a question. *Can I just stop and ask that?* I'm expecting him to say something like, I've been working all fucking day laying bricks, or the missus made me take the dog out for a walk in the bleedin' rain. Prejudice comes from 'pre' (before) and 'judging'. I've judged him before he's even into got to court.

So I am surprised when he says, 'In the morning I went to a meditation, Qigong.' *Is that what I once did to try and regulate my moon cycles?* 'And then I came home and I've been drawing and painting.'

'Drawing and painting?' I realise just how far out I have pre-judged. 'What do you paint?'
'I was painting my inner goddess.'

I am now open to him. Not sexually, but at least to have a conversation that is not about football, the weather or dog walking. 'For years,' he continues, 'my inner masculine and inner feminine have been in conflict, and I'm starting to get them to like each other.'

We meander through him talking about his wife, now ex, who by her admission, 'are not friends anymore,' but live under the same roof. As he says so I hear saliva get caught in the back of his throat. He swallows it down in front of me, a stranger. Poor bloke.

We get lost. Neither of us are sure where to go; I have no idea even where the Contact Improv jam is. He drives straight to a drive and heads up a steep incline, 'No, it's not here,' he mutters, and backs out again. I've never been. No idea. So we drive on. We stop at every left hand turn. I call a few people. No answer. He calls someone. No answer. I'm expecting him to flip. Under the pressure of a man lost, anything can happen. Though we've been having the goddess within conversation, I still feel his inner hooligan scraping to get out, to let off steam, to scream out, 'What The Fuck!' and thump the wheel in angry frustration.

'Goodness me,' he says, sat with the car idling. I'm actually really impressed. It's there, but he's handling it. I decide to go inside and feel how I'm doing. Quite peaceful. Not bothered about being late; I'm tired and wasn't even sure if I wanted to come anyway. This is new to me, feeling into myself, rather than the other. It feels quite exhilarating to not take on board his despair. If, indeed, that's what he is feeling. Who am I to say? He calls someone else, 'It's just me…Gary,' his voice dwindling off into nothingness, as if proclaiming himself a nobody. Self humiliation. I stay inside of me.

We find the place. It is actually where he thought it was, at the end of the steep drive where we first tried and turned around. Doubt just got in his way.

We were late, the others had already started, so we naturally made a pair for the first warm-up exercise. It was something I've never done before. The instructions were: touch the other, not in a soft, kind way, but experiment seeking out boundaries. It was designed to make us listen to the other's body. Gary is really sweet to me. Soft, shaky touch, uncertain. He never gets close to any of my limits. It feels a bit too frustratingly soft. 'You can go harder,' I whisper, but he doesn't.

Change around. My turn. I go with the instructions: don't just be kind. I whisper to him, 'Tell me when to stop,' and start with soft taps on his back and get stronger…and stronger…and SSSTTRrooooonger…I go up the scale until I am hitting him hard, thumping him, pinching him, pulling on his skin until it will stretch no more. It is affecting me inside. I feel like an aggressor. I can't take it: 'Shall I stop?' I plead.

'No, it's nice,' he says 'I've a strong tolerance for pain.'
But I don't and perhaps less for inflicting it. It feels on the edge of traumatic. I start again, stroking, tapping…and get harder…I get into it again, really pounding his back, and ask 'Are you OK?'
'Yes,' he says dreamily.

A few more slaps, my reactions are not so intense. I am dealing with this. Actually it's quite fun. I start again, now challenged to get to his limits. I hear my breath getting louder. The woman stroking the man next to us looks up out of her soft massaging dream, awoken by the slapping and thumping noises. It's a bit awkward. She and I smile at each other somewhat embarrassed, me for going for it, she because she isn't. But I get over it: I keep going. I'm getting into finding his limit, finding the line where he says, 'Stop!' But he doesn't. He is just smiling.

I stand on his back. All my 67 kilos. I stamp a little. It's hard to keep balance. Nothing. So I go to his arm and pull the skin. It feels like I'm de-skinning a chicken. 'I feel like I'm de-skinning a chicken,' I whisper.
'Thanks very much,' he mutters disgruntled – that was a limit: words, self images. I've heard, I won't say anymore.
'I'm pulling really hard are you OK?'
'Yes.'

It feels healthy, as if I were giving his fascia a good stretch out – it doesn't feel violent. I give up, I don't know how to be violent. I feel slightly numb emotionally while also feeling strangely energised, playful. I pretend to kick the shit out of him, without touching, and just as I playfully swing my leg again as if to bash his head like a football we are told to rejoin into a group circle. Time is up. Everyone gets up out of their dream-drift away from reality. I am exhilarated. I wonder where I can put all this pumped up energy streaming out of my released inner hooligan.

'A volunteer please,' says Joel. No one is able to respond, they are still coming out from deep relaxation. *I will! I want to!* I want to use this energy – I want to get going. 'I will,' I say as 'spiritually' as possible as if I were making a sacrifice. Joel explains the next exercise. 'Feel the weight of your partner on your arm. Feel the tension. Feel that point.' He leans on me, I lean on him. 'Now move it around your bodies and keep that point of tension.' We move with our hips touching, then our backs. He has a really nice steady tension.

I return to Gary and put the same weight onto him. I try to feel the tension: there is none. My weight is drifting towards him. He is not holding the weight. I feel the pressure in my calves, having to hold an unnatural balance. We move, hip to hip, I find my centre in the heels of my feet, not our hips, straining against his weightlessness. I cannot balance on him, there is nothing there. I will fall flat on my arse. He has withdrawn from the line, from the limit, trying to seek safety. I whisper 'Don't be afraid to use your weight,' but I don't think he understood.

I am getting nervous dancing with him. I'm reduced to dancing like a complete beginner. His weight is so hesitant; it makes me wonder what's going on for him. I wonder what is going on inside his head. *Where does he expect this to go?* I gulp. This closeness is uncomfortable…he's not groping, not at all, but it feels like it. I keep trying: I pull back my weight, try to find a common centre point, away from this heavy pressure in my heels. I try this lighter dance with him, but air comes between our contact, cracks of breath between us. Soon we drift apart.

—

On the way back in the car we talk again. I am now elated, energy is coming through me. I've been tumbling and dancing with a man who is so in his centre that he dominated the dance in a way that exhilarated me. I felt myself move in ways I've never moved before. He seemed so used to it, unaffected. He contained me in such a strong protection I felt completely safe. At one point I felt him hit me gently in the knees, and my legs collapsed into a fall and he caught me and whooshed me into a roll. *What pleasure!* The red carpet of a gentle landing, the strong wings of a silk take-off. We were both liberated knowing each of us were taking the responsibility of looking after our own safety, not the other. He moves around me, full contact, full pressure, light pressure, an exciting pathway through contrasting landscapes. I could never grow tired of this. I find myself flying through the air, weightless. Wow. I want more.

'I feel so open! So full of life!' I say to Gary, 'I feel so good! What a great night!'
'Yeeesssss,' he says pulling the word out for far too long, low gravelly tone. I wonder how he felt?
I want to share, so I do, ploughing through, ignoring whatever it is that he is not expressing, 'Isn't it amazing when someone in the field comes in who is much better, and how everyone's dancing improves?'
'Yours certainly did.' *Am I feeling him feeling intimidated?* I lost track of him in the dance. I don't know where he was at: he is not my responsibility. I let it slip. We chatter on a bit. I ask him how he came to Contact Improv.
'Ohh Tasmin. It was Tasmin who guided me here. I do her workshop, the 'Goddess Within' workshop. She's supported me all the way.' So much gratitude in his voice. And hope.

It seems that 'The Goddess Within' talk is safe territory for Gary: he knows what to think, what to say. Tasmin's trained him up. So we meander around her meadows a while. We talk about the interplay between the masculine and feminine within the psyche. It's a bit bland. I feel the same sensation again, how he isn't putting in his own weight.

So I go gently, and nose my way into weight between people while dancing. I don't say anything about the 'dance' between him and I, but we both know, I think, what we're talking about: no need to state the obvious. 'I've a problem with it. It is like when I'm with a woman in orgasm.' *Wow, that was a sharp u-bend!* Inside I am blinking furiously, delightfully. We're dancing now! 'I never know how much weight to give. So I pull back.' I am breathless with his honestly. 'It was a problem with my ex.'

74

Wow. What an insight! I flash to a sexual partner of mine who seemed to want to jump out, pull back, not connect as he was in orgasm. 'I know what you mean. I had a partner who seemed to want to completely pull out when he was coming. I found it insulting.'
'That's what my ex said.'

I look out of the windscreen; the headlamps are penetrating down the tunnel of the dark country lane. Hardly room to drive a single car width. This is Devon. 'It's actually my feminine within,' he says, 'my masculine has no problem with it. It's the female inside of me who is pulling back, not wanting to put too much pressure on the other, not wanting to hurt.'

I go inside. It's like, in that first exercise, when I was trying to push him to the limits of his pain. I got nowhere close. But I did have to go through my own limits in the middle of all that space. It was slightly traumatising. I didn't want to hurt. I didn't want to hurt anyone, any time. It's been instilled in me. And yet, I couldn't get to his limits. I didn't realise how much I have constrained myself, how much space there is out there. I'd said this in the sauna afterwards, and as I did I realised it is how I am in the world – in life – there is a lot more space for me than I have ever imagined, to be punchy, to go out and meet the world. No one is going to get hurt, quite the contrary. People could even be relieved! I begin to realise I am not pinned in. I mention it to Gary. 'Yes,' he says in his deep, flat voice, 'it was really pleasurable.'

I talk to him about limits, about the guy, Bryan, in Contact Improv in the states who got thrown out, not because he's a 'bad' person, but because he couldn't see the limits, couldn't get it, couldn't understand the idea of people's boundaries. I wrote a poem about it, and realised that it is us, the females, who set the line. I'm seeing it through Gary's eyes, trying to walk with him through this idea of limits and safety: where you can and where you can't put weight.

—

The sauna was too small for nine, so seven of us squeezed up on the bench and two stood. It was a bit weird us all being naked, but at the same time it wasn't really at all. We'd just been contacting with all of our bodies, clothes on, full body contact that included skin on arms, legs, stomachs, feet, hands, noses. This, though naked, was only shoulder to shoulder with normal sauna boundaries.

Later someone moved off the bench to go outside, to cool down under the starlit night. I was ready to sit. There was a space at the end, next to Gary, I sat there. After a while he moved, I think he thought imperceptibly, to brush his leg against mine. I moved, I think imperceptibly, away. After a time he shifted slightly away: a centimetre, at times, is bliss.

Gary was thirsty and went out for a drink. I relaxed into the space again. Meanwhile the guy who I'd danced with before, the one who had whirled me off my feet, came and sat in his place. Our skin brushed slightly. I left my leg where it was.

—

'The thing is,' I say as the hedgerows flash by under the spotlight of our headlamps, 'the line is changing all of the time. Each woman is completely different, so it's a matter of listening to each woman and where her limit is.'
'Tell me more,' he says, as we drive over a little ford, 'I'm new to all of this.'
His humbleness is so endearing. I want to help. I want to be there for him. It's so good sometimes to just talk about this basic stuff and realise how complicated it is.
'It's so hard for men!' I exclaim as we drive through a little ford: I just hadn't realised. 'Each woman is changing all of the time; if she has had a good day the line is different to a bad day, the time of the month, full moon, who she's just spoken with, if she's had chocolate or not, if she is feeling on for it, if she likes the guy or not. So many variables. And all this communicated non-verbally! Woa…I never realised how hard it is for men!'
The roads are so narrow. We come to a cross roads, and take a left. It feels like we are in a maze.
'It's hard. How can we ever know where a woman's limit is?' he asks dumbfounded.
'I guess you have to just listen.'

'It's not easy for women either,' I say later as we near the township of _____
⁴, 'it's not easy to maintain our limits, our lines. We have to spend a lot of time trying to keep men out.'

I am still slightly amazed that this man, with the tattoos up his arm, is learning to draw his inner goddess because he feels how it is opening him up and allowing peace to become part of him. His words go around my mind, 'The woman inside of me is starting to admit that there is a man in here too, without screaming at him, without him hurting her.'

After my exposition about lines he asks, 'So, like tell me, how do you begin to know how far to go with someone, how to know where their line is?' It's an honest question. He wants to have a decent relationship with a woman, wants to learn love, and wants to have sex. We all do.
'I don't know,' I say, 'it changes all of the time. It's not something you can just learn where someone's line is. I guess it's like we said: it's all about listening…I don't know.'
'With the inner female?'
'I guess. I don't know. I don't know what it is to be a man. I hardly know what it is to be a woman. I didn't realise until tonight how it is the feminine part of us that decides where the line is at any moment in time.'

As we whizz by hedgerows lit up like ghosts by the car's headlamps, it starts to gather ground in me that it's actually really hard to just hear – to be still enough to clear out our own noise – to listen to the other as well as ourselves as we constantly change, our limits moving in and out, our inner worlds shifting like weather patterns in the skies, while as each of us swirl around our ever-changing universe within us, the outer world too is also constantly changing, evolving, held on this planet as she too breathes into her own ever-changing life.

It's so difficult to stop the constant whirling within just to be able to begin to listen. 'Did you know,' I say, half in a dream, 'the heart looks like two ears?'

—

I say to Joseph, sat once again at the round wooden table in the kitchen, 'Don't you think it's amazing that everything is constantly changing, moving, breathing, living, dying? All of the time! Nothing is still. Nothing. We can only try to still ourselves and listen to who we are, where we are right now, where our limits are in the moment, and listen to the other, who they are being, where they are right now, where their limits are right now.'

He has his back to me, cooking his dinner on the stove, 'It's the only way we can move closer as human beings, as romantic partners, as friends, as communities…' I am in monologue, 'so that we can share together, from that deep place we are all searching for, going through ourselves together into that place of deep, eternal, still love…'

I hear his spoon clanging slightly on the edge of the pan.

What's inside?

Please look!
See me!
Ouch! The glare!
Don't look.
Look.
Don't look.
Come break down this door
I am suffocating inside.
A knock.
A shiver.
She bolts.

Creating or destroying in the ever changing present:
The know-how to handle ever increasing currents of life.

Formless Magik

The wood by the fireplace has gone.
The food for the potluck too.
They were in my hands.
Where have they gone?
Burnt, eaten, I know, but where?
How?
Structures collapsed into what?
What happens where we can't see?
And the us – the us
that went down to New Mexico
who, stunned by the dusk,
tumbled out of the van
into the middle of the road
to immerse ourselves in the exhilaration
of the dark blue skies,
the us who stared into space so limitless
and became suspended
in the silence of the earth
as it breathed into us
expanding with us
as far as the fading horizon –
where, just where, are they now?

The sky has never been the same.

I feel myself being constantly birthed into this world, into this newness, this present moment. Is anything ever the same?

A cloud forms. Its shape has never been before, never again. Even as I look it changes.

I look in the mirror. Is that me? Changing, changing, changing.

Every three days I have a new stomach lining.
Every month new skin.
Every three months a new skeleton.
Every year almost an entirely new body.

—

Marsyas, the Sileno, challenged Apollo to a flute competition. What was going on with Marsyas? Thought himself a god? Did he really think he could take on the ever-changing rivers of energies flowing, changing, surging through music and mould them with more grace than Apollo himself? Of course he lost! Apollo flays him alive. But Kerenyi wonders if it were a punishment, or if Apollo, actually having had to cheat in order to win, admires his effort and rewards him by stripping away his shaggy animal hide and so peeling away, like an onion, a skin of his psyche to reveal a purer more divine him.

—

Ascension or dissension?

—

Skill, preparation, technique. Anything will knock me if I don't know how to deal with it.

Can you handle, with grace and beauty, the energy streaming in through the windows of your soul?

—

'Will you play the trumpet for me?' asks Mercè. I have come to visit her, in her orange lounge. I've come straight from class, trumpet on my back.
'Erm….'
'Go on…'

I only do it because it is Mercè and I feel safe with her. I find it incredulous that I am opening up the trumpet case, putting the mouthpiece in, putting my music on a stand. My heart rate has sped up. I find it hard to talk. 'What do you want me to play?' as if she has a choice.
'Anything.'

What is this heart pumping all about? Am I excited to be playing for someone? Or terrified? I've never played for anyone else, not like this. This is a first. My ego is afraid of making a complete jack-ass of myself.

I put the trumpet to my lips and blow.

Time is suddenly going too fast for me to react. My brain has decided to clam up. I cannot get my eyes to focus. I am disassociating. *Which notes? Which valves?* I have to rely on unreliable muscle memory. I am blanking out. A white river of sensations is rushing through me. I have no space. I gasp into hyperventilation. Too much air? Too little air? My lungs sting.

My ego is red raw, too wired to be able to protect me from the glare of playing out of tune, mis-pitching, making mistakes. My face burns. I hang onto perfectionism like a priest onto dogma. I mangle notes squeezing them out through tense lips. Everything is happening too fast. I'm losing where I'm at. I want to throw down my trumpet and run.

I can barely hold on for the last line. I am in a marathon seeing the final sign too far away.

On the other side of trauma I unclench my fingers from the valves, my forearms are on fire. I look across to Mercè, no idea how that went. 'Wonderful,' she says. I can hardly believe her.

—

In the sports bar, music already too loud, I watch on life-size screens skiers and snowboarders jump off mountain sides, glide through the air, twist their body into an art form, to gently land and continue down the vertical mountain side. My body tingles with exhilaration.

How do they do that?

—

Years later I am in the brass band. Tony, the first solo cornet is not here. I am the soloist. We already know the pieces; we've practised them a lot. Les holds up his arms and conducts us in. I feel the piece is in my blood. As we play the music opens up to me; I feel into the space between the notes. The tempo is the same as when we couldn't play it, but now it feels we have more time inside of time. My fingers somehow move faster than my brain, rolling out a red carpet of notes. I feel secure, protected as I feel myself passing through petalled layers into the luxury of residing in the centre of each note.

I have slipped without knowing it into the centre of myself relaxing into the experience - feeling it more, giving shape to the music, finding the space to breathe my musicality into it. I become the music as it becomes me. I feel myself floating through notes, held by the embrace of the band. Les brings us to a close. Nods briefly. 'Next piece…' he says. I feel great: I was there.

How to stay in the centre?

I am stood in the middle of a field, ambling. A herd of cows at the far end of the field suddenly find me attractive. They run to me, excited. Excited about what? I forget they are not man eaters. I forget they are probably as scared as I am. I forget because they are so big. I have no experience of cows. They get closer, they begin to circle me, surround me. I don't know how to get out. They are within a metre of me. Part of me wants to scream. I stay still. Trying to show no fear. A cow comes up and sniffs my arms. *This is what dogs do right?* They are so big…I feel them all closing in. All around me big pink nostrils are so close I can feel their breath. I breathe as slowly as possible and realise I have to keep moving, slowly, without making any violent changes to my bodily movements. My legs are wobbling.

I move towards one of them in the direction of the gate. I imagine them stampeding me. They are heavy beasts. My heart races. I can only just bear this. I can only just stand this. The gate seems so far away. I stay within myself by brute force, calming myself as best I can. *Stay calm*, I say silently to myself. 'What do you want cows?' I say courageously out loud, 'I have no food for you!' and keep moving, as if I am simply ambling. *Show no fear!* They are now behind me, following me. I can hear the air going in and out of their nostrils. Inside I feel too close to imagined death. I hear my heart pumping around my head. *Don't panic,* I say to myself, *stay calm.* About two metres from the gate I cannot hold myself back any longer: I hurtle myself over the gate.

I lost it.

———

Can you stand firm even in the middle of your fears?

How long does it take you to scream?

———

Love, brings out all that is not love. Like absolute pure metal, brings out the impurities of impure metal. Can you stay innocent and open in the sea storms of love?

Parzival enters into the Fisher King's castle that magically arose in the middle ground only because he had attained the purity of being an innocent fool. Staying in his centre, he is accepted as friend, not foe.

———

'A cell,' says Filipe to the group of us Jungians, 'will fuse with another if it recognises the other as having the same qualities.' We listen, he is also a doctor, knows what he's talking about. 'However, if the other cell appears to be different, the cell will put up a defence mechanism and ward it off.'

———

How to know whether to merge with you, or not?

Chuck is an ex-boyfriend from so far back I've stopped counting. When we were living in Nepal together he told me this thing that I've never heard again anywhere else. Tantric sex is used by monks for heightening their awareness of consciousness by treading the razor-thin edge between losing themselves in impulsive instinct and disconnecting themselves from life and their own nature. They hold themselves in the middle of baying instincts. It takes a long time for the monk and the maiden to physically come together even to be able to touch. She sleeps in the same house for weeks. Slowly her mattress is moved towards his room. Once inside the room she sleeps beside the door for some time. Closer and closer she is moved towards his bed until they are touching, until they are making love, in a way that opens them to their divinity within.

—

Sarah killed all her husbands until Tobias came along. What was different about Tobias? He waited. He waited patiently and listened to her, to her energies, to his own energies and didn't advance until they were in sync.

When we fuse together, are bridges even necessary? Did he have to move towards her, or was she already there?

What I know is that he made love to her and only he did she not kill.

—

Mickey Mouse learnt the hard way. In *Fantasia* he didn't respect spells or magic, but simply looked for a quick way out from the work he had to do (on himself). In his sorcerer apprentice's mind he thinks that he can just dominate the magic like his master can. He gives no regard to the fact that he hasn't developed himself, his skills or his technique. He doesn't realise the implications, he doesn't see the personal work that is needed behind the scenes to contain the energy, to be able to dominate the energy; he just sees that he will not have to work. So he secrets a glance into the spell books and gets his mop to clean the floors and the bucket to swash out the water and before he knows it he has an inundation on his hands: buckets upon buckets of water and ineffectual mops. He has created destruction, and in the end days and days of work repairing what he's done.

He can start it up but he can't control the magic.

—

Meanwhile Chuck tells me, there are people who think of Tantric as something 'cool' to do, something that will get extra points on the 'who is more spiritual and totally making it towards enlightenment' game. We all play the points game I'm sure. I know I do. That's the game…we can't get out from being ourselves.

—

If Marsyas had contained the ever-changing energy of music with learned craft – surely he was rewarded? Surely Apollo stripped off his shaggy animal hide so underneath he could resemble more his god?

But if he wasn't able to handle the energy coming through him – surely he would have been eaten up by it, flayed alive by the music itself?

—

Mickey Mouse, without the timely return of his Master, could have drowned.

—

So, the cool spiritual wannabes go into Tantra, and they don't do the homework. They don't do all of the work to be able to contain the energy, to be able to keep their distance in order to not be hurled into the black hole of desire, they do not do the spiritual push-ups, so they don't have the strength of technique to walk the fine knife edge. They cannot stay in their centre once in the throes of desire. Instead, according to Chuck, they start wanting more and more sex, and then with more people, and then with children, animals and apparently progressively with urine, faeces and then blood. Blood apparently being the lowest of the low. The energy overrules them. They become slaves to it. No longer do they use the energy as a source, a tool, a power to create themselves, to become themselves, but are instead used and devoured by the power itself.

—

Mickey Mouse gets overwhelmed by the buckets and the mops taking on a life of their own. The deluge creeps further and further up the wall.

—

Do you want a relationship with me?

—

I don't know how true any of it is, I've never heard anything like this again after Chuck.

What I do know is that poison and medicine are the same. It depends only on the dose. How much technique do you have to hold big, fast streams of life coming your way?

And Marsyas plays alone, practising the flute, working out his technique, allowing the music to become him, containing it, giving it his shape. Music has become the single most important thing to him. He becomes the music as the music becomes him. But he doesn't let it overtake him. He doesn't lose himself within its power.

—

Àngel Priscini, another ex-boyfriend from before Chuck, once had a boyfriend who had a terminal illness. I remember talking to him about it, he was starting to get mighty pissed off with having to deal with his partner being devoured by the fears of his illness. Everything he did was about the illness, all he talked about was the illness. He had stopped being himself (with an illness), he had become the illness itself.

Just recently, I met again with Àngel Priscini. Sweet. We laughed, loving the time of our lives shared, as if the seventeen years since we'd separated had crumbled into dust and we were together momentarily as a couple. I ask him about the boyfriend with the terminal illness. 'Which?' he asks confused. It was ten or more years ago. I remind him about the bulk buying of toilet paper and bleach, in case of a supply issue, and, naughtily, that he used to rub lemon on his toes to make them softer so the boyfriend, with a toe fetish, could suck on them. 'Ohh yeah,' he says travelling through time, 'I bumped into him a couple of years back.'

I laugh, amazed. 'So he's still alive?'

'Yes,' he replies, 'probably still is, hobbling around in his fears.'

—

Will you dominate or be dominated? Can you find the way through the middle?

Facing the wrong way

Afraid to be wrong
she stuck to dogma
'This is how it is done.'
Missing out on what is.

Dogma. A picture of what once was, and is not anymore.

—

The sky is never the same.

—

Do you remember, sat outside Sebastian's house half-in half-out of his VW camper van. We in our tennis shorts, fueled by the high of a recent tennis match, feeling like gods? He asked you if you'll do the song writing course. You said 'I don't know…Bob Dylan never did song writing courses.' And it was then that I got it again, the same old message.

We need technique.

Everything, everyone, is unique and cannot fit into a map of what we have learnt of life, and yet without the maps, without fixing reality into some resemblance of stillness to be able to see patterns, we would not be able to develop technique to be able to mould life as it arises in this very moment.

We need to in-corpo-rate (in corpus: put in our body) technique, so we are free to surf the waves of the ever changing reality that swirls up and around us. Crafting with the arising of the ever-birthing present.

If a song comes to us from the land of songs, it is hard to craft it into reality if we have no tools. It will be a seed that falls onto hard ground, straight into the graveyard of songs.

We need technique to be able to love something into a beautiful, not monstrous, being.

—

The source of songs springs eternal.
The river runs through us. It is the never the same.
A poem runs through me, I can grasp it once. It will never return.

—

Hypothetically according to Planck theory, our atoms are moving in and out of us every $1/10^{44}$ of a second.

—

Arising and passing away, arising and passing away.
How much can you withstand of everything changing?

—

Do you want to try? You and me.

—

I have never had a kiss that is the same. Even from the same person.

I have never had an emotion that is the same. I have never fallen in love the same way, or got angry with someone the same way, or walked the same steps, even when I tread in my own footsteps in the snow.

—

'I have never felt like this,' I say to you. I feel conflict; as I say it images of me saying the same to others Irish waterfall up through my mind. But it is the truth: I have never felt like this, ever. It was different when I last said it to someone else, and when I first said it in awe. This now with you can never be repeated.

—

Do you want to try?

—

I want to say 'my love' but we are not there yet. I want to say 'darling' but I cannot. I want to say to you that I am not the same as anyone you have ever met, nor the same as the person you met the first day you met me, nor the same as I will be tomorrow. I want to say I cannot promise you anything at all. I want to say that I do not know who you are and that I'm trying really hard to just listen to who you are being right now, without thinking that you are like someone else, or that you will be this way or that.

I want to say that the stories I have in my head, and the stories you have in your head, are just us as humans trying to make patterns of what has happened to us in our lives, what is happening between us, what may happen in the dreams of the future that we have picked up along the way, created when we were little, when we were big, when we stopped to dream. Stories can stay unchanging, stories can be maps, but stories are just not real. The map is not the territory.

—

The ever-birthing reality, chaos, swirls of unrepeatable life. How to cope?

Middle way

A string too tight will snap
too loose will not sound.
The just right tension
makes the violin sing.

The contact is firm, but not too hard. My body is moving by itself around this man, this stranger. We are a flowing dance in a river of bodies. Smooth. Divine. Heaven meeting earth.

—

An egg needs just the right about of heat to hatch. Not too much, not too little. Miracle

—

Like chemicals reacting, if we meet we will both be changed forever.

—

I want to say, 'Stay in this moment,' and, 'accept yourself as you are now and accept me as I am now,' so we can be together and kiss in a way that we have never done so before; it may be really soft and tender, it may have an erotic sting or be a big disappointment. Each time different.

I want to say I am in awe of this miracle of the two streams of life going through our bodies right now, in this space, intertwining. Our paths are crossing. How is it that you and I are on this planet in the same place at the same time, weaving our ever-changing patterns? How is it they even fit? It is a marvel that our waters ride alongside each other, like rivers into seas, one fresh river water, the other sea water, different waters flowing beside each other, never mixing.

Maybe the membrane between us, if we stay close, like Tobias did to Sarah, may break, and I may taste of your waters, your eternal waters, mixed with mine. So we can become innocent fools passing into the castle of the middle ground as I taste the difference in my sips of being as I feel your temperature, texture, form, so different from my own, and it may change the very essence of my being. Can we ever know god without unbecoming ourselves? Can we ever know each other without changing who we are?

—

Slowly you come towards me, and I stay as firmly in myself as I can, so you can see me, the me that is now. I move towards you so we can dance together, knowing that tomorrow all will be different. Only the shepherd can haphazard what will happen in the weather between our souls.

Meeting you after the brass band

We have finished music making
that which simply creates forms invisible
a dance on the sound of our souls.
After rehearsal I wait,
barely hearing the others, for you.

I see your face
stones held by winter rye
turn stars birthing in my stomach;
out of myself
I am gently lifted
a bird hurtling into the sun.

Inner silence is rarely heard
I stand by you drowning in red pride
the waterfall deafens.

Love plays us
our death resurrects the now
we are taken over:
we, simple invisible forms
danced.

Do you see the movement of dust
dancing under the windowpane?
It too.

One foot on the map,
one foot in the ever-changing.

I Miss You

Trapped
on this hard earth
I grasp onto twigs
unable to stroll
our maps
or swim between
our eyes.

Inside, I am crying. We're walking down the steep road, that as soon as we get to the bottom we will march back up again. I have my cornet in my hand and Sebastian has his trombone. It's one of those strange situations where behind it all, behind the scenes, inside I am crying, long streams of tears welling from deep within the hole of depression. But outside it's a warm summer's day and we are about to play in Ipplepen's summer fete. We chat about an older man, a person who I normally would not give a second glance to, who goes about with an enormous parrot on his shoulder. 'He seems all too happy to stop and let people admire and talk to him,' I say, begrudgingly.

'It's a curiosity. Everyone knows him,' says Sebastian.

'I think he does it for attention, as if it gives him a tool to be able to interact where maybe he couldn't.' *And put himself on a pedestal,* I think to myself, *it's a simple, crude technique.* I wonder if I'm letting the depression talk; I'm caught in that perspective a little too close to raw reality, its decoration stripped off, too close to the void. I'm in puritan hellfire land.

'How so? What an interesting idea.' Sebastian, with his sparkling trombone always ready to see others in a positive light. *Phew!* Critical bitch has been overlooked – and on we chatter. The extension to the conversation comes as an image in my head: I wonder whether to tell him about the guy with the Google glasses in the geek conference I went to.

—

'I think Reality is what we create,' I declare lounging on my sofa; Ricard is on his. They are both mini so my legs have to hang uncomfortably over the side.

I think of Walt Whitman's 'Blades of Grass'. Being a poet must be different to being a shelf stacker, a digger machine operator, a wet nurse, a dietician, a gardener, a dentist, a beggar, a bus driver, a workshop facilitator, a cow farmer, a psychiatric nurse, an editor of pharmaceutical bulletins, a remover of asbestos, a secretary for a stainless steel factory, a pig inseminator, a vendor of plastic flowers, a seamstress, a plumber, a conductor, a postman, a manager of a toy shop, a team manager of programmers for Google Earth, a baker, a mechanic, a grave digger, a primary school teaching assistant, a street portrait painter, a designer of pornographic web sites, a shoe maker, a charity shop volunteer, a nun, a midwife, an NGO worker, a GP, a MP, a CEO.

'I mean, for me, just having travelled for years around the world for no conscious reason must make my reality different. No?'

He nods, 'Everyone creates their own world, with the skills and techniques that they have learnt along the way. We all have the same amount of intelligence given to us, we just use it in different ways.'

'Like?'

'Well you put a lot of your energy into being creative, into searching for yourself. Others, put it into other areas…' I am about to say, *like what?* But he knows the way I respond before I do sometimes. 'Like a chef learns to cook, which you haven't put a lot of your intelligence into.'

Point taken. Ricard is still trying to teach me how to do paella, but I bail out, get bored. My map of skills in the kitchen is so rudimentary that it takes a lot of effort to get anywhere, so many unknowns, whereas I can zoom along my maps of psychology.

'I wonder if we all share a common, unchanging Truth?' He cranes his neck across the armrest of the sofa to look at me. 'Like,' I say, 'is there anything at all in the world that is unchanging? Is there anything that we can rely on to not go completely mad? Or is it just our own illusion?'

'I have an idea,' he says, confiding in his characteristically over-guarded way, 'that our creation of Reality is that Truth and Necessity are impossible to separate. In order to create we must have Needs and Truth. Our reality is like a good beer. No one wants beer without the froth on the top. Beer and froth cannot go one without the other. What's important are the proportions. Some people have too much froth-you say, froth?'

'Yes, froth.'

'We need froth, but it stops us seeing the Truth, because we always have a necessity of some sort. We are always interpreting the Truth with respect to our needs. It's the map, as you say, that map of Borges…?'

'Si.'

'We can reduce our individual necessities, but you cannot have Truth without Necessity, like you can't have beer without a head.' + We both laugh at the image being so simple. 'If we never experienced need, we would never be incented to do anything but exist as a blob.' 'But do you think we can ever experience Truth?'

'Never!' he shouts suddenly like an enraged Caballero entering into the field upon his horse. He holds up his arm. I imagine his sword cutting through reality.

But I don't agree with him. I think about times when I've sat in meditation halls and have felt myself become nothing but light. It's not happened more than a few moments a few times in my life, but those moments of eternity changed me forever. 'How about,' I say, 'we cannot experience Truth when we believe we are separate from it?'

'¿Que?'

'Like, when we stop identifying with our ego as separate entities.'

I can tell that we're diverging in our perspectives. Ricard is a thinker, not a feeler; he's a philosopher, not a meditator. He is happy to consider the stars, but I've never felt he's gone too far inside of himself: he's afraid to. One time he told me that if he let out from his heart everything he felt, he was scared he would have a heart attack and die. For real. He is able to go into the smallest quarks in his head, but he doesn't find it easy to go into his heart. The world and him seem separate, as if he were an experimenter observing an experiment.

I tread carefully, 'Like Rainer Maria Rilke?' I wait for him to nod, 'You know? in the Duino Elegies?' In the stillness I continue, 'He says that to get 'there' you must leave behind everything, even your own name, just as a child leaves behind a broken toy.' He stays silent. There is no way to get him out of his firm conclusion that a person cannot ever see the Truth, which is true, but is it a partial truth? Maybe we can never see the absolute Truth, because even if we did, we would not be able to remember it – to record [2] it in our hearts – enough to bring it back to conscious experience on the human plane…but….

I push on, 'Like Bernardo Nante said, remember? – 'Dios es donde vos no sos'. God is where you are not. Remember?'
'But even then…well, from where I am, we can never see the Truth as it is, only through the glasses of my own needs…and that is my reality.'
'I agree and I disagree,' I say bending my mind to his viewpoint, 'but if you have an absolute transparent ego, in that moment of eternity then you have no needs! You stop being you.'
'That's your reality!'
We laugh at the discordant ideas and the silent clashing sounds of swords around us. I love all this sparring.

'You cannot make beer without froth,' he goes back to his original gambit. His feet twiddle hanging over the sofa, 'You cannot have Truth without some Necessity. We cannot separate them. So…so…' he says looking at his walls lined with books as if asking for backup, 'I see it like a good beer has just the right amount of froth on the top.' He twiddles his thumbs that are resting on top of his round tummy in glee. 'And if it doesn't have any froth then we don't want it, it is too flat. At the same time if we are served a glass filled with froth and no beer, then we don't want that either – it's a bad deal – we want the real thing. Our reality needs a certain amount of froth: our human needs, as you put it, are inseparable from our perspective view of Truth.'
'So you think we are constantly balancing our reality with not too much froth, and not too little?'
'Exactamente.'

—

I sit at the end of the long monastery table with Alice and her dog. She has just burst out laughing after me saying, 'As I look around here, I see everyone's lost.' Her laughter confuses me. I was being serious. Though she's laughing, I can also tell that she wants to continue. 'So,' I add warily, 'do you think there is a place where people have found themselves?'
She mulls it over for a little while; I gaze at the familiar Jesus statue in the middle of the courtyard, eventually she responds, 'Even someone who has a project and is doing it, and totally believes in it, still doubts. I mean there may be a person making amazing music, but still wonders if it's their real path.'

'I find it SO hard to know what I want,' I whine.

'Me too.'

'I mean recently I've been asking people who are in some sort of distress, 'What do you need?' When I'm asked it, it makes me feel heard, and also when they say, 'Nothing,' it gets me off the hook from having to try to find a solution for their distress…' Honesty is a funny bugger, makes me feel so big and so small at the same time. 'But you know, when I do ask it, most people don't know what they want, or need.' Between us there is a gaze that feels like the sea reflecting the sun. 'Often all they ask for is a cup of tea!'

'Maybe the truth is that we have no real needs.'

I am blown away. *We have no needs?! We have no wants?! We do not have to become anything! We are just this now?* Ricard's beer and froth idea comes into my head. 'Do you want to go on with this, deeper down, or are you tired?'

'I'm tired and I need to go to the toilet.'

I hear her, but I do want to go on. 'I'm just going to zone out.' And so I do.

In there, eyes looking inwards, I have a series of images that literally make me laugh out loud.

'What?'

'This idea thing…'

'Tell me…'

'You said you didn't want to go there…'

'Just bloody tell me will yer?' she says, Northern to Northern. I smile. It is so nice to be sworn at by a Northerner, makes me feel loved.

'Well,' I march onwards, 'there is this idea that there is Truth,' I put my hand on the table and make an imaginary pile of Truth to my left, 'and then there is Reality,' I make a pile on the right, 'which is split into Truth with Necessity.' And I sort of divide it in the air. 'If we have no needs, like we just said, then we don't need to create an individual reality, and we just have: Truth. Which if you look at it the other way around, means that in Truth we have no needs or wants!'

It is so good to watch her laugh her head off.

—

I once was given tickets to see a David Ferrer tennis match along with private entry to the accompanying VIP party. I was excited, all fizzed up. Inside there were lots of people looking around expecting something to happen. I found myself comparing their shoes, their clothes, their look: fancy. I had been invited into the Xerox stand by the ticket giver in an unabashed attempt to woo me. Everything seemed fancy, but after a while the fizz started to feel a bit tiring and I stopped being so nervous and excited and felt myself swinging less between feeling both inferior and superior with the VIP badge around my neck and my everyday scruffy shoes on my feet. Actually, it would have been all rather disappointing if it hadn't been for free: sandwiches and paella on little bendy plastic plates and forks that threatened to snap in my mouth.

There were however lots of photographers around, which 'proved' that this was an important event – for important people – why else would we need our own paparazzi? After an hour or so of hanging around with nothing but preening going on, suddenly a famous Barça football player walked around who I didn't recognise. There was a hubbub. It lasted about fifteen minutes. It's probably how much they could pay him for. Without recognising him, I could only see him as another human. Once the star had gone the atmosphere turned back into more waiting around within the fizz of unknown expectation, more weighing up of social position, digestion of the lukewarm paella and a dull but increasing pitiful fury watching the construct of image valued over substance.

Frothy fizz, nothing but frothy fizz.

—

I lie in bed. Body heavy. Room dark. Unable to move. In the depths of depression I only see nature in its violence, birthing, dying. Plants wilt. Animals kill each other. We are nothing more than instincts. I am nothing but a piece of dust in the ever consuming evolution of the cosmos. I am nothing. I spit on the idea of decorative fizz in my life, feel contempt for anyone trying to get out of this pit. Anything but this truth of nature is bovine, feeble-minded, a ridiculous comedy of empty masks: humans unable to accept anything but flickering shadows of Truth.

'Go, go, go, said the bird: human kind
Cannot bear very much reality.'

T.S Eliot 'Four Quartets'

'Have you seen those Google glasses?' We are now half way down the hill in Ippelpen. I am walking simultaneously through grey clouds of depression and the sparkle of walking down the road with Sebastian in the summer sun, both of us carrying our brass instruments to the start of the merry parade. 'Noooo…' he says, with his characteristic long vowels full of interest in the other. He always shows such wonderful attention to people. A real smoothy.

'There was a guy once in a conference I went to…' A big lorry goes by. We are a sky blue crowd of band blazers. I feel like I'm in a musical army. We've got that power of numbers thing going on and forget that a big lorry could actually knock us over. He suddenly puts his hand towards me to protect me and goes out into the road. 'Watch out!' I say, his trombone feathery close.

Sebastian turns to me, as oblivious as I to any danger, 'a conference?' he says as if we were in a cocktail party and he were James Bond. I just love it.
'Yeah this little Italian squat man had Google glasses. Everyone was surrounding him. He had all the power. I couldn't help but be really nice to him too, so I could have a go. He gave me the next go on them…the others who were waiting were men…' We flash eyes in a spurt of laughter. 'Like the parrot man!'

'What were they like?'
'The glasses?'
'Yeah.'
I swallow, 'There's a little Perspex cube in the right upper corner of one of the glasses…'
'There's glass in the glasses?'
'No…nothing…just this little clear box…and it projects images on it…'
'Noooooo!' he says, as if we were nothing but famous personalities decorating glamour with our beauty.
'It has voice recognition,' I say, smiling, caught between wanting to glam up, and get to the end of my idea, 'so you say, 'Google glasses, image me a 'cat'', for example, and a google image of a cat appears…on this little box thing in the corner of your eye…'
We stall a little, there is a bottleneck in the road, blue blazers all coming to a stop, '…and you can say, 'Google glasses, show me where the nearest public phone is,' and it goes to Google maps and that blue line – you know when you ask for directions?' Incredulity flows out through my mind as if through holes of a sieve, 'Well,' I say, feeling myself go into a would-you-believe-it hairdresser tone, 'the line feels like it is coming out of your stomach…and you just follow it…so that you don't look at reality any longer…just the map in the corner of your eye, and the line changing in real time…'
'Nooooo!!!' Sebastian is pulling me out from the dark world of depression, into the fizz of the social.

'People kept walking into tables and chairs! The Italian kept having to call out, 'Watch out!' Reminding people how to walk!' We both laugh down our noses. 'I did it too…I almost banged into a table! I was looking at the little box, following the blue line, mesmerised…'

He comes out of the laughter with a muse, 'You know…it makes me wonder what is reality and what is real these days? The lines are blurring for me.'
'I know what you mean. It's pasted all over technology. People stuck on their iPhones, sucked in.'
'People with thousands of facebook 'friends' lonely as hell.'

We come to a standstill at the bottom of the hill. This is where we are going to start the parade. The May Queens, the little ones, dressed in white frilly dresses are coming out and beginning to group up behind us. They can't be more than seven years old. So cute. Our job is to fanfare them into the village field, where the May Pole is waiting.

'You know Jorge Borges?'
'No,' he says, the sun dazzles me as it reflects off his trombone.
'He's a bit like a Samuel Beckett of the Latino world…a magical realist…'
'Right…' I can tell from the way that his tone lifted at the end of the word that he has no idea what I'm talking about.
'Anyway,' out of the corner of my eye I see a little boy who makes me smile deep inside: white shorts that seem too big for his shinny little legs, white shirt

and black bowtie, pushing between grownups legs. It reminds me of an old black and white photo of my Dad: stiff but proud as he holds the May Crown more than sixty-five years ago. I feel like we are suddenly in the past.

'Borges wrote this story of a king who wanted a map so detailed that he calls in his cartographers and demands they draw up a new detailed map for him of his reign.' I pause listening in to see if he's interested. He's listening. I keep going. 'They come back to him a couple of days later and unroll the map on the table, 'NO!' he cries, 'I want a bigger map…!!!' So they bring him a bigger map…and roll it out on the floor.
'NOO!' he cries,' I take a breath…part of me is watching the little boys being made to stand behind the little May Queens. 'The cartographers scurry off – guillotines looming large in their minds – and a couple of days later they come back to the King.
'Sire,' they say, 'we have drawn for you a map that is one to one, which is as big as your land.'
'Yes,' the king says at last relieved, 'that is what I desire.'
'But where shall we put it, Sire?'
'Lay it over the land.'
And so they do, and the people get used to walking on the map. And all is fine… but after a time, as nature would have it, the land underneath changes, erodes. What is underneath is not the same as the map any more, the simulation has become a simulacra.' I had to look up the word simulacra when I first heard it, so I add, 'A simulation is a copy of something that also exists, but a simulacra is a copy of something that doesn't exist anymore.' Sebastian nods, as if slightly spellbound but I'm going to have to speed up the story, the band are starting to get into formation.
'But,' I say a bit more quickly, 'the people don't notice and keep walking on the map, unaware that they are really walking on thin air. The map has no meaning with respect to what is below.' I turn and look at him. *Did he get it?*

'What a good story!' Sebastian, always quick to complement. He has a natural way with him, says the right thing at the right time. 'How to make sense of reality if we don't have a map? And how to be in reality if our maps are out of date?'
'Aha! Yes Sir!' I say, cheered on, 'Or like what you say about technology: we look at Google now almost more than what is right in front of our noses. We forget about the trees, and the wind, and we think about getting Bill a strap for his tuba on eBay so he'll stop complaining that he can't march.'

The girls in their white dresses have got themselves lined up, the little boys look confused. 'Like we are on the maps too much, and the grass is growing under our feet without us noticing,' says Sebastian.

Les has got the band together, cornets at the back, there is a space for a trombone up front where Sebastian is not yet. We are taking on the semblance of something half professional – and suddenly the moment has arrived. We both dash into place. The drum bangs three times and we are off! We march, half panting wobbly notes up the hill.

'The pure masculine (not be confused with male, or man)', I pause.
Mercè nods, 'I see as represented by Apollo, – 'a': absence of; poly: 'many'.
'¡Ohh si! ¡Que bonito!'
She's got it! The absence of individual. It is the union of all things in one. 'So
Apollo is the absence of the multiple. You know? It's Light, the immutable laws,
the forms, pure ideas, consciousness…'
'…and it's sterile,' she says licking her lips.
'…and it's sterile,' I agree with gusto, 'it's the map,'
'But the map is not the mountain.'
'No, and looking at the map is not the same as sweating up the mountain side…'
'And having a picnic.'
'No, it is not.'
'But without a map we would become psychotic.'
'Floating around like jetsam in the ever changing…'
'Unable to anchor ourselves to achieve any goal.'
We smile. We are trying to convert the converted.

I laugh down my nose. I love Mercè. I love that we can meet here in the clouds
and yet still be pedestrian. 'Without maps we'd be fucked.'
'Meanwhile,' I continue, picking up my pen again and drawing a random knot of
curves on the serviette on the table of Mercè's regular, where she often stops to
have a coffee, 'reality, the feminine, the creative, that which is constantly
changing, is …'
'Chaos!'
'Si señora! It can never be predicted, there is not one map that exists for this
exact, precise moment.'

A moped honks its horn at a passing car. A bird glides diagonally over the road.
Mercè catches a certain ray of light in her cat eyes that reflect after her cataract
operation. I smile into her smile.
'This moment will never, ever repeat. This you. This me. Will never occur ever
again.'
'We are ever-changing reality.'
'There's no map for that.'

There is a slight pause in the air, and as if synchronised we both push our chairs
out. It's time to get going to Can Martí and lunch.

Constant Change

Never ending
waves of change
even the gods are under construction;
no place to get to
only to be.

Hermes Trismegistus taught, 'That which is Below corresponds to that which is Above, and that which is Above corresponds to that which is Below, to accomplish the miracle of the One Thing.'

—

'So let's say we need maps to make sense of our lives and yet we cannot reduce the ever changing to a static sterile map…how to we reconcile the two? The maps and the reality of living?' asks Mercè in her ever deep, ever wise questioning.
'Be more flexible in our maps? Not get stuck on what was, what should be but….' I want more ali-oli.
'Like our egos, I guess, they contain our sense of self, but if they are too inflexible…' she bites into a piece of rabbit.
'People with fixed ideas of who they are…' I say spooning the ali-oli onto my plate.
'¡Chungo!' she says, around the rabbit. 'People with big IDs: difficult people, living in their ideas of themselves disconnected from reality of who they actually are!'
'…and we also need a sense of self, else we'd be psychotically changing our ideas of our self image all of the time.'
'We need our ideas about reality to survive a reality we can't ever imagine!'
'Richard always gets in a tiz-woz about certain Platonists who confuse reality with Plato's Forms, as if the Forms themselves were actual reality.'
'Traps of the mind as the ground of reality ever changes!'
'Yep…' I say, getting confused, losing my sense of where I'm at. 'Like how to get the balance between our thinking mind and our feeling heart?'
'How's that going for you?' she says, looking at me more intensely over the table.

Inside my mind a power vacuum cleaner sucks up all this beauty that Mercè and I have been creating. Like a house of cards imploding into a vacuum, the world of the maps and woven ideas between us disappears, leaving me with what I was trying to ignore: a dark corner of my mind.

'Uf!' The noise comes out of my pouting lips, confused. Knife and fork hovering. *What to talk about? My thoughts or my feelings?* Right now I am thinking I would like to end the relationship with Ricard, right now I am grieving an end that hasn't happened. *What's real?*

'Talking of which I didn't call him to tell him I'm eating out…and you know how he likes everything controlled…'

—

'Can you believe that Reality is ever birthing?' I say to Sebastian as we wait in the car at a red light. We are going off to a Funk band rehearsal. It's my first night, I've got my trumpet in its gig-case cradled between my legs. 'Never again,' I say looking at him, 'will we ever be sat in this car, in this position, at this red light, in this rain, ever again…it will always be different.'

As we spend more and more time together I am beginning to feel I can relax with Sebastian. Going to brass band concerts, talking about his VW van that I borrowed from him and smashed the corner of within 15 minutes, and now going to Funk, I realise we are weaving a rich tapestry between us, which extends in a lattice work to others. As the windscreen wipers do their dance, I start to realise that intimacy, in the form of friendship and community has a lot to do with being able to spend time with each other. Beautiful simplicity.

Green light, we're off. The moment has ended as another begins.

Simply being together

Time trickling
delicately
between them,
with soft feelers
their presence
tendrilled gingerly
through the velvet
gently beginning
to see,
quietly
opening to
to be seen.

Paul and I are in the New Forest. We are doubly celebrating: my birthday and that we are miraculously together despite living on the opposite sides of the world. It feels like we have broken through a membrane of reality. It is so nice to be in this wonderful forest. It is so green, the trees so tall. I feel its beauty flowing through my blood. I feel my body relaxing, opening, becoming more natural, wilder, more real somehow. We have had a little picnic topped by a gluten-free birthday cake that my mum made for me and are wallowing in simply being - not having to talk or be super brilliant people forced to portray masks of being happy and successful covering over the pain of humanity with false smiles. We are just being us in the bliss of having space to be real. Human can be so restful.

Lying down on the ground, looking up through the trees, we watch the leaves rustle against the wispy white clouds in the light blue sky outlined by branches. Lush. I feel Paul's head close to mine. I feel myself in a soft cocoon of love. 'I've just been reading that,' Paul says quietly, his soft breath breaking the silence like a feather, 'if we went in a space ship for 20 years to another planet and then turned around and came back for 20 years, when we got back to earth again, that earth would have moved on 36,000 years and yet we would have experienced only 40 years.' I mull it over in my mind, working through ephemeral images. Time seems like a membrane. I once felt so deeply that it felt like a knowing that we are nothing but time flowing through us. 'It's hard to get my head around it…

,

'I know, me too…'

We walk back hand in hand, soft, easy, at peace. I imagine the trees. They live for 500 years, more. I will live for 90 maybe. I wonder if they are simply in a different time. 'I wonder if trees are just in a different time dimension. A different reality? I know that little plants dance and play, I read that once in 'La Vanguardia' Newspaper in Barcelona. They have great interviews on the back page. This was with a guy from Italia – whose name was Stefano someone – who took photos of plants growing, one frame an hour or something like that, so that we can see them in their time frame…and they play!' I squeeze Paul's hand and smile into his eyes. 'The young sunflowers didn't just turn their head to the sun, they practised moving, they moved all over the place, and it really did look like they were playing.' He moves into me, hip to hip and lifts me, contact dance style. I feel the delight of swinging around his body.

Back side by side I say, 'Can you imagine what it must be for trees to see us?'
'I guess they don't. I guess we are like flies to them, going too fast to be able to focus on, if at all – we are lightening fast. Too fast for tree vision.'
'It may take a decade for them to take a step…'
'Can you imagine if they moved?' he asks going into images where I am.
'You know how they drop their seed and new shoots shoot up, maybe that to them is a step, and that if we sped it all up,' in my head I try to .zip file time, 'so that in a video of a minute we see what moved over the course of a century, maybe they are all dancing together, moving over hills, or exchanging information, organising symbiosis, or going to war with other species…maybe… .ohh it seems so silly…'
'What?'
'Well, like maybe, they would seem to have a consciousness that is similar to ours, if we all lived in the same reality of Time?'

I remember watching the film, 'Inception' with Leonardo DiCaprio where there were four or so layers of reality and as the actors went down the layers, each layer became more and more instable. Right at the bottom, in the shared dream space of the unconscious mind, Leonardo discovers an idea he didn't know about that was planted into his mind by his father, and in that space, in that unconscious space that he has become conscious of, he has to feel his wound. In seeing it, he heals. His upper world changes. 'But what's interesting,' I say to Paul, 'is that as a collective we are becoming aware of different realities.'

Closing the Gap

How can I imagine
without stumbling upon my dreams?
I paste them over your face
as I dangle dangerously
over the gap between
fantasy and reality

Santiago Rodriguez was provocative. As a professor in the Masters in Jungian Psychology and Psychoanalysis he taught us about complexes. But he didn't want to do it by the books. He forced us to understand with our minds through direct experience. He did it by innervating our complexes - so that we would feel them. I know of two women who refused to go back to his class and one woman who actually dropped out of the course all together thanks to him and his rather unorthodox didactics.

I remember in one class he had been smoking while talking to us (which was simply and utterly prohibited in any public building, and doubly so as a lecturing professor) sat back on top of a desk. There was a can of Coca-Cola behind him. Without being aware of the can behind him, he kept pushing it ever so slightly with every wiggle…our eyes were glued to it, watching it each time it travelled a little closer to the edge. I was finding it hard to listen to his discourse, part of me wanting to see what would happen…wanting to see it fall. He talked on, oblivious. I was breathless to see how he would react.

He nudged it again.

We sit there. Listening, spellbound by the silence of the can on its hero journey.

Nudge.

I feel the collective consciousness of everyone but him in the room watching it get closer and closer to the edge. It's so right there, surely, now?…It's going to tip…just one nudge…go on…nudge…squiggle a bit again…go on…

Nudge.

I am in gleeful empty mind space. Anticipant.

Yolanda's voice breaks the spell, 'There's a can of coke behind you…it's about to fall…'

Was that a collective silent groan? Bummer! It's not going to happen. He turns around, sees the precarious can and with his quick mind says, 'You see? Complexes…you must have all have been watching that can. I've been sat here for a time…' Yolanda nods guilty as charged. We all sit there in dead stillness. We know him. Each shielding differently from being on the firing end of his sharp tongue. 'You see? The complex of being a good student overrode the idea of the can falling. You said nothing. You didn't want to stand out. You didn't want to speak up,' he says directly to Yolanda. 'The ego doesn't want that. The ego wants to stay safe, not take risks…but when you see that the can is about to fall, another complex, the 'saviour' or the 'I-don't-want-to-feel-the-guilt-of-seeing-it-fall-over-when-I-knew-it-could-happen complex' kicked in and overrode the 'good-quiet-student complex' and made you say something.'

Yolanda goes bright red.

That was when I 'got' what complexes are: our unconscious ever-working maps of how to deal with life as it arises chaotically all around us.

—

In the second year Rodriguez came back. Most groaned. I for some reason adored him.

So he's back. This teacher with the short-man complex, who has a big car and a big voice and a big personality, but is, quite simply, very small. He wears his knowledge of psychology like the old man in Devon who wears his parrot. He's teaching us about La Psicologia de Dos, The Psychology of Two. The idea is simple, and genius.

'You have to study all you can on psychopathic problems. Have Gabbard, Bowlby, Kernberg, Shapiro…' He looks out of the window as if he is a sensuous diva, 'Have them on your bedside table. Go to bed with them. Go to sleep with their words in your mind. It is our duty, as people wanting to be psychoanalysts or Jungian therapists, to read as much as possible about how personality disorders operate,' he moves down the room to another window and looks out. I wonder if he is trying to be romantic, dreamy.

'Memorize the maps in your head, integrate them, let them change you.' As he talks towards the window his tone is slightly flattened by the glass, 'You have to be well versed in the landscape of what hysteria is, what narcissism is, what psychosis is, what neurosis is…it is our duty to know, to create working maps so as to not get lost in the patient's psyche. It is our duty to be comfortable knowing where a person may be conceptually; and when that person walks through our therapy door,' he turns around with a dramatic pause, 'it is our duty to forget everything we know.'

He pauses and goes around the room staring at each of us in turn, deep into the eyes. I shift in my chair uncomfortably. He continues his idea, 'Each person is completely and utterly unique and does not fit into any mould – ever.' He stands there, as if he were very tall. 'E-ver.' Some students are scribbling down notes. I wonder if they are avoiding the eye contact. I draw what I hear. 'They need the space to express themselves in their unique position. If we try to fit a person into what we know, we are very, very bad therapists. But if we do not know the maps, we will, with our clients, get lost in the woods of the unconscious. A good therapist has a foot in both worlds.'

—

One world: Truth. One. Plato's forms. Archetypes. Natural Laws. Stable. Unchanging in human time. Pure. Perfect. Merged White Light. Sterile.

Another world: Reality. Multiple. The constantly birthing chaos of the present moment. Unrepeatable. Unpredictable. Light separated into rainbows of colours. Uncontrollable. Exploding constellations of imperfections. Vibrantly fertile.

Under the canopy of the trees Paul says, 'Like you and me.' I dangle in his silence.

'You and me what?'

'We have completely different realities.' I know to stay quiet, to give him space. He processes his words differently to me. Deeper, slower. I know I often go too fast, fizzing about, sprinting around the surface. 'Well….' he says as if his mouth is a harbour waiting for a submarine to come up from a thousand leagues under the sea. I know not to wait on the edge – I have learnt to not wait for his words with an over-eagerness, burning in a bonfire of excitement. I go off in my senses, drinking in the sunlight lime in the leaves. It slows me down, grounds me.

'There's the obvious,' he says slowly in his adorably deep, soft voice of wisdom, 'age,' pause, 'gender,' pause, 'where we come from,' pause. I let the shadows dance into my eyes. 'But also the way we are. Sometimes I feel we disconnect.' There is something so wonderful and terrifying about being with Paul - he tells me what he really believes in a totally non-judgmental way. I feel my heart start to pound into my eyes. 'I feel sometimes that you are in a mental space disconnected from the ground of emotions, of sensations, of anyone but yourself. Don't get me wrong - I love your theories and concepts, but sometimes they seem disconnected from what is actually happening.' It is easier to hear this in the woods, where ground is all around me. I feel safe. 'And then sometimes,' he continues, 'you scare me with your strong emotions. I don't know how to handle them. I have no map in the chaos of what happens between us.'

I know what he's saying. I feel his fear when I express intense emotions. It makes me feel unsafe as if it is not OK to express all of me. It's one of the unresolved things between us.

'Labels are good, you know, they help us make sense of all this swirling around us, but the labels aren't the same as what is actually happening…' his voice is soft, knowing we are both in a difficult place. It's courageous to be honest. 'You know you are too complicated to be put into a box.' I nod, staying open, letting it come into me along with the lime green leaves that are glowing behind him. 'I'm too complicated to be put into a box.' I nod keeping my eyes connected to his. I feel the discomfort of being so deep with him mingling with the elation of being so deep with him. The space between us feels so intimate, so hairline close and yet impossible to breach right now. Part of me wants to kiss him, hug with him, run away from him. 'You know that we would both die if we were forced to stay in the box.'

As we continue walking, Joseph Campbell comes to my aid, pulls me back into the mind - just as perfectionism kills creativity, it also kills love. 'In the past,' I say to Paul, getting close to the car park, 'I've idealised my partner. In my mind I've put him up on a pedestal, projected all my animus onto him, tried to ignore the nagging reality. But the boxed in princes turn into frogs you know?'

'The destructive power of idealism…' he says. I feel his lean body besides me. It is comforting while at the same time I feel if I launch into a full-on hug at any moment he could simply disappear. Such a fine balance between giving and clinging! I cannot lean on him as if he were 'mine' as if he were my support. I have to support myself. I don't like it. I do like it. I wish he would be my daddy. I am glad of all this freedom to be me, to be independent, to be a grown woman. All this freedom is terrifying and I want to go home to base camp. I lean on him. He disappears somewhere inside of himself. The ground underneath me shifts. I stand on my own two legs. It is OK. I am able to support myself. I always have actually, now I come to think of it. I am grateful. I am confused by the simplicity of it all.

'And I get disillusioned and disheartened,' I say, standing my own ground, 'and the little girl within, who still believes in the existence of perfect princes and 'The One', wants to run and start the search all over again.'

'And does it work?'

'Their masks slip off their faces, my pedestal crumbles underneath them…I've tainted their imperfect humanity by my blinding ideals.' I'm not sure from where all these words tumbling out of my mouth have come from.

'Yeah. Humanity is imperfect,' he replies slowly, mulling over our words, like an oxen pulling a heavy plough. Trees. Lime Green. Roots on the ground. 'If we strip away our ideals, if we rely less on our maps…you know?' The trees bend to listen, 'If we relate with compassion to the other's imperfections,' his words are hypnotising, 'knowing we are all imperfect,' he slows down his rhythm and stops beside me, '…surrendering to the beautiful imperfection of being human,' he looks me deep into the eyes, 'well, that's maybe where true love lies?'

In between us, birthing up through our realities is a stillness, a silence, so deep it binds us into this moment – right here, right now - as our two psyches open and join to make one. We kiss into the deep source of cool, fresh waters, remembering our real selves deep within.

———

'Do you fancy it?' Christopher says with a mild panic and surging excitement. This is his recurrent testing ground. He's constantly saying that he wants to do Tantric workshops but never does.

'Yes, OK.' I say hoping my confidence will cover over my nervousness. 'Let's do it. What do we need to do?'

'Nothing,' he says proudly, 'I've signed up already in case we wanted to.'

'How much was it?'

'Free. I guess it's more like a short introduction. The only thing is that we need internet.'

In the frantic preparations I pluck up the courage to ask next door if they will share their internet with me just for the afternoon. I don't tell them what it's for. They quite happily tell me I can use it, whenever I want to. It was the first step we made in a friendship that was to become deep and supportive. Beautiful neighbours.

Christopher and I are finally sat, bright eyed and bushy tailed, on the sheepskin rugs in my pad as we listen to the introduction of the OMing course. Orgasmic Meditation. They talk about how men have forgotten how to give, how women have forgotten how to receive. They talk about how people in general seem to have got stuck sexually and how OMing has broken their dam(n)ed walls letting the water flow through and around them, breaking through blockages, destroying them, taking everything with the flow; so that in the resulting space they can open again to the world of the sexual.

I am slightly breathless. I wonder if I'm holding my breath. Can I do this? I am going to be overwhelmed? My mind has gone into blank. My feelings are spiralling around the imminent doom of breaking down, exploding, finding myself being hurled into a bottomless void of psychic despair. But I also know I am slightly breathless from the excitement of entering into new territory, of the sight of distant horizons that could become mine. Fear and excitement for me at times are so difficult to distinguish.

The OMing workshop is live streamed. They have got through the introduction and now it is time for some warm up exercises. I am surprised and buoyed by the fact we simply have to talk to each other, clothes on. The exercise consists of telling a well known story, and the other can say, at any point, 'Change!' and you have to change a part of the story. When it's my turn I choose Little Red Riding Hood.

'Once there was a little girl who had a red cape on, and was walking into town to go to the market,'
'Change!' says Christopher, eyes bright in the connection we are feeling, us two sat alone in the safety of my living room, doing something that for us is on the edge.
'…to go to buy a fork-lift truck. It was a long way to go. The path took her through woods, that were dark and scary,'
'Change!'
'…that were bright and full of yellow flowers of every kind. Daffodils and tulips and little yellow flowers and,' I realise I don't know any more yellow flowers, so I move on, 'and suddenly a wolf sprang out,'
'Change!'
'…and suddenly a…erm…a rabbit came out from under a yellow flower and said, 'Little Red Riding Hood, I am going to eat you!'
'Change!'
'…I am going to throw myself into a pot and sacrifice myself so that you don't have to go to market and can play and dance all day,'
'Change!'
'…so you can go back to your grandma and share a rabbit stew.'
'Change!'

Suddenly it is getting much easier to improv. I'm flowing, released from having to stick to some standard, to a story, free to explore my own imagination.
'So you can go home and eat your grandma, and become the woman of the house. But Little Red Riding Hood said, 'You know I don't want to eat my

grandma, or eat you even, I feel I am fully ready now to become a vegan. And from that day onwards she didn't eat anything that had moved more than 5 centimetres in their life.'

'Change!'

'…and from that day onwards she kept a secret store of sausages which she never ate in public and pretended she only ate grass lichen.'

Then it is time for feedback, which Christopher and I, being the only live participants in the room, do together as well. It feels as if we are opening up to each other as a couple. It feels like we are getting to the juice. 'It was so liberating being able to go out of the box!' he says.

'Yes!' I beam, 'I feel as if we were showing ourselves, sharing parts of ourselves, rather than sharing a story someone else made up.'

'In sexual pleasure,' says the facilitator on the computer screen, she's talking to six attendees in the studio, 'we can follow where we are taken by our bodies, we don't have to get anywhere.' The penny drops. I've been trying to force myself along the story of a sexual myth that says, 'You have not had successful sex until you orgasm.'

That evening I let myself follow the scent of the trail. I am being lifted to the skies, I can feel my body tingling, something taking over, I am on the upwards spiral into heavenly bliss. Something makes me slow down. I do not panic, not today, not after the workshop. I allow myself to be, to explore what is. I swoop down, back down to earth in such a relaxed state that I realise that I am in the middle of a beautiful, wonderful, mind-blowing massage. This doesn't have to go anywhere.

Spiralling Delight in the Way of the Middle

We do not reach climax
and push on over into
roller coasters of screeches
that echo through the skies
kamikaze free-falling
into the slumped relief
of exhausted egos,
but come down
following the trail
allowing what is
to overtake us
to become us.
In the valley after the climb
I feel rivers of orgasm
in the stillness of the lake
in the beauty of being here,
me inside me seeing you
smiling into the flight path

between our eyes.
Muscles relax and open
into soft sheens of
sparkling pleasure.
I open more
dark, moist, velvet;
Slow, ohh so slow,
we pulse
vibrantly alive.
Down
in this picnic of the senses
we lie in the lee
of a wind singing rock
deep within our bodies.
Realms within realms
I feel worlds opening before me
amazed at these secret gardens.
The stillness of being here with you
rises me,
pushes me once again:
I am a kite taking to the skies.

I am in the Monastery of Dreams, in a contact jam. I have been dancing hard, sweating slightly, on a high of energetic movement. The music changes, the beat is slower, softer. I do not want to slow. I do not want soft. I keep pounding. I begin to feel ridiculous, as if there were nothing underneath me, as if I were out of sync with the world. My mind says, *Allow yourself to slow, allow yourself to go down. Remember OMing!* So I do. My body slows down, goes in, goes deeper. *Ahhhh! Yes!* Yes, this too is nourishing, this too. *Yes.* It feels sublime to let my body enter into this place, velvet soft swirls sensual in their very nature. I cannot open my eyes afraid to see someone looking at me being so sensual in 'public'. I cannot open my eyes, because I don't want to lose this feeling. I am me with me. I am a living, breathing, sensual being. I swim like silverfish through the soft joy of existing. I am lying on the floor feeling it hold me like a mother in her arms.

A new song. Faster. I do not have the lightness of energy to move fast. I want to stay here, in this dark, earthy velvet. I want to stay with this sensuality. I do not want to move fast. The music does not stop. It continues with the faster beat. I remember how I felt before this slow joy of mine: I didn't want to come down here. Now I don't want to go up. I move the easy things to move a little faster - ankles, wrists, toes - while lying down still. Little riverlets of faster are silently caressing me to roll. I do. I roll, feeling my body change gears. In the momentum of the second roll, my legs bend and push to standing. I bounce to the rhythm of the song. Soon I am moving, moving and dancing and laughing and cannot remember why I wanted to stay so slow, not when I could be feeling this!

———

'**I guess,**' **says Paul,** '**one of the gifts of living well,** is being able to follow what is, rather than what one thinks it should be.'

'Yeah…' I say stroking his arm as he pushes me with his pelvis against the driver door of the car.

'Not,' he says softly into my ear, 'confusing Plato's forms with reality.' I close my eyes, in the dark I see golden patterns on the inside of my eyelids, they get brighter as I feel the joy of my lips spread into a Cheshire Cat smile. I am butter in his hands. 'Not,' his mouth now on my lips, 'maps', our tongues meet, he pulls away into a muffled, 'but this, here, now…'

Our bodies silently take over the conversation. Inside I feel myself diving into this kiss letting it take me in a gentle flow of current, spiralling in soft curves of underwater caves, swirling through into the skies. I let go. I leave myself to be moved by this that is happening so sweetly between us. I feel him also abandoning himself to the moment.

A click opens within. Feeling held I open into nothingness. Joy, Love, Peace. A wonderfully warm, comforting sensation of 'Home'. I feel our bodies becoming a single waterfall as we merge into One.

Later, hand on the wheel, driving us out of the New Forest, I say across to Paul in the passenger seat, 'Let's try and meet each other as human beings?' And returning to planet earth I add, 'I am never going to be perfect.'
'Me neither.'
'That's what I'm worried about,' I laugh.

It's a joke but it's also true: it's terrifying.

Less Froth

I realise in the pit of my heart
we will never be my fairytale.
I mourn for the image
I wanted us to become;
forced into this ravine to see
the ups and downs
as an unyielding constant
– green rolling hills
mountains
valleys
lakes –
I but a piece of dust floating
in the immensity.
This will never be my flat map of stillness
to trace gently under my finger pad
but continues to arise non-stop all around me
uncontrollably new.

*Avoiding the balance of the light
and the dark: playing god with
consequences.*

Clear Becoming

I hide away from
barbed-wire words
you afraid of my silence.
Cold war kitchen.
Ghosts relating:
my father your mother
my mother your father
– sacks of potatoes
bending our backs
warping our hearts.
Let's drop the whole thing!
Let's separate out
like Psyche did the grains
with the help of mice
so we can come together
you and me
just as we are.

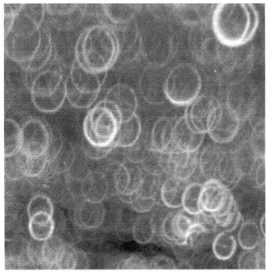

'You have to choose between all possible crappy outcomes of a situation,' Pete counsels me. He's told me this is the same advice a professor told him when he didn't know what to specialise in. I look into his eyes, feeling a splash of cold air – *what sort of advice is that to give to a doctor?* 'It was brilliant advice,' he grins, knowing I'm confused, '...he said to me, 'make a list of all of the specialities you'd like to do, write down all of the horrible things you'll have to do, all of the shit that goes with the job, and then chose the one that you can deal with best. You'll always be able to cope with the positives of any of the jobs, it's the negatives that have to be dealt with. So he advised not to choose a job just for the positive aspects else we'll never get through it.'

—

'I knew what I was getting into, you didn't.' How to know who you are about to live with from Craig's list? I mean, on screen I see the dimensions of the room, the price, the facts, but it doesn't say, 'Live-in Owner has the following psychological disorders...' Joseph who I also live with – thank god – did know. He's been her friend for ten years. He'd already had plenty of arguments with her, but living with her made it an easy move for him into the township of _____ [4], he didn't have to look for a place; it is clean, it is nice enough, it is fine. But, and it's a big but, there is Susanne. He knew that – I didn't.

—

Day three we have a house meeting, to show me the details of the house, to work out how we will all live together. I am blasted with a first inkling of the situation: I realise silence is the best way forward and as double security: agree to everything.

I am not particularly bothered either way on any of the issues. The issues being discussed hold a tone of grey that is creating a knot in my stomach. Things as important as 'Should We Have A Note In The Kitty To Say That We Have Paid...Or Not?' The discussions stretch like wormholes into a world of eternal spring cleaning I'd prefer to stay away from. It's on the edge of a type of absurd that my mind, in survival mode, twists into hilarity. 'Did you use My Conditioner this week?' Susanne, day two, had already told me under her breath that Joseph uses but doesn't restock. I have no idea at this point who Joseph is. From her words Susanne is a suffering saint. Joseph says that he hasn't used her fabric conditioner, 'I don't use it anyway, so I couldn't have.' It's getting into a fixed pattern of blame and excuse. 'Should We Share Laundry Soap?' The issues go on forever.

I have just come from living in a house where we all managed to wash our clothes and wash our plates and wash ourselves without having to ask each other how to do it – we used a technique called listening. Here it seems we are not.

—

The next day, in an art performance in town, I spot Susanne. I still do not know the danger. She comes up to me and pronounces, with sweet words that hold undercurrents of you-are-so-dead and how-dare-you-betray-me, 'Can we have a word?'

My body contracts. Neck pushes back, as if reversing.

I've been here before. Not with her. This is only day four of living with her. But I know this reaction, pinpricks of fear in the heart. This panic of unconscious reactive gas getting too close to a flame. I know it. I don't know how, but I do.

We go to a quiet place. I follow her as if being sent to the Head Master. I try to remember how my body sits down in a chair. Hyper alert, I am losing sense of how the world normally functions. She launches straight into, 'I didn't like the atmosphere in the house meeting last night. I didn't like the treatment. I didn't say anything about it last night but I felt there was a lack of respect. I don't have any problems with what we discussed, but there was a lack of kindness. I don't want to live in a house with people like that!' She spits it all out as if it were years of resentment. 'I've been in that house with others, and I have never encountered this. I was really worried, upset. I thought that I would wake up in the morning and it would be ok. But I wasn't. So I feel strongly that I have to talk to you. I've spoken to Joseph already.'

This is her welcome.

I am going into slight shock. I remember I had been silent most of the time. I remember watching her and seeing the flush on her face as she didn't know how to get through issues of 'Should We Share Salt Or Not'. As she leans further and further towards me, my heart pumping in front of my eyes, I begin to realise the question of flight or fight has become redundant: I want out; she is blocking me. 'I'm sorry,' I continue, as calmly as possible, 'but I cannot process your emotions for you.'

She erupts. I stand there. Grounding in my internal presence that is pulsating hard against my chest, up through my throat, crashing on the inside of my skull. Forced into a corner all I want right now is to leave my body. I cannot hear her words. All I can see is her ginger haired bob, frantically moving backwards and forwards.

—

'Hey Joseph, did Susanne speak to you today?' I say, as if casual chat.
'I wanted to warn you,' he says trying to evaporate an embarrassed air of being too late.

110

It turns out that she has problems wherever she goes. With people. They are always wrong. She is always right. Turns out, according to Joseph, that she has had plenty of problems with people in the house before. I feel the relief of realising this is not actually about me at all. 'She said to me,' I tell him, 'I want the atmosphere in the house to be friendly.'

'Funny way to start.'

'She said,' I am offloading, 'that she didn't want to be the one in charge, but for us all to be equals, all friends.'

'But it's her house!'

'It felt like we were in the barracks at one point. Her wanting us to wipe down the doors once a week…' 'I know and I know her. It's best to not confront her else it gets worse. Like the conditioner she was accusing me of using, I don't ever use it even if I had it, but I know her, that's why I didn't argue back. It's not worth it.'

'She must be really controlling her environment all of the time if she knows that you used her conditioner once and her fabric soap twice.'

'Ohh, that's not the worst of it.'

—

The next day, day five, we continue talking about Susanne, trying to process. She's gone off to London for four days, leaving behind her stink bomb. On the train she sends us both a text, 'I think we should have another meeting, to start over again.'

'Jesus! What more can we talk about over soap?' I'm starting to lose my patience.

'She means emotionally. She wants us all to be friends. She wants us to deal with her emotions and make them all alright.'

Meanwhile Joseph and I are using each other's milk, and cheese, and coffee and have no idea where we are up to. Neither of us really care. 'Ohh it'll work out…' he says when I check in with him, 'should do anyway.'

—

Day eight, we are both getting a little nervous because our freedom time with Susanne out of the house is coming to an end. Getting ready to pack our emotional bags and withdraw into the 'other' reality, we come to a new working conclusion. 'She is so vague! So vague!' he laments making himself a cup of coffee. This triggers me. Paul is vague. It is intensely annoying. You can never get a straight answer out from him on delicate matters such as, 'Are we a couple?'

'So,' says Joseph, 'I'm trying to set boundaries, because she may say, 'Oh we'll sort out the soap,' then I use the soap and she may be fine with it until one day she just blows up. So I'm going to push her to define the situation and say, 'Susanne what do you actually mean by that?' but if she stays vague I'm going to say, 'What I'm hearing is that you are OK sharing the soap and so I am going to use this soap until we have a further talk.' If she is too vague to set boundaries, I am setting them in my own head – else I'll go mad.'

'I get that. She's got no boundaries and yet the funny thing is that she is the one who wants to know that we know the rules, that we stay within her perceived limits, so that we will react as she expects us to, nothing unexpected, so there is no tension in the house and she is free to feel free!'

———

She's been in London now for four days doing her art work. It is actually really impressive: clean sharp lines of intricate delicate concepts. Clear forms, pristine ideas. Black and white. Perfect maps of a perfect world.

Four days without her and yet we have been talking about her nearly all of the time. She has become the centre of attention, without actually being here.

'She's like a ghost,' I lament with gusto, 'she's in all of our conversations, taking control of our free time even when she's not here!' I laugh. We change the subject. After a couple of minutes we get back to Susanne. It is addictive. 'Like how can we be friends, while she is bullying us, while she says she is being bullied?'

We both know that bully is too strong a word here, we've already worked our way around the nuances and have agreed, without having to write it down on a piece of paper, that despite her actions and words she is at heart a fair person, a wanna-be kind person with good intentions and that surely she must be totally unconscious of her affect on others? Being so cut off from her emotions, it seems she needs all these rules, all these detailed sculptured maps in constant working progress, to be able to cope with life. It seems that inside, things are going on too fast for her to cope with, uncontrollable…she needs somewhere, something, to stay fixed. So she chooses others and demands them not to change. She cannot cope with anything changing in her external world ever – people or things.

———

'I do understand – I see myself in her – but this moving around all the time between being our friend, being someone to save, and being this,' I do the two finger air quote thing, ''almost' bully, makes me wonder whether to live here or not. I mean look at all this that is going on, and I've only been here a week!'
'It's the vagueness that gets me, you never know how she will react.'

The light flicks on. Suddenly I get it.

'I think I've just got it! Chaaa dannnggg!!'
'What?'
'Well, everything has a positive and a negative. All jobs, all roles, all relationships have a positive and a negative side,' I think of Peter and deciding what specialism to go into as a doctor, 'She can't deal with negative emotions, so that if she puts herself, like you say, in a hinterland, she can surround herself in vagueness, then when the situation changes – and she can't cope – she can slip unnoticed into a different role in order to always stay only in the positive aspects.

All unconsciously probably…'

'Like?'

'Like as the owner of the house, she gets to be in control, so everything is done as she thinks it should be.' I stamp my fork on the table with each word, 'She sets the rules. So it's safe, she is the 'boss'. But then, because we have no voice, it moves into a her-against-us situation, creating distance between us, as if she were a 'tyrant'.'

'But it's impossible to have a friendship, based on equally, with someone who is not equal!'

'Exactly! That's the cost of her bossing us about – which is, actually, a valid solution if she stuck to it – but then she feels excluded, because she's not equal. So when she feels she's missing out, or there is too much distance between herself and others, feels rejected, she claims, 'I want everyone to be an equal here in this house!' I sigh into the impossible situation, 'Like you say, how to be friends and not have an equal say?'

'You need to be able to listen if we are all going to just muddle through as mates.' He's wiping the pots that he's just cooked with. 'Things become less clear as we each bring a little bit of ourselves to the shared story. Which means she loses control, she can't cope, she doesn't know who is using her soap and it swings her back into 'owner of the house' mistress of the rules that makes her feel safe again.'

We both stare into space, processing, digesting. I take a bite of my biscuit.

'I guess being vague is necessary for her psychologically, she feels comfort from all that grey space around her own boundaries, so the boundaries are diffuse when she needs them to be - a sort of hinterland - so she can sneak under the wires and be on either side of camp whenever one side gets a bit too much for her.'

'But it's impossible to have any kind of relationship and not accept that the other coming into our lives, will change us, will move our inner furniture around,' says Joseph wisely.

'Maybe relationships and intimacy are just too scary for her, you know? The mirror in the other, having to see all of ourselves, not just the good looking bits.'

—

This relationship with Paul is so vague. What are we? Partners?

—

Susanne is out of the house, so we can go deep into the conversation without suddenly being busted by her judgement. 'It's the vagueness in women, it's hard, it's hard to know where the line is, what they are actually wanting, feeling. It's so hard!'

CHhhhnannnnnnbuuuuuuuuuunnnng!

'I've just had a flash!'

'What? What?' I love the excitement of our conversations. We weren't talking about Paul, but I have been paralleling the conversation. 'I've just got the whole

vagueness thing with Paul. You remember we were talking about roles?'
'Yes?'
'I've just come across where the seed of vagueness may have sprouted.'

I suddenly realise that I'm going to have to break a limit, a personal moral boundary: to continue I'm going to have to share personal information about Paul. Joseph and I have shared so much about ourselves, so deep. This is no more exposing that our normal talk, but it is someone else's psychic material. I hold back, breathe in, feel into it. Joseph and I have been working through this issue for a week or more, would Paul mind if I told him, a person on the other side of the world? It would be different if he lived here. *Should I?* I feel a slight movement in my body. It has given me the answer. 'I'm going to break a confidence. Will you hold that? Will you hold it here, and not take it anywhere else?'
'You know I will.'

I get a sudden release, a permission to go on, to continue our knightly search for truth.

'Paul's father couldn't relate emotionally to his wife, Paul's mother. It sounds like she was highly emotional. She had seven children, Paul was the second. Paul was emotional. Paul was in touch with his emotions. And so she talked to him and over time made him into her emotional husband. Not her son. In a way he must have liked getting more attention from his mother than his siblings; being 'special' to mummy. But when he went to Berkeley, when it was his chance to get out into the world she sent him a letter. The first line went, 'I should be telling your father this but...' When he told me about it I had this explosive feeling in my chest, this feeling of pure anger of leave-me-the-fuck-alone. He loved his mother. He hated his mother. He was the darling child of his mother. He was his mother's prisoner not allowed out of the marital bond of emotional contract. Caught in concepts of what she expected of him. He was adored, he was made to feel bad if he found someone, another woman, to take her place.'

I feel my body getting heavy. Joseph is staring slightly off to the side - I guess he is creating an image of Paul and his mother. He breathes out long and heavy, 'Woowww,' his face is pale, 'that's hard. I feel for him. I feel myself panicking almost in that place of wanting to kill her and needing her love.'

'Emotional incest some would call it...' Suddenly I want to get a sharp knife and cut Paul, my love, out of his psychic spider web, but I can't, it's not my place to mother him either. I suddenly feel flattened by reality, 'It's like Susanne, if he keeps it vague, then he can keep running away from the shadows and lily-pad-jump wherever the spots of light are. When he wants to feel he is a good son, when he wants to feel his loving mother and that deep connection they had, he can withdraw a little from the world and 'mother' himself; and when he gets panicky of being trapped, of being in her psychic prison, he can be polyamorous, and go out into the world and be with lots of other women and love them all and be a wonderful partner to each of them without really having to define anything. But he never has to deal with the feelings of being trapped away from one role or

114

the other. He gets his cake and he gets to eat it.'

I remember complaining about him to Priscella, 'His best mate said of him,
'Vague is vague' and she's right.'
'But it sounds like he never really gets either, it sounds like he lives on his own
in a barricade in the hinterland.'
'Yes,' I say lips suddenly heavy, sticky, 'I miss him. He's far away. Relationship
on hold.'
'Have you talked about it?'
'Tried to, but, you know, it's all a bit vague.'

Vague is Vague

You do not say
'yes' or 'no';
unprepared
to allow in
the demons
from either side
you sit on the fence.

I watch you
my life on hold,
again.

PART III

Realising the Power of Choice
and Letting Go

Litres of conversation about learning
to state our needs and awakening
to what we want from life.

Coming Around

Candy cakes
to my harsh tongue,
sweet kisses
on the bruised remains
of past blows,
gingerly
I untangle
barbed wire
to give passage within,
he treads softly
through the mire
each step sweetens bitterness
each step jangles me
out of this dark, heavy sleep –
No longer so afraid now
to feel.

I'm feeling a little tipsy in the Bohemian Biergarten, on 13th near Pearl. I'm with my friend Lea from the world of Contact dance here in Boulder, CO. We've each ordered a large beer. Wow. I didn't expect them to be so big. I gasp, half in fear and half full of childish glee, 'It's only the afternoon!' and we both smile at each other, trying to lift them to our mouths. Life is good! We have instantly clicked into honest, where away from the gods of the dance floor we are able to comfortably admit to be human. It's so nice to take off masks and cloaks; nice to not have to worry if I'm good enough, if I'm accepted in this strangely familiar foreign country, and simply say, 'This is how I feel: what'ya think?' Bizarrely I feel extra comfortable with Lea because having lived in Nottingham, UK for a year she is talking in her 'British accent'. It's actually really convincing. I keep forgetting where I am.

It's not long before I say, 'You know, I'm slowly getting that I have to ask for my needs.'
'Beer?'
'More like, with men.'
'Ohh!' We smile.
'You know I'm slowly getting that if my needs aren't met in a relationship it's not his fault...actually...it's the other persons fault in the relationship.' I smile, being cheeky.
'Yours?'
'Yeahhh...'

We're sitting outside on the terrace bit. Boulderites are walking by, which means, a person dressed as a character from the Mad Hatter's Tea Party hardly gets a second glance. 'But.....' I say extending the u of my northern accent and stretching my neck to look to the skies, 'if you tell a man to buy you a box of chocolates and he does, is it really the same?'

The issue has actually come up from a story Lea's just been telling about her life. That's the beauty of these girl chats, you can never really tell who you are talking about...so I launch into the deep end, mustering up my bestest woman-of-the-world wisdom wondering if I'm talking to my friend or myself, or both?
'My mum and I have this silly tendency to hide within our psychic shells. Then if a man comes along and 'finds' us, then we have 'proof' of his love.'
'Ohh I think lots of women do that, don't they?'
'Hmmmm, I guess, but really we aren't 7 years old any longer. Hide and seek is so out of fashion!' We laugh, both comfortable having no idea where to go with this.

Georgina has come around for an impromptu breakfast. We meet in the narrows at the top of _____ [4]. 'Hug!' I nearly whop little Ray on the face. 'I didn't realise you were around there! I'm sorry.' He doesn't say anything. Georgina does her characteristic peal of laughter, 'You didn't see him on my back?'

It's hard to remember about little people when you're not a mother. It must seem inconceivable to a mother to not have children on the mind all of the time. I stroke little Ray's blonde hair. He's adorable. I'm rewarded by a wonderful smile. Why is it so wonderful to get a smile from a baby?

Back home, I ask Ray if he wants eggs. His mum says, 'Ohh yes, one, that would be great.'
'Do you want a half sausage?' I ask him,
His mum says, 'Ohh yes, please.'
'Do you want some orange juice?'
'Ohh no thanks, he's had a cold and well, best not.'
It's weird, I'm asking Ray, and his mum keeps talking for him. 'Stop butting in,' I say jokingly, 'I was talking to Ray!'
She peals, 'But he can't talk!!'

Later, we are coming to the end of our fry-up. Ray starts to whine. I look at him. Nothing seems amiss. Georgina looks at him, as if readjusting a satellite signal, 'You want the little bits of egg cut up more?' She doesn't wait for an answer. Cuts up the already minute pieces of egg, to me quite unnecessarily. Ray stops crying.

Ray and her are connected still. One psyche.

He still can't talk yet. How could it be otherwise?

—

'Will we ever grow out of expecting others to know what we want and need?' I ask Lea. 'Like, if I want a…' I look around searching for an example, nothing comes to mind…
'A bike?' she offers. We both look at the bike parking lot. There is a wonderful pink bike with big handle bars that I imagine belongs to a sassy chick. Sheer funk baby.
'Yeah, like I dream of cycling around and being a cute chic chick on my fab bike.' I like using English words when I'm in the States. I'm a linguist pervert.
'But I don't say anything to him outright - maybe a hint or a slight remark that he doesn't get. I feel like he doesn't care or love me. But actually he really just hasn't got that I want a bike.'
'Like when you talk in analogies, they think you are actually talking about what you are talking about!'

We laugh voraciously, and take a slug of our outrageously large beers.

'Yeah!' I say breathing in the sheer joy of communicating. The idea tickles us both that we can talk in many-tongued similes and chat about several things at once, without having to actually ever finish anything we are saying. Who knows where the conversation will slither to? This time we don't go off on a tangent: 'So, I don't say anything, I hide myself and my need inside, and then if someone, by sheer stroke of a miracle gives me a bike, it is 'evidence' that he is THE ONE. Underlined in Capitals.'
'And in bold.'
'Yes, **THE ONE**.'
We laugh in the absurdity of it all.

'But,' she says mimicking my British accent, 'the chances are that you will never get one.'
'The One or the bike?'
'Either!'
'Why? Why can't they hear? Women do! Women get other women without having to spell things out.'
'Because they are not women?'

Worlds of space suddenly open up between me and Paul. Men could be completely alien creatures for all I know. What must it be like to be inside of them? Like, are they really so interested only in sex and computers? Really? There must be a solution to gap this galactic divide.

'I guess,' I muse, 'with the man we have, we have to say, simply, clearly, 'I would like a bike.' And then he goes off dutifully and gets you a bike, or whatever it is that you need. Perhaps we even need to say which particular bike. But then when he delivers, does that mean that he loves you?'
We both ponder the situation, it's a bit sticky.

'Well, yes, to a degree. He wants everything to be good for you. He's actually gone out, for you, in his car, with his mission, and completed.'
'Or with his WiFi! But it is all rather perfunctory don't you think?'
And then I get this flash of brilliancy and pretend that I have known it all along, 'The deal is, that we don't actually want the 'bike', what we want is to be recognised within. Our inner needs met.'
'Ah ha!' says Lea, 'Wow, yeah, wooo.'
'I just made that up.'
'Sounds right to me.'

And so, given this encouragement I feel the permission to launch into one of my favourite fairytales with total freedom to ad-lib to my heart's content.

—

Sleeping Beauty is born on a wonderful summer afternoon and the fairies are invited to deal out her destiny. They take it in turns with the gifts they bestow upon her and say that she will be fair and gentle and good and intelligent and great at cooking and creative and a wonderful friend and an intrepid traveller and wonderful on a trumpet until right at the end of the queue, the bitch fairy cuts through the atmosphere like ice and says, 'She'll die on a prick.'

Everyone gasps, there is no way out.

Or so it would seem. But everyone has forgotten about the littlest fairy who is late and has just caught the action after flying through the window. She pipes up, slightly out of breath, 'My wish is that she doesn't die but falls asleep!'

And so the court, the family, keep all pricks away from their precious little baby girl. Every man is vetted on arrival and none are allowed in through the back door. Especially when she hits puberty. But as the story would have it, as she is rummaging around places she shouldn't be, she finds herself in some dark dusty old place and encounters a prick. It turns nasty. Blood drops.

—

Surely we all have wounds? We have opened up, bright and bushy tailed and let ourselves be vulnerable and – bang! – we get hurt. Often as young whipper-snappers, our blood only just dropped, we have been blindsided by things not being sweet and soft, but hard and sharp. Too young to be able to cope with it at all. No resources. No experience. No one to turn to. Getting lost in a web of our own inexperience. Didn't know ourselves enough to set limits, to protect ourselves.

Sometimes it gets abusive, I'm sure we've all felt wronged. We have all felt hurt.

It is alarmingly not unusual that a woman is sexually abused, often within the family.

People can be pricks. Egos can get out of control. The fires within suddenly burning wildly out of control, wanting, wanting, wanting without regard for the other…

—

Blood falls. The red stains the white snowy floor. With open eyes she sees reality. Her psyche collapses, she shuts down - she falls asleep. Of course she keeps getting up each day, doing her life, but it is behind the cotton wool of denial. The woman she has become is sleep-walking through life, cut off from her emotions. Part of her, the part that has been damaged, becomes completely closed off - that bit falls sound asleep.

She becomes numb to love.

In its moment it's not a bad defence mechanism: it gets her through the day, allows her to function to some degree while she is still unable to deal with the pain of it all…but if it goes on too long without resolution the psychic area and her defensive actions become unconscious. She gets caught in a prison of her own making.

And it's not just her, apparently the whole court falls asleep. Her family refuses to talk about anything related to the incident. Best to keep mum. The psychic energy between them gets frozen; nothing is allowed to flow any more. They are in stalemate, everyone trapped in collusion not dealing with the horrible situation. No-one is prepared to talk about it. Leave the can of worms closed shut. The consequences seem unimaginable. How to even start dialoguing it?

Thorns start to grow, twisting and turning outside the castle into a veritable wall of defence. She becomes so sensitive to anyone approaching the area of damage that she spits out thorny, harsh words. Her words tell people in no unquestionable terms that she is unavailable. She discovers that if she thinks she is not worthy, she will not have to try and find love: she is unworthy of it. Safe. She becomes adept at putting people off, asking too much or too little of people, leading them astray, creating smoke screens of independence or being suffocatingly dependent: anything to keep them at a distance, anything to stop any possible development of love.

Unconsciously, in a self perpetuating loop, she lets the wrong people get close and in so doing feels justified in throwing them out and putting up extra defence mechanisms: 24/7 surveillance mines, barbed wire and a couple of mantraps just for measure.

Until, that is, there is a man, within her psyche or without – the outer world reflecting the inner – who with his sword of gentle understanding, is able to swipe through the thorny bushes, the harsh attitudes, the over-dependence or the standoffishness and get to the other side, get into the chambers of her heart. He manages to disengage all of her defence mechanisms.

This guy gets through her thorns by being true to himself, and to her.

He manages to glimpse through the thorns to who she really is and falls in love with what he can see. He chooses her over all the other maidens; though part of him would like to stay single and in the game, he manages to fight his instincts and be true to her. She feels the warmth of his love. Begins to believe in it. He melts her thorns by his constancy, his loving awareness, his innocent desire to be with her. He listens to her, softening her thorny words.

She begins to trust again. She begins to open again.

Eventually, their lips meet and his pure love for her passes between them. She awakens out from the numbness of having been hurt. She stirs back into the living. The wound begins to heal. She begins to believe in life again. She lets herself open to love.

—

'And, unless I am the only one, I think many of us women are operating on this fairy tale,' my hand wrapped in the handle of the beer glass.
'Yes,' agrees Lea, we are still coming out from the story, 'yes, we've all been hurt, we've all shut down part of ourselves…' she murmurs, 'and how to live a full life if parts of us are shut down?'
'Exactly!' We clink our less heavy beer glasses, I'm pretty sure I'll finish this

lager now.

'Wow, it's amazing! I thought Sleeping Beauty was just a story…I didn't realise.'

'I know! I love fairytales!'

'How do you know about them?'

'We studied them in the masters in Barcelona. They hold psychic information that we sense behind the surface. Did you know, Sleeping Beauty was published at the end of the 17th Century, but it was probably told for centuries before that?…Most of these myths are oral culture…'

'I thought it was Disney!'

'No…Disney have just been clever and taken all these masterpieces.'

'Woo… that story's been around a long time!'

'Yea, and there's a reason why people, and children, love hearing it, and telling it, and keep it alive through the generations.'

'It's comforting…'

———

'But can we keep living like that?' asks Lea, still wondering about this new man who keeps calling her, asking her on dates, but not moving onto the next level. 'Like, can we keep wanting men to come and recognise us, to fill in our gaps. Or has it got to the point, where we, god-damn-it, have to find the prince within, and do it for ourselves?'

'You mean find the man within?! Find our inner Princes, the Animus, the ones who can speak out our needs? Instead of some guy we've been hanging out with for a few days and demanding that he magically knows what we want?'

I didn't mean it like that, I was just theorising, but I realise I've delivered an under-the-belt blow. So I tread carefully, 'Can we not wake ourselves up out of own unconscious state, by giving up the fantasies and deciding by ourselves what we need?'

'I guess,' she says doubtfully.

A group of men go by on a vehicle which is also a bar that they are pedaling themselves. They are shouting and being generally obnoxious. Pricks. We have to wait for them to go by before we can continue. They are merrily, drunkenly, sucking up all the attention of everyone on the street.

They go around the corner. There is a collective sigh.

'I practiced it last night,' it feels like I'm telling her my secrets, 'in despair it was my last ditch effort. I was feeling ignored and unloved and wondered if everything was going wrong between me and Paul. Weeks ago he had told me to state my needs, but I'm so unpractised in even knowing my needs, I normally only work them out way later, sometimes weeks too late.'

'Me too.'

'But last night, sat on a terrace on Pearl Street, we were both in this thorny silence after me declaring how hurt I felt, I mean I was trying to open up, communicate my pain. He wasn't responding at all and suddenly I realised I felt really vulnerable, I had put myself out there. I felt I was dangling over a big, dark drop…'

'What did you do?'

'I told him that I needed reassurance…through the cold, frozen silence I launched my well aimed words, 'I really need reassurance. Like right now. It's a state of emergency.''

We both breathe in, female comprehension. 'Really that's what I said,' my words are changing a bit from that fear place to slight exhilaration of the newness of stating my needs through the power of vulnerability, 'It's so weird to try something new.' Walking into my mind I am accompanied by an familiar image, 'Do you know Antonio Machado?'

'No.'

'He's a Catalan songwriter. One of his famous lines is, 'Wayfarer there is no path, you make the path by walking.' I always imagine a path behind me as I cut myself through wild vegetation. 'If you are walking someone else's path, then it's their path, not your own.' Constantly going into the unknown. I breathe in suddenly filled with my own sense of power.

'And how did he take it? What did he say?'

'It was so weird, just to say it. I felt really vulnerable. But the silence melted like butter under the sun, and suddenly there was a clearing between us, as if the Prince, I guess my Animus, had hacked through some of the thorniness, and Paul stepped up and said some really sweet words to me, which he couldn't do before because of all the thorny silence.' Wow, sometimes it's so strange to hear about myself from the outside, from the perspective of the story teller.

'What did he say?'

'I can't remember!' We both laugh, startled at the irony, 'I guess the words in themselves weren't what I needed!'

'You needed him to step up!'

'Yea. I needed the reassurance that he gives a shit.'

'Yea!'

'And after his wonderful words, whatever they were, I felt really soft and warm.'

'Nice!'

'We ended up snogging in front of our king prawns!'

—

We swing back to Lea's side, 'You see this guy,' she says, 'the one I went on three dates with and who hasn't even tried to kiss me yet…?' I nod in a recognising fashion, 'all I want for him to do is to claim me. To come up to me as a Man, capital M, and say something like, 'I want you. I desire you,' without me having to feed him his lines. I want to feel myself as an attractive woman. I want to feel recognised that I have opened the door to him and my body and that at least he sees me, there in my psychic negligee, panting slightly. I'm not even sure if I want sex with him, but…' she pauses, trying to work out what she actually wants, 'I just want the situation recognised….or,' she says in a grave tone 'are we just friends?'

We both know that this cannot, surely be the case. She asks even though we both know he is calling every day and taking her out for meals. Friends do not do this.

Friends meet on the park benches, because it's cheaper.

'Tell him what you want maybe. Tell him how you feel. Ask him how he feels.'
'He would freak out!'
'Do you want him?'
'I don't know.'

My wise woman comes to the surface again, probably talking to myself more than to Lea, 'You want him to make the decision, you want him to be the instigator. You want him to be 'the Man'. But maybe before asking him if he wants a relationship with you, you should decide if you want a relationship with him?'
She darts me a murderous look, as if pained that a friend could be so cruel. 'Yes,' she says backing down a little, 'yes, maybe you are right.'
'The thing is,' I am now on automatic ramble (these are the times when I really need to listen to myself), 'that if we don't become our own princes we'll keep asking men to validate us, to heal our pains...'
'and our unworthiness,'
'and constant need for reaffirmation,'
'and confirmation of deserving to exist,'
'and feeling unlovable,' we laugh; we could go on forever.

I take a gulp, quite amazed how little beer is left in my litre glass, 'I've nearly finished!' I look over to hers, not far behind.
She says, 'Maybe we should get another one? Between us?'
I laugh, 'Why not?' We both like the waiter.
When he comes with his massive glass, we pour it into two. 'To us!'
'Yes, to us stating our needs!'
It's so nice to just relax guard for a while. To let life pour in.

'It's funny to see it all from a different angle isn't it?' she says, the sun shining through her hair.
'It so is...all this asking men to validate us: it's dangerous...'
'How do you see it?'
'Well, as if we, or I put myself in a position where I'm not actually seeing the man as he is, but instead as a potential magical prince who is going to make me feel good about being me and live happily ever after.' I make the international air violin symbol and sing, 'Love Story'.
'We could just be projecting onto a man, and wanting him to be who we want him to be!'
'Exactly! Without bothering to find out who he actually is...and then if we ask him, stating our needs, to fight through our complicated defence mechanisms and tell us that he wants us as a woman, that he desires us, that he is willing to run barefoot to the end of the world for us just because we've stated that we want a 70% chocolate bar, if he actually does it...'

In a flash I imagine me in some weird cosy pink outfit on a plush warm sofa, under a cosy blanket, as he, with a manly stubble, goes out into the driving rain at the dead of night, pulling his dark rain jacket up across his face. He knows that the shops have closed, but he's prepared to go on the hunt anyway, to get me my fix: dramatic imagination gone wild.

'Anyway,' I sigh reining in my imagination to some semblance of reality, 'if we haven't done our homework beforehand, we might just find out – once he's back with the said chocolate feast, once he's swiped through the thorns and merited entry with feats of bravery into our inner sanctum, once he has validated us and calmed our fears – that he's a complete prick!'
'Driven by some murky drive to be a superhero, unable to see anyone in the picture but himself!'
We both sit still as if watching a horror movie.
'Yeaaaaa….' I say in a creepy voice that even creeps me out.

'If,' I continue back in my own voice, 'we only ask him because we can't see through our own fears, needing to feel accepted and seen by someone, anyone, we'd better be ready for a surprise once he gets manly. He might not be the prince we were waiting for.'
'I guess,' she says hope tinged with sadness. 'The other can never fill the void that is in us.'
'We have to validate ourselves….'
'Nooooo…..'
'Ahhhhhhh!!!'
'But,' says my friend 'we do need relationships to be able to grow personally – to go into our shadows, into our wounds.'

And then we had to leave. Of course we were twenty minutes late, and we both had to go to the toilet, and continued talking rapid fire through the cubicles despite the obvious noise interference, waterfalls aside. As we got outside and were unlocking our bikes I said, 'I feel a bit high.'
'You don't get oxytocin just from men you know! You get it from doing what you love!'

Which is maybe the actual answer. Just to make life into what you love.
Because no one else is going to do it for you.

In My Own

I want to exist
from my own light
like the sun
that glows with giving
never needing
to suck back
to fill in a dark hole.

A chapter about a brilliant
performer I had to cut down to size.

Falling in Wound

Like rats
they hang upon the bar
drinking up their vomit
'Just one more'
they trick their mind
to fill the hole
of wanting.
Just one more
and I'll hit the road
please give me
just one more,
a glimpse,
a word,
a soft sweet touch
ohh kind stranger
my dealing spirit.

As soon as I look into Nick's eyes I feel it: I want him. My body comes alive, sparkling in unknown places. I can only look his way. Listening to him. Engaging with him. Attempting to attract him with my words, with my gaze, with this firework display within. I want him. His light blue eyes shine like solar flares; as I look inside I feel a vortex of delight feeling his aliveness as he looks as me long and penetratingly in headily, dizzyingly, vertiginously long eye contact, as if this overwhelming excitation were new to him too, as if our worlds were colliding. Deep below my body explodes.

My inner wise one warns: *This is a cocktail of the moment. A paper fire! It will burn out before you have a chance to even explore it.*

And yet…

———

'I get really pissed off with Alpha men,' he says, under the beams of his kitchen. William is slender, shorter maybe than me, probably weighs less. Soft spoken.

'Alpha men?'

He is fuelled by that undercover bitching that Eurovision was invented for. 'Yeah….the ones that stroll into the room and everyone notices, the ones that steal all the attention. The ones all the women are attracted to. So very, very into themselves,' he breathes out like a domesticated dragon, 'they shine out impossible potential promises that even they themselves believe - and bang! - all the women want some of him.' I watch him with the tea towel in hand, the plate he has dried is perfectly placed on the side. 'But as soon as they don't get what they want, they turn into bullies, into cry babies, they create havoc, until they get what they want again.' He swings his tea towel onto the chip on his shoulder. 'They are so very exciting and dramatic. Life happens around them like 'magic',' he gently spits out his irony. 'Women love them when they are in the positive. And when the shit hits the fan they come crying to men like me, to pick up the pieces.'

———

In the morning jam I get really confused. There are two men who have been triggering me all week, so that the only way to cope with their presence is imagining the pleasure of their complete absence. But here, this morning they are creating such a beautiful, holy, creative energy in the room that I cannot help but soften towards them. Nick who has been playing every woman off in the group is now playing the guitar with genuine innocence, ultra sensitively, and I begrudgingly feel wonder as the notes play themselves into patterns of beauty. On the other side of the chapel is the other alpha male who has already slept with two women and counting, and is now singing, weaving his voice in and out of the music so sweetly, so harmoniously it is angelic. I feel I am being treated to a sound bath of pure beauty. It is magical. It is divine. I struggle against it, but find I cannot help but surrender into it, feeling myself uplifted, moved.

—

After the jam Anna comes up to me, 'It was beautiful this morning wasn't it?'
'Yes!' I say, wholeheartedly. We are on the upper banister, overlooking the courtyard. 'It confused me.'
'Me too,' she admits. *Phew! I'm glad I'm not the only one.* 'I looked at Nick and saw how he has carved out space for himself again as the centre of attention, sat in the window.'
'Hmmmm….yeah…'
'And I looked at him and thought, 'He is really talented.''
'And he is,' I admit. It is undeniable.
'Yes and so creative! And he's quite amazing sometimes.'
'Yes…really…it's true.' I feel like a traitor to myself for just agreeing.
'But, he's not kind.'

Her words are like a bullet hitting the heart of the target. A sudden stillness reverberates through the air: the type that heralds a truth has been born.

'Do you see how he reacts when he doesn't get his own way? Yesterday he totally cut Petra off just because she didn't agree with him about some silly little detail in the performance.' It was watching the way he was around Petra that had made me realise, stones churning in my stomach, that he is a serial womaniser. It stings still. Shattered dreams. *Thank god I hadn't rushed in!* Petra's face of pain could have been mine. 'He was actually really nasty…' she says, 'especially after how he had led her on…' The stillness is working itself through me. 'And I looked at him,' her words aimed with perfect weight, 'and thought, *Yes, you are good looking, and talented, and amazing, but you are not kind.*' She searches into my eyes. 'I would prefer a post man,' she says quietly, 'and I'm not putting post men down – but you know what I mean?' I nod. 'I would prefer a man who is simple, and maybe not so amazing on the guitar, or talented, or with such fascinating stories, but someone who is kind. Kind to me.'

I feel like clouds have parted and a shy sun is suddenly given space to shine in my soul.

'Someone,' she adds, 'who is not just there for himself.'

The Giant Schnauzer

I

There are dogs
- aren't there? -
that will sit by a
child's blanket
left in the middle of the park
protecting their little charge.
Sometimes I can slip
passed the dog
if I am nice enough
kind enough
soft enough.
Inside
I am groundless
surrounded in the
wonder of this soft
sensitivity,
his delicate touch.
Floating in his irises
I open so deeply
I let him
enter into my heart.
But a sudden move
innocent enough
scares him -
he cries out
in alarm:
that's when the dog
springs into terrifying action.

II

I walk away from you
knowing what's inside.
Loving you.
Afraid of you.

The feminine relationship to
her true merit and recognising
her undiscovered but well-known secrets.

I

In your music
are high majestic vaults,
a cathedral
not of incense
and candlesticks
but the firmament
of your soul.

II

In you is the world.
Will you let it arise?

'You know I admire Bernardo, he dances Tango so well…' he tells me as we are sharing a coffee. I wait for the 'but', we have been talking about how some of the more talented men in the tango class have the technique to 'mould' the woman, so she becomes open and malleable to his slightest touch, as he whisks her around the dance floor creating such graceful steps with such ease. Wonderful technique! He moves her anyway he wants by listening deeply to the grain of her body movement as they entwine, so immersed she becomes one with the tango, with the music, with him. A carpenter creating a sculpture in harmony with the grain of his beloved wood, he listens to her body with an expertise that moves her in effortless grace. Who would not surrender to a man like that?

'But…' he laughs to himself, only just holding back the school boy snigger, 'he minces.'

Inside I sigh. 'He glides,' I say not too dreamily: I don't want to have to deal with his jealousy.

—

My relationship is on the rocks. I am putting on tights and trying to make what I'm doing right. I am meeting with this guy I met in the park because there is a possibility that he can offer me some work 'translating'. *Right. Yeah. Sure.* That's my story. *Right. Yeah. Sure.* I am putting on tights, which I don't normally do. *Why?* I have to look presentable. *Really though?* I am a trousers woman. *Tights?* I am alone in our bedroom. Ricard is in the next room. I feel guilty. It starts to crack through. To stay integrated I have to admit to myself: *I am not happy in this relationship and I am about to go on a date.*

Why this guy though?

I pull up the tights slowly, sensually and start to dream. When we met for a coffee he told me, 'I like to treat women as women, give them gifts, flowers, fine silk panties, chocolate, take them to the opera, get a box, make love behind the curtain.' At the time I thought it was all quite ridiculous but I thought about it for weeks. *Is this why I am doing this?* It comes as a jolt. *Am I looking to him to fulfil my dreams of how life should be?* I am about to risk everything for the scent of a dream. I feel like Cinderella dressing for the ball.

—

'I wonder,' I say to Mercè passing back the maria, 'I wonder if women are attracted to men to fulfil their dreams of a fantasised future and men are attracted to women because they fantasise every vagina is going to be a completely different experience?'

—

Cinderella sits happily in her power. Her Prince has come from out of his hidden, inaccessible world, searching for her: the slipper fits. Everyone is happy for her. With this new self image, holding her, she can flower into her power. She is the woman she always knew she was but couldn't access while she was being so dictated to, bullied, by the three hags of elder sisters, by the constant tirade of the critic introjected within her attacking every action, her every thought as she swept up the cinders of someone else's fire. In that brute, dirty state, she didn't have the resources to become all of her…she couldn't access her gifts within, didn't have the time or the energy…she hadn't got the resources to go on the courses she needed, didn't have the time to meditate, or write a book, or apply herself to becoming her higher self, she was just too exhausted.

Even so, something had pushed her forward and she'd had the balls to go to the dance. Tasting of that joy changed everything! Ohh what joy to swirl and fly within his graceful dance. How she felt herself release into beauty. How people saw it shining out from her happy face.

But it was a touch and go affair all the same – just before having to leave she felt herself wobbling about to collapse back into her old self, back into victim. But she'd made it. Fake it till you make it style. Back by the cinders of the fire, she'd felt bolstered by the memories of herself at the ball, holding herself like a princess: she stepped up, she let herself be seen…and in stepping up the 'Universe' helped her in her path. She smiles and sweeps, less afraid of the dark now.

The door opens, light streams in through her entire being. Her animus steps up, steps into the room. Her Prince! Their worlds collide. She feels deep within herself the protection of this masculine giving her direction, support, confidence to become her true self in all her glory. She slips effortlessly into these new shoes. She feels herself miraculously becoming who she had dreamed she was all along.

Sigh. Happy. Good feelings inside.

Arising

I dance until I can no more,
I wander until lost,
losing all control
exhaustion's soft hand
kneads me ready:
unable but to surrender
I drop

falling into my body.
In the swirls of sensations
I am a bird
taking to the skies
flying through form.
Energies arise
taking me over,
dissolving who I am
into a dance of
inner worlds;
beyond
in the eye of the storm
in awe of the stillness
that holds us all

e

s

i

r

I

'I don't know why I keep having these weird situations with men,' I
say, 'I mean, some of them have just been horrible,' I am in The Cott Inn having
the most delicious meal I have eaten all year. George is sat opposite, he has an air
about him like Mole from one of my children's books. He looks fifteen years his
junior, though he's actually pushing seventy. He's nervous, has talked about
himself and wondered if he has talked too much. 'No, you haven't!' I say, but
suddenly the spot light in on me. It's my turn to expose.

'Like that Jungian guy who abused his power?'
'Yeah, the one who told me my life had been a complete waste. It hurt.' I feel my
insides burning. It's much easier to listen.
'I imagine.'
'But it hit a nerve. Like maybe my life has been a waste? What do I have to show
for it?' I have an image of myself, out of my own water, shrivelling up. *Ouch.*
'You've travelled, you've experienced, you've loved, you've seen so much that
most others don't even dream of.'
'But I have no place in the world,' I remonstrate, 'I have nothing to give. I do not
know what I am doing.' I gulp. Seeing myself in such a horrible light.

'I mean, I sit at a temporary home and write, which may never get to be read by
anyone but Paul. I feel like a hermit here and when I do get out I have to go
everywhere on a bicycle because I own nothing – at forty-one!' I see images of
people in their standard two- or three-room homes with a garage and a car, their
children running in through the front door, school bags on their shoulders. 'I
don't even have any friends here,' and then feel bad for saying it, 'apart from a
few people like you…' Awkward. He nods. Goes red. 'If I left here no-one

would really even notice.'

'I would. I would miss you.' I go red. He looks me in the eyes, 'Will you just take back all that you just said? I don't allow people to talk like that about my friends.'

I gulp. *How?* A small shudder of panic fireworks in my stomach. *How can I reframe this?* I feel trapped. Part of me jeers about my present situation: *LOSER!* It shouts at me from inside my ears. Another part feels totally relieved to have been seen, to feel valid, to be recognised that I have something to say, that I have experienced life in my own unique way, that it is worth keeping working on this book thing even though I have no income. I summon up the courage to believe what I believe: it is true that people like to be with me. I am not who this ogre inside is telling me I am. But the ogre critic refuses to die without a fight and shouts, *Where's the money? You have nothing to your name! What's your life worth? Nothing but empty inflated words.*

In the confusion I stay silent.

'I feel when I am around you that you are a deeply spiritual person.' I nod quietly, hardly moving, rabbit eyes in the glare. 'We need you.'
I nod. Timid acquiescence. I am. I know this. I don't let myself believe it.
'And we need you!' he repeats.
'Why?' I say piqued, wanting to be flattered just a little more...*please?* Water to a desert.
'...because you are different. We need people who are different, to show that different exists.' My heart suddenly pumps with an upward movement, like the first gasp of a person coming around after being given mouth-to-mouth resuscitation. 'You are who you are – you inspire others to be more themselves...'

I sit back, filled with George's loving words, suddenly realising that just as I am right now, I am good enough. I can feel something inside that felt brittle-dry begin to soften, to want to shine. George continues, 'It feels like you are finding, what I like to say is, your 'Authentic Father', not the one that criticises you inside, not the harsh side of you that never lets you feel good about anything you are doing or saying, but the loving father who protects and cares for you and wants the best for you.'

Just by being with him, I feel this energy. Osmosis. I feel calmer, safer, the world stops spinning. I feel such deep gratitude - I have no idea how to say it to him, words slip slide around the emotion. So I just sit there, letting in his words, that by magic are turning into self-acceptance.

—

'It's incredible, you never can let your thoughts stop', Pieter says to me as lie in the life-saving shade of the Greek Wall on the beach at Empúries. His English is weird; I like it. But it is not just his English that makes him go slow and to the point. He is. He doesn't over think, stays quiet most of the time, observing, sensing. At times he seems to be completely still as if nothing were going on at all inside as he simply floats in what is around him. I feel the difference between my incessant story making and his silence as I go in and notice all these kamikaze thoughts leaving jet streams crisscrossed through my innerscape. But by him, these my thoughts, having been recognised, begin to slow down. I begin to slow down. I breathe out. Wooa. I notice the tension in my body. Body relaxes thankful.

Slower now the world is suddenly infinitely sweeter.

It's not his words that support me as much as being able to swim in his presence. Deep still, content waters.

I feel the breeze against my warm summer sun and delight.

—

At thirteen I thought I was the only person in the world without a boyfriend. On the brown saggy sofa I sat – begrudgingly in the bosom of my family – watching 'Pretty Woman' wishing desperately for another reality. I fell in love with Julia Roberts and her big lips and with Richard Gere and his gentleness. I fed on the visions coming out of the TV screen. I gorged on my imagination of what must have happened in the sex scene while Dad turned it off as he declared, 'This is NOT family viewing.' Even Mum groaned.

When I got the sound track on cassette I poured it into my veins. I had recently won a Sony walkman (with auto-reverse) in a church raffle and walked down Constable Drive singing, 'Ohh Pretty Woman, walking down the street!' and 'Mercy!' as loudly as I dared. It was the first time I had put music to my everyday life. I looked out from my world of sound tracks sensing everything around me with a heightened awareness, as if there were more colours wherever I looked. I imagined myself in a film. I was enraptured by the idea of being brought out from the dirty depths of society, being chosen by a powerful man and being given what I need to become my true self.

The Cinderella of 1990.

Some say that Cinderella was written in China in the 9th Century CE, and the shoe was a slipper of precious metal. I wriggle my toes in my size six and a half Campers, while reading that the ancient Chinese connected being sexy and beautiful with extreme smallness of foot. I've never been into high heels, bit wobbly for me, but it seems that I've always been into Cinderella.

While sat on the brown, itchy sofa watching the scenes in 'Pretty Woman' unfold on the wood framed telly, I had my first ever sexual fantasy: I am in the house (magically alone) with my boyfriend, my parents have somehow conveniently disappeared off the face of the earth. The boy has blonde hair, blue eyes, is tall, and sporty, he's top of the class and artistic and we play duets together – he on the piano me on the tuba. It goes without saying he's mad about me. I'm mad about him. We've put a blanket on the lounge floor and are having an indoors picnic: take-out pizza (that I've only ever seen on adverts). It feels titillating just imagining the freedom of not eating at the table. We are both mesmerised by 'Pretty Woman' on the VHS. Both loving it.

I dream about it for days. If not years. If not decades.

It's 2008. I'm thirty-four. I'm cycling along the sea front down near Barceloneta, coming back from work. I love that my work route goes along the sea front. Though it adds on fifteen minutes to the journey, it's a no-brainer. Cycling up and down the cycle path has given me a relationship with the sea. In the winter with my big thick gloves on watching the sunrise on the way to work; on the first warm spring days cycling in my work clothes seeing the nudists get an early start on their all-over body tan; big long stretches of empty beach on bad weather days; beaches crammed to madness on school holidays. It's meditation for me. I sit on my bike, pedalling and wondering. The action of my body in a rhythmic space lets my mind free up and change cogs.

I am going out with a man, Ricard, who is twice my age. When we got together I was 33 he was 67. We are madly in love. It's weird. It's like going out with a woman for the first time. I remember kissing Laia, my first and last girlfriend, and flashing a couple of times into my 'old' mindset. Colours shifted. Like a veil was taken away. My brain would jump back in bemused shock and say, 'Stop! Stop! There's been a mistake – this is a WOMAN!' It was weird, as much as it was exciting.

The same thing happens with Ricard from time to time: I suddenly realise I am kissing a man older than my father. Brain melt down. 'Stop, stop! I've stepped into the wrong film set!' And yet it is a relationship that I had only ever dreamt of before. We have a beautiful connection that is hard to describe with words, something that I've never experienced before. We fly into each other minds and discover whole new worlds invisible to the naked eye. It's the first time I discovered in a person's manner, the idea of the delicate silk of a petal to be so strong. It's the first time I've been accompanied in the landscapes of my mind, matched in endurance and encouraged to go on, shown new places and been seen. I hadn't realised how lonely I'd been. Our love is delicate, fine, beautiful. It could so easily have been crushed, and yet, we gave it protection, space to be. We give it the water of our emotions, the heat of our thoughts, and are creating a world between us that is one of the most beautiful places that I have experienced existing on this planet.

To Ricard

The time between us morphs
into the immortal
I laugh and cry with you
dove tailing into our world
vibrant, alive, alight,
perfectly hidden from Cronos.

'Yes, I will take it on the chin that this could be a father complex issue,' I say to Larissa, 'Yes, sure it could….' I look at her, open in my honesty, feeling vulnerable, 'I guess this is just my way of dealing with it.'

She softens, 'And there are always father/daughter issues in all relationships…'

'It's just so much more obvious in this one!' I laugh, seeing in my mind his grey beard and rotund potbelly.

Suddenly it really does seem absurd.

'And at the same time you seem so good together. He's such a cutie, and he loves you so, so much.'

'And I am really happy. It feels so…right.'

'So what more do you need?'

'But then I was cycling along the beach the other day, and I suddenly had to stop…a really strong intuition came into me…' I breathe in. I'm not sure if I'm ready to share this deep. I look out of the open doors of the cafe onto the terrace. A person in a bright red t-shirt hurtles down the street on one of those modern bikes that have no gears, speeding to the gym at the bottom of the harbour.

'What?' she asks, dark brown eyes ablaze.

How to explain this sudden collapse of images that have been holding me up, unbeknownst to me, for years? 'Well, it's quite obvious we're not going to have children. I mean it's possible, but really…?' I look up sheepishly, she looks at me with compassion, with a softness that lets me drop my defences a bit more. *Isn't it every woman's dream to have a child?* 'I mean, it used to be my dream to be a mother, to have a child and bring a little being up and mould them and shape them and give them all that I can so they have the best go at life; to see where that person's path will take them with all that I have given.' I pause. I hear what I'm saying, 'If you look at it from a certain point of view then it's all quite ego driven.'

'To have children,' says Larissa in her characteristic deepness, 'is to be selfish. To not have children is selfish. Especially you Julia, with all that you could give to humanity.' I feel a wave of pleasurable shock ride through my body. 'We have to choose for ourselves, and take the consequences of our selfish choice that we have made for ourselves and ourselves only, else we'll end up being those horrible mothers who say, 'After all I did for you!' We have to chose: to be a mother and have another being on this planet, with the all good bits and the bad bits, or to not have that being with all the good bits and the bad bits. But it has to be a selfish decision made for ourselves, so that we fully take on the responsibility of bearing the personal consequences.'

Something in my heart relaxes, as if I am in a shower and the day is being washed off. I feel lighter, 'So,' I say slowly, this is the first time I've ever said it, 'I think I've decided that I don't want children.'

'And that's what made you stop your bike?'

'No…' I go back to the scene in my head, 'what made me stop on my bike was that if I don't want to have children, then suddenly I realised I don't know why people have long term relationships. I couldn't work out why, if children aren't involved, why more of us, as a society, are attracted to people who are not the

same age.' I'm not explaining myself, 'I mean, like why do we even get together as partners?' A car honks, exasperated, by a group of rollerbladers. 'So I was mulling it all over, on my bike…and then….' She looks at me expectantly. 'Well…' it's almost embarrassing, 'I had a flash.' I breathe in. This honesty thing is awkward, humbling. Larissa is holding space, her beautiful introversion is giving me space and time to me process. 'So,' I look out to the street, palm trees, bobbling white of yachts sails in the harbour, a family eating ice cream. 'Well, I, erm, realised,' *Uff! this is embarrassing,* 'my unconscious reasons for entering into all of my relationships so far are based on films that I watched when I was twelve or thirteen!' *How long have I been driven by these unconscious patterns?* 'I mean, I was prepubescent grabbling with the world…and that is what I'm basing my present day relationships on. Talk about,' then the word escapes me, 'what's it called when someone transfers all their feelings onto an object rather than holding the feelings inside.'
'Transference? Displacement?'

'Yes, I guess at that age it was displacement! I mean I've based my entire adult emotional life on teenage displacement, on the films 'Pretty Woman' and 'Back to the Future'!' I look at her, sheepishly, laughing over my uncomfortable exposure. 'I mean, I've been trapped in the Cinderella complex all my life, waiting for the perfect man to make me into my higher self; along with this feeling that I can save the fucked up dynamics of my family, by going back in time, giving my parents the self confidence to stand up for who they really are,' she looks confused, 'you know? With Michael J Fox? I realised I've unconsciously got caught up on that scene where they are all in a really nice white kitchen – you know right at the end? We had horrible Formica false wood cupboards – and the smiling Mum and Dad have just come back from playing tennis, the kids are all happy doing their homework and the bully is now their worker pleased to be part of it all, cleaning their really nice, red sports car.'

I breathe in, and on the out breath say, 'That's what got in.'

I remember walking out of Marple Cinema with my two best friends. It was the first time I'd been allowed out without any parents. I was still a bit stunned from being thrown out of the film into the glare of fluorescent lights. As I stumbled down the aisle to the exit, I was overwhelmed by the idea of time travel. 'Are we here now or there then?' I'd asked, dazed by the storyline.
'You're in the now!' they'd laughed, as if I didn't know I was in Marple. As if I didn't know I was thirteen years old. But deep down part of me really was confused and excited.

'That's what I've been unconsciously going for, that's what I've been trying to achieve without my knowing,' I admit to Larissa, 'I've been unconsciously caught up in relationships repeating a pattern of needing to find a man to bring out my true inner worth,'
'Cinderella…'
'Yep. And for me to save a really difficult dynamic and transform it into a situation that is happy, stable and successful in their own white, pure, spotless

140

modernity, all firmly supported in their personal power.'
'That's not such a bad image!'
'It's unconscious! It's based on a thirteen-year-old's fantasies! It's not real! My dreams extended to having a picnic on the lounge floor and eating take-out pizza…' I laugh. As if getting out my duvet now and having a take-out gluten-free pizza would fulfil all of my emotional needs. 'It's time to move on.'
'Into the next millennium!'
'Yes!!! Into this millennium!'

We laugh, how weird to realise that we have lived in two different millenniums. That's momentous. I wonder what it will look like over the long term view, over centuries…I wonder what is happening in this era right now? What will the experts of the turn of the millennium say in a hundred or two-hundred years about what we are going through? We will never know – the trees obscures the wood.
'The question is,' I say, sipping the last of my cortado, 'if 'Pretty Woman' and 'Back to the Future' is not what I should be modelling myself on now, what then? If I don't want children, so what's the point of having a relationship?'

—

We are in the break of the concert. The band is playing for the Dartmouth Regatta. Above is grey. The weather is close. This is mid-summer. The band is fractious. It took a long time to settle enough to even play. Dennis, the elderly horn player, had been sat on his seat and realised, after a long time, he didn't have his instrument. We worry: he's been diagnosed with Alzheimer's. The whole of the trombone section turn up late and tumble in, stands falling like tall trees in a whirlwind.

We play the first half well enough. Today there's a stand-in conductor, Victor, who normally plays the tenor horn. He's a good conductor, but I'm used to Les. We know how Les brings us in, how we move from section to section with him. Following Victor, though he's clearer on his downbeat, is like trying to dance with a stranger.

Half way through the programme the band are all queuing up for their free cup of tea by the refreshments hut. It's started to drizzle. I'm staying dry under the bandstand. It seems there is no possibility of a drink that isn't caffeinated or loaded with sugar. I had asked earlier for a peppermint tea, or a chamomile – they looked at me as if I had asked for alien juice.

So I'm hanging around, proud of my light blue blazer, talking to a member of the audience who turns out to be Sebastian's mother-in-law, 'It sounds lovely!' she says beaming, 'It really does. The audience, as soon as you all play, start moving in their chairs.' She moves her body as if enthralled by the memories of the music. I'm surprised. It felt like we were playing out to no-one, playing into a vacuum. It's hard to feel an audience in the outdoors.
'We have a substitute conductor today,' I say by way of explanation, 'he's doing really well.' I don't mention that he had to finish a piece in the middle because

141

we had all repeated back to different places. It was actually a great piece of conducting, it could have gone horribly wrong and he saved the day, being cool and collected, finding the right moment to pull us all to a parallel stop that sounded somewhat plausible and almost together.

'Yes,' she continues with flecks of spirit flying out of her eyes, 'I went to see the West Eastern Divan Orchestra, you know the one with the Palestinians and the Israelis?' I gaze straight into her, neutral. *Haven't heard of it, but I can imagine.* 'There was a Palestinian on the harp and the conductor was able to bring in the violin player, an Israeli, just hearing it. How did he do that? It's amazing.'
'Yeah,' I say in a middle-of-the-road tone because I don't really get what she was saying.
'I once went to the Royal Philharmonic and the conductor didn't show up. They couldn't play! They just fell apart. I never realised before how important the conductor is.'
I like this woman, she's one of those grandmothers who instead of going old and wrinkly is opening up into the deep scent of her wisdom.

'Yes!' I say, I'm back on track, 'a couple of rehearsals ago we had a top notch professional conductor come in. He came to see us because he used to play in the band as a boy. He's worked his way up to the higher echelons of the musical world and with all his conductor training he's now the conductor for the Gurkhas in the Army.' I pause, savouring the memory. 'It was like he was a magician; he was so inside the music that he could touch it. I felt high playing for him. It was like he brought out everything we had inside of us. He surprised us by conjuring all this music we didn't know we had in us, up to the surface. We all became much, much, better players. It was as if he serpent charmed the music out of us, bringing out the best of our talent, making us come alive. It was like…' she looks at me expectantly, '…like when you get to dance with a man who knows how to dance?'
'I know what you mean…'
'When somehow the body clicks into a world of its own.'
'Yes,'
'And you feel your body floating, literally gliding, moved by something that is not you?' We look into each other's eyes as if sharing a deep secret of fathomless pleasure, 'To me it feels like the body is moving all by itself and inside I am just an observer on a beautiful journey…'
'Yes,' she says, 'I know what you mean.' There is a twinkle in her eye.
'And afterwards it feels like you've been in a fairytale?'
'Yes.' We both smile, sharing this secret joy. I feel myself soaking in it, as if it were actually happening. 'Though,' I come back to the reality of the band stand and the summer drizzle, 'there aren't many men around who *can* dance…if there were I would be out there dancing!'
'I don't think they like to sweat. Women don't tend to sweat.' I nod, though I think it's a pretty strange idea…*Really? Men are afraid of sweating besides women?*
'I wonder if it's also about technique?' I venture as another partial truth. 'As a society, it feels like we're losing it: that ability to take a woman and hold her,

142

mould her, bring out the best in her and create something beautiful.'

She looks at me quizzically. 'I mean on one side men are forgetting how to hold a woman, how to treat the feminine, how to bring her out, how to awaken her, but on the other hand it feels like men, and rightly so, have become afraid of women. I mean,' I say, knowing that I am getting into more chat and I should be getting my caffeined cuppa – I'll be late for the second half if I don't buck up, 'it's like women have become so masculine that any feminine is protected behind a fierce, growling dog.'

There is a millisecond of stunned silence and then we belly laugh, as if we had known each other for years.

Even though I'm getting a dry mouth, I go over it again in my head. It's awkward saying the obvious, 'It's just the word 'dominate' seems so taboo, how can a man dominate a woman these days?' I think of the King and the Queen in Alchemy. 'It's so un-PC. They are too scared to even try else the woman bite his hand off!' Air comes out of my mouth. I smile. But it's lopsided, awkward, bemused. 'How can he 'handle' her, boss her about? It's almost not allowed, frowned upon.' I stick my chest out like a Sergeant Major.
'We must all be so dreadfully independent now…' she adds with a sigh.
'But we are losing out on so much! Why can't we allow ourselves to let loose and completely lose control to another so we can swim in the sensations of him playing us like a musical instrument – letting him bring out that magic from within?' I've gone all poetic. *Can it really happen?*
'I know what you mean!' she says again.
'Ohh good,' I say relieved, 'normally people think I'm potty.' She smiles. I like her. I like her grandmotherlyness.

I would like to swim in her aura for longer, soaking up her deep calmness…but I can't dawdle. 'I've got to get my tea,' I say disappointedly.
'I'll come with you,' she says taking my elbow. I like that, feels like she enjoyed our conversation as much as I did.

Raising the Baton

He rises his arms
and holding stillness
gathers in the silence
aligning us
so to fly like birds
through the music
into the unwordable
sounds of our soul.

A couple of weeks later, we are in rehearsal. Les is on holiday, and Victor can't make it. We're desperate. How to have a band practise without a conductor? We jolly one of the band members on – who isn't a conductor – until he says that

he'll give it a go. 'I can't do the test piece though,' he admonishes, 'I'll ruin the work put in more than add to it!' But we don't listen.
'Go on, give it a go!'
He drops his round shoulders, thinks about it, says, 'OK.' But he's not convinced.

I didn't realise how brave of him it was. He stands in front of us all and conducts. He's obviously held a baton before but it's hard to follow him. We are playing the test piece, so we all know how fast it goes, but we all know that we have to follow one person, the conductor, else we'll all be in different places. Tonight I'm solo cornet – I'm the lead for the band and having to watch his hand – but I can't quite tell where his down beat is. I know this section has to go faster, but he's not conducting it that speed, he's going slower, *how much slower to play?* I sort of go with what I guess he is trying to do. It's hard, he's sight-reading the score.

'Stop!' he says, 'You were going too slowly Julia…' he uses a pedantic tone, as if admonishing a primary school child. He's trying to be soft and kind, but it's coming out wrong. In his low self-confidence he's overcompensating by putting himself on a pedestal. The dynamics in the room are shifting. I look over at the trombones, they are staring at the music sheet in a grimace. The conductor is talking to me as if I had no idea what was happening and that I went too slowly because I wasn't playing well and need to follow him properly. I feel heat rise up inside. I nod in submission. There is no way around this. I feel like a prisoner in front of the guard. 'O-K,' he says really slowly in a higher than normal voice, as if having to talk slowly so we will understand, 'let's do it again.' It's the right voice for a parent who is becoming exasperated. He starts us off, I play faster, but he doesn't really conduct any differently to before, it is like being in a knot and struggling to push through: how to get the right balance between loosening the knot and making it worse. *Faster? Slower?* The band is falling apart. We are watching him like he were our torturer. It's really unclear. Hard to follow. 'Stop!' He looks around, 'You are not following me!'

It is all I can do to not get off my chair and walk out.

Instead of floating, opening up to undreamt possibilities of interweaving my being and becoming subtle beauty that is expressed through my acquiescing body, instead of delighting in the pleasant surprise of being danced by a conductor in firm but gentle grace, I feel myself collapsed, closed down, veins boiling. I feel like I have been made into a much worse player than I actually am. I feel violated. Forced entry into my inner temple. Made guilty.

In short: I feel like shit.

———

Is it just me caught in the Cinderella Complex? I want to grow, I want to grow into the highest expression of myself. I mean we have to keep growing right? A plant never stops, a tree never stops, nature doesn't stop growing. We cannot stop growing. I want to keep growing into myself so that greater amounts of light can shine out through me, in every action I do, in every thought, in every intention. Isn't that what the joy of living is all about?

—

There is the miracle of sun right down here in Devon. It is not raining. I'm sat on the terrace of the Curator Cafe. I've met up with Diane for a tea and a chat. She and her man are into Tantra and David Deida. We are talking about how orgasm can be so satisfying if we allow it to be just as it is and not try and make it into something else.

'It's like suddenly when I allow myself to relax, all those feelings of trying to get to orgasm, and imagining how I should feel based on an idea – probably based on films and books – and feeling that what I'm feeling is wrong…sort of aren't there…' she makes brief eye-contact to see if I'm with her still. I nod. I think I know what she is saying. 'So like now that I can relax into what is, here, now, without changing it, I realise that all those sensations that I had been dismissing as not enough, are actually really beautiful, subtle, quite divine.'

We're on the same sort of path, at least it feels like it, but we'll never know… how can words portray what we do when we are in the midst of creating love? She is so confident that I feel really small in her presence.
'Yeaaaa…' I say, feeling really vulnerable, scared that maybe I've never experienced what she's talking about.
'If only we let ourselves relax more into what is naturally occurring, rather than trying to make something happen,' she remonstrates to the world at large. This is where I feel confident I have actually experienced this – at least in the backwards form.
'Uf,' I add and nod my head.
'But it's so hard to do!' The red sea parts between us. *Will it stay open?*
'Yes,' I sigh out, the end of the word nothing more than a long exhalation. I ride on the breath of realising that it's not just me who finds all this accepting-who-I-am-in-the-moment hard.
Relief. Relief. Relief. I open.

She continues, 'I don't know about you, but all sorts come up for me, all sorts of trauma, or emotions, or grief…and the opposite, beauty, pleasure, joy. Sometimes in the midst of it all I burst into tears…'
I suddenly feel much better over me lying in bed with Christopher and crying my eyes out. Especially when I'm never really sure about what. Waves of pent up emotion flowing through my eyes as he gently moves in and out of me, holding me, allowing me, giving me space to experience all this in his kind arms.
'It needs a strong, wise man for a woman to become feminine enough to allow herself to dance with the spirit of the moment. We need protection to be able to totally concentrate on ourselves, on what is going on inside, to be able to move and bring out all that is within us,' I nod. I am loving her sharing all this with me, 'It's essential that the man can give us all the protected space we need so that we can free up all that energy of having to protect ourselves, and to be able to use it instead to go within and create.'

I think of Vipassana, where we are fed and given a place to sleep: release for ten days from worrying about staying alive. Free from external pressure we can use our energy on having the courage to leave the surface reality behind and dive down into ourselves, deeper and deeper, allowing all to arise and pass away, arise and pass away without having to control anything.

'It's so important to allow our feminine to be able to express herself without it needing to be 'anything',' she does air finger quotations, 'or to go 'anywhere', but just be whatever it is in that precise moment.'
I sigh in imagined joy. I sigh in the joy of imagining. I am loving this.
'What magic in the ruthless willingness to accept things as they are!'
'Wow, what a thing to say!' I admire.
'I know!'

'I read about Cinderella,' I say to contribute to our bouquet of conversation, 'and the idea that she has two mothers, a bad step mother and a good fairy godmother…which I guess is the same as saying our connection to the feminine, to ourselves…'
'Wow, I've never looked at it like that…'
'Yeah…I love going into fairy stories…'
'Go on,' she sounds interested.
I feel myself grow inside, I'm not feeling so little any longer. I have something interesting to say, something that is nourishing for us both, 'Our connection to the positive feminine, like with a good mother, or as my friend George would say, our authentic mother, allows us to see ourselves as we are, and helps us to reveal who we are…'
'To the world?'
'And to ourselves?'
'Yeah,' she says leaning forward, beautiful long fingers resting on her cheek, 'and the bad mother?' I can't help but feel buoyed up by her attention.
'She treats 'the daughter',' I now do the air quotation sign, 'as a usurper and rival and tries to hold her back, tries to keep her back in the dirt of the cinders. You know like the wicked witch in…what was the fairy tale?'
'Snow White?'
'That's right, with the seven dwarfs!' I think about how the seven dwarfs are her emerging animus. 'The Wicked witch says, 'Mirror mirror on the wall who is the fairest of them all?'
'Not you!' says the mirror.
'Then destroy her!! I want to be the fairest! Destroy!!!'' I breathe in, pulling myself early enough out of my potential pantomime voice, 'Pretty wicked narcissism.'
She does not respond straight away, but looks at me, as if examining me. *Crikey, I've gone too far, she thinks I'm a loony tunes* 'How do you know all of this?'

Hearing her admiration, I suddenly feel exposed to positive feelings about myself in public, in plain view of another. It takes me all I can to stay up and not collapse. 'I've read it, I did a masters in Jungian Psychology. I just like it,' I say in the most neutral tone I can, instead of jumping up and down and shouting

'Whipppeeeeee!' or imploding in a hole of fear of having been an arrogant, self conceited, bad, bad person, bad.

'I just didn't realise that fairy stories held such deep stuff in them.'

'It's why they are told and retold. It's why they are so attractive.' Neutral voice. She sips her coffee. I venture onwards, wary of going 'too far' but too titillated to stop right now, 'The bad mother inside of us tells us we must never have what we want, someone else must have it instead. Like we just don't deserve to have a wonderful man, sensational sex, a deep loving connection,'

'Right...' we look into each other's eyes. We both feel it. Does any woman not feel it?

'Like as if it would be absurd to accept ourselves!' Air comes out of my nose as I laugh at the image of myself not accepting me. 'Meanwhile,' I say hoping to get back onto firmer ground, 'the good mother, the fairy godmother, says, 'Let the magic come through you': it allows you to see yourself as desirable (and desirous) as you are. This good mother energy uses her wand to help us see.' We smile. We've both felt this side too: that feeling inside of light shining out, of being wanted, of feeling high on our own beauty, of feeling our own value, connecting to our sensual movements, our inner worlds. 'Daring to desire to express our beauty...'

'...and it be received.'

'Yeah....' I feel so strong suddenly. 'When we side with the bad stepmother,' I say, 'we get off on frustrating ourselves,' Diane lifts an eyebrow, 'meanwhile when we believe in ourselves – and our magic – we can follow our desire healthily in a flow of *what is*.'

'And to allow that to happen, we need the strong support and protection of the masculine to contain us, so that we can go within and allow our magic free reign!'

I lift up my almost empty tea cup. She does too and we clink. 'Yes Ma'am!'

I

In the eye of the storm
I open to you.

II

Cracked open,
I feel past pains
of thorn touches
turn to silk.

III

My ear to your heart
I hear myself
tasting love
and doubt myself
no more.

PART IV

Going In -
Sex and Love and All It Spews Up

Chapter 12: Awakening

An intimate journey transporting me into
an animal roaring in the throes of being satisfied.

I

Fear of getting close
Feeling his shadow
so close
I wonder
why he doesn't
walk through it
lightly into love;
as I cower
in the corner
of my cave.

II

Gaining entry
The innocent fool
stood alone
like a clown
open, honest;
purity his only
protection.

Sarah ate every one of her lovers
– except Tobias.
Tobias waited.
Listened.
Allowed.
He moved forward
only when their worlds
pulsated as one.
He, the only one
not devoured,
he, the only one
allowed within.

No-one would come looking for her here, exhausted collapsed in her dark, damp cave. She lay alone, safe in her isolation.

———

Parzival bent down and crouched, began to stroke her long blonde hair. Her eyelids flickered, she was in there, feeling his touch. Her mouth moved slightly, as if to talk. He imagined from her posture she liked him close, stroking her hair, but there was no way to know. He looked into her face, his being open to her, emotions flowed up through him, emotions he had never felt before - too pure to be marred by names. He wanted to protect her, to care for her, to please her. His spirit quickened uncontrollably as he felt an overwhelming desire to be within her, to penetrate her beauty, to be held within the translucent membrane in the cave of her innocence, wrapped deep within its purity. But he didn't advance. He knew in his being he must wait. He knew he must be patient. Overtaken by an understanding that she must first feel this growing inside of him – sense it, yearn for it, want to taste it – he maintained a distance. Desiring her as if stones were turning in his stomach he wanted nothing more than to pour himself into her deepest alcoves but he knew: now is not impossible. She was not ready for him: to be allowed entry into where he wanted to reach her she must feel open to him at the depths of her being.

He would stay here beside her as long as it took, for as long as she needed.

She made a little noise, a moaned word, as if waking from a deep dream. He moved his hand softly to her cheeks and brushed them. She moved her face, it pressed feather light into his hand. He held her on the wisps of his air, the heat of his hand barely touching her. He held her softly, securely, now with both hands on either side, cradling her head, and slowly, so very slowly, moved his mouth towards her lips.

He felt her like a magnet, her barriers pushing him away, like to like. The air over his lips tingled. *Move forward? Withdraw?* In the emotional charge he lost control, found his body taking over.

They kissed.

A tiny electric wave passed from his lips to hers.

Butterfly energy moved subtly within her, whispering to her of her body. She lay, half asleep, feeling through the distance, separated from her body several valleys away.

———

The whole of the next day, he felt light. He moved in the woods feeling his animal nature, hunting, collecting wood, drinking from the stream. As the light began to dim from the sky he built a fire, burning the deadwood within himself. He felt himself changing. The memory of the sleeping beauty in her dark cave moved through his loins. She had not awakened, but he'd felt something within her moving. *Was it only in his imagination? Would she ever open her eyes to him? See him?* He had felt something indescribable, a movement from deep within heavy stone.

That night he went to her again. He crouched beside her on the hard rock floor watching her delicate features, marvelled as her chest moved so delicately with her breath. Again, he stroked her hair and though tangled and knotted took pleasure in how it smoothed out in places, how he saw glimmers of a diamond through this rough stone. Hardly daring, holding his breath, he edged towards her lips, his whole being caught in an intensity of awareness he could hardly bear. In the darkness he found her lips with his own. He felt her move towards him. Her lips moved slightly with his. It gave him courage within his heart. He moved his hand softly, slipping over the dirty ragged cotton, enthralled to touch her body for the first time. She lay still; the rising and falling of her chest quickened. She moved gently as if deep undercurrents of the sea were swaying her body awake. She moaned and turned over; turned away.

—

His fire grew throughout the next day. He became hard whenever he thought of her asleep in her cave. He was ready to penetrate through her defence, through her sleep state, he wanted to lull her awake with this that pulsated within him.

In the evening, he went to her again. Circling around her he wondered how to advance into her space. Again, he sat as he had the previous nights on the rocky floor and stroked her hair. It was slightly less matted, a little more familiar. Leaning on one arm he bent towards her face, her eyelids fluttered a butterfly message and gently, as if suspended in a dream, he kissed them. This time he felt her respond. She moved her mouth, opened her lips. She allowed herself to be defenceless, let her vulnerability be present. He moved slowly, pulling her gently towards him, letting his tongue dance upon the entry of her lips. Her body moved under him. He took courage and lay beside her, though part of him feared becoming trapped. He had no experience of who she was, she could become a wild, scared animal, snarling; but he didn't care - this within him was too strong to be afraid now. He, the innocent fool could do nothing but love this tattered soul, this beauty masquerading as derelict raggedness.

The length of his body touched hers, his hand moved over her shape, brushing it. She moaned and turned her head towards him. He kissed her, love surging through his loins he reined in his passion. He didn't want to scare her. He moved his lips down, gently kissing her chin, kissing down her throat, over her chest, and began circling her breasts. Through the threadbare cotton, he felt her nipples harden. Her body began to move in waves. Slight, inaudible moans escaped her parted lips. He wished, a stone in his throat, to see her eyes. They were closed, her head thrown up, as if looking through her eyelids to the entrance of the cave.

He slowly, gently, pulled her dress up to her thighs and took her gently with his fingers, afraid to go too fast, too soon. She continued, her legs pressed together, to writhe almost imperceptibly. He felt her mountain between his fingers and from the valley upwards began stroking it as softly as a feather. She was dry! *Should he stop?* He paused, fingers hovering. With the minutest of movement he felt her push herself onto his fingers. He slipped one inside her offering and was hit by the awe of her soft, wet warmth. He rubbed her gently, massaging her, wanting her with his swollen cock.

He moved down her body and took her wet vagina in his mouth, softly moving his tongue in and out of her entrance. Her legs opened, allowing him to go further into her with his tongue. He felt he would explode.

Kundry feels her back undulating on the soft ground, feeling waves of pleasure run through her body. Part of her is tense. *Is this an intrusion? Who is this being beside her?* She feels his body against hers, but through the fear she also feels pleasure. This path is unbearable. *Should she?* Something inside whispers for her to let go. She allows herself just a little more, then she'll push him away. His hands are roving softly over her body. She feels them, a soft tickle hovering around her shape, into her hollows, over her mounds. She had forgotten about her body in this way, she had forgotten the pleasure of sensing. Her vagina is pulsating, something bursting forth between her slit. The release surges through her body as his fingers reach her clitoris – her body stirs, awakening from a deep sleep. She feels as if she is under water, being moved by waves, slowly, gingerly, as if she were seaweed deep below the surface on the sea floor. Part of her wants to hold on tightly, to stop, to keep control. It doesn't feel safe to let go. She wants to stay in her head. She wants to stay in the safety zone of thoughts, even though they are of dread. She wants to stay within the enclosed circle of her taut, dormant, petrified muscles. She feels the terror of opening up. *What will it bring?*

Her body begins to rock, her voice lets out an inaudible moan. Her body is taking over, taking on a life of its own.

She feels him stroking her a little more firmly. The soft, firm way he is touching her makes her feel held, secure. She wants more. *Who is this man?* She has felt him come to her night after night, has felt his gentleness through her dreamless sleep, she has felt his light touch. He didn't feel dangerous. *But how can she tell?* Her body moans with each wave, wanting to go forward.

Sensations move through her legs, numbing and sparkling at the same time and begin to concentrate in her pelvis. She feels the warmth of his soft tongue dart within her vagina. The stream of energy moves her. She is losing herself, forgetting herself, sensing only herself and this man; this kind, gentle man.

He begins to lick her now with a greater confidence that wasn't there before, listening to her, hearing her in the movements of her body. Encouraged by her moans he licks softly with his tongue from the mouth of her vagina up her mound to the peak of her clitoris. His licks become slightly firmer, flicking at the end over her erect clitoris. Her body pulsates in rhythm with his tongue. He cannot think now, nor decide, he is simply becoming, moving his tongue inside and out, dancing within the deep listening of her breath, of her body, feeling himself dissolving into her energy, feeling himself throbbing and hard, ready to penetrate into her growing softness.

Her body pulsates in larger, higher waves. She is on a brink. She needs to decide: to go back, to go back to her state of defence, of safety, of being alone in the cave, or to go now with these sensations, to lose control, to allow this man to rock her into her body, to float under the waves of this deluge of sensations. An ecstatic white tingling moves up through her legs through her vagina and spreads into her womb: a rich, smooth swirling. Her muscles relax as sensations move up within her into her head, a soft, blissfully blinding, white light. She is nothing but this moment now. Nothing but white sensations coursing through her entire body. She feels his body quicken beside hers though barely touching. She feels him coming towards her, feels his desire. She wants him. Her body quickens, her breathing swirls into panting. She has lost control. Pleasure trickles through her vagina, running streams down her legs.

There is only one desire now: his cock in her mouth. She is nothing but the drive within her, no thoughts now enter her mind, nothing but desire and this white, beautiful light. She feels herself renouncing her humanity for the sake of the animal. It wakes her to herself, to her instincts, to cock.

She moves, moaning, trying to communicate her desire to him. He moves his body, unsure as to her needs, unsure if he's moving too fast, but something has taken hold of him, something is giving him courage to move his body, his shaft close to her mouth. He leaves space so she can make the final distance but the space between his cock and her mouth are torture to her; she swims through her dormant state, allowing her body to pick up the energy to move and as if in a dream, manoeuvres herself to put his cock between her lips. She hears him gasp.

As if jumping off the top of a waterfall she freefalls down his cock. She moves her tongue, moves her mouth, feels him and his potency within her. She feels him going blissfully into his body. She is a baby suckling, she is a whore sucking, she is a woman in pleasure, she is an animal in bliss. He moans, she feels it through her body, titillated by the power he is giving her.

He shifts to allow his tongue to meet her vagina again, to move deliriously in and out. She moves her mouth up and down his shaft as they unite in one rhythm. The animal within her groans with pleasure, adores his smooth, hard dick. Deep in praise she feels herself in a temple to it, venerating it, losing herself in a prayer of pleasure. As if from above she hears herself groan deeply, her breath coming up through her, a bubble coming up through water, before she returns back to the underwater world.

They rock on and on, time ceasing to exist.

Her body softens. His body hardens. They are expanding beyond their limits, entering into something bigger than each of them.

He is kneeling over her, her pussy in his mouth, dangling his dick over her suckling mouth. She feels his buttocks being pulled apart by his posture. Feeling the shift from retiring to advancing, she moves her hand to let her fingers slide down his back. She realises she has permission, she can touch him as she desires, it ripples through her being as she explores her pleasure. Her fingers slide into the crack between his mounds, and feels for his anus. Her dry finger meets his dry entrance. She massages him slightly, power surging through her, this is her last decision: to become the animal or to retreat. She decides to slide her finger into her mouth, wetting it with desire.

Sensing her finger moving over his anus, he moans. Wants it deeper. Electricity moves around them in a circle between his mouth and her vagina, up through her stomach, crossing through with the contact of her breasts against his lower stomach. Magnetized by his penis in her mouth, she feels her lust concentrating around her lips: the animal awakes out of the cave of oblivion. No thoughts, no feelings, just sensations running through her body: his cock, her vagina, fingers touching, stroking, the contact of her breasts on his stomach. Her back arches, her legs release and tense in pleasure, twitching. Her body is coming alive. Her tongue extending far out from her mouth stimulates her. She is writhing like a snake, her arms move to his back, holding on to him, letting go of herself. She is no longer in control – her animal is. She wants his dick in her mouth forever, she wants these sensations in her vagina to never end. Her body moves all by itself, she flows, uncontrolled, flailing in pleasure.

When it seems she can take no more, both of their bodies sense a peak, an opening, a need. He turns his body around. She needs to see. Slowly she opens her eyes, allowing them to unpeel. They meet face to face. In the invisible tunnel between their eyes, each feel their worlds unending. They kiss with a fury of passion that startles them both. They are electrified, they are consumed by lines of light flashing between them, connecting.

Eyes locked, listening deeply, he penetrates her.

Timeless darkness rocks them together. Each thrust closer to becoming one. Groans mingling, he is deep within her. She feels his presence throughout her whole body, entering her, occupying her. The animal instinct jerks through her, insatiable wanting pushing against his hard member, her groaning ever stronger as she grinds against his cock. The energy within her, the animal inside, has taken on a life of its own, her body is moving in ways unknown to her, exciting her. An arch stretches through her back, opening out her chest, she is vulnerable, free. Her toes clench almost to cramping, her legs spread in butter soft abandonment.

The waves of pleasure grow bigger and bigger. With her mind completely closed down, her body is in control now. She rides wave after wave of pleasure, of natural movement lead by her vagina. Impulses run up through her spine. Groans run up through her throat, her neck extends upwards to the roof of the cave allowing the sound to resonate, echoing loud moans of pleasure. The waves get more intense, her groans louder, faster, peaking closer and closer. Together they are merging into one state, one being, caught in time eternal.

Given over to pleasure, it rides through her, becoming her, pushing her higher and higher, further and further away from herself, into herself. White water crashing upwards she flies inwards towards the deep familiar stars. Her body is fire, white hot searing fire, burning through her every cell. She arches her back, throws her head back again, opens her throat wide to allow passage to that within her. Her muscles are too exhausted now to take control; she too ecstatic to care, falling into blissful nothingness, merging with that which is dancing her, pulsating through her. Panting, she feels sound rising up through her being. A final membrane of tension gives way, and suddenly, as if at the centre of a star, from deep within a surge of light explodes softly, violently in her, passing through every crack in her being, expanding, destroying: she is nothing but an explosion hurtling through space.

Flying at the speed of light, over the distance her voice lets out a birthing scream. Deep within the scream, in the eye of the storm, she recognises herself.

Recreating

I want only
this now:
you, me
our bodies
burning as One
in the heights;
the fire destroying
anew
that which was me,
that which was you.

Climbing into heaven and falling, through
shards of painful exposure, back down
into uncomfortable, tighter 'I' suits.

No End to Becoming

Eternal
destruction
and
construction
leaving
and
returning
into ourselves;
don't convert
what converts you
into an end:
don't stop time
with an idol.

We rush to yoga. I am in fast mode, pushing Paul along, enjoying sharing my life in the township of _____ [4]. We get there late; I knock on the door to let us in. They are already lying on the floor in Shavasana. My mate is there, Alexa, the one I can have a good northern laugh with. 'Relax!' I whisper like a Sergeant Major. We laugh, titillated by secret ribaldry in this place where the idea is to not laugh. I am pumping, moving fast. I get out my yoga mat, trying not to be really noisy, and try slip in under the sheets of the yogic breath. I'm breathing fast. *How to still this panting?*

At the end of the yoga class, we move into Shavasana again, as slow as snails. Sara, the facilitator, does the whole thing (that my logical brain thinks is silly): she roots us down into the earth, past 'crystal caves' (yeah, yeah, yeah) and as I do so I feel my breath softening more. My body is relaxed from the hour and a half of yoga. I am going in, deeper in, past the crystal caves of my insides. I am feeling (or imagining?) light coming up through these roots, feeling myself as a field, as little snowdrops, warmed by the sun, nourished by the earth. I feel my system going into butter soft, into forgetting who I am, where I am: into (just?) being. I hear my breath. I feel my body. Sensations. Waves of something invisible. Tingling. Weight. Airiness. Stomach and chest moving with the waves of inhalation, exhalation. I am sinking further in. Further. Further. Pleasure. Juice.

Time has stayed up on some forgotten surface. I feel myself expanding into soft awareness of presence.

I stay in this place for an eternity of nothingness. Being.

'When you are ready, put your right hand under your neck and turn gently onto your right side.'

Woooah….Outside?…. I had forgotten….. Move?

I stay still. I stay in my nothingness…I cannot move…..want not to…..brain not logic…..*stay here*….peace….*don't have to move*…..freedom….world….waves come over me….pleasure….warm duvet of breathing….*stay in this place*… ..lovely…..soft…..safe…..ahhhh…

I hear the others moving. I don't. I can't.

The idea of time comes crashing in, soft waves up on the surface.

The others are rustling. I don't.

I do – I make the Hercules effort to move my fingers.

Are the others sat up?

I crane power my hand under my neck. I am heavy. Very heavy. This is an uphill battle.

Within

Find the eternal
Here-Now
for there is nothing
outside of time.

I admire the Knights Templar, the ones who explored in honesty, in naked truths, round the backside of the established church, the ones who were strong enough of character to continue through the realities of their psyches even at the risk of being killed by dogmatic, torturing priests.

The crafted statues the Knights Templar often have a saint with an open and a closed book. The outer world and the inner world: somehow they have to unite.

—

In alchemy, the person who connects worlds is Mercury. Running up and down in his winged boots and matching winged hat. Fancy. He has a staff with entwined snakes that Pharmacies use now as a symbol of health. His role as mediator and 'keeper of boundaries' bridges between the upper and lower worlds. Mercury is the silver flow that connects inside and outside, above and below; the Presence of Universal Oneness and our unique us-ness, our instincts with our divinity.

The Kiss in the Alley by the Chippie

For a moment of eternity
there were no shadows.

Love, brings out all that is not love.

—

From: <julia.butterflypress@gmail.com>
To: <christopher.bond@gmail.com>

One of the things I've learnt with Paul is that the coming in and out of a merged state is where we learn most – against 'the rub' of who I have been and who I am becoming. Coming out is where suddenly we see ourselves...not as gods anymore...but as imperfect humans...it is the horror mirror of the funfair park...we see how we have distorted our gods within and are petrified...

So that is where I am now...you and me, me and you...after feeling such sublime love, I suddenly feel apprehension. I suddenly feel a fear of who you are. I suddenly realise that I may have seen you as a projection of the perfect knight of the round table. The energy between us is so strong, it could be so overpowering. I go into altered states just kissing you. Can we manage to control it rather than be controlled by it? Control is the wrong word. Like Marsyas, can we allow the energy to flow through us to become a servant to our higher selves, or will we try to manipulate it with our egos and be flayed alive? And being flayed alive...is that good or bad? Up or down? Is it being stripped of ego clothing becoming closer to our truths? Unveiled. Revealed.

When I am scared I intellectualise.
I am scared.
I feel vulnerable.
I feel excited.
I am suddenly not sure how I feel.

Julia xxx

—

We are in the final rehearsal stood on the altar inside St. Peter's - a white-washed Greek church that has been plonked on top of an ancient temple site sometime in the last couple of thousand years.

Orpheus has been voice training us for months for this rather ambitious program that includes pieces from Rachmaninoff, pieces that stretch back to the medieval times, deep pieces praising the Virgin Mary. Spring. Few of us, if any, are religious. The others scoff at the idea of a pregnant virgin - but I don't. My strong feelings of ancient, deep blasphemy made me pipe up in one rehearsal; I get angry when people make assumptions without going into what it's really about. I get angry with dogma, within church goers and church haters. I feel hot anger rising through me when people limit their enquiries to the superficial as if they have reached a final goal, and then use inappropriate generalisations as if they hold the only, obvious truth. Oblivious even to the idea of partial truths.

'Virgin Mary who is pregnant!' they scoff, their thinking ended, corroded in the obvious.

So I breathe in ready to launch out into their disbelief. 'Mary comes from the same roots as Mar, Sea: water, emotions.' I say as an introduction and though I have a map in my head, a sort of Celtic Cross, I don't expand into it, I just stay as simple as I can, walking along this knife edge between two different worlds. 'If we are able to enter into a state of nothingness,' they are all looking at me, sheet music in their hands. I go into that vulnerable place where they can hurl laughter, or they can dismiss me by saying that we should get on with singing, 'If we can go into that place of settled emotions, of settled thoughts, if we are able to make the inside our minds virgin and clear, if we can manage to be filled with nothing but nothingness - we become the temple: the virgin empty temple,' I imagine a bare inner temple, nothing, nothing outside, nothing inside, nothing, 'and in that state of receptivity the divine can enter and can pregnate within us.' I remember the scene in Wagner's Parzival as light comes down into the temple from the heavens above.

They look at me, startled, not sure. In their faces I see they are looking around the edges, wondering if I'm pulling their leg. It seems so obvious to me! I think back to experiences in Vipassana, white pure light, that feeling of bliss. *How to explain?* I want to say it is where Rainer Maria Rilke says that to go to that place we must leave behind even our names like a child leaves behind their broken toys. I want to say it is where the Divine becomes human for the sake of humankind, and the human becomes divine for the sake of Divinity. But I don't; I've already pushed them too far. Virgin. Pregnant. It makes sense to me. In fact, from where I'm looking it's the only way. Mundus Imaginalis. Corbin. I want to say so much, express so much, but I know that it's something you have to feel, not think.

I say, hopelessly, 'Clean water transmits light.' I am dangling and do not know how to go forward or to come back, hanging into words that are useless without experience.

Orpheus, the conductor looks at me, smiles in what I imagine as a sort of Masonic nod and says, 'OK, back to the beginning.'

———

So, after months of rehearsal we are ready to sing in front of an audience. We get ready to sing Rachmaninoff. It is a stirring piece. It's midday, tonight is the concert. Gnawing pre-concert anxiety is putting me into a heightened sense of hyper awareness: this is getting real. Orpheus tunes us with το παιχνίδι, the 'toy', his little electric keyboard.

We sing.

I sing.

Behind a veil

Through the membrane
to where I am not I,
deeper into true self.

I feel the notes deep in myself. The pieces are so well known now they are part of me, words surging through without having to think. I sing. I feel my heart expanding. I feel myself merging with the music. I feel myself pouring into that which is occurring between our eight voices. I feel myself feeling the open empty temple. The Virgin Mar. I feel myself in bliss. My voice sings somewhere as I fly through the harmonies. I forget I have a body. Forget I have a voice. Forget I am singing. I just am. Being. I am being sung. Blissful invisible me. Harmonic virgin me. Me. Not me. We are birds flying in the formation of starlings, swooping through the skies, carried on the thermals of our emotions, carried in the crescendos and drops of our voices, feeling my heart beat as if someone else's. Feeling myself in pure, innocent expression. Entering a place that is eternally not here.

Orpheus conducts us to the close of the piece. Everything is lighter: my eyes feel so open, heart so full. The silence after the final note is exquisite. Maybe this is it, the reason to sing, to hear the silence of afterward. The deep velvet of stillness after the birdsong. In the silence we are all one. Floating. Being held in its satin sheets.

Orpheus brings down his baton. We let out our breath in quiet controlled sighs. He nods. It is broken. We are human beings again. We sit down. We drink our water. He mentions that after 'B' we were a bit loud. On the repeat we have to pay attention. Someone laughs. 'OK,' says our beloved conductor, 'let's move onto the Langue d'Oc song.'

On the altar, I stand back from this world, in a flash I crash into the human me. I feel excruciatingly vulnerable. Naked. Regaining sense. Scrambling for my ego jacket. I cannot quite remember what happened. I have no image of what I was doing: no self judgement, no control. 'I' was not there. *Were the others? Were the others watching? Seeing? Judging? What was I doing? Was I out of control?* I just remember being 'out there'. *Did I make a fool of myself?* All I remember is expanding happily – *but was I singing in tune? Too loud? Was it a mess? Did I take up too much space?* All my complexes come out. The ego is pulling on its suit again, complaining about being forgotten, crying out all the more intensely for attention, using 'my' fears to get it back in control, using anything to get back in power. I feel my face red. I peer out through the corner of my eyes to detect any smirks. Paranoia.

———

'Synchronicity,' says Pedro from our little Jungian study group, 'is when things happen as if from another world, with hidden meaning to show us more of ourselves.' We all sit quietly mulling over our own ideas on synchronicity.

'What's the difference between that and mere coincidence?' asks Gregorio.
'Well…they are coincidences, significant coincidences…' pipes in Pau pushing up his Woody Allen glasses.
'But they are not meaningless…' adds Pedro, battling for centre stage, 'So two things happen at the same time, 'a coincidence' – acausal – so they appear to be separate and yet are meaningfully related.'
'Who connects that rope of meaning? Like us, and is it real? Or something greater than us? Where does the meaning come from?' I ask. Such a hard thing to talk about.
'I read that it is as if we were aware of a 2D plane,' Pedro taps the table, 'but there are other dimensions out there,' he picks up his half empty wine glass, 'so when we see just a filled in circle,' he lowers the base of the glass to be beside the table top, 'we think it is just a solid circle of clear transparent material,' he lowers the glass, 'but then it rapidly becomes a small circle, as if completely disconnected from the previous circle,' he puts the glass so the wine is level with the table top, 'and then it opens out into a larger filled circle with a colour of red,' he moves his glass up to where there is no wine, 'and then, on our 2D mentality, it becomes an empty circle.' I think I see what he's saying. 'We don't

necessarily connect the different images on our 2D plane, they all seem disconnected, but from a different vision, 3D it is obvious they are connected in the form of a wine glass.'

I try to imagine something more complicated, that would have massively different shapes, that to us would seem totally disconnected on a 2D plane, but connected on a 3D, but I can't. I try to imagine on our 3D plane a shape going through it from a 5D plane. But I can't, at all. I've have a bit too much wine.

—

In the other Jungian group, who meet midday in the library, we are all soberly delving into the subject of synchronicity. How to know what is what? *How to know if something is actually synchronicity or just a figment of our imaginations?* Lola tells us about a personal experience. She gives us a rather long winded tale about a mystic experience she had when walking the Camino de Santiago across Spain. With each step so important to her she peppers the whole story with details, but it's understandable: her beloved lifelong partner of fifty years had recently died, collapsing on the street on his way to join her in their favourite afternoon cafe. He was a few metres from the door. She never had a chance to say goodbye.

Flaying in all of the resulting space of her new life, she decides to walk the Camino, to find herself again. To heal from the shock. She tells us about her journey full of wonderfully big coincidences and small miracles. She culminates the story in how at a certain moment, placing her stone on one of the heaps of other pilgrims' stones she felt her spirit rise up into the skies – and his coming down. Near her the leaves on the trees suddenly rustle loudly. Expanded into an altered state it seems obvious the trees were confirming for her, as if angels, what she was feeling. The air had been still all morning. The rustling stops, as abruptly as it began. She feels sure it is him. It is a feeling deep inside, a remembering. She feels touched by his love. He had managed to give her their loving farewell.

Afterward she wonders out loud to our little group in the library: *Was it real?*

Our leader, Filipe, who does not like to be called leader, the one who has read the most, experienced a lot, searched a lot, comes to wonderful conclusions a lot, and thrives on being the invisible leader with his narcissism only just under control, says, 'The problem with these experiences experienced with the heart in a transparent state of flexible ego is that afterwards, in that most vulnerable time, logic steps in and tells us it is just a mere coincidence and not to be so soft headed.'

Commander Logic comes storming in cracking its whip. Ego, having made a pact long ago with Logic, sneers and pulls back on its strait-jacket of control.

Sudden ghastly awareness. Vulnerable, heart raw, exposure. *What is real?*

—

Even before the big blow up with my brother we still had to be careful about the minefields between us, the church goer and the world goer. So we're talking, he's in his bath in his enormous house in England, and I'm sat in the small dark Catalan study, filled with Spanish books on philosophy, mysticism, psychology, the sexual relationship, and general topics of inescapable curiosity. Though we haven't spoken for six months we are laughing, fuelling the fragile image we want to portray of closeness.

We've been chatting and sharing for a long time, almost an hour. I'm getting ready to close. He is telling me about how some Jehovah Witnesses came around. How he talked to them. I stay quiet. Minefield aware. I think he is trying to show me that he is open to other religions; *Is he?* He talks about Jews, is saying something about them that he doesn't agree with – when the line goes dead.

He has money. I do not. I don't know whether to call him back. I don't know if I am being a bad sister to think, *Well, we were almost finished anyway* …and leave it at that. I don't know if I should spend fifty pence to make an international call to say, 'OK, well nice speaking.' Ending conversations are hard. We cannot say, 'Speak to you soon,' because we won't. I should call. I don't want to. I don't want to just waste money on a phone call for no real reason; it will just be awkward anyway. So I don't. I have nothing more to say. But I think I should. I walk to the window, stare out through the dirty panes to the little patio garden, vibrantly green. I stare through my sun drenched leafy friends and worry. *Am I being a bad sister? A bad person?*

After a few minutes the phone rings – it's my brother on his mobile phone. His fast words sown hastily together with desperation, 'I was in the bath and the batteries on the land line went dead…' Inside I laugh, relieved. 'I just wanted you to know,' he continues quick-fire, 'I have no issue with the Jews.'

Afterwards I wonder about how my mother would have reacted in the same situation. How would she have coped in the void of the connection going dead? I imagine she would have tried to call back straight away in her desperation to cover over any fear drenched thoughts of being a 'bad mother', getting into a flap, punching the numbers on the phone to reconnect ASAP. I imagine her gasping, half jokey voice, 'I just called the wrong number!' and in our joint laughter, fears being assuaged.

My brother calls to cover up doubts of the expansiveness of his religious views.

I stand by the window worrying if I am a good enough sister, or not.

—

I mean things just happen sometimes. For no reason that we are conscious of. It just happens. Batteries fail.

When the Planck level collapses randomly between us, we project into the gap, into the ensuing void, the monsters within us desperate to get out of the cage we hold them in.

—

Love brings out all that is not love.

—

Our images collapse. Our maps collapse. We collapse in agony.

Our ignorance cannot help us anymore. We flounder in the dark. It is not as we thought - what is then? The unknown looms.

—

We could say 'monsters', there's more finesse in saying, 'our impurities' or as the Buddhists say 'Saṅkhāra' (fabrications). Jungians would say innervated complexes and that we need healthy complexes to be able to function in the world. We need a 'Mother Complex' to be able to be a mother. But most of us have incomplete patterns in the constellation of our complexes: spanners in the works, knotty constricted areas in our images that impede us from flowing through time. Knots, mistakes, holes that need healing.

—

'I was sat in the bath on the house phone, and the battery went dead,' my bro says again to make sure we've got it straight. Nothing, it would seem, to do with either of our complexes.

Maybe I am not such a bad sister?

It's hard to let go of old my old monster friends, I want them back in *my* cage. Who am I without them?

—

'It got confusing,' Bernard says. I am on Pearl Street in Boulder having a Bhakti Chai latte after the Sunday morning jam. It is horribly sweet. I wanted to try it, tempted by the spiritual name. All I can think about is candida - wish I'd stuck to water. Bernard, however, is one of those rare people who is totally genuine. He's drinking a beer, midday. Why? Because he likes it. He's just recounted a story about a Touch and Play workshop he went to one weekend in the next state, New Mexico.

Touch and Play is an extension of Contact Improvisation where people play with broadened boundaries that include the erotic and sexual limits. He said that they went into a yurt that was a bit too small, and they were all naked and oiled up. Unfortunately the floor was not quite flat enough: everyone slid into a doughy pile on one side of the yurt. By 'confusing' he later explains, 'I would put my hand out and think, *Oh what's that?* and it would be a breast, or arms, or parts of people that I couldn't define, and at one point a fanny slid all over my face.' I ask him if all the men had hard-ons. 'No,' he says calmly, 'it wasn't quite like that, it came and went, the energy was a bit all over the place. Sometimes it was more like a logistical issue, and there was a big German guy, not quite in his body, who did things like dive over the top of everyone – and suddenly I'd have a pair of balls on me. He brought the energy down, stopped it being too erotic.' Sat there in the middle of *The Laughing Goat* he looks across the sticky table to me as if to say, *You know what I mean?*

The answer is *No*. I can only imagine, and it's scary just to do that.

'I came out of the yurt with my friend,' he continues, 'and as we walked away he confided to me how full on it had felt to him. 'What went on there?' I'd felt the women were really going for it. We laughed a bit about it, but he said sort of embarrassed (because it's embarrassing for a bloke), that he felt subtly attacked by some of the women. They were rubbing themselves all over us in that provocative way while saying, 'I'm not being provocative.' But you know I totally agreed with him – it was all so edgy.'
'You didn't enjoy it?'
'It wasn't exactly that, more that I felt threatened…it was hard to know how to respond.'

I sit, listening. Sip a bit of my tea. I love living by proxy. It's so safe. 'So the next day,' he says, 'the women called a meeting. They were angry. They said they felt unsafe. Claimed it had not been nourishing in the way they were expecting it to be. They were upset. They felt their limits had been violated.' I raise my eyebrows, 'I know,' he says, 'What to do? We men just hung our heads, confused. The women asked to do it again, this time just by themselves, just women. I just felt it was all so…well…you know…we are so easily accused by women, but to me the story they were saying just wasn't what I felt had happened – at all. Anyway, that afternoon they did their dance and came out telling everyone how different it was, how nourishing, just what they had wanted.'

He lets out a long breath of air. I can see him reliving the story, getting worked up over it again. Bernard is a man who is more in contact with his emotions than the average woman. I feel myself wanting to stand up for men, against the unfair treatment from projecting women wielding so much power with the ever-available trump card that we-have-been-repressed-for-centuries-by-you-macho-pigs. Poor buggers are scared to breathe.

'So, I asked to talk to the woman who had been the most vocal in her complaints. She was 'coincidentally' the one who had been rubbing herself so profusely against my friend – on all of us actually – but mostly against him.'
'Ahhh…right…' Things are starting to clear.
'I told her how I felt about it all, that it had not just been 'the men', but that 'the women' had also played their part in the whole episode.' Bernard is so good at expressing his feelings, he would have really framed it well.
'And did she listen?'
'Yea, to give her her due, she did. She heard me.'
'And,' I say as Devil's advocate, 'she'd already got want she wanted by then.'
'Exactly. She'd had her fun. She'd made her point. But,' Bernard says, ever fair, 'she was open to what I said.' *How it had been in that tent with only naked women?* 'I told her that I felt as if the boundaries had been crossed by both sexes,' he puts his cup on the kitchen table, as if playing chess. 'Eventually she admitted to me that she had crossed her own boundaries.'
'Publically?'

'No only to me.' Seems so unfair. 'She said that she realised that she was going to have to reclaim a lot of her own projections. She said that she had felt herself get out of control, and that yes, on hindsight it had been an unfair accusation against the men.' I feel the air clearing, '…then she said, 'Sorry'.'

We sit in the silence of it for a while. Feeling it. Feeling what was going on. Feeling how we would have been if we had been in that woman's position. 'I guess,' I say, 'as a woman, sometimes I get carried away too. I leave behind all my judgement, and I just go for what my body wants, what my instincts want.' I remember that animal sex, writhing like a snake. 'Revelling in that Dionysian realm, in that altered state, can be so addictive!'
Bernard stays quiet, listening.
'Sometimes afterwards, when I come back into 'here' I am left with a feeling of emptiness, of purity, smooth in that peaceful feeling of being satisfied,' I look across our crammed tiny Laughing Goat table without seeing, 'even you know, healed?' I am staring at the window that has thick tape around it, a quick fix, 'but other times I'm left with a feeling that I cannot cope with; vague memories of sensations that I cannot accept in myself, of being impure, feeling like a whore, of shattered limitations that scratch me raw when I resurface.' I breathe out, *does this ever end?* 'It doesn't help that I went to Catholic school. It goes down deep: no sex before marriage and all that; sure fire tickets to Hell Realms.' I go for my tea, but there is none left.

'It's then that my logic kicks in, my ego comes back, and protects me, and tells me how it wasn't my fault, but the fault of others, or of alcohol, or that I was manipulated. I feel humiliated that I let myself fall into such an obvious trap. I was set up and the aggressor must be punished. That's when my paranoia takes centre stage.'

—

I am beside the swimming pool in our friend Angelika's hotel, 'Estella' in Piso Livadi. Helga and I are at home here, she's from Germany, I'm from England, both living in Paros. I am just about to have sex with my ex, Agapius. I feel it. He feels it. We are beginning to incubate our libidos, soft warmth. Tumescence is overflowing into the air around us.

Paul, my primary partner, is in the States. We are experimenting with polyamory. Neither of us really knows what we are doing. I ask Paul for consent to go through the door that Agapius has knocked on. Paul eventually gives his consent. I have the green light. But I'm still not sure. I'm sitting on amber.

So, I call in feminine council. Helga is a wonderful listener. We sit on sun beds wrapped in beach towels, protected against the sun. She tells me her story. We are not gossiping, though it may seem like it, we are trying to make sense of who we are. She tells me how the man from the restaurant, Alexandros, her ex who she met the year before, who had a wife, has now split from his wife and now has another girlfriend. She tells me how she doesn't really know how to feel about it. She and Alexandros separated. He didn't really have time for her. She didn't have time for him, or rather she did have time for him but didn't want to spend her time with him. But she misses him. She misses being in bed with him. She misses sex. She keeps going, unravelling the knot, until we come to the unusual (for us) conclusion that actually she doesn't want him as a partner, doesn't want to be the wife, or the girlfriend – just the lover.

She puts her hands over her mouth. 'But my grandma would be horrified…'
'I know! I know…it's a mind fuck isn't it?!'
We nod, silently united in confusion.

I wrap my beach towel around me a little tighter. 'We go on all these patterns we've been told are correct,' I murmur watching the moving pattern of the light on the swimming pool floor, 'I cannot believe that I am considering having sex with another man who is not my partner…it makes me feel like a loose woman, like a bad person.'
'Like, as if, we are not allowed to just be who we want to be. We have to stay within some sort of safe role.'
'Yes! Because if not 'they' will call us.'
'Call us sluts, and whores, and bad women…'
'Just like at school!' I have an image of the playground. 'Where we picked up our sexual attitudes. Trained by other eleven year olds!'
'The horror of letting go! Of relaxing into our desires!'
'There were 'good' girls, or 'slags'.'

I feel myself breathing in really deeply with her, our eyes being opened to realising: we have been programmed. Long thin shadows of a palm tree flicker over her face.
She says really softly, 'Maybe all that is just not true?'
The water is azure. The white squares on the bottom of the pool move around, bigger, smaller, elongating as they are danced by water. 'Maybe, it's OK,' I say wondering if it is ok, 'to just want to have him as a lover. To just admit it?'

Our eyes are locked into each other, supporting each other through these rings of fire, destroying our infernal, internal patterns.

'Maybe,' she says 'it is perfectly alright to make love with more than one man? If everyone knows and is fine with it?'
'Perhaps,' I say thrown into clashing emotions, 'it is OK now that we are adults, to make our own rules up. To take our own responsibility for how we want to live?' I gulp. *Can I really be so simple? Where has the fear come from? Why aren't we all doing this all of time?*
'Perhaps,' she laughs on this roller coaster between us, 'it is time to forget what they used to say as little children on the playground thirty years ago!'

We laugh into the hot, dry afternoon. In the air between us I breathe in a freedom that I had never imagined could be OK.

It's more than OK. It's me.

I do not have to be anything other than what I am.

Through skin

Renouncing my very being
slipping through the barrier
that removes me from my name
I surrender to all.

Red pill or blue pill? This is Leo's last chance: to take either the blue pill and wake up in bed, believing whatever he wants to, or the red pill, to stay in Wonderland and find out how deep the rabbit hole goes.

I took the red pill. We each took the red pill.

I remember in Crete with you, my darling Paul, as we joined our spirits, in the beauty of one dance. I felt myself soaking in your love, beginning to believe once again that it existed. I remember how we walked alone along beaches barely awake from their winter rest, how we breathed in ballets of figures of eights. Me, Universe, You, Universe, Me, Universe, You. How the clothes between us felt so heavy, how it felt so natural to be on the other side of your skin. Merged in this space where our joined presence becomes more than just us. Where we slipped into the realm of gods.

—

Morpheus says, 'remember: all I'm offering is the truth. Nothing more.'

The Art of Traversing

Passing through skin
the ancient walls crumble
allowing in
more than was
so within
can emanate
the tiny
but omnipotent
transformation.

And I also remember the next day, as we fell from Eden, from that which seemed so eternal to that which is finite, as we fell back into time, into our bodies. We fell out from the depth of the moment where light is timeless, and suddenly found ourselves in with the passing of time, climbing back up into 'reality'. As we fell from the Eternal, back into the jaws of Cronos, as we separated from each other's light, I separated within myself. I saw fractions of myself in the shards of mirrors as I fell, shattering back into humanhood. Like a leaf falling from the tree seeing itself for the first time.

—

'The truth. Nothing more.'

—

I remember screaming.

Looming Large

I find myself
with no contact
around my body
mind freefalling
to that flat surface of water
reflection looming
larger and larger:
I see myself
and scream.

—

In that place, falling between no-man's land, there is a mirror: it is a place where we walk into the dark pages of children's stories, where we spy through the door lock, shaped like a temple, into the corridor of monsters. Suddenly the door is forced open from the other side. We plunge, sucked into our depths. Angels now a forgotten realm. I remember thinking through otherwise scrambled thoughts of horror that only when we separate do we see ourselves as separate selves, forced to see our egoic forms of terror.

I remember feeling that only when we merge do I see my own soul.

I remember wanting to stay in eternity forever.

I remember falling and wishing I had never known what I had seen, for to live without it feels like torture.

I remember wishing back my ignorance.

Unable to stay in the Eternal

In the depth of the well
submerged in
nameless being
the soul realised
it was divine
and it hurt.

Paul and I have taken ceremonies together, we have joined as one, we have allowed ourselves to dissolve into the oneness of something that is bigger than both of us. It is sublime. It is Love. It is who we are when we remove the clothes of our individuality, when we go so far within ourselves that we become universal, where he is me and I am him and we are. The great I AM. It is mystical, it is marvel, it is awe.

Next day, having returned to the realm of human, we are exhausted. Flying so close to the sun has used up so much energy that we are tumbling apart, we lie on the bed, and feel the distance between us like daggers. I feel myself with feelings that are not beauty and light, but instead paranoia and fear. I cannot accept myself like this. This is inhuman. I feel jealous of him and his separate life to mine. I feel cracks in our love. I feel dreadful. I am seeing myself in the fall out, from the place of heavenly bliss. In the fall from Eden I see my ego.

I scream.

Sometimes he holds me.

Sometimes he walks out on me.

We are human again. It is unbearable.

—

After making love with Agapius all afternoon, I return to the world, after expressing myself in a way I have never done. I have shared my love with two men. I return back, after having reached a place of joint tantric heaven. I am totally and blissfully satisfied, sexually, emotionally, physically, intuitively… I float for a while. Feel changed inside. *Can I hold it?*

I leave Agapius' little white washed house on the other side of the island to return to my own. Carless I have got used to going around the island on my bicycle or by hitching. Today is a hitch day. I decide to walk along the sea. I feel blessed by the wonderful surprise of a new path, one I never knew existed. I am in sublime softness, connected to the sea, to the clouds, to the flowers. I take photo after photo, feeling myself slide into a state of oneness, hoping that I will be able to reconnect to it in the future through my photos. Dusk is soon upon me. I really ought to start getting home; no-one picks up a hitcher after dark.

I stand by the road, face glowing, and expect in this sublime state to be picked up straight away. I am not. I am not perturbed. I put my thumb out to the next car: they swing by, speeding up to pass me. This is not so unusual, it can take up to five cars on this sleepy little island. Most people trust. Another car goes by, and another, and again, and more. It's getting darker. I start to walk a little. Another car doesn't stop. *Surely I'm not going to have to walk all the way home?* Cars are going by as if I am the devil. I begin to wonder if I have broken my karma. *Is this punishment from God?* I do not think but more feel this Catholic terror. Inside I am beginning to fear something has changed in my energies: *perhaps from now on, no one will ever pick me up?* A car goes by. Up until now I have always been a 'good' girl. But now I have entered into that other category of woman, one who sleeps with more than one man. *Have I changed my 'karma'? Is this how it will always be from now on?* Another car. Thumb out. I pray. It goes past. *Did I break a sacrament?* I keep walking. The voice that says, *Don't be silly!* is waning, sounds less convincing. I am going into slight panic. *Have I fucked up?*

I put my thumb out, smiling tensely. A jeep with a surf board pulls up. 'Euharisto! Thank you! Euharisto!' I say, 'You don't know how much this means to me. Thank you!'
'No sweat. It's fine. No biggie,' his voice says *chill dude.*
I realise that to get down on my knees right now is not appropriate.

He is going to Paroikia by the main road, I live on the old road. He offers to go the long way round for me, but I say that I would like to walk across the mountain track. He drops me off. Now the sky is turning into a beautiful electric dark blue. I feel like I have been redeemed. I have said my Hail Mary's and I'm out of confession.

The path across the mountain is beautiful. I love it. I feel so good. It is that time of night that makes great photos. At the end of this dirt road is a beautiful white Greek orthodox church. This is a winner – a great pic. I swivel my bag around from my back and fumble for my SLR. I pull off the lens cap smiling. Turn it on. Point. Frame. I press down for focus, it doesn't happen. I panic. I try again, this time it focuses as if turning some large rusty press, as if there were donkeys inside pulling a creaky mill wheel. The camera sounds out a heavy groan. *What?* This is my trusty camera. This is my gift from Paul. *It's broken? Won't focus? Was I not redeemed? Am I guilty as charged? Is this now my life? This constant breaking, nothing smooth?* I am so used to everything going well, of being aided by the Universe, of everything that happens to me being a gift. *Is it over?*

I try again: it is definitely not working. It is broken.

I drag my heals, kick up some dust. Wondering. *Do our actions affect us so? In the fall out after the love making, in the coming back down into the earth of my individuality, am I seeing a mirror of myself? Am I the loose woman, the slag, who deserves no better? A quick turn of fate and suddenly…*

I have walked this mountain path dozens of times. I have never seen a soul. Suddenly, coming from behind me, a man on a moped stops. He offers me a lift. My head does an about turn. I am being offered a lift. *What?!* 'Nai, parakalo, euharisto!' I get on the back of his banger and he takes me the last kilometre to outside my house. 'Euharisto poli!' *Was that redemption? Was that the Universe saying, 'Don't be so hard on yourself?'* I walk into the house, and under the kitchen light pull out my camera. I focus on the table. It does. I focus on the distant door. It does. It is not broken! *Was it the diminished light?* The battery sign flashes. *It was low on battery! There was no light.* It is not broken at all. Redeemed.

'God' was not punishing me. Catholic priests are not trying to burn me in a pyre. The list of sacraments we had to say on rote whenever the Head Master came into our primary school class is still just a list. It is ok. I have not been damned. I have not committed a sin. I will not be eternally punished. The old bonds of Catholic upbringing fall agonisingly slowly from my shoulders. *Will I ever be free?*

Lying down on my bed, I begin to realise how much I project onto the world. How the world is a simple mirror for me to see who I think I am being. The world doesn't care if I have made beautiful love with a man, with the consent of my partner. The world is just mountains and sky and sea.

I am. Nothing more, nothing less.

What I think I am, is how I feel I am, as I look at this world and my experiences.

I begin to realise, I am free.

Forced into Knighthood

You cannot jump
over the wall to liberty
but must break through
the anguish and the fear
with the passion of pain
until broken
you become whole
again.

A curry in the park with suncream on.

Anew

Out from nowhere
I am surprised by me
aching with love.

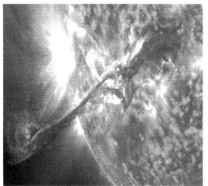

The guy with the funny eye comes limping across sporting a take-out box. I'm sat in the park eating a curry from the market. As I watch his ungraceful movements I sort of relive how at the age of two he flew out of a swing and suffered slight brain damage. I imagine it every time I see him, I feel his mother's devastation, the feeling of impotence mixed in with post hoc guilt.

Part of me doesn't really want to talk to anyone. I am just enjoying the fish. But he asks me after a few nice silent moments, what I have been doing in my week. My mind goes blank. Fork hangs empty on limp wrist. My mind can't seem to crank up to moving into the past or future. *Am I losing my memory? I have no idea. What to say?* I begrudge having to express myself. I want to stay in my hole. 'Ohh,' I mutter 'just the same as usual.'

Which is what? I wonder. He looks at me quizzically. I search, reel out 'Brass band, pottery class, tennis, modelling, you know…writing…you know,' I'm repeating myself. *What did I do?* The sun is really strong, nice for England, there is a little child running headlong down a hill, delight beaming out all over her face, 'and then,' I say, which is truer perhaps of where I myself have been, 'I've been falling in love…'

He gulps awkwardly. Tries to simulate normality. He's let the cat out of the bag: *Did he think there was something between us?* 'That's nice,' he says slowly. Ironically I warm to him as he holds himself back.
'Yeah, it's joy with fear,' I say to not seem to be rubbing it in.

He looks at me. I know he is Buddhist. I also know that he is a soft soul trying hard to work through this thing called life. I say, 'I am finding that I don't experience simple emotions any longer, it's more a sort of happiness with fear, peace with anguish, terror of the void along with hopefulness…'

He seems perfectly settled and ready for a natter. I know this guy can take emotional conversations, he won't suddenly internally combust. We've shared insights before so I know he go there. I know he is soft and wise in a way that is surprising. I also know he's needy. 'You know,' I say realising this you-know thing is turning into a verbal tick, 'love is terrifying. It can heal but it can also destroy.' I take another mouthful. It's yummy.
'Oh, I don't agree with that,' he says. Inside I jump a little as my interest is piqued, though to be honest I can't really respect him on this one particular topic because I know that he has never had a girlfriend. And I don't think it's because he's handicapped: I think it's because he's scared. *Am I being too harsh?* But it's what I think. He's such a lovely person, but so desperate for attention. He talks about his mother a lot even though he must be in his mid-forties. 'Love,' he continues, having just come back from a Buddhist camp up in the Lake District,

'is what we all are, it's what makes the world, it's the source of all.'

I know what he's getting at, I've done my fair share of sitting in meditation halls. But I'm talking human love, relationships, 'tits and arse' - not spirituality. It turns over all those feelings from Agapius. Only last week he posted on Facebook, 'The consciousness in you and the consciousness in me, apparently two, really one, seek unity and that is love. Nisargadatta Maharaj.' And I get that, and I agree. But I also get Agapius. He, the great healer - who really does heal people by connecting himself and them to wonderful feelings he calls 'Universal Love' - after a certain depth in our relationship couldn't bear his love for me because it meant him having to look at his own shadow.

I've been around the houses with this one so many times and the fish curry is so good. So good. I want to just eat my fish curry. Not think, not delve into my past. 'Well,' I say obligingly, as if cranking up an old disused engine, 'you know, I see us like a wire. Electricity runs through it. Electricity isn't 'good' or 'bad' but if we don't have a strong enough wire, then it will burn us up, short circuit us.'

I guess it's that Marsyas conundrum again. How much can this, my container, take to craft love into something beautiful, while not being destroyed in the attempt? But under the summer sun the idea never reaches critical mass and simply flickers through my sluggish mind and out again. The heat is sapping my energy.

———

I remember pillow-talking with Paul. 'Love,' I whisper, 'is so powerful. This relationship is burning down into all of my dark caverns, and bringing up all sorts of shit.'
'Like?'
'Ohh you know, childhood stuff…' I suddenly feel really vulnerable. He looks at me, listening. 'It's like you hold up a mirror and it's so clear that it burns through me and in its light I see parts of me I don't care to admit to.'

I want him to take me out of this uncomfortableness. But he doesn't. He holds me. This is what I'm talking about…this mirror of his silent holding without saying a word. I am forced to see myself alone, feeling painfully witnessed.

'Icarus flew too close to the sun,' I say, scrambling for a throw line out from the rising sea of emotions, 'maybe he should have prepared himself before flying… you know?' I smile, protected by comedy, 'A little sunscreen could have made a big difference!'

The Silent Puppeteers

Trying to find who I am
I stumble through images
stored in the attic
of childhood dreams.
How to kill
my teddy bears?

We are talking for the millionth time about Polyamory, 'I want to do it,' Paul states, 'I want to do it with you.'

'But for me to be able to even enter into those emotional swamps I need to have a stable container between us beforehand, else we could break open.' I've been here so many times with him, and yet somehow I can't get him to understand me. He doesn't want to. His map is set, not open to updates.

'What do you mean?'

'Like just you and me for a time, monogamous, a year, two years, to have a strong enough base, to have a foundation that can withstand the hurricane of emotions if someone else comes into our relationship. I don't know that I can contain you loving someone else right now, we are not stable enough, we haven't bonded in a way that I feel safe enough. There is only a certain amount of emotional intensity that I can take.' He looks at me as if I were talking in a foreign language. 'Even this love that I feel for you right now, I'm finding hard to contain, let alone if other people were adding to it.'

—

The wire turns red.

—

My hair is tussled softly as the leaves sing out the breeze. It's such a beautiful day to be out. British summer sun. On the safety of the park bench I continue telling my fellow curry connoisseur about being terrified by love. 'Love is terrifying to my brain…' *What's his name? Nigel?* I look down at my plate, trying to remember. It's all nearly gone. I must have been eating like a pig.

An Empty Plate

Unable to stop the whirling of the innards
reacting to this,
commenting about that,
overflowing with memories of past joys,
chewing on future fears,
comparing.
Unable to stop, to be.
The here and now disappearing
into volcanic expressions of nothingness.
Without warning,
as if in a flash –
an empty plate staring its epitaph:
Not Tasted, But Consumed.

'Well,' Nigel says. He talks slowly due to his disability, 'There is love, and then,' he says delicately, 'there is attachment.' It is as if he has to search for each word. 'Attachment isn't bad as such,' the trees rustle, the little girls run back up the slope, 'but I think maybe it's the attachment which destroys us. Love doesn't.' He's got a point. Clinging on. Love addiction. Complexes.

'Yeah,' I say, 'yeah, I guess I swim in my attachment, I can't see it, like fish can't see water, so I see love being the thing that brings out all that is not love, but really maybe, like you say maybe love breaks down my attachment…or…'

It's hard talking about stuff I have no idea about.

'But Love, Love is beautiful,' he says, 'Love is….' he looks at me, unsure whether to go on, his eyes dart backwards and forwards, 'Love for me is this simple idea, 'I wish the other to be happy.''

I sit back. I put my plastic fork down for a moment. Yes, actually that is really beautiful. I think of Paul so far away in the States. 'I have a partner in the States,' I say. 'We're practising Polyamory.' I don't explain. I don't apologise. I state and move on. That's why I like living in _____ [4], – it's hard to cause waves.

'Being so far away he's decided he is ready to open into another relationship. And I am happy that he is happier, but the self cherishing part of the mind, the ego, has started to fantasise that he will get to the same level of intimacy phobia that he got to with me, and…' an image flashes through of him actually being really happy with Syna, seeing her once or twice a week, she being happy seeing him once or twice a week, of both of them being happy, 'I fantasised that then he would want out, he would want to not be with her and would yearn for me, want me.' I pick up my fork and fish for fish. 'ME!' It's fun to exaggerate, if indeed I am. 'It's hard.' I feel the sun on my neck. I'm getting hot under the collar.

He listens well, this man; he gives me space to continue. It is a joy to go slower. My mind begins to relax and instead of going fast forward begins to sink a little into greater depth. 'It took a lot of spiritual muscle, or consciousness, or whatever it was, to turn my mind around and be happy for him. To want him to be happy without me. To wish him his own happiness. Hard.'

'Well…yes,' he says. Pause. Space. Time just to be. In the blanks I silently thank him for not demonizing, just humanising.

'I think maybe that was one of the greatest feats of love I have done in my life,' I dangle my fork, and stare out not seeing the park, but Paul in Boulder, in his house, and me, here, 'Sitting alone five thousand miles away and instead of wishing him to fail without me being there, to turn it around and wish him happiness without me. I guess…' I say, slightly startled at myself, 'I was disconnecting attachment from love…' I stare out into the lush green of the park, and realise that actually it's true: I have done well. I pop in a forkful of fish.

'Maybe you learnt to love yourself under whatever conditions, alone or with someone?' his tone is so hesitant and yet firm that I can't help but be touched by his loving words. Somehow his softness has let me see myself less harshly. I suddenly feel really glad I opened up to him.

'Attachment is so hard,' Nigel says, a wind rustles through the tree's summer green, 'we get so attached to our self cherishing.' His tongue lolls a little in his mouth. 'I meditate a lot on Love,' his face lights up just saying it. 'There is a

Rinpoche that says that love is the heat of the fire, but not burning.' He looks at me, straining to talk, 'He says we are connected to the Essence of Love when there is a voice inside that says, 'I'm OK,' and, and,' he swallows, 'when we say, 'I'm not OK,' it is when we are disconnected.'

What a beautiful image. I imagine myself meditating on it too. I wonder how to fill up, connect to the light, feel that 'I'm OK' more, instead of this consistent worrying and fear. I wonder if my budding practise of automatic writing will help and the idea that a therapist said of meditating in the light that I did a couple of times. Suddenly I am consumed by anxiety that I am not doing enough, that I am being left behind in the dark. That everyone else is entering into Love, connecting to an 'OK-ness' without me.

It takes me an eternity to come out from the dark vortex. Pheeewwww. I hear the leaves dancing in the breeze. I step back onto a firmer part of myself, almost kissing the ground. *I am OK. It's all OK.* I wander back into the conversation, 'I wonder if you and I are talking about different loves? It sounds like you are talking about divine love. I'm talking about human love,' I get that image again of a tube of white light speckled with dark patches, like dust, like bits of coal. To receive 'love' as we humans love, it also needs an acceptance of what it brings with it. I think of all the times I've been hurt by my loving, wonderful mother who loves me with all her human heart, and who also, because she is human, has unconscious drives, 'it's not pure, it comes packaged with all sorts of other emotions, some of them not very loving. I think you are talking about a spiritual Love, a pure Love that isn't human. I think you are talking about divine Love, that we as humans, unless we become not human, unless we are ego-less, can never fully experience.' I look down: no fish left, just some veggies and rice.
'Really?'
'Yea dude, it's hard to love! Maybe it's even impossible for humans to love purely. We've got so many needs…attachments…unresolved issues.' The light with the dark bits in, the dark swirling 'pips' of shadow material. *How to translate it into words?* 'It's all part and parcel of being human.'
'Really?'
'Yeah dude,' I say, for comradeship and distance. 'I mean, how to love without the fear of losing, which brings up our 'stuff'. Like who are we if the love object is taken away?' He looks at me as if I were going mad. 'I have this idea that getting close to someone, and feeling for them, feeling love for them, brings out our light AND our shadows.'
'Attachments…'
'Yeah…everything is highlighted, so suddenly even the little things are hard to handle.' He forks some fish – lucky bugger. 'And so instead of blaming ourselves, we blame the other.' Heavy breath out. *Go towards Christopher, go away from Christopher?* 'It's brave to get close to someone, because it is like putting a magnifying glass to who we are and our undergarment emotions.' He looks me in the eye to see if that was meant to be funny. A little spark flashes between us. He laughs.

'Yeah,' he says in his slow spitty drawl, 'but when we love we feel so differently!' he pops in the fish.

'But do we feel differently, or do we simply feel everything more intensely?' I watch him chewing, 'Maybe that's why people shy away from intimacy. It's hard to hold. Hard to see the reality of our naked selves.'

He chews on it. 'But is that love?'

'It's the best I can do! I guess it's the golden carpet to get to know ourselves, to see who we are. In Vipassana they talk about purifying metal. To make an impure metal 100% pure, you need a ring of that same metal that is already 100% pure. Then you pass the impure through the middle of the ring of the pure metal and it draws out all the impurities. I think that is what Love does, as we pass our human love through its ring. I just know when I love a man it's not 100% pure love.' I am still hungry. 'When I get closer than I ever have to someone and I feel a love that is 'purer' or 'deeper' than I've felt before, it also brings out all my deeper shit, all my shadows in a greater intensity too. Love brings out all that is not Love.' He looks at me with his funny eye. I can't tell which one to look into. 'But Love is pure…nothing is purer than Love!'

'Divine Love is pure, yes, but human love, well…I've never experienced it as pure, not even mother love.'

Maybe all I've ever experienced is addiction to an ideal of love…even? I feel red raw exposure in a gaping hole of terror: *have I ever even experienced for another human being, anything other than addiction to a concept of love?* I feel the sun beating down on the back of my neck. I'm glad I put sun cream on.

Becoming Love

Remove the cloaks
of your patched up images of God,
take off all those ideals
all those ideas
that choke you of warmth!
Instead surrender
until you are
bare in essence
without even a name,
submerged in self -
nakedly not you.

'Jung,' I say confidently, 'said that Love is the only thing we can experience in our (human) psyche that bridges to a consciousness outside of its own consciousness,' I'm grabbling, 'or something like that…love is like a bridge to something more than us,' and then it flashes, it flashes through me like a flash. *How to explain?* A sort of different 2D clear membrane goes through me diagonally and I just suddenly get it, 'we have all experienced something greater than ourselves, something that is not us, we have all had glimpses of Love.' It doesn't sound half as powerful in words. The awe of dissolving into something far greater than us, far more powerful, and the fear of not knowing how will we be when we come out again, into our human bodies? How will it change us? 'I mean,' I continue, 'It's scary as hell because it can burn us alive! It creates so much change!'

Nigel looks at me, intrigued. I just don't know how to explain myself. 'We're just humans. I mean….' *What do I mean?* 'My love wavers in and out. I don't know that it's ever that pure really,' three little girls are running bonkers down the grassy slope. 'Plato said that Eros, the Greek god of love, is fickle…and that we have created Ethos, ethics, to bridge the gap.' One little girls falls over, laughing her head off. 'I mean we wouldn't have to have any rules, wouldn't have any human laws, if we all acted out of love all of the time.'
'And being vulnerable to someone else is hard…' he adds.
'Especially if Eros suddenly goes for a trip to the supermarket and we end up staring hungrily at some imperfect human who we can tell is not going to satisfy us.'

—

After ten days of sitting in silent meditation, I feel myself dissolve into a flow of light that rampages through my body as if I am in the middle of Niagara Falls flowing upwards. I use all my energy to stay still: to not move a muscle of my body, nor my mind. I feel myself in blissful surrender. Complete trust. The flow becomes me and at the same time I contain it within my invisible subtle body.

Something inside decides to completely let go. Fear dissolves into Awe. I become invisible. I become me that is not me. Light.

Ecstatic.

Peace.

Roars of silence.

Immersed in Love.

For a sip of eternity I am transported into a state of bliss, where words are left behind, where my 'I' is left behind, where I am nothing but this light, this bliss.

Minutes normally. Once an afternoon.

Maybe only for minutes, but afterwards, returning to 'here' I feel changed, as if inside has 'clicked' into a new way of being, as if I have shifted inside. Forever changed, brimming over in Gratitude.

I just know that the few times that I have experienced deep love, in the purest state that I can manage, it has changed my entire being, which has changed my entire life.

—

181

Courage, cor, heart.

It takes courage to believe in Love. It takes courage to love. It can split us apart and put us back together in ways that we cannot even imagine.

—

I walk out of the park. I'm a little too hot, but calm inside. I've got my plastic bag with my empty Styrofoam container inside of it smashed to flat. I feel happy. I feel enlivened. I'm so happy to have spoken to that guy, Nigel, if that's his name. It's as if a love were coming out of him, passing through all his needs for attention and his unusual ways – if only one takes the time to look, to receive. Just having opened to a conversation with him, a slow verse, I feel as if he has done me such a huge favour. He's stopped me sprinting ever onwards and helped me dig down. And down there I feel a still lake of light comforting me. I feel temporarily fulfilled. I post my flat rubbish into the park's bin, feeling something has clicked into place.

Finding Love Again

Relief,
awful relief
tumbles up to the surface
rage of repressed love
flotsam of pain
I strangle in what was once my only defence:
my loneliness is broken.

A long overwhelming,
exhausting chapter about being trapped
in our maps, disconnected from the earth
of reality, written like a Catherine wheel
in which no attention is left to linger too
long, anywhere at all.

Turning to Stone

In her lean body
wonder woman
seeks perfection
whizzing
through her mind
petrifying all emotions
into sterility,
staying safe
up in the clouds.

'Let me tell you about what I'm doing,' Trevon says. We've already had ten minutes about him and the issues he has with people we know in common. He has this defiant energy, a hidden spouting of aggression that pushes me away. Unpleasant. And yet as I get to know him I wonder if I am wrong?

He's so talented, surely he… he…can't be what I see right now?

—

'It's so interesting,' I say to Christopher, '…interesting? Is that the word? Terrifying maybe is more suitable,' I laugh, my chuckles letting out the nervy scaredy-cat within, 'that as I get to know people, if I keep going into greater and greater intimacy, eventually, sooner or later, I hit a sort of bed rock of issues, of not liking them, of not being able to accept them.'
'Fuck yeah. Most people really annoy me.'
By the glow of the wood fire, my fingers stroke the grain of wood on the long wooden table we are sat at in the Seven Stars pub. 'I mean on the surface it's all OK. I like nearly everyone. It's just as I get to know people more…'
'Yep…' he takes a slug of his lager.

I linger in the middle of the sentence, not sure really how to go on. I wonder if the more I am comfortable in my own skin, the more I can accept and move on through others' issues. 'But even so,' I venture, 'with every single human I've ever met, I eventually get to this base rock.'
'Is it really a base rock?'
'Well like strata…of ego defence.'
'That's life…'
'I mean you think you are talking to the prince, and suddenly he converts into a frog.'

He laughs, a deep guttural laugh through his long, beautiful neck. He makes a manly noise with his pint thumping it back on the table and declares, 'I'd prefer to say, 'The Incredible Hulk'.'
'Erm, they are both just green…'
'Yeahhhh….' and he flexes his muscles. Me likes.
But in another part I feel a fear flutter through me.

—

I'm sat in the cafe with Mercè. I look over at her and her Swedish blue eyes captured in her Catalan face and swim softly in her energy. I love her so. It suddenly seemed so obvious when a past-life therapist said that Mercè and I have

184

had past lives together. It didn't feel any surprise just a deep sense of reassurance.

'So,' I tell her as if I am a journalism on the scent of a story, 'I'm starting to get the idea of hysteria and narcissism and how they fit like hand and glove...it's fascinating.'
'Dime!'
'Well...it seems hysteria is just after Sleeping Beauty wakes up. Can you image? She's lying there, all warm and nice, and in that sleepy, dark place, and as she opens her eyes a little, and starts to remember where she is...she remembers...all those emotions come flooding back, all the reasons that disassociated her and repressed her into sleep – into that deep frozen state – are still there.' I lean towards her a little on her sofa.
'As she wakes up, so do her emotions.'
'Si!' says Mercè.

I fall back into the cushions and lap up her characteristic enthusiasm, as she adds, intrigued as I am in the matter, 'And we cannot feel just the good emotions – just the emotions of the prince's kiss, we can't just feel all the nice stuff – emotions are indiscriminate! If you want to feel you have to feel ALL of them!' I smile, breathing it in.
'Yeah!' I say part inwardly, 'The prince's kiss has awoken her – and *all* of her feelings!'
'Claro, can you imagine waking up out of a deep sleep to be faced with that mix? Love and all that mierda - all she fell asleep to avoid!'
'Uf! It's enough to want to doze back into sleep...'
'Unless the prince is particularly...'
'Sexy!' I sip from the little white café cup. 'Imagine the friction...'
'Of a sexy prince?'
'Yeah, like you want him and yet opening up to him brings all the feelings of the last time you were hurt – maybe you know – even abused...?'
'Ouch.'
I realise that my scatty brain has wandered off the original path. I also realise I have to tread much more carefully suddenly as her history rears its ugly head in my memory. 'Yeah, so,' I put the little cup back into its little saucer, 'instead of actually feeling, she goes into her glass tower, analysing, reducing any feeling that may come up by controlling it, forcing it into a thought,' I think of me in Greece, falling, falling into my heart - it was terrifying, '*as if* she were feeling them. As if analysing, talking about all those undigested feelings were actually feeling them, as if talking about them were resolving them.'
'Until the pressure cooker blows.' *Woa, scary.*

—

I ask James's best friend about Liz, James's ex, 'She's always processing something 'deep' that she'll 'tell you about later.'' I ask James later. 'Sounds about right...' he says. Sad sigh.

Once on a road trip, James tells me all about his nine-year relationship with Liz.

'When she was four or five her father tried to drown her once in the bath,' he says hands on the wheel. We've had a beautiful trip together. It's brought us together and in the confidence of this new space between us, he's opening up. Telling me more about himself, and his relationships. I am intrigued. Listening to him pour out this story, without being prompted. A rare insight.

'Did she imagine it, do you think, or do you think it really James happened? I mean he may have been playing about with her, washing her hair, and pretending to want to kill her…' Even as I say it I realise that it really isn't appropriate to even play kill with little children.

'She was the last of a line of girls. He wanted a boy. It sounds like consciously or unconscious he really did want her dead.' He stares down the open road, 'I guess he felt she was another burden weighing down his prison, pulling him away from freedom.'

We cruise down the straight, straight road. There is horizon for as far as we can see. Dry. Dusty. I feel like I am in Thelma and Louise. 'He was a classic case of psychopathological narcissism. It was always all about just him. He's still a nasty jerk.'

I'm amazed how open James is talking: driving seems to lull him, 'Apparently he would make up stories for the children at night-time and there would always been a girl who was killed…and it would always be the youngest, and there would always be the names of all the brothers and sisters, except, Liz.' He stares down the road of the past. 'Who knows how true it all is, but the thing is, she believes it,' he says, his words sound like they are reliving past pain, 'it makes no difference if it's true or not.'

———

As he sorts out the music that he's just written for me to play Trevon half concentrates on his words, 'I was really upset the way that he treated me,' he continues, apparently oblivious to if I am interested or not, 'I'm an Empath,' he says grandly, 'I get too involved in others problems…but I'm going to stand up to them. I think it may help them see the error of their ways.'

He flickers his attention across to me, ascertaining that I am still in agreement. But actually I'm just listening passively. Waiting. I've gotten bored. I keep looking around to all these toys in here, all this recording equipment. I want to get going. But he's in charge. He's sat in front of his computer with the massive screen, going around and around in circles about people from the tennis club and how a year ago they hurt him. It's like he's collected a list of things they did wrong to him and savours it like a stamp collection.

'So,' he says, 'I've got a tight time schedule today,' in a tone as if I were pushing him out of time. I listen. 'We've really got to get on.'
'Yes,' I say relieved.

———

We are in Gregorio's favourite restaurant on the Plaza de Libertad, for the lunch time special. On the next table is a set of couples entering the third age. Dressed to 'kill', they are power struggling through social acceptance, the females both have bleached blown-dried hair that looks like candy floss. They are speaking in Catalan. The plumper woman, who is dominating the whole table, has just said for about the fourth time, 'I don't know why he did it! I don't know why he just up and left. I'm his mother. Does he have the right? Does he?' There is a feeling of repetitive, tired agony in the air.

A chronic victim of subtle, but constant, emotional abuse, her husband's eyes are downcast; disengaging. I bet he just gave up…decades ago.

Her question lingers like a loaded gun. She's clearly not expecting an answer because she is giving no space for anyone else to talk. 'After all I did for him…' she glances around the table, like a martyr, not leaving anything to chance, like a night watch on emotional patrol.

I would like to stand up and slap her.

———

I love plane journeys. Sometimes I just lounge around in the joy of doing nothing, other times a conversation can strike up with the stranger in the next seat that is totally unexpected. I get a thrill glimpsing into people's lives. Planes are fertile picking ground: there is an enormous freedom knowing we'll never ever see each other again. I've heard the most amazing stories on planes and trains. The faster they go, the further the distance, the deeper the sharing. Masks off. Transport companions are a rare gift to show yourself as a true being, totally risk free. I remember a guy once telling me how he had been fucking his brother's wife for five years and that he didn't know how to get out of the dangerous but addictive knot. Today I am sat next to a couple. They are sat looking out of the window - my favourite seat. Though I can't see out passed their heads, in recompense I stretch my legs out into the aisle.

———

'So, let me tell you about where I'm at,' Trevon looks across. *Did you not just do that in the kitchen?* The music he's written is still in his hands. I start to feel tense, controlled: this is freaky passive aggression. I am forced to sit still on the little drummer's button seat, as if I were nothing but a sounding board for him to paint image after image of himself upon. 'I've been doing a course in Berklee, online, to get more technique with music production.' He rambles on, throwing in words like sound remixing, synthesize, hybrid arranging. I'm getting nervous. *Maybe I won't be able to do this?* 'So this is a project to create a sound track, for this scene…' he swivels in his big leather executive chair around to his computer, 'I've just composed this, in the hour before you came.' He's talking really, really quickly now.

———

We start with pleasantries. One of them has to go to the toilet mid flight. ''Cuse'

'No worries.'
'Good book?'
'Yes…' etc etc.

By the time we have to put our table trays into the upright position for landing she is talking as fast as she can to get it all out before the plane comes to a standstill and we can unbuckle. He's sat in the middle. She's leaning right over him telling me about her mother-in-law, his mother, who is simply unable to manage any change, or any emotion whatsoever. 'What happened…' the girl said, with obvious relish – *Is this the first time she's got to tell her side? Her suffering, her pain: or the fiftieth?* – 'her daughter was in hospital, she was in a coma for a long time. The doctors were on the fence. They didn't know. After a few weeks, she couldn't take it anymore and walked out. She left her daughter for dead. Gave up on her. Her husband, his dad,' she nods towards her husband, as if he were a prop, 'just stayed by the bedside. She got angry at him, but left him to it. She thought he was only dragging it out; only harming himself. 'Time to move on,' she said.'

She looks me in the eye, but I am looking at a propeller, imagining the scene, imagining her walking down those sterile white corridors, defiantly, high heels echoing her aloneness, a slight wobble to her walk from being too long sat in an uncomfortable hospital chair; big revolving automatic doors at the end of the tunnel, turning her resolve around from 'yes' to 'no'. She ignores her pain, as she begins to ignore her doubt. 'But the thing is,' says the woman by the window seat, 'that her daughter recovered.' My eyes open wide. I feel air coming in under the lids. 'Woooow!' I say, I can't help it. In my mind I'm imagining the collapse I would feel if that had happened to me.
'Yea…' says her husband, the brother, the son. Head down.

His wife doesn't seem to hear him. She seems to have un-emotionalised this whole saga throughout the years of having to suffer his mother being a monster, a control freak, of being unable to attend to anyone's emotions, least her own. This is not compassion land. Not any longer. This is marital cold war. The stark reality: his mother makes their lives impossible. They both know it. I hear dozens of midnight arguments woven between her words. It is clearly not easy for either of them. 'She never got over it. Never forgave herself. Can't–won't–talk about it. Refuses to feel a thing,' she says, as if it were nothing but pure gossip.

Suddenly I see it: the mother cannot ever open up the doors to her emotions, because waiting there, banging on the door, are the monsters: a queue of undigested emotional nightmares. If she so much as inches towards an emotion she'd be hit by a swarm of them bursting out: images of herself giving up on the life of her little girl – of her walking out on someone who needed her, of betraying someone she dearly loves. I imagine the automatic swinging doors of the Hospital she walked through jeering out in her mind, *What Sort Of Person Are You?*

Emotions strong enough to kill.

Sharp Tongue

As I watched
I felt all too well
her desolate isolation
as she swung her sword
of steely intellect
fending off
with witty sharpness
anything real
coming her way.

She must realise she is destroying her family, her loved ones lives, at least unconsciously? Add that to the pile of undigested emotions behind the door. The monsters bay to the full moon.

Her one, inflexible, dogmatic response: close down.

'It's like she's dead. We all have to be so bloody careful, stepping on egg-shells. And still she explodes at the slightest. It's destroying us.'
'And her too…' says the son, the husband, trapped between worlds.

—

As I listen to Trevon's spiel, I realise that he has not invited me here to play music with him at all but to play the trumpet for a piece in his sound track. I feel duped and at the same time excited…we're not going to jam (which I'm rubbish at) we're going to record a sound track for his school work.

'So, here is what I want you to play,' he clicks play on his computer. Above is the film scene it's to go with, below the sheet music. It's not in my key. Trumpet is in B flat. This is in C.
'Can you transpose it?' he asks.
'Kind of…' I'm doubtful.
'I'll just write it down quickly for you.' And hence starts the search for the manuscript book. It could be anywhere. It feels like we'll never get going at this rate.

—

'I mean she was on a completely different page,' _____ [4], says, over the pillow. 'I had gone around to hers to end the relationship.' He is opening up, to deep within, to a him decades ago. 'Relationship!'' he scoffs, 'We'd only slept together a few times…it felt all wrong.' I listen, wondering where this is going, and what it has to do with us right now, not connecting sexually. 'I feel like I've been raped by her,' I look at him over the pillow. I need to gulp, but I don't want to draw attention to myself. 'She said that she was on the pill, but she wasn't.' *Is this about him being unable to trust in the feminine?* 'She'd tacked up a poster of the Virgin of Guadalupe over the bed…' I raise my eyebrows in question, 'She aids in fertility.'

'She wanted to get pregnant?'

'I guess…I didn't know…' It is agonising to go back there. 'I wanted to pull out, but she said, 'It's OK!' and held me. I didn't pull out. I didn't! I just didn't!' his looks down, impotent to change the past, closes his eyes. Pain seeps out through his eyelids.

—

'All it takes is an ejaculation,' says _____, terrified. He lies on the bed exhausted after running around as a single dad. He can't cope. Emotions. Logistics. Food. School. Friends. Accidents. He is on constant overwhelm: too much to have penetrative sex. Only wants to talk about it. To feel by proxy.

—

'Soon I will be free,' says _____ yearning for the day the kids are old enough to be independent. We've been talking about his relationships, with an intimacy that opens new worlds of the male to me. It's healing to hear how _____, my friend, is so similar to boyfriends that I've gotten close to: I can hear without it becoming personal. He swims in ideas and concepts about how he wants to connect sexually to women, how easily he talks about it, how he dreams about it, how difficult it is to him to actually do it. Abject fear keeps it all in his head.

—

'My mother didn't let me enter into my manhood properly: two psychologists have said that to me,' says _____ as if he were talking about what's happening in the newspaper. 'One said that she didn't know what compromises my brother had to make to get out as he did.' He's making a chicken omelette. I think of *Mother and Child Reunion* by Simon and Garfunkel. *Is that synchronicity?* 'It's scared me for life. I never know if I'm being man enough.'

—

We are all a child of a man.

We are all a child of a woman.

—

'It's often women who develop Histrionic Personality Disorder…' I continue telling Mercè as I sip the last cold sip of my coffee and she makes a rollie.

'We should say feminines, no? The feminine within the man as well – the anima?'

I look at her: I've been caught out at my own game. We've had the when-I-mean-feminine-I-mean-the-feminine-in-woman-and-in-men, conversation so many times…but it's so easy to slip back into gender…

'Yeah,' I say bowing to her superior technique, 'so, yeah, hysterics are, in the way I see it, 'feminines',' I do the two fingers in the air thing that make me feel like a hippy-cum-brownie guide, her fingers roll the tobacco, 'who are unable to process emotions, and so they are swimming in them all of the time.'

Mercè and I talk to each other intensely, deeply and yet in a wonderfully relaxed, comfortable way. We both have brains that convert concepts into images, so we can go far together, and we can go there quickly, flying sometimes. It's exhilarating. 'But,' I continue, distracted by a desire to smoke, 'their emotions can fire up without warning, because they are so unattended to.'

'Go on,' she says. I watch her rolling. *I'm really not going to smoke. I've promised myself.*

'They dissociate, falling into the place where Kundry, or Sleeping Beauty, have shut down into. They can't get out, can't process the emotions, be it anger, or sadness, or feelings they consider unacceptable. They've shut down part of their psyche, it's gone to 'sleep'.' Air quotation marks again.

'But,' she says, looking up at a weird angle into my eyes as she licks the paper, 'isn't hysteria also about creating attention from a father who didn't give enough attention or inadequate attention, and the little girl learns to use drama to get him to notice her?'

'Could it be an extension of the same thing? The little girl who cannot accept that her Dad doesn't pay her enough attention, would prefer her 'dead' at times...' I say remembering that road trip and James telling me about Liz and her dad.

'Wow imagine! It's hard enough as it is as an adult to not be liked by someone, but imagine as a little kiddie feeling that a person you are dependent on is wishing, if only for half an hour, that you didn't exist...'

'Easier to cover over her own reactive emotions with melodrama, that she knows deep down aren't true.'

'And gets her attention.'

'But with time can't remember what is, and what isn't, real anymore.'

'Or,' I muse, taking a different tack, 'she develops sexualised behaviour or some other inappropriate behaviour to get her Daddy's attention...'

'Yeah, which as a teenager becomes a dangerous adaptive behaviour...men flock to her like flies to shit.'

We pause for a little breath. She lights her cigarette, takes the first drag. Satisfaction smokes out of her. I feel an involuntary psychic jerk, I want to smoke, but I'm not going to.

'You know like a Catherine wheel...?' I say watching her inhale a second time.

'What is?' she says after puffing out the last bit of smoke from the corner of her mouth. It's like watching clouds in the sky.

'Melodrama. Talking, for attention, and bringing up all those emotions so intensely – as if processing them – but not feeling them.'

'Throwing emotions into the air, so that no-one will get to see what is underneath?'

'Did I tell you about that guy I recorded with?'

'No...' says Mercè exhaling smoke.

'Control freak. Tried to control everything, including my thoughts about him. As if he couldn't leave anything to chance,' I say watching her smoke, 'in case someone were to see what was underneath.' I breathe out, it's making me tense just remembering. 'Like the dude was 'creative', but so fucking chaotic to work with.'

'Like the Catherine wheel you talked about! Attention spinning…'

'Yeah, burning up. But also magic somehow…'

'The type you wouldn't want, even in an emergency, to get into their car?'

'No way! He'd be so distracted by everything around him, as if danger could spring up anytime, from anywhere – he'd crash!'

—

Trevor starts writing down the notes. Black dots between the lines. I see that he is struggling to concentrate. 'I'm just going to concentrate on this. I'm doing it so fast. It's easy to make mistakes. So I'm just going to be quiet for a time. I wrote this only this morning. So, yeah…well…'

I see he's actually going really slowly as if forcing his attention through the hubbub in his head.

—

I am sat in William's car. We are talking about the woman who, last night, ended their relationship. 'She's so intelligent,' he sighs as we both stare through his windscreen, 'she goes from point one, to point two, to point fifty in a second. It takes me a time just to catch up.' I look, past the water marks on the windscreen, at the telegraph post, how the lines come out of it at the top, wires spreading out, like my ideas sometimes, bursting into several directions. I'm thinking that just because she has a sound theory, it doesn't mean it's right. 'The problem is,' he says, 'just because she's intelligent doesn't mean she's always right.' I'm shocked how close we are in our lines of thought.

'The thing is,' he says, 'I can't argue my side, because she's picked holes in it before I've even finished.'

I wonder about her father. I can hear him in there, disgruntled. 'How about her parents?'

'She's always thought that they never really loved her.'

Another woman escaping into the safety of her mind!

It suddenly dawns on me that she has two masters and a PhD.

—

When he hands over the manuscript, I look at what he's written. It's covered with mistakes. It takes time to work out what he's done. Double time because when I ask him – with the possibility of him having made a mistake – he's not very receptive…at all. He goes into defensive excuses instantly. I just want to know what notes he wants me to play for his project and where. I have to tread so carefully, on fine egg shells, but if I can't read what he's written, I can't play it. And we're here to play.

'Are there really two bars rest at the beginning?' I ask, I don't know. I don't know this piece. This piece didn't exist an hour ago, it's come from out of his head.

'That's what it says here, on the computer.' He plays it. *I'm supposed to know what's in his head?* OK I get it, the first bar is white noise from the scene. 'OK yeah, I get it.' As if I were the one confused.

—

Agapius is the silent type. Able to sit out and enjoy wherever he is. He adores coffee, wakes up every morning and goes through his ceremony. Gets out the coffee maker, adds cold water slowly, gazes at the mineral water falling out of the bottle as if it were a world heritage waterfall, puts in the required amount of coffee – two and a half heaped table spoons – lovingly taps the coffee mountain down so it's compact. Slowly, slowly, twists the top of the coffee maker on until it is tight as tight. Puts it on the stove. Reaches for the lighter, turns the stove on, and lights the blue flame. He brings out the tin of Carnation condensed milk stroking the side, gets the metal sugar holder out. Opens the drawer for the teaspoon. Stands, waiting, admiring, getting ready to enjoy his morning coffee.

I have watched him do this every day. I am never sure if he will remember me even though we have just made love. I watch him get out one mug. I watch him pour the coffee like an artist. He adds the milk, stirs in the sugar, slowly, gingerly. Sits down with one mug.

'Is that just for you?' I ask.
'Ohh Babes,' he says disappointedly, as if I had totally let him down, no faith in him, 'I've made this one for both of us.' Romantic gesture. Again. But I don't drink carnation, I'm lactose intolerant and I don't take sugar.

Is it really possible that he just totally forgot I existed?

—

I have professional head phones on, the clarity of them is amazing. I love it. I'm playing into a professional microphone, like you see on the movies, with that mesh thing in front. I play the third take. I am loving this.

—

After a couple of months of being together I'm at Christopher's. His house is his den. Stig of the dump. It should say on the door: 'Outsiders stay out!' I know I am privileged to be allowed into his horribly untidy kitchen. I am one of the chosen few. This is the realm of Christopher and his private world. I sit on a wobbly chair, socked feet on a nasty carpet and pretend it's not weird, trying to find anomalies to the rule that a person's home represents their inner world.

We are sipping wine and eating nibbles before he cooks me an ordinary meal that somehow is infused with a magic aura. The reason I can ignore all the mess is that he is making me feel like a princess. He says to me, 'You're amazing.' I feel a rush of hot energy up through my body. My face flames into red: I feel as if I am about to burst in pleasure. 'You said that,' he continues, 'and I am.'

What?

—

Trevon and I are really getting into it. We've settled. Both of us. We are in

193

deep concentration. I feel alive. 'OK,' he says remarkably calmly, 'let's go over the second phrase.' He clicks his mouse. We are slowly learning to work together.

—

I call Paul. This has been another crucial moment in our history of polyamory. It is not easy. At all. But we've had past hurdles that we've already learned to get around. This time feels different, as if he's prepared to be more open. He is ready to open to a new relationship. I give my consent. He's on the other side of the world… Somehow going through the process together is bringing us closer together again. 'And then,' he says 'there's this third woman that asked *me* over okcupid.com.'

'Wow,' I say, strangely distant to any emotion, protected by my relationship with Christopher. But it is there, I'm just not letting it get out of control. This is one of the reasons why I'm in this polyamory game, to learn to deal with the hard stuff. So far the dates have all fizzled out. So I'm not going to rise to the bait.

'Yeah…Lora is going to cook us a dinner.'

'You three?'

'Yeah, it's so sweet of her.' It's rising again. The imagery is too easy to access. It is the kitchen where Lora, Paul's flatmate, cooked us dinner. Lora is *my* friend.

'I hope that goes well for you…' I say forcing myself into a different emotional landscape.

'Thanks love,' says Paul, 'it means a lot to me that you are with me in this.'

I'm OK with him having dinner with a woman, in 'our' kitchen, with 'our' friend…it's the 'our' bed thing that I'm not letting myself mull over.

—

'Are you pleased with that? Do you need to do it again?' asks Trevon.

'No,' I say, almost holding my breath. 'It felt right, I think it was good.'

'Good, I think we've got it all! Let's mix it!'

—

'Did you sleep together?' he's been skirting around the issue. I just really need to know.

'It was really sweet. Gentle.'

I gulp quietly. Breathe in. A question tumbles out, 'Did you need a pill?'

'No!' he says proudly. I float for a while, disorientated. I feel proud for him too. And me. After all the work we've done on 'it' together. Then without warning a flash consumes me in its fire: he could do it. He *could!* He wasn't afraid of her. He was afraid of me at first. Not with *her*. He told me he always had an issue at the beginning. He connected to her. It wasn't just sex…he…he…he…he *made love* with her!

'Wow,' I say, through the inner storms, 'that's great, isn't it?'

'Yeah,' he says softly, full of love.

Full of love for who?

—

194

I put the phone down and the damn breaks. I burst into sobs.

Something cracks inside. I am being sucked into a swirling void of angry depression as it reaches out its tentacles into all my fears. I have not felt like this for a long, long time.

In the bathroom mirror I look at myself through volcanoes of tears. My face is Edvard Munch's Scream. The observer within me says to the mirror image, *You have a choice: you don't have to go there. Your relationship with Paul is still there. You can suffer over this as if it were a threat, or you can have faith in the relationship knowing that you love each other.*

—

Next day I throw I Ching. It says, 'When you do not contend, nothing contends with you: that is real power.'

—

I sit on the drummer's stool by Trevon's computer, and watch. 'You see here, I'm moving the wavelengths on that note you played?' I sit there, listening, loving it.

—

I decide to wait. I don't want to intrude. This is Paul's time, he too needs to process…and I want to digest it by myself so as to not vomit it all out onto him. I'll sleep on it. Tomorrow. I'll wait for him to call tomorrow.

He doesn't.

The next day I send a mail explaining that I'm finding it really hard that he's slept with another woman. That I give him my consent etc. but that it is really hard to deal with it emotionally. I would like some support.

Nothing.

My emotions are starting to harden.

A day later he writes a one liner, 'I need space and am taking my space.'

My mental response: *You can just fuck off.*

I hold back from communicating through his silence, for days, until I can withstand it no more. Boiling up from the wells of anger I send a mail, telling him how I feel. No-holds-barred.

'Wow,' he emails back, 'you are blind-siding me. I've been waiting for three days to hear from you and process together.'

—

Is that coffee for me?

—

That old gas-lighting gag?

—

I just stay mad. I don't want to have a relationship with someone with such low emotional intelligence. I feel too tired over our ridiculous relationship to care anymore. Let him do what he wants.

He doesn't call.

He doesn't write.

I don't care.

—

We listen to the recording. 'There!' I say, 'That bit, it's too abrupt. It needs it to slowly taper off…'
'I can do that…' I watch his mouse doing its stuff…this is amazing.

We listen again. The trumpet note is beautifully rounded. 'I love this! I love playing. This is just so exciting!'
'Isn't it? Concentrating, going into that space…'
'Yeah!' I say, incredulously.

—

One night I am writing. My finger slips and instead of going onto the web for the dictionary, it goes onto Skype. He has tried to call. Once. Today. I resist. I do not want to call back. It's late. I'm tired. I can't be bothered. Someone inside of me, who I am not conscious of, calls him.

He is sad.

Why?

He doesn't know why I am so distant.

I explain everything. Really simply. Like he were a kid.

'I missed all of that.'

I actually feel comforted by his honesty.

In the light of his day he repeats, 'I'm really sorry.' His attention is divided, 'I'm reading over your mails now. I missed it all. I guess I just didn't want to see.'

It's hard to accept simple. But it is actually all there is to it. He was in his own world, unconscious of anyone else.

In my heart I begin to break up the equation, 'not there = not being loved'. He hasn't stopped loving me. He hasn't rejected me. He was just up his own arse.

The pain subsides a little. This is not about me.

We are sitting in a car in the dusty car park in front of the beach at Paroikia. Athena is crying. She has relationship issues with her new wonderful partner and is scared she's with another narcissist. But it sounds more like she is processing unprocessed emotions from her ex-relationship because she's entering into the same spaces with this new one. Triggered.

'I served him for 38 years while he went off and played the Executive, working all hours, networking in parties, cruising around with the rich and famous. I did events for him in the house, hosted all sorts of important people, all for him. I was there for him twenty-four seven. And then one day, he just walked out. No explanation.' I look out through the windscreen to the clear blue of the Aegean sea. It's beautiful. 'Nothing,' she says, still dismayed. I know this story, not hers, but I've heard it so many times from other women. 'I can't get over him. It's like narcissists don't just get into you like a knife, they come in like chewing gum and stick to all of you. It's like being in a jungle trying to remove all of his tentacles. I feel so angry. So used. So...'

I know.

So.

—

I have been teaching English for twelve years. I feel I know about it. I have taught all levels and all types in lots of different ways: individual classes, UB university classes, private classes in cafes, on a podium in front of sixty nurses at the Red Cross, a one-on-one to an 80 year old, kiddies classes, I've even taught friends who wanted to try learning while smoking marijuana.

So I see it coming when this guy, Juan Miguel from Mexico, comes to me. He's a cousin of my friend Luna and is paying me twenty-five euros an hour. He says, 'I want to do my own method. I think I can be speaking English perfectly in a month, with one or two hours per week,' he says (in Spanish).
'I've been teaching English for 12 years, and to be honest I'm not sure it's possible.' (In Spanish).
'Believe me! I'll pay you. I'll show you how it's possible.' (In Spanish). I'm in this for the money. If he wants to pay me and not teach, fine. 'I just want you to talk to me, and I'll just talk back. I just need to concentrate.' (In Spanish).

*Right, sure!...*but part of me breaks under the conviction of his words*: have I been doing this wrong for years?*

—

'So, I'll work on this for the next couple of days. I just wanted to show you what can be done.' He swivels around on his black leather control chair in the middle of his recording studio. 'Great,' I say putting my trumpet away.
'Let me show you my favourite composer...'

The super powers of the narcissistic personality disorder can get extreme. Truly believing themselves saviours of the world. One, very short lived disastrous boyfriend, Mark, told my dad, after my dad had enquired what sort of job he would like to do (once he stops being unemployed), 'I would like to hold conferences where people come to listen. Not in the hundreds, but in the thousands.' My Dad told me afterwards, sheepishly. For the first time ever I appreciated my Dad's viewpoint.

We are sat in his tiny kitchen, low angled ceilings that were once attic space and give an uneasy hue of claustrophobia. Mark says, cradling his super-food smoothie, 'Over the New Year I did a plant ceremony. I was visited by Christ.' He looks at me meaningfully. 'I felt like him: I have a message for the world.'

I want to laugh, but I know not to.

Actually I should have run.

—

Out of the music again, Trevon and I are now just two human beings again having to relate clumsily to each other. It feels like it feels dangerous to him.

—

We sit down at the round table and I ask, 'What is your name?' (In English) 'Juan Miguel,' he beams back, as if to say, *You see, you see? This is working?!!* He seems to fail to recognise I am talking very, very slowly, and articulating my words like Wallis and Gromit. 'Where are you from?'
'ParDON?'
'Where–are–you–from?' I cannot slow down any more.
'I from MeGico.' I have already been told to not correct him.
'What do you like to do?'
'ParDON?'
'What–do–you–do–in–your–free–time?'
'What?'
'Hobbies?'
'Xobbies?'
'Yes.'
'I like ski. I like horse.'
'What do you NOT like to do?'
'I not like to do cook, I not do read.'

I keep going, but after five minutes cannot stand it. I get out a piece of paper to explain the present simple. 'TO DO'. He cannot stand it. 'No, no, I want not this. We talk just. We talk just.'

The seconds seem not to tick.

—

Trevon is going so fast now. 'That one's a bit wooden. Orchestral.' He flips back to the search engine, looking for a better version to play for me. We've only

198

listened to it for a couple of seconds. His mind is speeding up again. He's pulling me along. I'm getting frantically excited. I feel myself wanting to compose music. I think of the brass band. *Maybe I could compose for them?*
'Listen to this one!'
'Can you send me his name?'
He opens gmail. Cuts and pastes. 'I'm sending it now!' Presses send. Message Error.
'You've got to put my email address in.'

It's starting again: his speed up into crazy control freak land that is out of control.

—

In the restaurant, after the disastrous 'class', he tells me how he is the centre of his family and without him they would all be miserable and spiral off into death. 'It is a big responsibility,' he says gravely in Spanish. He tells me how he never knew his father. How he decided to go on a search for him. Travelled for weeks around Mexico. *Ahh,* I think, *Absent Father.* Eventually he found where he lived. When he got there, he had died the week before.

Hearing him, the whole narcissist picture gets sharper. Poor sod. Like how is he supposed to know what 'good enough' is, if he had to go through adolescence alone? No masculine figure heralding the path out into the world. This guy, Juan Miguel, has gone completely over the top, overshooting the idea of what good enough could be, with grandiose images of himself, just to avoid the devouring nightmare of not being 'good enough', of not being 'man' enough.

Easy to see why, but, whoooieee, he's really gone over the top.

—

Imagining walking up the mountain, doesn't get you to the top. The map is not the territory. We cannot cover reality over with our mental maps and pretend that we are the king of the castle.
Just because we can imagine ourselves as superheroes doesn't mean that we are.
Just because we can imagine something doesn't mean it is (possible).

I have met so many men who in their hearts of hearts secretly wait to be discovered as the next Jesus Christ, the next James Bond, the next king of rap. I kid you not. They have the headlines already written.

I wonder what the little boys of today are watching – in their imaginations whose sword do they swing? When they drift off to sleep who do they imagine they are protected by? What kind of hero are they pretending to be so deeply within themselves these defenceless little boys, that in decades to come it will be second nature to believe they can still become it?

—

Apparently Trevon wrote a soundtrack for 'The Breakfast Club'. It was my favourite adolescent film. Smack bang in the middle of the eighties. I'm amazed. I'm amazed that this man here, who is so scatty, was chosen from all of the amazing musicians in the whole wide world to make the music for that scene. *Wow, this guy sitting here did that. Well done Trevon.* I mention it.

'Well thanks for that…' he says visibly pleased and trying to hold it back, 'but well…'

The way he says it, a doubt creeps into my mind. Here we are doing a project for a master's course, for him to write a piece for a scene of a movie. 'The Breakfast Club' is a massive hit. *Is it possible that his 'Breakfast Club' piece was also a music college assignment, over the original music? I mean did he really do that? I don't know how to ask him if it's for real. So I don't.*[6]

—

The narcissists that I have loved all have a similar pattern. The mother. She's normally been inappropriately close. The Father. Absent. The Mothers treated their sons as emotional partners in lieu of the dick-head narcissists they married, sorry I mean, emotionally shut-down husbands.

To narcissists people are 'things' to be used with the ever unachievable goal of maintaining his never big enough, never amazing enough image. Let's understate it: a wife to a husband who after a couple of years of marriage, forgets she exists, at least as a feeling human, and treats her as an asset – cook, cleaner, child minder, housekeeper of his fort as he goes out 'decorated' with a woman on his arm, or pays her attention as a sex slave – tends to have unmet emotional needs.

The wife turns to her children.

She looks to them now to fulfil her dreams.

The narcissist as a son never had his image reflected back to him with any reliable sense of reality: his mother was either totally unrealistic with him, drowning him in her own fantasies, or simply, blatantly absent. How, then, to know what good enough is?

Hard.

And very, very annoying.

These young men, walking the rocky path into manhood, pick up scraps of information from their absent, often narcissistic fathers and faithfully copy him. They know what they are doing. They've been on the other side of the story as their father took advantage of their mother. Their new manly freedom is chained down by the guilt of leaving behind their mothers.

—

'So I'm sat there, I was about fifteen and she says, 'Son, we can't continue like this. I am your mother.' And pretty much from that day onwards, after her being the most important person in the world to me, isn't there for me. Disappears. I didn't know what I'd done.'
We're having another heart-to-heart. It feels intimate, at least as if we are preparing the ground to be intimate. *Did the mother feel a sexual attraction? Him*

to her? Her to him? Do they still? Or maybe he was just too clingy and needed to grow up. I listen, trying to make sense of now, of then.

'It was like as if from then on she expected me to do what she needed, but I wasn't going to get anything of the good stuff from her anymore.'

'Like what?'

'You know, the juicy closeness.'

—

Little Joey screams out, full of emotional rage, mouth open to her covered boob. His mother, in her own agonising cloud of uprising guilt, body depleted, drained of vitality, tired, overwhelmed, is trying to wean him.

—

My best friend tells me over my mum's kitchen table, as we scoff leftover turkey sandwiches and mince pies, 'When I went to Uni, Mum just said, 'You contact me when you need, but from now on you're on your own now,' and that, pretty much, was it. It seemed so unfair! I didn't get any of what she used to give me. I felt really angry about it actually.' *Wow*, I think, *their stories are so similar.* 'It was as if we weren't even friends anymore, but I still had to comply, doing stuff I didn't want to do, as her son.'

—

A different pillow: 'Mum was in hospital again, you know? With cancer. She was in and out of that damned place all her life. Dad was about sixty-five, he seemed SO old. I suddenly thought, *what happens if she dies this time?* I was about nine. She would have been about forty-five. I remember it: I was walking down the street with an ice-cream, all on my tod. I looked around and saw all these people, and I wondered what would happen to me if they both died – I'd be completely alone. We'd only been in Greece a year or so, I didn't really know anyone, couldn't talk Greek yet…and there and then I decided that I had to train myself not to love her. Just in case.'

—

We have just made love and lying together in the juicy, sticky aftermath, he's opening up, and lo and behold, out comes his mother. 'When I got to Berkley, I got a letter from her, the first line was, 'I should be telling your Dad this but…' I mean even as I went to University, so far, far away, she was trying to devour me. I was trying to move out into my own life, find women, have a partner of my own. I mean she should have been telling all those emotions to my Dad. But he never understood. I did. He didn't.'

—

A boy doesn't get what he needs from his emotionally starved mother or his shut down father but it is a misnomer to hate them. He needs them. So he overcompensates somehow, excusing them, saving them like superheroes – mimicking the gods they would need to be to bend reality.

The anger behind it all is never resolved, instead years later it is projected onto others who they relate with. Women are bitches. Men are dangerous competitors

201

to beat and dominate. The only way out is to keep hiding in their imagery of who they think they are: better.

Don't mess with their image, they'll go for attack.

The image is the only shield that protects them from feeling. Protecting them from the anger and hatred they felt for their mother, the heart rendering disappointment of seeing their fathers as nothing but pathetic.

Are they pathetic? They wonder in moments of tantalisingly close self inspection.

No! Instead of accepting the truth of themselves, the imagery escalates, ever further and further away from human.

—

Just before we close everything down I say as professionally as possible, so as not to make it the slightest bit personal. 'I'm not sure I do like that effect…' 'Yea, yea, yeah…' Trevon says quickly, smoothing over, 'I'll smooth that over once you've gone.'

I'm not sure he's heard what I was referring to.

—

I feel for this guy who thinks that he is going to learn English in four one-hour lessons when others take years. He's invited me quite grandly to a greasy cafe; part of me likes being treated to lunch. 'Narcissists are up in the skies,' I say to him as if making idle conversation, 'floating in images of being superheroes, which is a normal healthy stage for little boys, but not for adults.' The waitress comes with two plates of all day breakfast that already look like Dali's clock wilting over the side. 'It's like narcissists find reality too scary, as if they have to be superheroes to get through a normal day.' I stay extra alert to not affect his armour, extra alert to not be on the firing end of him feeling slighted. Juan Miguel scoffs, undoing his knife and fork from the paper serviette. He has no idea that this is about him. 'So they fly in the skies. They can't connect with any ground feelings at all. It is not safe. They would have to land in the fires of anger that they feel towards their devouring mothers, fuelled by their rampant, scathing rage towards their absent fathers.'

Juan Miguel is losing any interest he may have had. He's picked up the salt cellar and is examining it. But he's still listening; not interrupting. I keep ploughing through. *Why am I doing this?* 'Meanwhile their mother,' the salt cellar has much interest, 'either slowly resents his growing maleness, or worse, holds onto him as a phantom lover and cannot let him go. He's stuck! Can't stay home and can't go out into the world to find his own life, his own woman.' Juan Miguel laughs through his nose. Surprisingly – he is listening. 'She controls him, as an extension of herself…' He puts salt on his floppy chips. 'Do you know Parzival?' He looks up, I know he doesn't. I know he can't say he doesn't. 'One of the oldest myths in European lore; King Arthur – and all that.' I'm desperately trying not to go too deep. 'The brave, innocent fool, Parzival, walks over the bridge and

202

leaves his mother crumbling, perhaps even for dead, without even glancing back.' I reach for the salt, 'But the weak, they never get over the bridge, they go back and stay with her and resent her for it forever as they watch life from the sidelines.'

He is quiet. I can't work out if he's followed me or if I've wasted my breath. Anything that is not him at the centre is useless to him. Ironically this is all about him, and perhaps he senses it, perhaps that is why there is this wall of silence.

—

Trevon plays back the music again. I can't help but get a thrill from hearing myself recorded.

—

'Because they don't feel any of their own,' I say to Mercè, 'narcissists love orchestrating other's emotions.' I laugh as I see an image, 'Like throwing water bombs at people!'
'What an image! Boy tyrant!'
'Aim straight at a hysterical woman carrying all the weight of unprocessed emotions, give them a tiny pinch: they explode!'
'Like little boys pulling legs off an insect.'
'And safe! Because they aren't his emotions at all; and there he has a whole fridge of varying emotional tastes to experience vicariously, without having to ever get out his own.'
'And if they are caught guilty, they are so good at turning everything around!'
'Yes ma'am! Fuck are they good at dodging the bullet!'
'How do they do it?'
'How do they dare to do it?' I think about it, 'Like Agapius, he would say something really upsetting. I wouldn't even notice at first. But after a while I'd say, 'Wow, darling, that really upset me!' and he'd reply saying something like…erm…' I imagine him smiling in the sun, totally unruffled. Totally James Bond. It happened so many times. 'But darling,' he'd say force field around the maiden ship on full alert, 'can't you see how easily upset you become over anything at all?' And I'd get confused wondering if it were true.'

'Yeah,' says Mercè, 'I had an ex who'd bring up unrelated emotional stuff he thought would trigger me. Sometimes it wasn't even true.'
'Like what?'
'Like, 'Oh cariño, you sound the same as when that dress didn't look good on you!' Ignoring any emotion I may actually have had while deftly fabricating others. He had a way of getting under my skin. He knew how to make me mad.'
'And in such a deeply sweet, 'caring' way, as if he were protecting you?'
'Yes, like an angel.'

'It confused me,' I add, 'would make me feel insecure. I'd seriously wonder if I was being hysterical and totally drama queening out.' I breathe in, feeling my throat tighten just remembering all that crap I used to put up with. 'I'd start to think he'd leave me and I'd become addicted to this sort of magic that he created all around him.'

'And then cry?'
'Sometimes…'
'Meanwhile he's got away with whatever it was he'd done!'

—

Athena cries out through her tears in the car parked in front of the eternal waves of the Aegean, 'I served him all of my life, and when he got into a position of power, he left me. Just like that. As if I meant nothing to him. As if thirty-eight years of serving him were nothing at all…'

I say nothing. I know how she is feeling. There is no answer. Instead I watch the waves crashing against the shore.

—

How long can a narcissist keep up his magic?

A Break

You weren't there
and I was glad
so I could just
be normal for a while.

Christopher goes into panic. This is getting too intimate for him. He complains that our relationship is stopping him achieving his dream of being a rock star. He is 43. He says that the conventional life, the wife, the home, the family, is death for him. He complains that our relationship is opening up his feelings, opening up his heart, so that he wants to express himself, as a musician, and that puts into jeopardy his work, his flat, his security. I wonder if he realises that he's just said, 'You make me dream. You stop me dreaming.'
'I really don't think this has anything to do with me,' I say surprisingly detached.
'I am exhausted keeping up the mask,' he says accusingly, lying down on the bank in Leechwell Park.
'Then take it off,' I say.
'You're talking to me like you were a teacher,' he replies caustically. I think he should really say, *Like a mummy.*
'Because you are being like a fucking little boy.'
'Now you are being real.'

He's always looking for the bitch mother inside of me. He can easily bring her out. This is where we work, I need to express her, this psychic part of me that is crazy angry at the masculine for not accepting me as I am, for not seeing me as more than a projection for their own self-aggrandisement. Daddy crap. I'm not taking it anymore. 'I do not feel threatened by this,' I hear myself, amazed with myself, 'this has nothing do to with me. I'm sorry it's not working out for you. Good luck.'

And I walk.

And I don't look back.
When he's a man, he can come back.
With pleasure.
If it happens.

—

One of the factors of overcoming addiction is knowing that we have a choice.

—

I bump into my friend and yoga teacher, Sara, in the town square. 'Dude!' We hug.
'What's going down?' she asks.
'I'm actually feeling really proud of myself,' I say brimming over, playfully pushing out my chest.
'Why? What've you done this time?' she says. I like the feel of her arm down mine. I like how she is familiar and comfortable enough with her body to share it. I like the feminine of it all. 'For the first time in my life, I didn't consciously accept someone else's projections of me! Someone just said stuff to me that in the past would have sent me reeling, but today I just saw that it was all about him. Nothing more. Maybe he's never actually seen me for who I really am.'
'Woo, that's wonderful. That's wonderful when it happens,' she has a beaming smile.
'Yes,' I say, soaking in the sun.

'And you?' I ask and like opening a treasure trove she tells me her new secret. A new man who is much, much younger. Juicy!

—

'So I really have to get going,' Trevon says without making a move. I can feel the tension growing between us again. It's been there the whole time, except when we were deep in concentration playing and recording music, but now it's ramped up again. He's just messing about on his computer for no real reason, demanding my constant attention as if he were a little boy and me his mummy. He wants me to approve all of his favourite music, without considering for a moment if I have any of my own. I'm getting tired. Now that we have come out from that space of making music – I really want to run. I don't like this. I don't want to have to sit here listening to him and his fast, draining, words.

—

Snuggled at home one day, alone, I read, 'It is more obvious when a man has intimacy issues, the woman can run after him, but if he ever turns around, she feels the same issues, and runs herself.'

I am running. I do not want this.

There is a tick box of situations that people with intimacy issues have, such as geographical distance, unsuitable partners, age gaps, people with addictions, situations that are never going to turn out well.

I tick them all.

I feel my legs start to wobble. Literally. They are jittering.

'Intimacy issues often occur as messages from your parents. What sacrifices did they have to make on their freedom in order to have intimacy? Did your father have a job that was dreary?' asks the book.

Suddenly, I weep uncontrollably.

The world seems as far away and as ethereal as sea level does when diving at the bottom of the depths. I have image after image of me not being able to commit to a country, to a job, to a set of friends, to a house, to a man, to a sexual orientation, not even to this planet.

For the first time I haven't taken on a partner's projection of me. Haven't tried to perform for him. Haven't tried to save him from his intimacy issues. For the first time I cannot continue to cover over my own issues with someone else's.

I feel sick.
I want to vomit.
I cannot take this.
I want to run.
I want to see more, *is this an exit from the prison?*

—

Being with these people is torture. I can hide in my dormitory - a spacious empty guest wing - but still I can feel the breath of their existence on my neck, I feel them judging me, I feel them demanding of me, I feel claustrophobic. I need space. I hate people.

I need to get out of the artist's residency. I go for a walk. But somehow the smell of them follows me down the road. This is not getting away, this is playing hide and seek and having to shut down who I am so they will not find me. I have all my attention on them, this is not space, this is not me in my own world; this is my world being invaded, being polluted, being jammed full of others. *I need out! I need out!* I sit by an ancient washing well, eyes closed in a pretence of meditation trying block out the world. Perhaps I look serene from the outside world, but inside I am desiring death – *is that the only escape?*

The biggest rat I've ever seen comes out from the hedgerow. It has killed something. Dirty horrible rats. *Disease carriers!* I close my eyes again, only to hear a sparrow in a nearby tree squawking. *Even the birds are fighting?*

I notice a *Matrix* style déjà vu: a strange repeating discord within. *This is projection Julia. Be careful this is projection!* I open my eyes to look out and fair enough there are two sparrow scrapping over branch space.

My instincts kick in. Back in the Monastery of Dreams there is so much fighting underneath all those placid smiles! Underneath the compliments so frequently given to each other is a layer of stinking psyche, of abnormal psychology. Under the shining surface reality of us all living wonderfully in community, so modern, so 'sharing and caring', are monsters wanting to dominate everyone else. Everyone is fighting.

I feel overwhelm. Am thrown back to being a little girl, feeling I have to publically cover over the fact that our family is not fine actually. To keep up the pretence of perfection, keep up the spick and span British, 'Everything is fine here thank you very much,' attitude while in our home we are all fighting like passive aggressive dogs. *How to make my parents happy so I won't be rejected? How to survive the Monastery of Dreams?*

I panic. I go within again. *Actually,* a voice within whispers, *it is natural. Birds sometimes fight. Sometimes they are in peace. But they are not ideal. It is normal for people's egos to fight when they are in close contact. It's human.*

My parents fought, silently, behind the scenes of being a perfect family. Ghosts of resentments. No words to express. No system to be able to step out from the socially defined image of 'life' being fine and dandy. Forced to pretend.

Suddenly with adult eyes I realise: *of course they fought!* Any psyche coming into contact will eventually have discord. Emotions give rise to change, angry fires burn old drift wood that is otherwise blocking our natural expression. Fighting is natural. It's normal. Even in repressed England.

I suddenly realise, again, that my parents are just normal human beings! It doesn't mean what I made it mean.

———

I come out of the recording studio super high. I love, love, love doing creative stuff. We've recorded the sound track. I'm still high from having the headphones on and being all plugged in, playing my trumpet into a real sound studio microphone as if I were in a film. My narcissism has been so well fed that I am high as a kite.

———

What an enormous disparity between reality and the erroneous, fantastical maps of the media, as they attempt to archetype our idea of family. All those corrosive adverts of billowing curtains, vomit free clean white sheets, all the family in bed together, happy, fully present to the beautiful gift of togetherness, or else strolling through the park, a breeze playing in their sun drenched hair, smiles on their faces that can sell toothpaste, one parent happily pushing a pram, another playing delightfully with children full of joyful expression.

When I walk through the park – using my eyes and not the television screen to see – I see parents leaning on the pram for moral support, dark rings under their eyes, exhausted from not having slept well: not for a night, but for three years... or more. Others bend down, back groaning to pick up the ball, again, as the child gallivants almost uncontrollably around the thankfully open space. They throw the ball to their offspring, arm heavy, impotently waiting for evening to come when they will have the little ones fed, bathed, PJ's on, and eventually, after an eternity of coaxing, joy of joys: asleep! Now the parents can stop being parents for a golden hour or two and can live their own lives – if they are not too tired.

As a single woman, left on the (golden) shelf, I frequently ask parents through my confusion, 'Are you glad you had children?' Most say, 'I wouldn't change it for the world, but…' or 'You get on with it, you can't put them back.' Many say something around the lines of: the ninety-five percent of sacrifice, of suffering, of screaming, of wanting to run, is worth it for those brief, ephemeral moments when, all is well, when the little one looks into your eyes and pours in love. When they learn to walk, or ride a bike, or become more human.

Many mothers say, I don't know why nobody told me what it was really like.

I remember my best friend and mother of three going for a blessedly single swim in the sea and fighting against the urge to keep swimming into the horizon.

I ruminated with a mother who had a five and a seven year old, about how we all dream suddenly when a woman becomes pregnant, how society as a whole, me included, gets so romantic: colours in the world seem so vibrantly that fairy tales seem to come alive, we breathe deeply, brimming over with such expectant hope for the future. 'Because if not,' said the haggard face of the mother, ten years my junior, 'no-one would do it.'

Even good parents, and maybe especially the good ones   though loving their children deeply – in the space of the twenty-four hours of the day, admit to feeling on the brink of collapsing faced by the void dark spiralling hole of constant and utter child caring. Even a good parent cannot get away from the fact they are often screaming out, craving silence. Yearning temporarily for the death of all the noise (makers).

—

It is simply human. We are all human.

We are all children of humans.

—

I wonder if being wished dead, is not what later, as adults, we have made it mean, as we sit in the psychoanalyst's chair remembering our childhood fear.

—

Walking home, with my trumpet on my back, I storm down my favourite path, down by the river. The sun shines through the trees. I barely notice their emerald beauty. I rush on with so many ideas in my head that I barely notice where I am. I do not hear the rush of the water as its white crests fall down the weir. I forget about the canopy of trees along the river path. I am swirling in my mind.

I make a superhuman effort to slow down. Part of me resists slow not wanting to lose all this firework energy. *You won't,* says the wise one inside, *it will deepen if you let it settle. Use this energy well. Ground it.*

Part of me wants to stop to look at the river. I keep going fuelled on by Trevon's G-force. I have just sat in his recording studio for two hours, being nothing but a sounding board with lips and lungs to play the trumpet for him. I hardly got a word in edgeways. It was annoying. My breath speeds up. The trees disappear.

As I escape back into the freedom of being Trevon-less, I begin to realise that it is OK not to be drama, or the centre of attention. It's OK just to be human. Actually it's perfectly fine to be a human. In fact I like it more than the constant frazzle of trying to be something more. Icarus burnt his wings – I'm ready just to walk.

I slow down.

I breathe properly.

It's ok just to be.

I breathe.

It's ok.

Really.

It's ok.

It is wonderful to breathe.

As I slow I start to see the wood.

Haiku: Ungrasping from co-dependence

I plug into you
contact lost with my own Source
hurt you are not god.

A talk with a stranger in my kitchen
about finding the right balance in
facing our shadows.

Amazing Grace in an eggshell

The heat
just right to hatch:
too much it hard boils;
too little it can't hatch.
Just the right amount:
Middle Way,
birthing life.

'The difference between medicine and poison is Consciousness...' I listen as words come tumbling out of my own mouth, something is saying them through me. An image of Ricard's eggs hatches in my mind: if you heat an egg it will boil, if you don't give it heat it will stay raw; but just the right amount, and bingo! Life creates. It's amazing. Simply amazing.

It seems too much to work out how to say it all, so I simply add, 'It's all a question of quantity. I mean if you drink too much water it would kill you.'

I'm not sure how we've got in so deep so quickly. I'm talking to someone in my kitchen with a French name that I keep missing. We only shook hands an hour ago. This is the first time we've really spoken. We are getting along quite nicely in the hearth of the house as I tuck into some cheese and gluten free oat cakes.

'Yes,' she says, 'I 'ave a friend who drank too much water.' I love how French people talk, flat tones as if it were nothing that her friend faced death, and...'
'And died?'
'No they got him to the 'ospital first,' she says next to the sink.

I suddenly feel really thirsty, get up to get a glass and laugh to find that she has beaten me to it. I stand in line at the sink, chuckling in our shared joke.

It's strange meeting someone for the first time in your own kitchen. We are art digs. She's an artist staying in one of the spare rooms here in Susanne's house. It's more awkward meeting a stranger in my familiar surroundings, there's not much to hide behind. I go back to my oat biscuits like psychic shields.

'If you drink too much water, at first it cleans the system and then it does not,' she says. I like this level of science; I'm comfortable in this conference.
'I guess we need flora and the water eventually washes out the flora?'
'Flora?' We fall into a vocab gap. *How to say? Gut. Flora.* 'Like bacteria. We need it to process, to digest. We need stuff in our system to do stuff.' Bit vague; but she doesn't seem to mind either. We are both working, I think, with images. She nods, going for another sip of water. Meanwhile back at the table I've still got margarine on my knife. Had enough cheese. Not sure what to do.

Turns out she's doing a dance project on touch. I can't quite get what it is about, but something about touch diaries and going out into the field and experimenting with different types of touch, trying to reduce or eliminate the other senses. She's just come in from being outside in the woods nearby, on the tarmac cycle path I guess. It was completely dark. Foreign to her. All she had was her arms for sensing. 'I freaked out a little. I 'ad no idea where I was, the only way out was to keep walking.'

I imagine her fingers in the dark brushing poisonous plants that were used for murder or committing suicide: Hemlock, Monkshood, Foxglove, Yew, Deadly Nightshade, Death Cap fungus. In small doses they could be medicine, but all the same I'm guessing, hoping, there are none of those plants along the cycle path for night time freaked out gropers.

'Wow, the project has a lot of scope.' I say coming out from my margarine dilemma. 'I can't even quite get what you are doing, it seems so theoretical and yet it is something that we are doing all of the time.' I back up my statement with a present moment experience of touching: I feel the wooden table, feel the grains of it with my finger pads. It is as if the table top opens to me. 'You know those flotation tanks?' I ask.
'Yes, I 'ave been in one…very nice, very relaxing.'
'They used them in Japan in the war for torture. Too much and you go mad. You lose sense of yourself. You lose all your senses.'
'Oh, that is very interesting…' I'm sort of glad she said that. I feel a little stream of flowing relief. It's a weird conversation to be having just before going to bed and having only spoken to the person for five minutes. She seems as bonkers as I am - comfortable with the non-lineal flow of conversation.

I decide on another oat cake but just with margarine. I can't leave any evidence because I've got it stealth like out of Susanne's margarine tub. Best to leave no trace. I say, as the oak cake snaps down the middle due to my hack handed spreading of the margarine, 'It's that balance between medicine and poison again.'

As she starts putting her groceries into her newly assigned cupboard space, I think about wounds, how sometimes we can go into wounds and heal them, and other times just be re-traumatised.

———

The documentary was actually quite good despite the Civic Centre's uncomfortable chairs. *Arise* is about women around the world and how they are recognising and coming into their power and creating social projects that naturally affect their society and our earth. It was really uplifting. In Denver, CO, they are planting veggies in public spaces and then giving the harvest to institutions that protect women who have been abused. All good stuff…growing stuff in front gardens, disused plots and roundabouts, creating community. There is a scene in it about touch that I want to tell the French woman.

'One scene had this wonderful woman, healthy, big smile, who said that at first many of the children don't want to get their hands dirty…Ug! No!' The French touch artist looks at me, amused. 'The film then shoots her hands caressing the land, feeling the soil between them, and her saying that after a while they realise how wonderful it is to touch mother earth, to feel her in our own hands.' I smile, just remembering the scene. 'It made me want to garden myself. To just do it again!'

I look up and make spiders with my hands. I don't know why. It's somehow to do with touching more.

'I like to jardin, but now I do not. Not in London. But in France I love to be in my mother's jardin.'

'Yeah, me too,' I say admiring the way she holds her body. 'We should all be gardening everywhere. This documentary showed how they had plants growing in the emergency exits in America in the Second World War! Apparently 40% of all vegetable production came from front gardens, and terraces, and anywhere you could grow!'

'In the Second World War?'

'Yes!'

'Amazing!' We both smile. I imagine the world becoming covered with edibles. *Wow, what a difference that would make!* I imagine people just going out and picking dinner, rather than having to work at something unpleasant to buy a car to get them there and on the way buying plastic wrapped dinners in too brightly lit supermarkets. 'But children, they don't want to get dirty now,' she says moving like a ballet dancer as she floats a tub of almond butter into her cubbyhole.

I suddenly feel a bit guilty that I haven't really done much more than type for work in the last couple of months. I have the same first reaction as the kids: I have to break through my own programming too. 'I think it's because we are indoctrinating these children with photoshopped models, with commercials of perfect cleanliness, of how to create an image that is perfectly germ free. And wherever they go they are told, by OCD adults, to wash their hands in disinfectant soap.'

'Ohh yes. And we need bacteria, we were talking about this today in our meeting,' she sort of handshakes herself as each hand touches the other, one upside down. 'Yes. It is like in the schools, they are so...' she pauses ever so slightly searching for the right word in English, 'compact in, all the people so close, viruses spread. And they all wash their hands all of the time, but the viruses come anyway, because they don't open the windows and let new air in.' I am suddenly very glad to be a kitchen with just one other person who appears to be healthy. She says, 'We are all so afraid of everything! So afraid of germs and bacteria and dying!'

We drink a little water, in a companionable silence.

I find myself branching off into a completely new topic that somehow seems completely related, 'Have you seen 'Game of Thrones'?'

'No, but I've heard of it.' I really like that she is about as TV literate as me. 'There's a dwarf in it, and they try and piss him off calling him 'Dwarf!'' I breathe out, somewhat deflated, suddenly aware that this is an idea I've had, that I hold it in images and have never said it out loud. I don't know how to. It's an image of movements between self and the world and being able to hold our own image, with all of its truths, because we have accepted it. It's not a word thing. She is looking at me, nodding, encouraging. It feels like she is more than ready to try and get what I'm trying to say. 'So,' I continue, a little wary, because in words it seems so simple, 'he says, 'Yes, I am a dwarf.' In claiming what he is, in claiming the insulted words as an honest description, he protects himself. No one can say anything to rile him about being a dwarf, because he just goes ahead and says, 'Yes, I'm a dwarf.' He accepts his reality as it is.'

It really affected me. I'm not sure I'm getting the message across. It's like being invisible because the external is one and the same, there is no edge of resistance, it cannot grate against the internal image. Truth with truth. Free pass to flow smoothly through the world. I look into her eyes to try and see her. *Did she get it?* It's about someone trying to throw an image onto someone else to hurt them, and yet if we accept ourselves as we are, we resonate with the image, and it doesn't do anything, it doesn't knock our image of ourselves, because it IS the image we have of ourselves - we have accepted ourselves as we are. And conversely if their 'insult' doesn't hold, because we don't identify with it, then it simply misses its target. It flows around us, like water off a duck's back.

I am swirling in images to share. I think about telling her how later on the dwarf was trying to show this to the bastard of the king. The bastard was getting all worked up, but eventually the dwarf got it through to him, and he realised that it's not such a big deal to be a bastard. He is still alive, still a person, he still exists, breathes, feels, senses. Yes he is a bastard, but he is not just a bastard: there is much more to him than that one image of himself. The dwarf taught the bastard to accept the word and to begin to remove his own stigma towards it.

The message to me seems to be to claim ourselves as we are. I decide to stick with, 'It's just that if we admit to who we really are, our faults, our actual state, if we have courage to see ourselves as we are, then…'
'Yes,' she says. *Oh I think she's got it.* It wasn't all in vain…Suddenly I feel really connected to her.

Jollied on I say something I have not thought, nor felt, until it comes out of my lips in a spontaneous combustion of intuition, 'If we just accept the condition that we are human and that actually we are going to die…' I get up to clean my glass, and turn around to her, 'then nothing can scare us! Nothing can really take us away from enjoying this life, instead of fighting against it all the time trying to stay alive.'

We both stand there, in still amazement of this epiphany. I feel a hallowed silence come between us. A respect. A sudden deepening in our souls, as we both stand on our own two feet with greater balance. Yes, we will die. Yes, we accept it. Yes. Shoulders relax. 'Yes, well,' I say suddenly embarrassed, 'that's the sort of thing I write about.'

We head off to our separate beds particularly well hydrated.

Bliss of the Absolute Middle

How to stand
on a dome
of ice?

PART V

Raw Life-Giving Vulnerability

The vulnerability of the middle path.

Raw

Over the kitchen table
we chat.
Going deep into
where his story
becomes mine
- becomes everyone's -
I get confused as to who
he's talking about,
him or me?
Something inside me
jumps out
uncomfortably described
in his pain.
Honest,
vulnerable
alive.

'Sometimes I feel I'm one step away from being found out to be a fraud.' Les, the conductor, and I are having a rare one-to-one conversation while we wait for the Morris Dancers to stop flaunting themselves around the summer fair.

He's a psychiatric nurse, and is allowing me a glimmer into his innerscape. Deep, soft eyes. He's one of those rare souls who genuinely care about people and the world and instead of just talking incessantly about what could be done, does stuff, like conducting the band, and somehow – I'm not sure how – is there for others in a way that is far more than just being a conductor: he lets off a feeling of love that seems to run through his bones.

I feel so much more confident about myself and the world when he's around. He's the type of person you want to talk to, to open up to, to share yourself with. I think it's because he has that rare skill of not judging while having his own opinion. He tells me in no uncertain terms what he thinks of me, giving me new angles of perception (not always as I would like to see myself), that he says in such a kind, deep way that I also feel seen, sensed, supported. The two or so times that I've spoken to him properly, I've felt so seen by him in his soft, kind shower of non-judging that I've dropped down to a level of honesty of expressing myself in such a way that I've surprised myself – that I've gotten closer to myself.

So it comes as a surprise to me that he doubts himself, that he doubts himself like I do. I've so often felt alone in my dread of the sound of a knock on the door, of a 'polite' notice, of my mobile ringing with an unknown number. It feels reassuring to know I'm accompanied in the unsubstantiated but substantial fear of being told, 'Game's up! You've been clocked!' or, 'Our records show us – you're a fake,' or 'You don't even know what you are about, how can you help/teach/be in any capacity with *others*?'

I shudder a little in the summer marquee recalling that vulnerable place of trying to be in a world that feels so much bigger than I can ever be. Inside I have visual sensations of worlds imploding, too close to the void of eternal dread of 'being found out', while, curiously, feeling safe sat next to Les feeling the same. I can see his are just fears, nothing more. From a safe distance it all suddenly seems absurd.

I wonder if this constant awareness of the void is how Les feels as he treats mothers with broken bonds to their little children. I look at him, a lighthouse in the storm of human chaos. I hang on to his normality like a life buoy. He's a regular fish and chips sort of guy. I imagine him with his family, eating in their caravan, watching the windows steam up. Nothing fake about him. No grandiose maps, just as it is. Beside him by osmosis I feel grounded. Strong roots hold the tree through any storm. I feel – in that big, tall, overweight body – his strength to be able to show frailty, the courage to be able to emit the message that he is full of doubt of himself: it's his strength and his curse – vulnerability.

Even when he's being a bossy-boots there is always a soft edge to him, so that he never closes me down. And in situations just like this, sat in the chaos of this local village fair in the diffused light of the marquee tent that slanting at quite an angle, the metal legs on his chair digging into the soft ground reducing it to near primary school proportions, the Morris Dancers shouting and clanging wooden sticks, I can't help but open up to him.

'I'm sure,' I say, 'you're a great psychiatric nurse,' his eyes look at me, inside his iris they are flickering, as if afraid to look at something he really wants and yet is afraid of at the same time. How to say, *You stay present in your vulnerability, so it gives others the chance to experience their own? I like being beside you, it gives me a chance to feel my own frailty?* 'What I mean is:' I say indirectly, 'you're great at holding other's emotions, hearing them, letting them be, giving them space to get out.'
'That's what the others tell me,' he says, 'but after a while, the waters rise and I can't do it anymore, it's too much…and I blow.' A tick flashes across his left eye. He's feeling exposed.

I want to say more. I see Victor, move ever so slightly, leaning his big weight forward onto one leg. He's looking over at the Morris Dancers and their red, white and blue silk handkerchiefs bobbing up and down as if upside-down clouds about to burst rainbows. His horn is in its case, the baton in his hand.

I want to cover over this vulnerable space that's opened up between Les and me with soothing words.

I want to paste over these vulnerable feelings I'm feeling beside him: fragility, impotency, self-doubt of being forced into a world much, much bigger than me.

There is a sudden cry; the silk colours drop all at once. I want to say to Les, as if he didn't know, that we need people like him able to be there and guide mothers with broken bonds to their babies; we need people like him humble enough to question themselves instead of someone numbed by routine assessments unemotionally spouting off from some expensive university gained intellectual map; we need people like him who doubt themselves enough to stay awake to be present with people when everyone else has given up on them. I want to tell him how powerful I find his simple kindness.

I want to say all this and more but I can't, we've got our mouthpieces to our lips – Victor's on his feet, arms raised, hovering his enormous body over us, ready to beat us in.

—

It's not easy to know how much to clean the toilets. They look clean enough to me so I wipe them superficially. I've been volunteering here in the Vipassana centre for months and still haven't quite got over how much to do. Setting my own standards is an emotionally fraught business. There is no boss to order me about; I have to find my own balance in and amongst other women, who coming only for a ten-day stint, use their fresh energy to blitz every nook and cranny, afraid of being told they are not doing enough. I was (a bit) like that at the beginning, that is until I burnt out.

Perfectionism is easy: you know when it is perfect and you know when it is not. It's obvious and it's so, so easy to find imperfections. When it is not perfect you just keep going. Generally it is not.

Perfectionism has burnt me out. It's not my friend. It takes me hand in hand to Exhaustion. But still as I clean I worry, trying to be more than I am. Worrying my image will break and people will see within. *Am I enough?*

—

'Do you remember that Slovakian girl who was like a motor? She never stopped?' I ask Emily, as I bend down for the toilet cleaner.
'Aha…'
'What did you think of her?'
'Erm…sort of arrogantly humble…' she paces around near the cleaning cupboard, 'Does that make sense?'
'Ohh yes!' I say. Waves of relief. *It's not just me after all!*
'It was as if she couldn't leave anything to chance. So that no-one could ever complain about her work,' Em says putting on rubber gloves.
'Impenetrable, like?' I look at her, but she's looking for something. 'Do you remember she wouldn't stop even for a break, not even on her days off?' Mop in hand now Em looks at the floor. I feel a wave of gladness come over me that I'm not the only person who felt such… *What was it? Bitterness? Anger?*
'I was repulsed by her to be honest…I'm not sure why.'
'I know what you mean. I tried to connect to her, felt sorry for her, but it felt like there was no way in. It was something to do with her pushing ever onwards to the next clean…desperately clinging to the perfect, making it impossible for us to ever criticise anything about her at all.' Em starts to mop a random corner, though she should be in the shower block really. 'Somehow,' I say reaching for the bog brush, 'it made me want to knock her off her pedestal.'
'Yeah, I know what you mean…she was sort of smug and yet totally pathetic…'
'As if giving her a slap would wake her up.' I watch the legs of the blue cleaner drip around the rim of the toilet bowl. Looks like the legs of wine in a wineglass. I hear Em clatter into the shower room.

I'm two toilets down when she comes back in, mopless, 'You know it was like she distanced herself from us mere mortals…'
'Yeah,' I say stretching out my back, 'invulnerable somehow, pushing us away.'
'Inflexible…'
'I don't know how she kept it up,' I say, genuinely amazed. Nice to be standing

tall after bending down over bogs. 'I mean, she made us all look like slack asses.'
'You were!' snorts Em.
I look for a reality check in her eyes. They are sparkling with friendship. It's a joke, but she means it too for real. I reel in the truth of the mirror. *But would Em be able to keep this pace up for more than a few weeks? She's off tomorrow. I'm going to miss her.*

I'm putting all the sanitary bins back into the cubicles. The floors are done now, but I'm still thinking about Lenka, the woman from Slovakia. I'm imagining her following me around making my life hell. For apparently no reason at all my mind noses into what it is to be a 'baddie'. *Why am I thinking of that now?* A stream of baddies from various films flash through my mind, their stories, their attitudes, layer one on top of the other. Suddenly I realise: they are all attempting to be invulnerable.

—

'I would *not* go hitchhiking with that knot in your t-shirt,' I tell Irena, the age gap between us suddenly converting me into grandmother advisor. This is a girl who has been raped, this is a girl who is trying to find her way through the world back to a place where she can feel safe, as if she needs to go back in and recreate the same story but this time with a different ending, with her ending, with her empowerment of being able to defend herself. 'Unknot your t-shirt,' I say as unprotectively as possible.

—

'The middle path,' said Buddha. He twirls a flower in his hand.

Something inside Mahākāśyapa clicks; he 'gets it'.

—

In Contact Improvisation I am leaning on another, eyes closed. We are creating a series of balance points between us, harmonious. With every change there is a new balance. Our bodies move by themselves.

I'm on my feet, leaning in with my shoulder, he leans in with his shoulder, balancing on one leg, the other is beautifully straight. He moves slightly, the tension between us is strong. I feel safe like there's a thick nautical rope between us, strong enough to put all our weight into so the other can feel supported too. Later we are both lying on the floor, our legs entangled, the pressure between them is light, fairy like. Fairy hair. Soft tickle. We push against each other into a stand, enter into a twirl, and he lifts me, he has all my weight, I push my arms and legs out like a star, evening out my weight so I'll be lighter for him.

So many points of balance! So many middle ways. Not too much, not too little. Harmonious balancing between two. Between me and him. Between me and the world. Between me and myself. We find balance too in me moving slowly, him fast; me falling hard into his softness, him high above while I'm low below. The balancing point always changing! Sometimes we are mirroring sometimes we are different, but the point of balance is always moving, changing, moving, changing: we are in flow, it is dancing us. We are the dance.

—

Exhilarating, petrifying, sensual, sexual, boring, annoying, repulsive, pleasing, creative…the deeper the dance the more we open to that which is. Uncontrolled vulnerability.

—

There are quite a few huffs and puffs over the kilos and kilos of carrots. Miranda is talking. The idea is that, like the hundred people meditating in the hall, we as volunteers talk the minimum possible, to stay in our bodies, to be with sensations, but in the kitchen it's hard, we aren't segregated here, and: there are men around. 'It was this amazing experience,' my ears pick up, 'I went out of my body, I could see myself down below, as if I were floating on the ceiling. I felt such a very big, big – ¡grande! – expansion, as if I were becoming the cosmos. Oh it was the most!' As much as I try not to be jealous, I am. I can't help feeling belittled hearing of a wonderful experience that I have never had, and after years of doing this stuff. I've no idea how she felt, what she experienced is beyond mine. As my eyes stare into my teacup, as if I'm not bothered one iota, I feel waves of sensations through my body…hot…cold… slight tickles…a torrent of tightness around my throat. I feel small, unheard, pathetic.

Staring into my dandelion tea, feigning nonchalance, I am all ears. 'I have to talk to the AT about it, I really do,' declares Miranda happily.

—

'I felt myself leave my body, and hover a while, and then I saw myself from below. It felt as if I were expanding into the cosmos,' I say to the AT, the Assistant Teacher. I'm translating. This is my role. I look at him, trying to stay as neutral as possible in my tone and choice of words. 'Very good,' he says looking at her. 'Muy bien,' I say staring into space. I wonder how she is feeling; am I projecting onto her shiny eyes of expectation? I'm feeling that she's feeling excited to hear something like: 'What a deeply nourishing experience. Yes, this is the first real step. Well done. I have been observing you. You are ready to proceed to the advanced course. The world needs you. Welcome!' I too want to hear him tell her that she is anything other than this we are being now: frail human beings without a coherent idea of what it means to be alive. Inside, trying to be detached, I am desperate to hear what he's going to say after she's explained this amazing experience.

He looks at her, waiting for the right words to come. We sit hardly breathing, in heavily baited silence.

'Very good,' he says, 'All experiences are experiences. Return to sensations. Do not let yourself get distracted. Return to sensations. Everything else is a distraction.'

I translate to her. She looks at him blank with disbelief. I feel it too. *That's it?*

223

He smiles compassionately.

———

Is there no more than this?

This is it.

Here. Now.

Really: this is it!

No more, no less.

Awakening

                Live,
                 raw
               delicate.
      The protective glass
               lifted;
                there
           becomes here
               tingling
             with fear,
           with pleasure.
          Contact again,
           with real life,
            with my life,
              with me;
           ever changing.

I watch Paul dancing Contact Improv with a woman who teaches it. They just keep moving, finding new points of balance, playing in the gaps, swirling. Making art, bringing grace and form into the space between them. I feel the life in their dance and gasp.

———

'I don't know if I like Contact,' I say to Paul, 'I just don't know what I'm doing. I feel vulnerable without any rules, or set movements. I mean I just feel so exposed.' I huff my vision through the window into the sky, 'Like sometimes it works and other times I'm just so clumsy and without any thing to hide behind I feel so vulnerable.'

He pauses, characteristically, allowing me space to feel it all and says, 'That's the point sweetie.'

———

This is it?

Nothing more?

This is me?

You make the path by walking

Fuck off! Guru me? Ha!
Make your own path!
Stand exposed
raw you, in
naked

v

u

l

n

e

r

a

b

i?

l

i

t

y

as you smash up against
not knowing
floating unprotected
– nobody knowing –
no plans, no maps, no recipes for life.

I can't be your guru
a tabula rasa for your ideal life,
for when you desire
without lifting a finger

225

           piling your damp paper dreams
           onto the fantasy of my shoulders
            you'll scream out in agony
     as you watch them decay into sterile dust
       and then you'll scream all the more
            – now to sacrifice me –
          rather than seeing the reality
            of who you haven't become.

I am kneeling beside Ben in the chapel on the dance mats. He's an older man, wiry with horribly unkempt beard, who has spent his life hiding from vulnerability in the library of his mind - and so he's interesting to talk to. Safe. Deeply intellectual thoughts about the world. I ask, 'Will you tell me again what you said yesterday about intimacy and vulnerability?'

He looks into his mental files, definitions, conclusions, investigations closed. Frowns in concentration until suddenly his face lights up: information located. 'Shared vulnerability,' he looks into space as if reading something, 'both opening up to the possibility of being hurt.'

Danger?

           I feel so vulnerable
          reaching into this light
             as if it were fire
             that would burn
             rather than love
            that will nourish.

Trust.

Opening up.

Vulnerable.

Trusting another.

Trusting myself.

Feel sick.

Breath hard.

Deep down swirling.

Underneath it all I hear a voice, 'It is OK, it is OK, it is OK.' *Is it the voice of desperation? Is it the voice of gentle wisdom?*

Should I believe?

Hearing more, Seeing more

I

Dry brittle bones
dozing in the comfort zone.

Wet yourself:
wade into something new.

Push through the unknown
'til you know nothing any more.

II

He spirals back to basics
re-learning what he
already knows,
innocent fool,
seeing further in:
a smaller pattern
within the same;
he sees
further into himself.

III

Being listened to
he hears more of himself.

I am in panic being on stage in front of all of these people. Back stage I have already gone through terror as I put on random clown's clothes. Terror edged with fun. Most of me wants to run away but somehow I've managed to stay there in the wings of the stage with my legs burning out, going into wobble.

I have a police jacket on, a pink frilly ballerina's skirt, rainbow tights and a pair of wellingtons. On my head I've strapped on a straw summer hat with a pair of swimming goggles. I dump the red sunglasses. It's too much.

It is my turn to go on stage. I gulp.

My whole being now wants to run the other way but the sergeant major in my head makes me march on stage. If I'm going to do this, I might as well ramp it up. So I march in backwards, forcing myself on stage in a Monti Python style from the Ministry of Funny Walks.

I get to the centre of the stage. I have not received any instructions of what I need to do as yet. No map. No schema of what I should be doing. No idea what is going to happen. Will I be brave enough, good enough? I am in limbo. I look out into the audience. My heart is pumping so loudly that I want to make it quieten so I can at least hear something. I say, 'Shush,' really loudly, and hold my hand over my heart as if making it be quiet.

I stand there petrified.

I look out to the audience from far, far inside. I feel very, very small inside a rapidly receding body that is in a very big hall.

I don't feel like I'm here, and yet, I feel totally and utterly naked as if people can see right into me, into this pounding fear.

The audience are laughing their heads off.

———

'What will you do with this one wonderful life?' asks Mary Oliver. I stare at the white ceiling in blind panic.

———

Existential fear. Question after question swirl through my mind colliding, colluding, collecting, stir-frying doubts into sharp edged fears. I shatter into paranoia, electrocuted on the table of shock sensations crashing the bitter taste of aspirin through my system; anus scrunching with the agony of psyches' nails scratching down a blackboard; jaw clenched into pain. Tears and snot hang weights onto my head, neck sags under the pressure, unable to stay upright…I look away from the mirror, too scared to see.

———

'Clowning is about being vulnerable and connecting through it to the audience – letting them see us in the most fragile state of this thing called being a human – it is cathartic in the manner that on some level they recognise themselves and they laugh it out,' says Àngel, who is leading this workshop, having transformed himself yet again and now at the age of forty-five is an expert on clowning. That's a long way from selling chickens in the street in Argentina.

———

I am with Angelika, in Greece. She is my good friend. We are so similar, despite her being old enough to be my mother. We are in the valley between Paroikia and Naoussa. You can see my house further down in Kamares, nestled between dry fields of olive trees and the noisy bird sanctuary. Either side is the Aegean sea, twinkling in the sun. We are watering her vegetables. I'm on cucumbers. 'I just have no idea what life is about…' I say, dumbfounded. 'Nobody knows what life is about,' she says humbly, meekly, 'I mean, just look around you. Nobody gets it…' She stops watering for a moment, in the change of sound I look up. 'It's all just too big to get.' Her arms sweep across the valley.

Her honest, innocent words fly like birds straight into my heart.

Staying Open

So brave
not to worry,
to be right now
with the future
roller coastering on,
hurtling towards us
into its black unknown.

I think back to the clown workshops where I suddenly realised that what made the audience laugh was my vulnerability. Showing them, in my eyes, that I really, really did not know what to do, burning in their gaze…that I was *really* improvising and that I was actually really, really scared. It was in these moments the audience truly connected with me, humans to human. Was it relief in feeling that no-one is alone in this wyrd game called 'Life'? It made them laugh their heads off. I really wasn't doing anything funny at all. I was just feeling; feeling for me and for them: and in that bridge magic happened.

—

'You really should take up clowning,' a professional French clown says to me, her big round face full of tenderness, 'you're a natural.'
I smile. I feel horrified. I don't think my heart could take it.

—

Joy. Pain. Sorrow. Happiness. Peace. Panic. Fear. Love.

Human. *How to stay open to all of this?*

Fish Blind to Water

It is there
all around us
waiting patiently.
Nothing can it really do
until we feel its kisses
and slowly begin to
creep out of our dreams
waking up to our gifts
ready to accept
ourselves.

We're playing the last bars from a medley of the music track from the film 'Grease'. Victor's baton does a swish as if he's knotting an invisible bow. I lower my cornet slowly away from my mouth. He wipes the sweat of his brow. I drop my cornet into my lap, hearing a few embarrassed quiet groans. We're not playing so well, some of us got a bar out. It's not easy to conduct. Hard to hold the band together.

'I've been thinking,' I say sideways to Les as he puts the next piece of music on the stand, 'I'm not sure we have to get 'better' at anything at all actually.' I secure the fluttering music with a peg on my side of the stand, he does the same on the other. 'I'm wondering if it's more about how much we can actually hold?' My voice is a bit weird bending forward, cornet digging into my stomach. 'You know? To be able to hold life, as it is, right now?' A breeze gets under the sheet music. 'I mean everyone can be charming on a beautiful summer's day, but the question is: when the storm hits, how much can we hold as we each navigate through our inner weather?' The breeze whips up a corner of the music. I put the other peg to secure it at the base and sit back, unjamming cornet from stomach.

'You know?' I continue, 'The ability to just be – to just be!' Cosmic joke. So simple! So difficult! I come back to earth, notice the marquee sloping off to the right. 'It's so hard to just 'let it be' with the whole 'good' or 'bad' thing going on...you know?' I keep staring ahead at the angles of the marquee. 'To not squeeze the life out of everything in a desperate measure to control it all, make it perfect?'
'What?' he says. I turn around to his eyes sparkling in the sun, his attention is on pulling his chair out from the earth again.
'You know, like, can we stay calm instead of...'
But I don't have time to say anything else, Victor's arms are in the air, counting us in.

Forgetting to Remember

'Good' or 'Bad'
how do I know?
For a moment
of strength
I lay down my stories,
let go,
surrender,
become what is.

Opening to you, I am forced to see me;
my images crash against deeper truth.

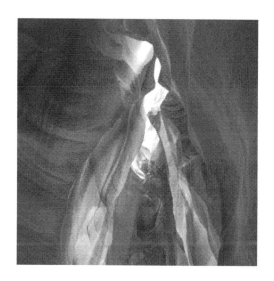

231

You look into me

and see

what?

Who am I?

What am I?

?

Dinner party chatter around our
instinctual need to teeter on the edge.

Odysseus

Strapped to the mast
I cannot get away:
forced to stay open
to the sheerness of the waves
crashing
dark and heaving
within myself.

Raw naked depths
pull the roots of my hair
blood rushes
tempest storms whiplash,
psychic swirls
dislodge past wounds;
flotsam flying.
Hit, I hurt.

Sinking in claustrophobia
I pant in this minute space
desperately open,
drowning in terror.

Under the
crashing waves far above,
deep inside
I discover
a new sense of calm.

New found Ithaca.

'But what is competition for you?' asks Lucien sat as if comfortable on the sheep skin rug on my floor, arms wrapped around himself, hugging his legs. I wonder if he unconsciously feels me looking at his posture oozing with vulnerability, fragility. *I wish I had a sofa.* He shifts his body and sits like an Indian chief…it feels like something is moving inside of him. Lucien is Christopher's friend from life drawing. Thin, tall, a whittled down psyche after living in the midst of emotional chaos and the high drama of having teenagers. It feels as if his hair is still on end from his recent 'holiday'. It is quite clear that this, here, is an oasis of calm, an eye in the storm. I can almost hear his psyche panting, catching its spirit.

It's a precious night for all of us. Co-ordinating a night where the three of us are free and the men childless, feels like a miracle. Lucien is an über-sensitive, highly intelligent artist, his conversation a delight to swim in. Christopher on his second bottle of wine, seems surprisingly compos mentis, 'To me,' he says, 'it's almost like a male way of showing love.'

—

I have a flash of Paul admitting that being in bed with a woman was terrifying. 'Each woman is so different, and we have no way of knowing what each woman expects.' I get what he's saying. I'm feeling it too, but I'm too embarrassed to say that I am not satisfied; or rather I want him to discover how my body receives pleasure without me telling him. Why not just tell him? 'We, or at least I, don't have the courage to ask a woman to show me her body,' says Paul, maintaining a soft eye gaze. This is my chance, but suddenly, I draw a blank. How does my body receive pleasure?

I would like to get out of this fumbling about in the dark routine, we've been motoring on primal survival instincts and it would be nice to become a little more subtle. *How to explain, I like a tongue here, under my armpit. I like eye contact. I like strokes that only touch hairs. Sometimes I like it really, really slow, but not for too long else I drift off. Sometimes I like it fast and furious, but it is like a grace note, not to be overused. I like clitoral stimulation more than penetration.* I nod in agreement, as if attending a lecture. Missed it. Missed opportunity. Flaked out.

'So that's why men find sport to be more important often than sex. A man can understand another man's body. Sport, for lots of men, and contact dance for me, is a dialogue between bodies that understand each other,' his voice low, soft, vulnerable.

—

The two men are on the opposite side of the table and as much as I feel accepted in our little trio, I'm feeling a sort of two men connection of which I'm not part. I'm wondering if it is a realm of sensing that I have no antennae for. Maybe I'm just projecting, but it doesn't take away that I feel an impasse between us, as if they were both in one airport and I in another.

'Is it true that men, when there are no women around, are not competitive?' I ask, 'A man told me that the other day,' I feel like an investigator into the realm of man.
'Ohh I'm not sure about that,' Christopher says almost instantly, 'at the Manifest camp there's all sorts of competition.'
'But what is competition?' Lucien asks, a timid edge in the air.
'It's almost like a male way of showing love.' I think I get what Christopher is saying. *Is it a way for men to be close without the fear of it becoming sexual?*
'I've always considered competition to be 'bad'…' says Lucien. His words hang in the air, the quietness shouts out pain, shouts out trauma. Christopher hears it in the silence. It is a joy to be with two sensitive men.
'In what way 'bad'?' he asks uber gently.
'Well, sort of taking from the other, making the other feel bad…' he makes eye contact with Christopher, pleading to be kind, to be soft. Christopher is so kind. He is a soft, sensitive soul, but it feels he's not sure where to go with it. So he gives space, holds space. Strong, confident, fortress style.

———

In the soft, protected silence an image runs through my head of black kids in Africa somewhere getting close enough to the goal and then passing the ball to the opponents. The westerner introducing football to them was exasperated, 'Why are you passing the ball to the opponents now? You had a clear shot at goal!' They look at him confused. Silence. 'Why?' he insists.

One of the older boys says, softly, as if explaining something very, very simple, 'We don't want the others to feel bad. If we win it means they feel bad, if they win, we feel bad. We don't want to feel bad.'

———

'Maybe there is good competition and bad competition?' I speak out loud a possible conclusion to my internal images.
'Yea, maybe?' says Christopher on the trail again, 'I read this thing' he says, 'that being highly excited puts you into a set of bodily responses,' he puts his elbow on his other hand and swings his forearm like a speed dial, 'and it's where we want to be, totally alert to life, but at a given moment', he pauses, 'it can totally swing into terror.' He swings his arm dramatically in the opposite direction. Twisted.

We sit there for a heartbeat, imagining the horror.

———

What would happen if we didn't contain our animal instincts?

———

Five minutes later Lucien says, 'You've triggered me with this 'good' competition thing, like what do you mean by 'good' competition?' He is asking the masculine in Christopher. He doesn't see my masculine. It annoys me.

Christopher says, 'I guess good competition could be when you spar with the other, when you pit your wits against the other, when you both practise with each other and raise each other's game.' Lucien hugs his knees. That silence is there again. Christopher the kind giant becomes quiet, waits, gives time for what needs to come out - gives Lucien space. We sit without moving. I hear my breathing. I realise I am privileged to be the proverbial fly on the wall, watching two sensitive men in their interaction. *Is this how the world operates when I'm not there?*

'I was always small for my age, was late going into puberty, I was in my mind a lot...' I imagine Lucien in the library, feeling safe in his mind, safe from the harsh world, '...competition for me feels like being on the floor, being stamped on, kicked, sometimes...' he pauses, breathes in with the horror of the memory, 'being completely beaten up on the playground...'

We know about English state schools. We just, unfortunately, do. I don't want to go there. I stay wallflower.

———

Fight/flight. Our eternal trauma played out over and over again.

———

'What is good competition again?' Lucien is beautiful in his vulnerability. I would like to go hug him. But this manly comradeship is what they want, not a mummy solution. They want to get through this thicket of psyche and not to be held back with a feminine hug that softens them, pulls them away from squaring up to the issue, fighting with the discernment of their swords, with their mental sharpness.

'I wonder if good competition,' Christopher says, 'is going into a safe container? Maybe it's having all that excitement of the kill,' he makes fists of both hands, 'and being able to let it all out, but in such a way that it is contained and restrained from pushing over into terror, so that it isn't death-like dangerous – you know? – but held within the safe limits of a container so that we can experience the excitement of our inner forces, of our instincts?'

Over the table I look at Christopher, so beautiful with his sweatband that he's using like an Alice-band, and realise that even in this drunken state, he is kind and intelligent and lets wisdom through him. I feel myself gorging on his image. I feel like a man, loving looking at him across the table, as if he were a stranger. It's weird to see him in mate mode, as a separate individual. I'm trying to digest seeing him in a different light. 'Competition could just be an opportunity to explore contained instincts.'
'Yes! Christopher, yes!' I bubble out from my silence, I can't control my instinct to spurt out, 'Yes! Like sex?'

'Yes,' says Christopher quietly with a protective tone that holds wisps of a secret garden far away from here. *Did I break a boundary?*

Privately, Christopher and I are learning that good sex needs a solid container. We did a Orgasmic Meditation (OMing) course together which taught us to set up 'the nest' in the same way each time, so that when we OM we have a container that we can trust. Timing it for fifteen minutes is a part of the container, the ceremony of starting and ending in the same way, the reassurance that we know what to do at certain points along the journey also help relax into the contained space, so that I can really let go, can really let myself break free, trusting that the container is there waiting to collect me again. The container lets me feel safe enough to explore and experience boundless freedom within its safeguarded limits. I realise I'm knocking that very container, bringing it out into a world of more than just him and I.

Christopher, who is not one for sharing private stuff, covers over my inappropriateness. He turns to Lucien, they make eye contact in a few milliseconds of silences, where in that space I'm sure I see Lucien's eyes say to Christopher, 'It's fine, it's fine, carry on.' There is a tenderness between them, a nobility that I feel so grateful for. Humbled.

Christopher armours himself again, back onto the scent of warfare, 'It's like kick-boxing. It is so good to feel met. I mean I am there fighting and I could kill the other, I'm trying to kill the other, but the other defends, and tries to kill me…and it's electrifying: I love it! To be in those instincts to kill…!' his voice drops a little at the end, suddenly unsure of himself, wondering if in the exuberance of his honest expression he has lost track of what is correct to admit to. Around him a did-I-go-too-far feeling starts to quiver. The image of him wanting to kill, floats in the air, as if over a cliff. But he is in safe company: there is ground below. It is held.

Lucien smiles, nods, tries to look comfortable, stays silent. I give my bit of ground, 'I guess it has to feel real? Like you really could kill, to be able to feel the instincts pump through you, but in a container that makes it safe? I wonder if it has to feel real for the hormones to kick in?'

I feel now like I'm covering for him. It's exciting to be so close to an edge, and vulnerable.

———

The night before Christopher and I went to a party at Scott Islington's house. I had totally surprised myself. Christopher and I were going out for the first time as a couple into 'public'. *How were we going to do this?* How to shift from the dizzying freedom of singledom into being in the confines of a couple? At the door Scott comes out. He's a flirt. He's a hippy trustafarian who has come from rich stock and has a beautiful castle house in the countryside where he puts on gigs and parties which are infamous. I have only ever interacted with him as a single woman who also loves to flirt. So we do. I like to imagine myself being his lover even though I don't think, but don't know, that I would ever actually really want to - but I love the potential, I love that air of tension between us, I love the hug and the kiss that slightly brushes the side of my lips that smacks of friendship on the edge. Something vague, undefined, embraces this new friendship. It is softly electrifying. It feels safe to flirt with a flirt, it feels contained, safe, comfortable. But for it to actually have those real feelings of desire, there has to be an actual possibility.

And there and then I find myself pushing Christopher away, pretending that I hardly know him.

—

'Yes,' says Christopher musing, 'it has to be a safe container, yes of course, but it also has to feel real with unsafe edges...'

—

One summer I hiked through the Pyrenees on my own for four days. I saw a short-cut on the map: a clear dotted line representing a footpath. I followed it twenty minutes to a ridge, and then it disappeared over the top. *Did it? Could it? Really?* I searched around for the footpath. I kept checking the map. *It must be here*, my inside voice said to me, *It has to be...* The ground did appear to have a slight path before it dropped off between two cliffs. Nothing else seemed remotely possible. So I went for it. A classic case of believing map over reality. If there are dots on the map there must be a path, *surely?*

It started steep. I am a mountaineer, I was brought up walking in mountains and felt confident enough even as it started to get a bit hairy...but half way down, I begin to feel myself start to wobble. I look down and suddenly feel the fifty metre drop below me. I had pushed on slowly and steadily, but now realise that I am actually almost vertically rock climbing and that the drop down, if I slip, could – for real – kill me. I am shocked to be in proper, real danger. Right then my legs start to wobble.

'Don't go on me now!' I order sternly, talking out loud. My nerves are running up and down my body so fast that I begin to lose form of where I end and where the outside world begins. Dad's voice training me as a kid comes through me, 'Always three points of contact.' My free leg swings wildly, trying to find a new footing. I can't see down: it's vertical. My hands are sweating. I want to pass out. I can't: I am dangling on a rock face. I have to stay alert. I cannot relax. *Do not relax!* I just have to keep going, excruciatingly. *Hold on!* Part of me wants to give up, as if this were a game in a gym. *Keep going, slowly, slowly, keep going...* I am not sure if I can keep edging down the cliff face.

Time suddenly becomes irrelevant: I am in one big NOW. I am hyper alert using all my energy to stay alive. Each movement counts. I am too intensely alive. I am burning energy fast. I feel my breath; I feel every muscle in my body. I feel myself clinging onto my inner strength while feeling the terror of my weakness grow exponentially. *How long will I last?* There are so many sensations streaming through me that it is all I can do not to give in, to not let go of the rock. I want to just disassociate and go blank. *This is not a joke,* I realise.

Concentrate!! You cannot just let yourself die.

—

On the sheep skin rug, Christopher continues, 'Yes,' he says as much to himself, 'competition is about having a safe container, to let the animal out. To be the beast that we are; to experience the high of terror.'

—

The conversation has shifted. Lucien is on a roll. We are talking about men and women's sensitivities. 'I wonder if men are more sensitive somehow…like women are more cerebral, they think more, unlike we have been told in history classes.' He pauses and we all agree in the silence of the pause. 'We are like our sexual organs,' he turns to me, 'you women,' I have become the token woman, 'have your sexual organs well hidden, protected, but we have them outside. They could be cut off. But even more sensitive is that we have, at the tip, a gland that is internal, or should be internal, and it is exposed, out there.'
Christopher opens up in flowering admiration, 'Wow,' he says, 'You are a guru!!'
They float in manly comradeship that flickers in the sensitivity between their eyes like a candle bravely shedding off the dark. I don't get a thing. *What?*
'Maybe,' says Lucien encouraged, 'we men are more connected to the earth, to flowers, to sensitivity, and it is women who are more in the symbolic realm? More conceptual?'

I notice that the two men have hair on their faces, they have hairy bodies, surely they are closer to animals? Or am I being a post-feminist pig?

—

I think back to Jules, a fucking genius of a man who I was desperately not falling in love with. My heart stood bravely still, ticking loudly into a fireproof jacket in the middle of consuming, licking flames. *How long do these jackets work for?*

He stands, facilitating his performers' workshop entitled 'Everything comes Alive when Contradictions Accumulate'. In his gravelly deep confidence-inducing voice his words slip-slide through his American accent. 'Lee Strasburg', he says, his head cocks still to the side for a brief moment, honing in on us - my still head is suddenly in a sea of nods - 'worked with actors for decades and came up with this idea of why actors get scared to really *Go There*.' He stands in front of us - I can't help but stare, mesmerised, drinking him in. 'This was after watching hundreds of people who decide to dedicate *their lives* to acting…'

He strides to the edge of the taped-off square: our magic box to step into, to allow ourselves to step out of the prison we normally put ourselves into, barred daily by our wild, desperate attempts to be 'acceptable'. He stands as if ready to bow for a massive audience. 'These people,' he says, 'dedicate all their vital energies to letting people see them,' I could just look at him all day, 'but they stumble, according to Lee Strasburg for fear of three things,' he holds up three fingers defiantly and with his other hand grabs the first finger, 'fear of looking psychotic,' second finger, 'fear of being too erotic,' third finger, 'fear of being too violent.'

———

I wonder if the fear of becoming an animal is the fear of slipping back? Our evolution as humanity is so slow, we are still so violent and war like, even in our love relationships. We are so hairy in our feelings, so groping in our sex, so starving in our continual need to sustain and protect ourselves. We disconnect at the drop of a hat from the source of our higher selves; we are so easily triggered into unconscious behaviour.

I wonder if the fear of becoming an animal is the fear of losing ourselves to our own violence that boils volcanically within, of being devoured by our wild, uncontrollable instincts that swing at us, looming towards us from the wilds separated only by a gossamer veil, so dangerously close to the uncontrollable, so easy to fall into our animal instincts that are but a membrane away. It's petrifying even to gaze into the void, let alone fall into it.

I wonder if the call of the wild is too strong for those who cannot trust themselves.

———

Fight or flight? Glaring contact with our life facing possible death.

On the cusp on humanity

We drag ourselves onwards
evolving tantalisingly slowly,
erect and hairless
we drop our clubs
afraid to return to animal;
floundering in the dark
we grab onto sex,
violence,
the rush of forced
awareness
as the moment is stripped
from all but death
glimmering but a membrane away,
as if going into the wound
will heal,
as if calling forth our wild
will tame us of our burning fires.

I am hanging on the rock. I do not want to die. I realise I am alone, very, very alone. My insistence on not taking a mobile phone is suddenly dangerously absurd. I wanted to be in the wilds, but not this wild. My heart beat resounds around my whole body. My brain is finding it hard to just keep working. My hands are beginning to shake. I have to keep wiping the sweat off them. My legs are an almost uncontrollable solid wobble. *I seriously don't know if I can do this.* There is no way I am going back up, it's closer down than up. I need to get to a horizontal. *I cannot bear this!*

Another saner voice says, *There is no choice. You **have** to bear it.* I want to scream into this void of nothingness. I am on the edge. I cling to the rock, petrified. I want to eject from here. Ctrl Z. Give up. I panic: there is no escape route. A part inside of me commands: *Do not panic!* Strong tone. Sergeant Major. *Do not stop. Keep edging down. Keep moving. You can do this. Stay calm.* Out loud, I whisper desperately to myself, 'Stay calm.' I can only half believe I have it in me. My voice is warbling. A cry wants to sob up through my throat, *Stay calm. Please – stay calm.*

I look down. *Don't look down*, something inside says softly but sternly. My stomach rolls. It's not just the vertigo, but the fear that my legs, lost to reason, will just jump off by themselves.

At home sat comfortably on my sofa I read in Milan Kundera's *The Unbearable Lightness of Being*, 'Anyone whose goal is 'something higher' must expect someday to suffer vertigo. What is vertigo? Fear of falling? No, Vertigo is something other than fear of falling. It is the voice of the emptiness below us which tempts and lures us, it is the desire to fall, against which, terrified, we defend ourselves.'

I reach the bottom of the rock face. I am scrambling on all fours over loose rocks and scree, the incline is still dangerously steep, my legs can barely keep me up. I cannot sit down yet. A fall now could still seriously harm. I look down, it seems like the valley is light years away. *This is still dangerous. Don't give up. Don't relax. Keep going!* Something inside of me guides. My brain screams out, *I cannot keep concentrating like this!* My legs scream, *I am pumped up with blood, I cannot hold you much longer.* My heart is pounding unable to speak, my mouth is in it.

As the vertical, step by painful step, curves back into a more horizontal, the silent fear subsides so slowly that in itself it is tormenting.

At the bottom of the rocky valley, I reach a path. I let myself collapse. I am in trauma. I am unending waves of relief. I want to cry. I want to laugh. I do not know what I am. Who I am. I am alive.

'The solution is in the wound,' I say to the men, 'The Fisher King...'
'That was a great film!' says Christopher.
'Parzival?'
'With Robbie Williams and Jeff Bridges?'
'I'm talking about Parzival. Wolfram. Thirteenth Century?'

'Erm…no…' he laughs.

Sometimes I worry about him and I being on such different pages. I glance across to Lucien – *did he see that?* – and feel supported by his quiet nod. I keep going, this idea is in my head and demands birth: 'The Fisher King,' I continue, trying not to sound pedantic, 'has a wound in his side, it could be the trauma like we were talking about – you know any sort of trauma really: being bullied, or the trauma of being born, or the trauma of becoming an animal, or the trauma of fights and flights, the trauma of destructive passion and…' I realise that I'm going on…they are not the only ones drinking.

'Anyway, he has this wound in his side, and the only way for it to stop hurting is to put the lance into it laced with poison.' Should I mention the lance is the direction we focus our awareness of consciousness? They are looking a bit blank. I breathe in. I am a little overwhelmed in my inebriated state, my tongue seems so slow. It's an uphill battle to put words to my inner world, to make these flashing images into a catchable one liner for these two sensitive, intelligent men who are slowly getting more swozzled.

'So, yeah,' I decide to cut it as short as possible, 'the only way for it to stop hurting is to put into the bottom of the wound the same poison that caused it.' I've lost them. I don't know how to say it any simpler.

'Alchemists say that the solution is in the wound,' I say hopefully.

———

As far as I have read, people who have had near death experiences seem to come back to living with a completely new awareness of what life is. They appear to have discovered deeper values, tend to live life more than they did before, have a quiet calmness, a confidence about life itself. Some claim to have felt 'god'.

What is it? What happened? How?

What did they experience deep inside?

———

'I wonder,' says Lucien, who is back to hugging his legs, 'if competition, you know, fighting in that safe container, allows us to be completely in the moment. To be so concentrated that we have no choice but to bring all of ourselves into the moment, to be absolutely present to all that is happening right now?'
I look at him with pure admiration. 'Wowwwww! That's a great idea! Like as if in that moment we suddenly become more conscious?' In my head I imagine an increment of light, a sudden jolt into a higher level of consciousness than we have ever felt before…a step up into the brighter, lighter, more expansive.
'Yeah, like we experience a dose of being absolutely conscious?'

Sensing death

Sharp.
Alert.
Each
movement
hyper defined.
In and out
bare,
raw.
No future,
no past,
no ego shouting
greedy demands.
I am nothing
but this now,
sensing the
infinitesimal,
feeling nothing
but an intense
brilliance
of simply
being alive.

Maybe we go into the wound to peel off all that is not now? Maybe we go into danger without protection so that we can get closer to that light deep inside of us? Maybe we need the intensity to get our ego's out of the way, away from past and future, distracting it by dealing with intense panic of staying alive, while we get to glimpse through and experience a dose of death; of the lighter, brighter, more expansive?

Perhaps it is only by going down into a wound, into an experience that stretches our consciousness to such a degree that a mere slip from awareness could potentially re-traumatise us, that we get to see what is on the other side, deep down inside of us?

—

I'm back to thinking of the bottom of the trauma being a place where time stops, where we get to experience a heightened awareness of our humanity, 'Being so aware of consciousness, do you think it frees us up? Sort of knocks through blockages within us?' I ponder.
'What do you mean?' Christopher pours himself another sneaky wine. He sees me spotting his covert operation, but like a good spy, covers over any allegations by a public declaration of transparency, 'Anyone?' We shake our heads.
Undeterred I continue, 'Like the killer instinct that you talked about, like going out into war and killing, which through competition is somehow abated...like...'
'Hmmm maybe...' Christopher is still dealing with being caught.
'Like when I come out of a changing room, after sport, I always feel so relaxed,

my body is relaxed. I feel on top of the world. I feel happy and harmonious…as if the tension that I dragged myself to the tennis court with, or any anger or fear or aggression that I was carrying through the day, is somehow let out, gone for a while. I feel more space inside of myself. Freed up.' Lucien is here so I can't say: *after animal sex with you, Christopher, I feel sublime. Like an angel.*
Christopher murmurs, 'Yes, as if we have cleaned ourselves out from the inside? Flowing more?' Lucien unlocks his legs and murmurs something I can't hear.

—

Lucien has left. Christopher has left. The evening has flown through my veins, words through my mind. I feel happily empty.

Alive

Palatable
slipping on my throat
as she confides
deep pain
- his death -
deeply tender,
sticky sweet on Adam's apple.
I hear myself swallow;
luxuriously alive
chokingly aware
of my essence.

A rather sweaty conversation about
sexual freedom without responsibility
and explosions of confusion.

In my power

Present in my body:
this is me!
Looking out
through my own eyes,
I breathe into this,
my experience.
He, besides me,
is part
but not the focus:
I am.
I am at the centre
creating
my universe
one god amongst billions.

I am toasty warm in bed, drinking in Erich Fromm. As I open the leaves of 'The Art of Loving', something inside me opens too. His words swirl inside of me, caressing me with his wisdom. I love the idea that Love is something that we need to practice to be able to love. His dancing words say how people just like me have confused the problem of love, by thinking it is about *being loved*, instead of *loving*. We march on blindly, unconcerned about our capacity to love, concentrating all our angst on how to be loved, how to make ourselves loveable. As we get all roused up trying to find someone who will and can love us, we are misled by the illusion that it's easy to love another.

I love long Sunday mornings in bed. The duvet and I have become one as I meander in and out of the sliver river of his words whispering how we are all strangers, separated from each other, until one fateful day a wall between two of us breaks down and – joy of joys! –we feel close and merge it would seem magically into a state of oneness. I smile as I read how this moment of oneness is one of the most exhilarating, exiting experiences in life. Yes sir! But suddenly I gulp, cold water splashing over the words: 'falling in love' he warns is even more 'amazing' and 'wonderful' and 'miraculous' for those who have shut themselves off, isolated, without enough nourishing love in their lives. I breathe out tensely, prickly uncomfortable.

The miracle, my wise friend continues to tell me, when combined with sex, is a ticking bomb. I breathe in, feel my eyes closing, remembering. I arch my back. But, he continues to warn twisting me around the sheets: this type of love is a paper fire and by its very nature just isn't lasting. As the couple get to know each other, the intimacy that they had taken for granted as magical and mysterious slowly turns into a nightmare scenario of differences, antagonisms, and disappointment, until their mutual boredom kills off whatever is left. Ahhhhhh! I bite my lower lip. Push against the pillow. Try to get away. Fromm has caught me at my weakest. He has me in the palm of hand as he describes how people run into these sexual, intimate paper fires totally unaware that the intensity of their infatuation, this 'being crazy in love' is only really proving, I grip the page, 'the degree of their preceding loneliness.'

———

All I knew about Tasmin before last night was a Facebook issue.

She posted a sophisticated, photoshopped, black and white shot of a nubile young man naked in the height of his sexual prowess, aesthetically contoured shadows highlight his rippling shining muscles, horns coming out of his beautiful head, his knee covering the part we all want to see. Arousing. She had written underneath, 'This is the kind of faun I'd love to explore my sexuality with!' *Me too!* I think frivolously.

—

Later in the day I go make a tea in the kitchen. Joseph is there. 'Did you see what Tasmin posted?' I ask for no conscious reason.
'Yes,' his neck stiffens. His upended hairs on the back of his neck warn – be on the alert. 'What do you think?' he asks. I can tell from his tone to take this seriously, *very* seriously.
'Not much,' I say in my most levelled voice, 'you?'

The way he starts off so quickly, so mentally prepared I can tell he's been waiting to get it out. 'I find it insulting. Demeaning!' I feel him launching into a swimming pool of difficult murky emotions, 'I mean if it were the other way around…' he spits out, 'if it were a man with some bunny girl saying, 'I'll like to explore my sexuality with her!' he would be hounded for being sexist. Ostracised.'

I see what he means – I hadn't considered it like that – I just hadn't put any thought into it at all to be honest. I stay quiet, my only defence is innocence. 'I find it intimidating…' he says, anger covering over insecurity, 'I mean, are we all suddenly supposed to be like him? It's hard enough as it is, wondering if I'll be good enough without having someone expecting me to be a hunk of a faun. I want to write something in a comment…but I don't know what. I don't know if I will be understood.'

—

A week later I am in the kitchen, with Joseph. We are blissfully without the owner of the house around. 'It was really good last night, shame you couldn't make it,' I say.
'Yeah? I'm glad you enjoyed it.'
'It was a good dance, that good dancer was there again, you know Robert? The one who knows Paul in the States?'
'Ohh, I still haven't met him,' there is a genuine openness alongside a feeling of threat woven into the space between his words.

I know that I'm treading on thin ice here, but I need to process and Joseph is the man to process with. 'And then in the sauna afterwards Tasmin spoke about an Osho workshop.'
'Oh right…' he says nonchalantly, we both know that the faun photo is hanging (potently) in the air, nagging him about his sexuality. I tread carefully…

—

Once I've got used to it, it is divine to be naked in the sauna after the dance. I am sat at the end, now next to Robert. It's delicious because we are all in a body floppy state of peace after having danced, having touched, having communicated through our skins, bodies nourished. There is a feeling of having dived into the hidden worlds of touching, of cranking ourselves open again into caves of vulnerability together, of tasting unbounded intimacy in a shared dance within our little group of seven that is not easily found in our non-touching society.

We laugh and talk. The conversation rambles onto Osho Leila. There is a big Christmas course coming up, something tantric, apparently. Tasmin is leading the conversation. She is shining loud. I begin to find her irritating. She is triggering me. 'It was wonderful over the days,' she exults, 'to see the group ascend into a higher state of consciousness…expanding out…it's so frequently only me, me on my own…but this time it was ALL of us.' *Is she being arrogant?* I check my inner critic. *Am I being sceptical here or cynical?* She, happy in her own world, continues unabashedly, 'Each day we expanded more, opened more, into this state…' she pauses as we all grabble about, trying confusedly to imagine something that we cannot.

I stare out of the window, listening, keeping my energy to myself. How to know what is true in this incessant talk, how much is fantasy and how much is reality? It so often feels like people are giving out an advertising campaign of their feats, photoshopped somewhat out of the reality of what really happened, of what really is. The more I get to meet these people, the more I hear echoes of loneliness. Gingerly I take what she is saying as a partial truth: it is fantasy and it is real.

A young souled, fortyish, curly blond-haired guy, sat close to her, is nodding vigorously. There is an energy building between them. She is enjoying being venerated. I imagine he is imagining it could go further. 'Yes!' he says in excited tones, 'We all need to explore more! To become more conscious!' They are exchanging words fuelled with passionate ego.

There is a lot of big talk, in that little sauna, about transforming energy through sex, about reaching down into the depths of the animal instinct and transmuting it, of humans accepting themselves as they are, of exploring the power of sexuality, of exploring self power, of inner transformation through the acceptance of sexuality. My ground is shaking slightly. I agree with all that she and our fellow sweaterers are saying. I agree with my mind but my body is in a state of tense rejection. I stare out of the window, the fields are in darkness. Stars are twinkling. They reassure me: they will not stop existing right now. They at least, are stable.

'On the last day,' she tells us, 'I was walking through the garden, and saw a man. I looked across at him. I felt it. I went up to him and opened myself to him. I wanted to explore my sexuality. I wanted to feel my power.' I cannot help but feel honoured to be allowed into her sharing. 'We fucked. It was amazing. We were just like animals. Doing it. Afterwards, done, we didn't talk, we just moved away, continued on our way. Nothing to say.'

The curly blond is now wide open rabbit eyed. His wanting her is palpable. 'Like an animal,' he says almost breathlessly, 'but staying conscious, right?' I feel him trying to impress her by the muscles of his insight, by the strength of his spirituality, 'being like an animal but staying conscious?'

She nods at him, looking him in the eyes for a long time. It's awkward, as if we are all colluding somehow in their game. It is so surreal I even wonder if I'm imagining all this sexual tension. 'I have never felt so free in all my life. Free and expansive and full of my own power. I felt my power. The power of my sexuality in all its glory. It was all about me, not about him. He has his own story. There was no need to share, or to talk. I just walked away.' As I stare silently out towards the stars, I imagine the blond curls through the dark of the sauna bobbing up and down as he gulps through his images: fucking and walking away! Pure masculine heaven.

Meanwhile I sink further into conflict. Yes, I love the idea of being so free as to be able to fuck whoever I want, whenever I want. What honest adult wouldn't? But, and it's a big but, a butt that gets in the way…something doesn't sit well here for me. Is this me being old school? Is this me imprisoned in a self limiting belief system that squashes any real juice out from my dry, frigid life? Am I too inflexible, too old school, too closed to allow life in with all its intense colours? Too afraid for the wilds of intimacy? Or is it something else? Is this Eastern 'Tantra' gone Western berserk?

I am becoming increasingly uncomfortable. I cannot work out why. I feel shadowy monsters lurking inside, ready to snarl. Part of me admires what she is saying. Part of me wants it…I feel jealous of her experience, of her dominating this space here in the sauna with her stories of greatness. She has been to a place of sexual prowess where I cannot even imagine. I feel my body reacting in repulsion. I am confused. *Would I do it?* I feel so small. So fear ridden. *Would I like to go to Osho Leila? Yes! No!* I feel fear. *Yes, I would. No, I would not like that at all.* I cannot imagine myself fucking just to feel myself and my power. It seems so masculine. A warped masculine. It feels to me that after all the work we have done as women we are falling into being nothing but masculinised sex maniacs. I feel drawn to it. To the experience of it. Of being able to see it from within. Maybe from the inside it is completely different to this, my observer's stance. I start to wonder about my own ideas of sex.

In my dry mind I am bogged down with questions that flash through my inner vision in images. I see an open feminine-being receiving. I see energies going up through her, as she is a channel, a filtering cleaning system of her and other's energies. If we open up as a feminine-being, what are we receiving? Are we purifying machines of others' karma? We receive semen, we receive energy – do we also receive the masculine's karma too? Is it our sexual role to take all that 'energetic history' into our receiving psyches and process it? If so we have to be careful what and whose energies we take on. We have to be careful with what 'gifts' the masculine is coming to us with, coming in us with and leaving with us. What's in the white explosion he's left us to deal with? Sometimes after sex I feel great; sometimes I feel heavy, sad, not myself – in short I feel shit. Why is that? Is it to do with his stuff as much as my own? We need to know that we can handle it.

I remember being in QPR (Queens Park Rangers) and being taught to head the ball harder than the ball comes to us. Somehow it didn't hurt if I wellied it with my forehead but it stung like hell if I just let it land on my head: knocked me out a little. *Is it about our attitude, our stance? How much do we let in? Can we control it?* Even so I feel that we need to know and feel the other deeply before we go 'there'. Intimacy is feral. I don't want to be sweeping out someone else's dirty water like Mickey Mouse in the 'The Sorcerer's Apprentice'.

I wish Goethe had been to Osho Leila and had written about it instead of me having to try make sense of all this fuzzy confusion in the darkness of my unknowing.

I want the conversation to end.

'After the course ended,' she's on a roll, no one can compete with her now: she has the whole stage and she's going out on a limb, fuelled by the deep silence of our intense reaction to her monologue. I sit breathing shallowly, almost holding my breath, like a little kid behind a curtain in hide-and-seek. I am living by proxy, listening to her words, quivering, 'after it was all over, Leo, the facilitator, came over to me and asked me if I wanted a session!' She squeals with joy. The young man holds fixed eye contact…he is temptingly close to the bait. He smiles, nods, hopes. 'I said,' I hear a warped sense of amazement in her voice, 'you have space for ME???!!!''

She laughs. The blond laughs. I hear people smile, wanting to be in on the joke. I feel like I am in a horror film. Something inside of her laugh sounds like an ego gone mad, like an axe murderer coming home to kill. I sit there staring fixedly at the stars. *Am I being unfair?* Perhaps I'm projecting my fears onto her, but her ego seems so hungrily titillated in knowing she'd been chosen out from all the other women – though surely too that is warped perception if he had a full timetable? This guy has cherry picked out the women he wants from a group of attendees and has somehow made each one feel amazing special, singled out. *How does he do it?*

'I mean,' she revels, 'he had booked times with so many women, and still he had space for me!' Her voice is filled with…undeniable glee? I hear alarm bells. I'm starting to really pull out. I am holding onto the stars. She is on her stage here in the sauna. My brain is whirling around all sort of concepts of scenarios of group collective consciousness and if the individual ego is functioning here at all? *How has it occurred that she, a beautiful woman, is delighted to be on a list of women he has chosen to fuck?* A voice that has not spoken yet, an older male voice asks (is he thinking the same as I am?) 'Can he ask women while he's facilitating the group?'
'There's a rule,' she answers seriously, her words taking on the gravitational weight of important instruction, 'that while he is facilitating he cannot propose to any woman, but once the workshop is over,' her words lighten, 'he is a free man, and can go to any woman.' I am not sure if she has disassociated, words are

flying out of her. It doesn't feel very controlled. 'So, anyway, I went to the session. It was amazing. Amazing sex,' she pauses: this is the point she's been working towards, 'A-*maz*-ing,' she says again.

Amazing?

I sit, grizzling. Sweat running. I suddenly have no idea what amazing sex is. *Have I ever been close? Have I had it? Am I missing out on something because of my limitations? Am I hounding myself into a prison? I want to try it!* My mind swings around: *he goes about fucking ALL the pretty women? Did he ask the ugly ones? I mean is that ethical in any sense?* Is he not simply preying on some sort of collective hysteria he himself has built up over the course of the workshop, preying on beautiful women blinded by days of opening and expanding and losing sense of their individual ego. *Is it OK?* Or is it that he wisely chose with deep experience only those women he has seen throughout the week who would be capable of holding the experience and has truly given them a great gift?

I sit distancing myself as much as I can, staring out of the window, waiting for this intense discomfort to end.

—

Sat on a sofa a week later I'm still confused over the whole thing, I mean I've read some of Osho and it reads well. Correct. It's gives the right feeling of light, of freedom, of out-pouring of love. I ask William, 'But all this sex?'
He says 'He's one of the mutant rebel gurus, who came across to the west.'
A mutual rebel guru? 'What's that?'
'They come across to the west to say, 'You think you know what spirituality is? Then think again!''

I have an image flash through of uptight rule-abiding women who go ballistic if you ever step out of line of what the guru has deemed. I particularly remember a woman almost stamping her foot, 'The incense sticks HAVE to be HERE!!!' I wonder that she didn't break the sticks as she pointed hysterically to the altar table. Did she recognise the irony of not being calm? So many followers - afraid of the not being 'spiritual' enough and messing up in the invisible spiritual world - give their power away, give their own decision making process away – give themselves away – to follow blindly: too afraid to make their own path.

Then I think of people who have that drained look on their face of not having fucked in years. The Spanish even have a word for women who are nasty all of the time 'Mala follada' (badly fucked) – it's one of the worst insults you can deal out. Whereas the men are full of 'mala leche', bad milk. 'Milk' being the semen which in this case has 'gone off'.

—

'I just get filled with doubt and come back too far,' Joseph says across the kitchen table. I guess it is the inner critic telling him he's not worthy, just like his mother did throughout his childhood. So many men out there with mother complexes, so many mothers out there with father complexes. Deep work.

So many people hiding.

—

I talk to Paul over Skype. 'What've you been doing?'
'Working too hard. Again.'
Hiding behind work, hiding from the world of people.
Broken record.

—

I wonder how the tantric sex guru gets all those women to drop their limits?

—

In Chile there was a guy, Claudio, who kept showing me attention all week long. We were jammed into a raft everyday on a course to be white water rafting guides. I pushed him off, everyday. I found his big swollen lips repulsive. Didn't like his black curly hair. He became pesky, but I also hadn't realised how much I liked having someone admire me.

We were all invited, the whole group of us, to a pizza place opening night. There had been quite a lot of wine, and to make matters less controlled, I was premenstrual. My friend and I decided to leave, we'd had enough, we were off the next day: an early start travelling onwards and upwards up through South America. The guy, Claudio, came out of the restaurant running around me, singing some Spanish love song I couldn't understand, and showering me with rose petals. It did it for me. It worked.

OK, why not?

The next day I woke up crying because we would have to part. I was sat on the hostel chair, by a little coffee table with a round brown tinted glass top sobbing over someone who the day before I hadn't been one bit interested in.

—

Sex for me is dangerous. Emotions fly too fast for me to grasp. It has taken me years to wake up from the kaleidoscope of intimacy, alarmed at who I so easily gave my power away to, in heavy, clumsy attempts to reclaim my mighty animus warrior from his sunken chest. So many tangled knots to unravel myself from. How much wasted time!

—

'Sex can be dangerous,' Joseph says after my recounting of the Osho sex stories from the sauna. It jolts me. Telling him the story about the sauna last night I've gotten into a haze of imagining someone else's story, of imagining a connection to a different level of consciousness, of trance, of expanding sexual power where one can just be – god damn it – who one simply is, and allow all of the parts within to come out and fuck, fuck, fuck. Conscious animals digging down into a deeper purity.
'I'm not sure if I would do anything like that, and yet…' my words hover in the air.

'Me neither,' says Joseph hearing me, 'or maybe I should say, 'Me too!''
'I know! I don't know if I'm ready to do something like that, if I ever will be, if I already am?'
Joseph pours a cup of tea. 'Sex really can be very dangerous, it's not to be messed around with.'
'Yes,' I say and fall back down to earth through Logic's wind tunnel. Thud! 'For a woman it can mean a story for the next eighteen years, until the baby becomes independent, not even then – but for the rest of our lives…and for someone who doesn't want to have children – that's horrific.'
'Oh I didn't mean that,' he says, 'I meant I have it programmed into me that sex can be dangerous if a man lets it out completely, that it can be dangerous for women.' *What is he talking about?* 'Partly I think from my mother's strict protestant upbringing.' I shudder. I have no idea what he is saying, but I imagine violence.

———

'The thing is,' my darling Paul says as we lie together by the hearth, warming in the security of our little fire, just him and me, safe in his arms, 'is that we all think it's acceptable to go out and dance in a nightclub and be erotic, feeling sexual attraction and going out looking for it. We hide it away, we have sex behind closed doors, we don't share.' We are talking now about the erotic dance jam that Norbert held in Paul's house in the States as a leaving party. It makes me feel uncomfortable. 'The dance is safe,' he assures me, 'it's a way to explore sex in community: to remove negative feelings from sex, to allow ourselves to be erotic in safe places. It's not going to go far, we all know each other, so why can't we just express it? In a dance? Honestly. Together.'

My head is on his chest, I concentrate on my breathing, on the sensations going through my body. I'm out of my comfort zone. I'm standing firm in the onslaught of my fears. 'Sex and eroticism,' he continues 'is a frontier of human consciousness, and we can be there as spiritual warriors, pushing through into a new paradigm where sex is not shamed, where sex is good.'

———

I have invited two new friends around to my house for dinner, Jenny and Diane. I know them – like English people seem to know each other – I know facts about them, but not really how they feel, or who they really are inside. We have drank a bottle of wine, and in some weird sort of masculine way, after the meal I have resorted to a smoke, as if this were something normal for me. I'm still edgy. I don't feel comfortable. I feel constricted by rules of behaviour. I guess I'm trying to break through with the ridiculous smoking gag.

Osho Leila comes up in conversation. I say as casually as possible, 'I've heard about courses there…are they as intense as they seem?'
'What?'
'Like free sex and all that?'
'Ohh you are talking about the Tantric Sex Courses,' says Diane knowledgeably.
'Really?' I have no idea what attitude they have towards them, how they feel, but

I launch recklessly into, 'I heard a story once, about how this woman decided to go for it and experience her own sexual power and so fucked a guy in the garden. Afterwards they didn't talk, they just walked off in separate directions.'
'Like a man!'
'Yes!' I relax, feeling mirrored, 'My whole body recoiled from the story, like, it just felt so wrong…and yet…' We have moved from the table to the sofas. I feel them go into slight panic. 'And yet,' *Should I? Should I say?* I rush into it, not letting myself have too much time to think, 'I want to try it…to know…to be able to know it as a personal experience, rather than hearsay.'

'Wow!' says Diane who has taken up the three person sofa for herself. It is really nice to see her relaxed, it half relaxes me. 'That's honest!'
'You are going to do a course like that aren't you?' Jenny asks her, craning her neck towards her from the armchair.
'Nooo….' she says laughing, 'I'm going to do a course which is about sexuality, about intimacy, but it doesn't have actual sex in it.'
I am piqued. I want to know. I want to know for myself. 'What is it?'
'It's meditating, talks, eye gazing, exercises with others, but always with clothes on.'
'Don't you want to do the Tantric thing?' In comparison it seems quite lame.
'No, I don't feel ready for it.' I like that the field between us is clearing; I'm beginning to know who I am talking to. 'My partner taught those courses for five years…' She allows silence to let it sink in to us.
'Wow,' I say, breaking the silence, 'that must feel really intimidating!'
'A-ha…' she gazes into me. I feel her feeling her feelings acknowledged. 'He would be naked with his ex-partner and show groups how to massage each other.'
'You mean touch each other's genitals?'
'Yes….'

I reel back in shock. This is not just something that is happening in one part of the woods, it's happening all over the place. Without me.
'Did the participants all have sex?'
'No, it's well boundaried. In these places you don't ever have to do what you don't want to do. They are quite safe,' she is used to talking about this, 'well held. Contained. You are free to go as far as you like.' She is so calm, so sure. I admire her and her honesty of knowing herself well enough to know that she's not ready to go there.
'Ohhhhhh…..' I pressure cooker release just a little bit of the tension…the wanting and not wanting. 'I get so confused by it all…' and look to the painting on the wall of a cockerel. Nice relaxed strokes, the cock picking at grain, his hind feathers the centre of the piece. A sun shining hazily through an abstract background.
'I guess,' says Diane, 'it's all quite a different story on the inside, once you are there, experiencing it, rather than how we feel about it now, on the outside.' I look at her, gracefully sprawled on the sofa.
I get an image of a point outside of a circle and a point within a circle. Different landscapes. 'Yes,' I admit, 'you're right, maybe I am experiencing more my fear

of it than the reality of it?'

I assume that since we are talking about Tantric Sex that they will know about OM. 'I remember being completely repulsed by OMing, thinking that I would never do it,' I say, 'and now it feels perfectly natural.'
'OMing?' asks Jenny.
'Yeah, what's OMing?' asks Diane.
'Orgasmic Meditation.' I say, and launch back into safe territory. I feel like I've played a trump card. Fucking ego, always wanting to 'win'.

Kitchen table chat

We both keep glancing
towards the clock
things to do
but neither of us
can get away
from being ourselves.

'When I hear these stories, like the one in the sauna yesterday, Paul's erotic dances and you remember I told you that story about the Touch and Play in the States?'
'No?'
'You know, in that yurt on a slant? The one with the woman sliding all over everyone?'
'Ohh yes, the women were up for it and then they weren't?'
'Yeah,' I swallow, carving out a bit of time before plunging into my uncomfort zone, 'Well,' I look at the teaspoon shining a deformed reflection on my face, 'When I hear those stories, I feel my body get horny.' I adjust my position on the wooden kitchen chair. 'I feel like going and doing it, just jumping in and experimenting with my own limits, and then I get really scared and want to run away.' I love living with Joseph. I need to get work done, but instead here we are again in the kitchen, discussing life and the world. 'It's like when a man comes close to me, who I am attracted to, and he is clearly offering me his body, I get all excited and think, 'Why not!! Animal sex! Yeah baby, bring it on!' but then I swing into the complex of nun, of purity and sainthood and think, 'How will this affect my psyche, how will it affect my purity.' I'm just not sure what sex is at all. I have no idea.'

He looks across the kitchen to me, 'What do you mean?'
'Well of course I know penis into vagina makes baby, but on an alchemical level, what is it? How does it affect us?' All my boundaries wobble all over the place: confused lines in the sand. 'In that space, where I lose control, often all my complexes swing out of control and I can't help but react.'
'We all do…' he says softly.
'Like I wonder, if the feminine,' I always have to stop and clear this word up, 'I don't mean woman, I mean the feminine within a woman or within a man…'

259

'I'm with you.'

'…I wonder if the feminine soaks in, is receptive to the karma of the masculine?'

'The masculine not necessarily being the man…'

'Correct. I mean does the feminine take all the karmic shit from the masculine who is releasing them and help 'him' purify it, heal it?' It's here, that old nugget of an idea from Symbology classes with Raimon Arola and the Psychoanalysis classes with Malka. I'm saying it out-loud instead of just thinking it, 'I just feel that the feminine absorbs, allows entrance, the masculine penetrates and ejaculates.' It's so simple, and yet the truth hides in the simple because it is where it is most easily overlooked. Looked at superficially it's seems silly simple.

'I don't know…could be? I knew a Jewish woman who said a similar thing. And actually I've heard the goddess-within-women say that the energies of men can stay inside of a woman and interact with hers for years – but I think that's just more 'sauna' talk…'

'I mean even that - it's scary bonkers! But I really don't know what's true…and then as soon as my wandering mind tumbles into concepts I shut down and want only to be a 'pure' entity. Suddenly I have all these impasses, all these thorns to stop any prince from entering the palace and kissing me.'

———

Left at the kitchen table alone, finishing off my cup of tea I wonder if it is destructive for Tasmin to be filled with all this sexual animal power that allows her to feel it her right to go and fuck like an animal? Or is this her in her glorious masculine and it's completely safe? Has she ripped off some shaggy hide and is more in contact with her true being? Does she regret it ever, secretly within?

I keep living it by proxy.

I remember coming out of the sauna and asking her how it felt coming down, back into society. 'Hard,' she said 'really hard. Some of the others haven't got over it yet.'

Virgin Maria
Slut Lilith
Virgin Maria
Slut Lilith
Virgin Maria
Slut Lilith

I flick back to the start of the book 'The Art of Loving.' Erich (we are on first name terms now) tells me, as I wrap myself tighter into the duvet, that he wants people to understand that that love is not easy, not something that can be indulged in by any old Tom, Dick or Harry, regardless of the maturity they may have reached. I shudder. He says, quite candidly that all attempts to love are bound to fail unless he or she begins to actively work on their all the corners of their personality, developing ones total personality, becoming well rounded beings, because love is simply not going to 'just happen' especially if we are unable to love even our neighbor with 'true humility, courage, faith and discipline.' It is only by developing these qualities that we can experience true love, but we would rather continue in the illusion that we simply fall in love while clinging to sentimental claptrap devoid of any real qualities. This lack of any true value in our society has made it that true love is so rare in our day.

We do not fall in love, he says, but we have to be in love. I sigh in a cocktail of despair mixed with hope as he concludes bravely: the capacity to love continues to remain a rare achievement indeed.

—

I sigh. I realise that without knowing it I have been wanting it easy. What is it that I am actually looking for and am I prepared to work for it?

Cinderella Freaks Out

I want you
to come
here
with that magic wand
between your legs
and make me all better.

Chapter 20: Walking the Knife Edge

*Admitting to the animal within and letting
it out of the cage for a long, wild, satisfying run.*

Unleashing

Pinstriped women
absorbed in black sips
wired on a power
far from their own.
Curves ironed out,
controlled seriousness
cages their goddess within;
protecting from...
from what?

Where is the feminine?

Why shudder from
the dark voids
that destroy
as they create?

Where are the she-s with
soft curved fertile mounds
who frolic in pleasure,
lounging luxuriously
in the totality
of their entire beings,
imbibing in the thrill
of plump summer fruits,
tongues licking
tantalising trickles
of sweet meanderings
and sinking into the senses
being devouring by it all
as they dance frenzied
screaming into the night?

How do I get to *her* from *here*?

I write this smelling like a whore. I like it.

—

Neither of us know where we stand really with fantasy, and yet, it is there. It's hard to work out where to go with it. 'At Uni,' I say, 'back in the 90s, we all read 'The Secret Garden,' by Nancy Friday. It was sensitive, innocent, gave me a freedom to explore as it opened up to the door for me to fantasise.'

'Like what?' _____ [4] is always wanting to dig for sexual dirt. I ignore him. I'm talking theory now.

'The book explains how fantasies are fine, healthy, good to have.'

'I'd say!' _____ declares over-confidently. I know he is tormented over sex and all it brings up for him. Is he perverted for thinking certain things? He gets off on feeling twisted and then crucifies himself afterwards having tainted any purity he feels he has left. Impotency a constant threat of self punishment.

'It taught me how there is a world of difference between having a fantasy – and in the book there were gang rape fantasies, incest, animals; all sorts! – and them actually coming into reality. We'd be horrified if our fantasies came true.'

_____ looks down.

'But then,' I frown a little, 'it gets confusing, because these days there is all this talk about tantra and being in the moment, fully living the experience as it is, staying in the body - not floating out into the mind and fantasies. I mean does fantasy stop us being in the present moment, because we are imagining something, somewhere else…or connects us more?'

'Yea…' says _____, his eyes have gone somewhere else. I look at his beautiful face. It is as if he suddenly wakes up again, his eyes focus and he says, quite confidently, 'I guess all fantasies are unconscious elements, unworked traumas that want to be expressed…'

I look into him. I know some of the places he goes in his fantasies. I get scared.

We dangle in between sentences.

The silence eats at me: 'Soooo,' I say trying to assuage my uprising discomfort, getting back into the safety of theory, 'I guess both are good? We have to work to become conscious of our repressed traumas, but not get trapped into only being able to be turned on with our fantasies…'

'And being able to simply stay conscious and experience what is, here and now?' We both look at each other confused.

—

'Call me,' he says, 'Text me!' he shouts from the door. He's late. We've just had amazing sex. The door slams. He is going to be really late to pick up his son. We shouldn't have. We really shouldn't have. I think that's why it was so exciting.

—

It's the middle of the night and his very presence suddenly feels intrusive. He likes a candle on; the flickers over stimulate me. Because he gets hot so quickly I opened the window with joy hours before he arrived, wrapped in the love of loving him, caring for him, but now in the dark hours the screeches from the fucking seagulls are annoying the hell out of me. I'm trying to ignore them and go back to sleep. My legs feel tense, as if it's not ok to spread out. I don't spread out normally, I am lying just how I would normally, but as if frozen: a tensed not moving, straining to relax. I have the intense need to stretch and move out over all of MY bed. I try not to touch him. *Maybe I can pretend he's not here.*

Eventually I get up and close the window. I need to make this back into my space.

—

'Are you OK?'
'Yeah, kinda. I got a bit freaked out in the night.'
'Yeah?' Soft. Vulnerable. I don't know if I can be honest. He's being so loving. But I need space. I feel claustrophobic. I don't know if I want a big hairy beast in my life. This animal. This human animal. I don't know if I want to open up my life and have to accommodate another, anywhere other than in my mind where it is clean and safe and just me. I look into his soft grey eyes and part of me melts.
'Well…it's just…that…' I pause and instead of forcing out words, let them come out themselves, 'I had nightmares.' That is also true. Then without me realising it slips out round the back, 'It was hard to share my bed.'
'Yeah…' he empathises.
'Did you sleep OK?' I want to turn this around.
'On and off. I think if I could lie-in now and I didn't have to pick up Jalil I'd be OK.'
I have not budged much. I am still wondering if I want this bigness in my life. 'I found it really hard actually.'
'Yeah?' his voice always goes softer when he feels I have hard emotions.
'I just found it, a bit, erm, claustrophobic…like, erm…' I swallow, 'made me want to run.'
'We just have to go slow, that's all.'

I feel a sudden flash of rage. I hate it when he does these easy solutions, the one sentence answer, when he blanks over difficult issues with his guru voice. It's as if he can't be arsed listening to me, but pulls an 'all sizes fit' card out of his top pocket. I feel hatred flash through me. It's surprising. I've not felt like this for him before. My eyes dart back and forth, honesty is spilling out of my guts, 'What happens if we start to hate each other?'
'Well,' he says, still with his guru voice, 'we'll work through it.'

The one liner again. Any filtering system of expression is rapidly dissolving. The words slip out through my level tone, 'I feel anger when you give me those…' as I let myself be totally, utterly honest I start to feel lighter, 'those one liners, as if you know the truth about everything. I got a flash of anger of you giving me a simple answer, a solution. Making life easy. A cover up plaster to not have to deal with anything 'unpleasant.''

He looks at me alarmed but curious, as if to say, *give me more. Yes! Honest truthful emotions.* 'When you do that cover-over shit, I get so fucking angry at you that…' I search for words, 'that,' I say feeling into it, *where is this going?* The words slip out of my lips, 'I get turned on.'

We are gazing into each other's eyes feeling the intensity of peering into each other's wildness. Intense intimacy. This is it. My body is reacting.
'I read on the bible of intimacy – facebook,' he says, there is a silent guffaw that bridges a spark between our eyes, 'that a woman on the TNT page said that you have to hate the other a little to have good sex.'

The question floats in the air. Sounds like bullshit to me, but I can't deny: I am being really turned on. This is not my idea of angel sex with its nurturing massage and deep, quiet, gentle listening to the other. This is not what I dream of. This is animal. My lips open. My tongue licks him. I have no feelings, just desire.

———

I feel like I want to hurt him, to make him suffer. Make him do penance for all he has done wrong, to me, to the world. To make him confess to everything that proves he is not a god. I want him to see his humanity, I want to push his face in the vomit of his shitty human unconsciousness. I want him to break him open to his pain, so he can start dealing with it. I want to punish him for being so fucking weak. I want to get my revenge on his impotency. I want him to pay for not being who I want him to be.

We go into our fantasy making, as our bodies move over each other's, hands radar over each other's skin like a heavy night watch. I can smell him. His scent. His particular scent. I am wet. 'I'm going to have to make you watch me fucking other men. Not to turn you on, but to humiliate you.'
'Ohh yes,' half groan, 'and to show me who is a real man.'
'Yes,' I lick him, 'you'll just have to watch.'
'And be tied to the chair…can't touch.'
'Can't touch.' Our bodies are shifting into a new pace, the image we are creating is moving my body, my 'I' has less and less control.
'And the man is telling me how real men are, how big his penis is, how he is penetrating you for as long as he wants.'
'Yessss.'
We ride that wave.

'I am left abandoned and you reach orgasm with another man…'
I am living this. 'You have a massive hard-on…but you can't use it.'
'Yes, yes, yes,' his lips smother my words. I have his penis in my hands, hard, big. I feel a sudden shift inside of me. I do not want to punish now. I do not want to hate him. I want him to be my man.

'And you get out of the cage, and push the man away, and penetrate me.'
'Yes! My penis is sliding over his come, perfect preparation for me…'
'Yes.…' his fingers slip in and out of me. I am going into that land where I am not me. I am losing sense of anything but him, holding me, moulding me, making me into a sexual creature of his exclusive making, 'You are hard, and big, and the man runs away because he's scared of you.' His body puts all his weight onto mine. Deep, gurgling delight. I delve into the safety of him dominating me. I feel secure, loved, and sexualised. I am an object. It turns me on, I feel my hips push back, back arching in pleasure.

———

I am animal. I am in the throes of sensations. My body is writhing; I have his penis in my mouth, loving it. I have my fingers on my clit, as if another were there, I am nothing but sex. They use me for their own sex. I use them for sex. We are animals. This is not making love. This is sex. There are no fluffy love making feelings here, this is instinctual. From a small recess in my mind, I observe the deep pleasure of my body moving in its own rhythm…I have become lost to the sex…the sex is me…I am the dancer and the danced, I am the music. I am animal. It is divine.

———

'You have to go!' His son. Pick up. School. He's scrambling around for his shirt. I cannot stop putting my lips around his cock. He thrusts backwards and forwards, trying to button up buttons… 'One last.…' the deadline is turning us both on, the prohibition of what we are doing, my body is writhing like a snake, 'I need to take you, you're mine. You're my sex slave. I'm going to invite my friends around to fuck you with me.'
I have my hands on my clit, I feel it. I want to be used. I want to be nothing but sensations of sex. I want to have to serve him as my master. 'And then I'll serve you drinks?'
'Yes.'
'I'm your sex slave?' *Why does that turn me on?* Animal. Animal. Instincts. Animal.

He comes as I do.

———

Downstairs he moves around, trying to gather up all his scattered stuff. 'Truth,' I hear him demand half muttering to himself.

'Text me!' Door slam. He runs down the stairs. He's going to be late.

———

Lying in bed I realise that I do not want to text him. I am not going to text him. *Why not?* Another says, *I am not 'on tap'.* Suddenly I know not to text him. I want him to work for me. *Why? Why make him suffer?* I say to myself. *Why play these games?*

The animal inside is in control. The animal knows how to play the game with his

266

animal. I will not give in to him. He needs the hunt. I'll pull back and make space for him to feel his manhood in its raw nature, going into the fray, going for the kill, dragging his trophy back home through the woods. He doesn't want some dead animal delivered to his door. He needs to rise above the little boy inside crumbling over not getting a text, to feel the humiliation so as to rise above it, to come into his power and hunt me. His masculine animal needs it. I will not make this easy for him. I can feel it's what he wants, needs. I feel myself tested: Am I a nice girl to walk over, or a wild women to respect?

—

I would normally feel so scared of letting out this animal, but somehow this morning I feel in peace. Deep peace. Fulfilled. Satiated. I fantasise about wandering around my house in my lingerie, no knickers on, doing my chores, working, being silky sexual, touching myself whenever I desire, walking down the street, men smelling me, yearning from a distance. I feel like a goddess.

—

'To get to heaven we have to go through hell,' I say to him later on that evening, a candle is flickers between us in the restaurant, 'according to Milton.'

—

I wonder – as I gaze out of the window, happily spent, hoping he gets to his son before it's too much of a disaster – if this thing about becoming an animal is what is so scary about intimacy. Losing control to the 'lower' parts of ourselves, to our animal instincts. Part of me is delighted that he would give me time over his son. Animal warfare. As much as on a conscious level I really like Jalil, as much as I want to create good relationships with his children, as much as we are managing all of it really well, lovingly, this animal also needs her fill, needs to know that I have sway. Needs to know I'm not always at the bottom of the priority list.

The priority list is not a sign of his emotions. I know, at least my conscious woman part knows, that the priority list is about his responsibilities, and nothing to do with how he feels about me…

…but the animal wants her share of the kill.

Animal Song

Irresponsible to anything
but this here now
I breathe you in.
Morning airs refresh
after humid closeness.
I smell you through my pores
I feel the imprint of your lips
on my soft, warm skin
so relaxed I wonder I can walk.
We glide down the pavement
angelically having flown through
the sensuality of matter
of screams
of ropes
of red raw buttocks
sweetly stinging
singing our animal song.

Putting the base back on the cross,
going through Dionysus to Apollo
(or 'hell' to 'heaven')

The Modern Woman: Heavy Ground

Repressing her animal power
her hips turn into hind
- a heavy anchor of agony -
as she elopes high
into to her mind
terrified
that her light fluffy sweetness
may fly her away
kidnapped
on the wings of anger.

So much life! I ooze in bed, feeling sublime in the wake of being taken over by the fiery animal. Having lost conscious control I feel myself wrapped in a world of beauty, warmth, softness. I am light silk held by the sweet depths of the earth. I swim deep and relaxed in a balance of being connected, vibrant and alive. Of being all that I am, of being as small as I am. Of pure acceptance of what is.

Why do I so often negate this part of myself?

—

Why am I so afraid to get here, to this wondrous dwelling place? I gaze softly out of the skylight.
Well, says my wise person within, *because of the part within that gives so much fear.*
Which is that? A seagull dives, wings open, down through a current.
The Animal.
But why, if the animal leads to here? All my energies feel aligned, I feel smooth, I feel at one!
Well, continues the wise one, *remember she can destroy.* A seagull screeches. I nod. But still I feel divine.
But worse than that, she can create.

—

I know what pressure to use, I know what I like - minute movements impossible to describe. With the deep knowing of my feminine, it is effortless to be in this mellow, soft place. I am buoyed on cushions of desire, my muscles float in ease. It is soothing, calming, and like silk flowing I soon slip into a different world, far from the skylight above, far from the soaring seagulls. I feel my whole self begin a well known path constantly changing as divine pleasure overtakes me...

—

I am balancing, as if on a dome of ice, between neither thinking nor feeling. A divine emptiness in my mind. I am vaguely aware of my body's limits but acutely aware of its sensations further and further in. With my closed eyes, my body is see-through: I am not clear where my skin ends or where my energy expands out to. There is so much space. The longed for place I can at last relax into. Fly into. Be in. Body full of ever new, remembered sensations. Earth. Sky. Worlds inside collide in fusion. I tumble down further into myself, deep within a cave, a void, a velvet breathing of wondrous dark. I hear my breathing, deep, calm, rasping. Mind is clear.

Shimmering flat on the surface of a calm lake. The wicked step mother of my ego has danced itself to death before the ball. Words are absent, floating high above on the surface of the water. I am deep within, further down where words, and ego and mind only peer in from high above. I soar, empty, sipping of the waters of a nothing that is simply divine. Suddenly I don't care about the neighbours, my head arches to the sky, 'It' waterfall rushes loud out through my mouth. I am divinely crucified, having reached for a moment of eternity the centre of pleasure that's spiralling out from my very being.

———

Afterwards sprawled on my bed over a wet towel, cool vibrator touching my warm inner thigh, I am used, finished, satisfied. I wonder if this is the best way to prepare myself for Christopher: being a well oiled oasis rather than a white virgin bride? To be sensual curves and watered lush mounds, self fulfilled, ready for him to take his pleasure…land well worked, fruits dropping heavily from the boughs? Why not?

———

Where did this idea of being desert dry, of being virgin, sacred, scared, brittle, come from?

I lie in the warm sheets watching the seagulls as ideas and intuitions swoop in flights my mind.

———

I dream back to being in Nepal and reading an article in a fanzine. I have a series of imagines:

Nepalese women dominated by men throughout their entire lives.

As little girls, when they only feel but don't know what sexuality is, they are promised to much older men.

End of story. No experience of sexual freedom away from him, or probably with him. He sleeps in the bed. She sleeps on the floor, serving him.

The husband dies, of course before her. His child bride is just coming into her sexual maturity as a woman, tracing the faint lines of her sexual power.

But instead she is forced, by tradition, to burn alive on the funeral pyre along with her dead husband.

Some are not killed. They walk around with horrible burn scars all over their body - for life. Not sexy.

Modern Nepali's don't do this anymore. The woman is married instead to the dead man's brother.

She lies now on his brother's floor.

She is never allowed to explore herself. *Why?*

I remember the fanzine concluding with breathtaking erudition: it is because men are afraid of women's power.

—

A sudden flash: The Church. Catholic schools. Saying the sacraments. No sex before marriage. Prepubescent. Measuring my breasts for growth with a wooden ruler. The joy of secretly finding a pube – at last! The day I realised, round the back of the music rooms that all our parents must have 'done it.' Disgust. Intrigue. Can it be so 'bad'? The priest telling us from his pulpit that, 'masturbation will lead us to hell'. My mum not knowing what the word masturbation meant, but when she got home and looked it up in the dictionary being 'disgusted' - with the priest, or with the act?

—

The fucking church, removing us from our power. Eliminating the feminine as men dress in black dresses and make us adore them on the altar. The trinity: Father, Son and Holy Ghost. Air, Water, Fire. As if there were only three elements, as if they were all masculine. What about Earth? What about the feminine? Jung writes that the church raped us of quaternity. The Church knocked out sensuality from the rituals, 'purified us' of sensations.

—

I wonder, for the first time, if self pleasuring every day is real spirituality? Connecting to myself, connecting to another, connecting to that which is more than us? Is that a trinity? And if I add my body is that a quaternary? Does that begin to integrate the four elements, air/earth fire/water so that as I balance between the two poles I find the centre? I find 'god'? I find myself balancing on that dome of ice – is this a wormhole in the middle of the cross?

How to get there?

Be.

—

Maria. Mary. Mar. Sea. Emotions. Flat lake, serene. The virgin mind, the temple.

—

Birthing out creation. Origin. VITRIOL [7].

—

The temple – in the calm interior; the ego waiting outside in the outer courtyard – is the only place where we can ever experience something greater than ourselves. Letting down our own defensive walls, so as to enter into the temple, the unknown, is the only way to become impregnated with a higher consciousness. It makes no difference in that virgin state if we have had sex or not, or indeed if we are having sex right then. Being alive, alert, awake in that precise moment of eternity, here-now bringing our minds out of the future and the past, out of worry, out of pain, out of thought, of feeling, out of everything. Converting our body and mind into a pure, empty temple, opening ourselves for divinity to enter us.

Pregnant virgins.

—

I am so relaxed that I sink like water into the horizon and find myself wanting only to dance alone in the chapel while the others have a bar-b-que on the other side of the monastery. The floor is covered by a dance mat and I roll and move and find my legs swinging through the air slowly, softly, breathing space into what is. I am barely aware of who is making the movements. Is it me or am I being shaped, moulded by something that is not 'me'? I do not care, I am so into the experience, so wide into the sensations, the joy of being, the peace of acceptance of this here, now, that I feel I am flying through space, connected so firmly to ground.

My voice spontaneously begins to sing 'Amazing Grace' with such feeling that I am nothing but this outside movement, this inner world where my heart is so open it has become a temple. I get so into the words that they become me and my experience so harmoniously. 'Wretch' so well seems to describe how I exist when I am out of this state. I was lost, swirling in the mind of who I should be, where I should go, what I should do. And then this. Peace. Harmony. Being right here, right now, virgin state. I am found. I am rolling in Grace over the black dance mats, under the arched painted ceiling of the chapel. I was blind, I was seeing nothing but projection of my inner battles to reach equilibrium and now I am balancing in perfect sight. I feel I am worshipping 'God', by becoming It. It is ecstatic.

—

Etymology. Ecstasy (n.)

Late 14c., extasie 'elation,' from Old French estaise 'ecstasy, rapture,' from Late Latin extasis, from Greek ekstasis 'entrancement, astonishment, insanity; any displacement or removal from the proper place,' in New Testament 'a trance,' from existanai 'displace, put out of place,' also 'drive out of one's mind' (existanai phrenon), from ek 'out' (see ex-) + histanai 'to place, cause to stand,' from PIE root *stā- 'to stand'.

Used by 17c. mystical writers for 'a state of rapture that stupefied the body while the soul contemplated divine things,' which probably helped the meaning shift to 'exalted state of good feeling' (1610s).

—

'If you want to become good at an art you practise every day,' Jean-Luc is teaching us in the Aegean School of Fine Art. I love to hang out with him, his art is so mystic somehow while also being grounded in his body: a wonderful mix of this world and another. He has trained his eyes to see so much more than I can. 'Same with music. Same with any art. Regular practise allows our gifts to be honed in the flow of your art, so that even though most times it's not happening, when the genie does come out of the wall, when the muse impregnates us, when we are connected to creation,' his hands move in an outward expansion, 'it doesn't miss us, but catches us with our brush in our hand, or,' he glances across to me, 'with our instrument to our lips.' He smiles. 'If we are ready, we can allow it to flow through us easily: that is art.'

—

I am walking along the beach with Jean-Luc. 'Wow, look at that colour!' he says. He brings me out of my thoughts into the silence of seeing. Wow, yes. I nearly didn't notice. 'Wow,' I say to him, 'You have such wonderful sight…' I know that he is seeing the world so much more intensely than I.
'I don't think it's any different to yours…'
'I don't know…I don't see like you do. You see colours and textures and can remember colours from the days before and compare…you have such a gift!'
'Ohh I don't think so. It's just a matter of training. Take my dad. He's a perfumier, he can pick out and discern really subtle smells. He doesn't have a better nose, he's just trained himself.'

—

Rolling around on the chapel dance floor in a morning meditation, I wonder: *is the point of life to enter into the world as deeply as we can by honing our senses?* Being a musician I realise that I hear music deeper than others, can pick out sounds more easily, am amazed when people confuse the sounds of different instruments. As I dance with these dancers I see how far behind I am in the expression of movement. I watch Mara taste her food to such a depth, mesmerised by her sensing, my plate empty, gobbled up, barely remembered. Five senses, and more, all for us to deepen our experience of life with.

—

I start to do self pleasuring every day. At first I find it really hard. Something doesn't feel right. A blockage. I need to stay here. I want to stay in sex-less land where it is safe and comfortable. I want to save myself for him. I haven't had sexual feelings for a month. Why would I do it right now, just as _____ [4] and I are coming back together? I want to save myself in this virgin white dress of purity. But I don't, I keep moving through this, struggling out from my programming.

—

Sprawled on my bed, wet, relaxed, satisfied. Thoughts begin to return, slow trains, wisps of ideas. I realise that maybe I should be taking the responsibility of fulfilling my own sexual needs instead of waiting for someone else to do so. Then when we come together we can share freely of ourselves, cleanly without agendas.

But I get worried – could I get caught up in this sexual oasis? How much can I allow into me? Can I create with it, rather than be destroyed by it?

Could I get sucked in, as it takes over my life and I become addicted to wanting it, needing it, as it seeps into all my decisions, creating havoc in my life? Am I strong enough to allow this to be healing, rather than poison? Can I contain it sufficiently so as to create with it, rather than letting it overtake me? How much of the animal can I allow into the china shop of my life?

Despite all the questions, through the clouds of fear I hear its call. It is electrifying. It is life!

—

From my pillow I watch the birds fly over the skylight - a television to the outside world. It begins to sink in that living is about being able to open to the moment, to be able to dive in, to be able to immerse myself in what is, without barriers of the mind telling me what is 'right' and what is 'wrong'; being able to trust in what is happening in my body, being able to trust my senses to lead me rather than what I have learnt to believe - following the path of what is, rather than trying to construct a path from my head. I watch the birds float lazily in the summer air – such simple pleasure in their soaring!

Gazing at a seagull flying across the diagonal of the skylight I begin to realise that so much about life is about being able to connect to It, to be able to take pleasure in the simple that is happening as life unfolds (rather than what we think should be happening) and so bypassing what is 'right' or 'wrong', 'good' and 'bad'. Suddenly no birds, empty sky. I realise that everything, every pleasure, every pain, every object, every experience is a portal to a deeper reality. My body is a laboratory: a huge doorway to deeperness.

A seagull sings a trashy squawk of a symphony. I want to learn to sense more and more. I want to open to what is and in so doing allow myself to open to who I am - including the animal, the shadow parts, so much so that I am able to accept them as much as the parts of me that are easy to accept.

If I practice to be present to what is, down through the eternal spiral of time, I begin to see that I don't need anyone else to give me pleasure, that I can sink myself into the pleasures of simply being alive, the pleasure of my body and senses unfolding into life. I do not need anyone else to bring magic into my life if I am surrounded by it, so that when I come together with someone else, we can each share this that we have collected within: a golden mist of Being.

I realise am able to trust –myself and It - enough to lose control. I decide to allow myself to open up to the sublime.

Sublimation

Let us go to the depths
of our animal instincts
so we may thrash and roar
into exhaustion
until we can no more
but surrender
bursting forth
into the heavens.

PART VI

Real Intimacy

A short chapter on the foolishness
of being caught up in confusing
'deep' with 'deep thinking'.

Letting go

Straight out of the red hot fire
the potato burns her fingers
quick as a flash
she drops it.
Why would you not?

It's 1am. Lucien has just left.
Christopher and I are by the door. You can feel it in the air that we are all as happy as each other to have had a nice night. Three sensitive beings, artists, soft, kind, inquisitive. Somehow we bring out the best in each other, like the conversation we had about competition. It feels like we are a triangulation of astrological planets that works well in the conjunct.

I am however still befuddled by their male communication that I didn't seem to hear, or get into. I feel him wanting to hug and kiss, but I need to process. I push his chest away with my words. I am still feeling on the edge of a dance that I could only watch. 'Sometimes I wonder if I didn't get something, if I just didn't hear, or understand something.' He stands back from the hug, he's still sensitive even when he's drunk as a fart; his body posture says I-am-ready-to-listen. I feel like a little girl in the play ground, it all seems so petty after such a wonderful evening, but it's nagging me. 'Like you when you said 'Wow, Lucien, you're a genius!!' but I didn't understand a thing – did I not get it? What did I not get?'

'Probably nothing to get,' he says honestly, wanting to move on. *Nothing to get in words? Or nothing to get at all. Are there whole worlds that I am kept out of by this incessant thinking?*

—

I think about what Chrispy said at Christmas about his mother. They were watching a typically English, absurd comedy program. The type my brother laughs his head off to while I sit dumbfounded at the idiocy. I just don't get it. It's more than that - I am disturbed by it. 'Mum just didn't get the simplicity of it,' Chrispy says, 'she kept trying, looking for something really complicated.'
'Yeah, I get that - looking for something more intelligent? I really do, I get it - like because she doesn't understand, she thinks it must be something more difficult she's not seeing, not something simpler?'
'Yeah, she kept wanting it to be something more than it was, or something else, looking for something that wasn't there. Getting further and further away from the point of it.'
'So it was harder and harder to get?'
'Yeah, and she kept asking me 'Is it that?' As if I could just explain it to her logically. In the end I wished I'd watched it alone.'

—

I feel relieved. I come out of my prison of thoughts. There probably was nothing to get, nothing to think.

Underneath I still sense I missed out.

Underneath I sense him trying to transmit to me, 'Just whole worlds to sense'.

———

Paul has an allure, a je ne sais quoi. An attractive quiet, strong confidence of knowing, of being in control, of deep wisdom. We'd been travelling around the Greek islands for a couple of weeks, and somehow I'd felt that I couldn't connect to him as deeply as I wanted to, that the conversations, the wisdom, the energy that I wanted to flow between us in conversation wasn't happening. I wondered what I was doing wrong. I was attracted to him, deeply in love with him, and yet felt a disconnection deep down. It felt that if only he could open up to me I could tap into this deep source that gives him so much confidence in life, so that we could enjoy it together. If only he would share whatever it was that was behind the curtain.

At the breakfast table, on the terrace of the hotel in the middle of the dry craggy mountains of Crete, I keep mining. 'What's behind the curtain?!' I say as if in jest. So elusive, so close, I just want to peek, like honey to bees, like paint to artists, like nectar to the emotionally starved. Eventually he cedes, he stops playing the master of the magic trick. He looks me straight in the eyes, 'You want to know what is behind the curtain?' I hear the soft honesty in his voice; I hear he is going to open the theatre curtains for me, to see the set in his inner scenery, to show me the workings, to unveil his mind, his beauty.
'Yes...' I half whisper, feeling myself become lighter in his gaze, feeling myself become so close to him that I hold my breath so as not to move.
'There is...' he says slowly, looking me deep into the eyes, 'nothing.'

———

I'm walking to the shrink's office. I'm never sure if it's a good idea to come here, there is always an edge. *Is that edge me? Is it her?* There is something about her that I don't like. *Is that me projecting me?* It's all so confusing. I mean this is the first time I've done any long term treatment. I liked her well enough as a professor on the masters course; but now, she seems so narrow minded. *Can that be true?* My mind goes on and on. I press the door bell.

'It seems that you are a searcher?'
'Yes.'
'But eventually you will have to drop that idea.'
I feel panic inside. *Stop searching? Like just GIVE UP? No way. No. Why would anyone say that?*
'The thing is,' she says, 'searchers search, they don't find. Eventually you are going to have to stop searching in order to find.' I look at her as if she has just stabbed me with a dagger. 'So you can become a finder.'

———

I swim in Pieter's peace, in the open space of his presence. By him I feel the quality of his soft velvet of genuine sensing, silently being in the world without filters. 'I am just a fool,' he says in his slow, bad English. 'I like to make my life simple.' Each word seems to come up from such a deep place, like an iceberg floating to the surface. I feel like a fly buzzing about, going fast over the surface, only buzzing about theories, never actually landing, never getting into what's at hand. 'It is like you cannot turn off your thinking,' he says with his slow, nourishing compassion as if I were a leper.

—

We are sat in 'Rumours', our favourite restaurant in town. We've asked for the steak deal. His with pepper sauce. Both rare. Red wine. That's the deal. That's our deal. It is our familiar routine so that we can relax into the evening. I'm mining again. 'What I came away with that night...' says Christopher, 'is Lucien saying about the internal gland being on the end of the penis.' He knows that I am still triggered by this vague sense of missing out. *But what?*
'Was there anything more to get than that?'
'Well,' he says, 'No...that's it. The image.'

I listen. I sense. I do not use my thoughts. I do not push mental ideas forward like the Red Queen desperate to get somewhere while getting nowhere. I am not going to get myself into a pant to get to the next point, trying too hard to jump over the void below. I do not want to skim the surface rather than sinking down into something deeper, slower, more real.

I sit in silence. I hold back mental ideas and sense – feel! - I let myself be comfortable being uncomfortable.

Liberated from the race of running off into thoughts, I find it in me to simply listen to this moment, and as I do it opens to me. This here, waiting for steaks. Christopher. Me. Candle flickers. I allow the energy that is here to enter me, rather than pushing it away wanting something else - I leave my 'should' behind in the antechamber. Instead of demanding more and more explanation, more need to understand, it begins to settle into me that there is nothing more than this – *this is it*. This is sufficient. Watching the candle flicker, this dark, smooth, velvet feeling of sitting here with a beautiful man who I love, wrapped in the romance of the situation: it all begins to acknowledge itself in me. I begin to feel it. I am here, I have entered into this moment. My body softens. As I quieten into a greater stillness, I realise how much I had been missing out on clinging to the inside of my ever running mind.

Life is now, taste it. Open to what is around you. I go with it. Sink into it.

After a silence, which I would normally find uncomfortable, as if a whale were surfacing from deep down under, he says in the space the silence made, the space he needed to go down into himself, 'That's it,' his words sound like they are rising out of a meditation, 'it's like the concepts in my head all turned upside down. Like everything changed.'
I look into him, grateful. 'Right...' I say softly, delighted by a glimmer of 'getting it', 'nothing more to 'explain' – more that the images in your head all shifted?'
'Yes, everything shifted. That's it. Nothing more, nothing less.' He smiles into my eyes.
'Nothing more to be said. Nothing more to be analysed. Nothing more to be

understood?' I say, feeling my shoulders go back, my back arch, my head cocking slightly to the side as I lean in feeling proud, feeling sexy. Cheshire cat smile.

'Exactly.'

And we clink our glasses, feeling somehow that something between us has shifted.

———

This is it. There is nothing more than this. This is it. This is life. No rehearsal, it's now.

———

I look up to the trees. I'm walking alone.

I wonder about Christopher and I, about if we will ever have more than hours together, if we will ever spend long periods of time together. I think of the weekend on, weekend off, the children, his job, my hobbies, his hobbies, all of which are barriers to spending time together doing nothing, time being real.

A long breath brings me out of my mental prison and suddenly I see the trees again. This is it. This is now. Christopher and I are this. I am now alone in the trees. Nothing more. Nothing less. Nothing more is necessary. Suddenly I relax realising that there is no mountain to climb. In fact nothing at all to do: only to be alive, sensing who I am, as I am, in this moment, here, now.

I have been missing the fluttering mosaics of leaves in the lime green of the translucent sunlight.

———

And suddenly I realise there is no need to be more.

That which connects us all

The tree listens
accepts what is
without need
nor expectations
asks us to drop our desires
and enter into
unfolding infinities
as it soaks in the luxury
of simply being.

Not Quite a Chapter at All: 'Who I Really Am'

*A stand alone section that didn't really fit
into any other chapter but is probably one
of the most crucial messages in the book:*

**intimacy is the space to fall into
who we actually are.**

Coming into power

Is this really me?
I feel as if I am remembering
who I have always been
instead of this constant hiding.

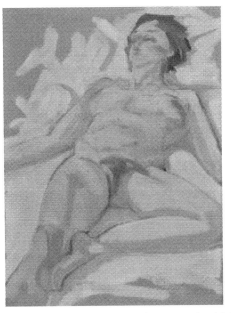

I am slightly snuffling being slightly poorly in bed. A cold is coming on and all the emotions that have been coming up have exhausted me. Greg, the owner of the flat, needs to come around. He's a friend, but this is business. 'Yes, OK.' I text, 'but I'm not up for too much conversation.'

He rings the doorbell. I drag myself out of bed. He has brought lemons. Kind. Sweet. I sit and listen to him. I am being strong, so much so I wonder if there is anything actually the matter with me.

He leaves.

I go back to bed. Slump.

It feels like too much to get changed and go out and shop for lunch. I wonder if Christopher will call, if he will find out, if he will come to the rescue. I realise I am not the old me any longer. I remember that I am OK alone and that I also know how to state my needs. I realise that I do not need to be afraid of Christopher seeing me in this state, weak and pathetic, we have built bridges of light between us so we don't have to be so afraid of the shadows separating us in the eye-less dark. I text, 'I'm a little poorly.' For the first time in my life I don't try and make myself look more poorly than I am, merely to warrant attention. I have the right to be a little poorly and still care for myself. I don't have to be on death's doorstep before I begin to slow into a stop. 'I wonder if you could bring me a pie?' Straight forward. I imagine Christopher happy with the information of knowing exactly what to do.

He replies, 'Awwww, I'll come around at 12.30 with a pie and some TLC.' I burst into tears. All my body goes into the cold flu, my joints ache, the energy drains from my body. With his support and protection I can afford to let myself go. I can release. No need to be strong any more.

Is this intimacy? This no need to 'keep it up'? I don't have to brave with Christopher when I'm feeling not brave. I don't have to be with the social mask on that is acceptable and attractive. I do not have to protect myself from Christopher, he is already inside. Inside my complicated defence systems. Inside the illusion of my social masks of me being perfectly in control of my perfectly wonderful life. Christopher has beaten through the thicket of thorns around my castle: I can respond to him how I actually am - not how I would like to be, or how I would like to be seen. The fact is I simply cannot hold up the imagery with him, he knows how to see through it. He is in the intimacy of my inner chambers, looking at the pale skin of my psyche, the festering wounds that I cannot see - and he is not running away but nursing me. I even trust him enough to dig in the dagger to bring out the puss. This is not Hollywood.

Mirror mirror on the wall

With the others I stand strong
firm, not noticing this
is my public face.
But when you hold me
I collapse
into who I really am.

Moving past the show biz,
through the perfect image,
into a deeper Now.

To be alone

My darling
I feel so whole
walking through
pale green leaves and autumn skies
protected by branches from the rain -
impish joy arises from my dryness!
I savour softness within
as my feet sink into the mud of the earth.
I get close and whisper to the trees,
hugging them I feel my peace
this is my presence
this is how I love...
Alone, I greet myself
less a stranger now
surprised at the delicacy
surprised how far I've come
laughing sweetly
at the simplicity of it all.

As I clean the bathroom sink, a conversation starts up in my head.

I don't really realise I'm even having it as get on with scrubbing. It's almost like listening to a radio talk show echoing through my mind, except the sentences seem to come through in blocks rather than individual words. *It's impossible to 'stay clean',* the voice reports, *simply by living we are dirtying where we are.* I take all the toiletries off the sink. I don't like doing that. Not sure why. Electric toothbrush, toothpaste, soap. I put each one on the closed toilet seat. *Cleaners around the world know it is just impossible that things stay sparkly clean.* Dental floss. Nail brush. Toilet seat. *It's impossible even to not harm.* An image flashes up of monks who sweep the floor in front of them in order to not step on insects and kill them. *Like what Joseph Campbell says,* an image flashes up of a buffalo falling off a cliff, *when he talks about how the very fact of life means that we have to kill to stay alive.* I squirt cleaning liquid on the porcelain sink. *Even vegans eat from fields of grain that have killed local wildlife and habitat.*

I like it when the big bits of grime give way to the white shine of clean porcelain. *It's impossible to get away from harming and killing and dirtying. Ever.* I run the taps and swish the water around. I watch it as if I were a tourist watching a waterfall, half mesmerised, while cleaning off the residue. *It's impossible to be perfect human beings. We'll always eventually step over someone's line and hurt them or dirty the psychic space between us.* I polish the taps, get the sponge right into the difficult bits underneath. It makes me feel like I've really got it together when I have sparkly clean, new-looking taps. *It's not the idea of never being dirty, it's knowing how to clean up after oneself.*

An image flashes of Christopher's grotty bathroom, a place where sponge and cleaning fluids rarely make a star appearance. I feel my body scrunch up a bit. *It really is disgusting. I don't know how he lives like that. It doesn't take that long to clean up after yourself.* I move toothbrush et al off from the toilet seat. *He doesn't clean up much after himself in arguments either...actually...now that I come to think about it...makes a mess and leaves a mess.* I put each of toiletries back onto the sparkling clean sink. *But then there are all those mothers who don't trust their children to make mistakes, over-protecting, devouring their own children.* I imagine a child who is not allowed to swing much in a playground swing, smile half dead. Toothbrush. *Safe, clean, sterile environments.*

I suddenly feel so grateful to have been given the space to make a complete mess of my life. Toothpaste. I remember that argument I had with Melissa in Greece, a full-on heated argument, she was almost stranger then, and how we managed to both sit down at the table, after I had almost walked out, and had the strength of character to talk about what had just happened to us. It's hard to be honest, and own my own feelings. It's hard to fall, after an attack, into unprotected who-I-am being-ness. It's hard to tell her how I actually really feel, as it uncovers, all too quickly, that I am not 'perfect' and she is not all to blame, but to share truthfully how I really feel. Fear. Panic. Realising that I'm doing something stupid and can't stop for fear of a different consequence. My true feelings for her, how I was scared of her. How it reminded me and so triggered me because of situations in the past that have nothing to do with her. Projection. Turns out, through our joint courageous, vulnerable honesty that she had been relating to her mother complex; I had been relating to my father complex. They go hand in glove. Nail brush. Heavy duty critics both of them. Soap. And going through that process brought us together, made us good friends, gave us an unusual level of trust between us. *'Cos of course if we'd gone through that, we don't need to be afraid of it happening again, 'cos if it does we know already we can deal with our tough crap.* I lift up the toilet seat. A sound of something hitting the floor. *And all those moments of reaching rock bottom and getting through it.* I have to lean right in to pick up the dental floss from the floor between the dust by the outlet pipe. Grim. Inside my body goes into a squeam, imagining all the germs around the packaging of the dental floss. I wash it under the tap. *The house where I lived on the side of the mountain in Greece and me collapsing into abject fear and panic for days on end… It gives me strength now…somehow…I know I can do it.* I squirt toilet cleaner around the bowl. *I'm learning how to cope with myself as a flawed imperfect being who is going to mess up probably quite regularly.* Toilet brush around the basin. I feel empowered, I am cleaning the shit off the porcelain without a flinch. Old hand. Years of cleaning toilets in YHAs and mediation centres.

I suddenly realise how far I've come along on my own journey. I've learnt to say sorry when it's due, to own my own feelings, to let others have their own, different versions of events. *I am the only one who knows what it is to be me.* I get the sponge. I like the squeak of clean against the rim of the toilet basin. My hands are a bit sweaty in the rubber gloves. Strangely as I clean my environment I get dirty.

———

Under the water of the shower I realise we do not need to be so fucking scared about going over someone else's line, of invading their space, if we know how to clean up after ourselves. I don't have to be constantly on the alert that I may be hurting someone and so hide behind sterile ideas or safe thoughts of difficult feelings – creating a massive space of hinterland between myself and the world of other. Relief streams up as realisation showers down that it is impossible to stay perfect, even to stay with a perfect image. It is impossible to be a perfect girlfriend. Impossible to have a perfect boyfriend. Relationships are not a fixed, easy 'match' like children playing snap – but a journey. It suddenly feels like a meandering eternal valley of respect, getting close, something happening, being open to find a way to repair a situation, giving space again, becoming separate, going into myself as an individual, returning to relate with other, enjoying, getting close, messing up, giving space…being.

———

We've just been in a tunnel that has great acoustics in Boulder. It was Kieran's idea, to go and make music with whatever we have. Tubes, pieces of garage plastic and empty jars. Harry brought a Hoover handle. I brought my trumpet – I hadn't quite got the plan. It was wonderful, free and terribly exposing: the three of us in a pedestrian tunnel, in the pouring rain, making sounds.

On the outside it just looked like three beings having fun, playing with sounds, but it was not fraught-free, not on the inside. I would get into it, lose myself, only to come out of it again with paranoia, feeling the raw edges of vulnerability. Playing, according to Kerenyi, is only playing when you are not conscious you are playing. The minute you realise you are playing, you become an observer watching play.

A Flash of Eternity

Play is play
till in a funny little blip
our minds tell us:
we are but playing.

Life is life
till stuck in a pose,
we forget to play
the ever changing.

Ohh but when we play!
When we manage
to become
not childish
but child-like
separated no more
from becoming the
the ever flowing
that delivers our hearts into
the secret place hidden within time
- Eternity -
and for a breath-giving instant
we are nothing but our naked selves!

The playing bit was 'awesome'. I felt like we were merging, as if I had become the music, that the music was me. I was the dance and the dancer, we were the dance and the dancers. I felt as if I were in my element. But I would also, more so, come out and observe myself, I would stop playing and observe the play. It was terrifying. Questions wanted to destroy the play: *Is it good enough? Am I being rhythmic enough?* When I did bigger, braver expressions, *Am I being annoying? Am I crashing my own rhythm into what they are doing? Am I missing some sensitivity?*

The questions pushed me to stop expressing myself so much, to listen to the others, observe. I would be listening so much that I couldn't hear myself, sometimes couldn't bear myself. I swing from one fear extreme to the other, like a monkey mind on Duracell: *Am I being too quiet? Am I not putting enough of myself into it? Am I making it dribble into meaningless sound?* And then without rhyme nor reason I would just really get into it, stop thinking, stop feeling, and be there, feeling the sounds we were making, amazed at this experience, amazed at being with two others in this. Forgetting who I am. Amazed as doors swing wide to a different unknown but remembered world. Making love through music.

Kieran had to go and wait on tables so Harry and I chatted just outside the tunnel. I have my car keys in one hand, trumpet in the other. I am ready to go; tired from all the concentrating and waves of emotions. I'm waiting to deliver a yes-it-was-really-nice-to-be-with-you-just-now / how-interesting / well-I-hope-you-have-a-good-week and get into the car. He wants to talk about the pain of a separation from a woman who I don't like. I don't want to know. The woman is the same woman my partner, Paul, grieves over, the one who he was 'polyamorous' with, without my consent or knowledge. It cuts deep: to me he was simply unfaithful. It brings up too much pain. I just don't want to hear how wonderful she is from this other star-struck man. Paul hurt me the way he handled his relationship with her. Paul still grieves it has ended. It's a thorn in my side.

It starts to rain – sudden, heavy sheets. I've not delivered my line, he is mid sentence, I want to be in the car. Alone. 'Let's go into the car,' I shout between the noise of pouring rain.

'False intimacy,' he says as we stare through the sheet of water that has taken over the role of my windscreen, 'is actually something that gets in the way of intimacy.' Harry is judgemental, the type who it is difficult to be normal with. I feel that I have to know everything, to have read every single book and have experienced all there is within his field of vision, else I am not worthy. *False intimacy? What's that?* I brave social rejection: 'What's false intimacy?' 'I read it in a book by [name of person I've never heard of].' I nod a knowing nod. I do. I admit it, even then talking about false intimacy, somehow I can't admit to him I don't know someone, something. 'She says, that false intimacy is when you tell your partner everything that has ever happened to you, everything that you have ever felt, all of the past traumas and pain in your life.'

Phewwiieeeee! Thank god I haven't told him anything about me and Paul! Thank god I didn't explain that I lay for an hour or more with him on the bed last night crying about an abusive relationship I'd had with a woman, ten years ago. I felt as if I were showing Paul my inner wounds, covered in snot. Paper tissues scattered on the floor. I felt I was opening up to him in truth. Showing him my real self. He holding me through my raw expression. It felt reassuring that he cared enough to stay, to listen. The image flips uncomfortably: *Did he or was he stoically 'sitting it out'?*

'Real intimacy,' says Harry, as if he has thought of this himself, 'is when you are able to just be with each other in the moment. And accept it as it is. Rather than trying to make it be something else. It is about being naked and vulnerable with someone else and not running away into dreams or fantasies of the future or talking about the past - but just staying in the here and now, as it is.'
Meanwhile my fingers play with the keys impotently dangling from the ignition. I would really like to not be in this intimate situation with this guy. I don't feel good close to him. His breath smells. I want to drive off and have my lunch.

———

'Do you like his art?' I ask Joseph. He and Christopher have known each other longer than I have.
'Yeah...' he says, glances at me, assessing. I stay perfectly still, and then almost imperceptibly lift my shoulders and eyebrows at the same time. I'm hoping my honest expectancy will open his honest opinion, 'Well...' he says, slowly, softly. His voice is changing railway tracks.

I sit with my '?'

He breathes in; takes the plunge. 'I find he draws ideas of art, rather than art itself.' Got it. Click. Suddenly our whole relationship clicks into place. 'It's as if he isn't expressing himself, but an idea of what he thinks art is.' Months of waiting for a relationship to happen stream through my calendar head, months of yearning for real intimacy instead of us just talking about it, of actual intimacy rather than preparing for it, waiting for the ideas of who we want to become to be made real. I realise, with a sudden blast of icy cold air, we are not a relationship, only a concept of a partnership – in potential – and what potential! But we've never stepped out of the land of ideas. Never got off the map. Never stepped into working reality. I guess it could never live up to what we've got in our heads.

———

On the way home the rain is really hard on the metal roof of the car. 'Wow,' I say to myself out loud, mercifully alone again, 'real intimacy is being able to just be next to each other without freaking out.'

I find it so hard to let go! To just let myself be in the simplicity of the unknown. I'm always trying (fruitlessly!) to control & make things 'safe' or 'right' or 'better' with some sort of idea about how things should be, (where do I get this from? Childhood? society? Films? Parents?) rather than just being in the moment. I tense up trying to make it 'work' (& not who knows what I'm doing unconsciously...)

'Intimate' seems to mean letting myself (alone or together) go into a purer space, naked, unveiled in front of WHAT IS. Being in it. As it is. So easy! And yet I continually cover up, unable to accept what's happening around me – like puttin make-up all over my psyche trying to make me & things appear as I think I should see them – rather than just allowing myself to see what is. How to just relax into what is?

... and is this the inner temple?

Pure.
Empty.
Open.

Ego — a see-through membrane where my past, my fears, my joys, defense mechanisms dreams, even my name ('like Rilke's poem) are left behind like a child leaves behind a broken toy. When I've been there before, it really is 'child's play — but once we are adults it's so difficult to get to!!

Simple is so hard! Unknown so scary!

That Brazilian Guy who gave us a CI Jam warm-up said 'Do not look for contact, nor avoid contact, just allow.'

I do have the courage to surrender.
I want to remember to be free, free from all I think 'I' am.
To just be! To naturally come into contact if & when it arises — & not in some false way because I've made it happen & I want

it to — & then allow the dance to go
where it wants to go: connecting, dancing,
sharing, retiring, re-establishing distance.
A natural flow like all others. I get into
this crazy place where I feel I should be
buzzing in some dramatic 'amazing' high
of intense connection with a partner all
of the time... why???
On top of it all I try to control it, addicted
to that high, blocking any natural rhythm
— and then I'm out of sync! So I feel
I have to control again... to get the
frustration out from not being 'there'
anymore. Blah, Blah, Blah.

Goal: ALLOW MYSELF TO RELEASE — allow
the dance of intimacy to take me & the other
where it naturally flows — & to trust it!
I'm going to just be, & allow space so I can
be surprised by what arises. And 'surprise'
is stuff coming up from the unconscious —
gifts of the unconscious — surprise

because we haven't previously been conscious of it — else it wouldn't be a surprise... ha!

I guess the deal is that the 'surprises' are not all 'wonderful' & 'amazing' images of me, me, ME!

Whenever I get close to someone, I get scared of separating — like in ceremonies with Paul, after that intense intimacy we have to come back to earth — & in the fall out, the fall from Eden — it is like from being whole, harmonious, complete, suddenly I am crashing into splinters of ghastly mirrors: which are also true, and when I've been able to withstand listening to them, show me something essential about who I am (being), & it gives me a truer picture of who I am. But it's scary! Hard. Feels like attack. Why is it so hard to accept my ugly unharmonious bits? I guess this is what

I'm actually afraid of: nice surprise or not?

But whenever I've been intimate with someone & released into the dance of it, when distance has come after great closeness, it has had a sacred flavour, like new space has been created in my/our being — an expansion where I can breathe more freely, that nourishes me.

And, when I've managed to feel the bliss of meeting someone <u>as they are</u> — warts and all! — & have been accepted as I am. there's been a dissolution.

Is this the way to discover my/our natural & simple self?

Recreation
Dissolution
Recreation
Dissolution
Recreation
Dissolution
} Is this 'becoming'??

Yet still the flames of intimacy scare me.
Why?

Where the Truth hides

Simple -
so difficult
to achieve

S   e   p   t   in
D   l   u   t   o   n
          T   u   h
               s   a
                         e
          r   d   p
a   I   l   o
s   s   t   i   o   l
                    n
          t   l   u   t
               o   r
                    n
                    u
               t
               h
s   e   p   r   t   i   o   n
d   i   s   s   l   u   t   n
          t   r   u   h
               s   a
                    e
     l   r   d   p
       a   r   l   o
       a   ti   o   n l   s

298

t   l   u   t

o r

n

u

t

h

s   e   p   a   r   t   i   o   n

d   i   s   s   l   u   t   i   n

t   r   u   h

s

a s

e   t   s   u

r   p   i   o   i   t

i   n

d

i   n

r

t

u

h

separation

dissolution

truth

I am in the car on the way back from playing music in the tunnel with Kieran and Harry. The rain is still lashing down. The metal roof is playing heavy raindrop music at triple forte. Without knowing it we are leading up to the hundred year flood. As the windscreen wipers tirelessly flash clarity onto the blurry world, I drive along Broadway and wonder if it's actually possible to be intimate with someone if I am not intimate with myself. The wipers wish-wash. On the next flash of clear windscreen I wonder if intimacy has anything to do with going to therapists and digging out the old wounds and complexes and fears – wish wash – *though surely that helps to clear the airs?* – wish wash – But can we not just drop it all – like a hot potato that is burning our fingers straight out of the fire? – wish wash – Why do we need therapy if intimacy is in fact the ability to be in the moment – wish wash – without making any mental schemes of what's happening – wish wash – without trying to wrangle the present onto a map of what I've already experienced – wish wash – and can therefore control – wish wash.

Is it simply a matter of being naked, unveiled, allowing – wish wash – of what is in the very moment? – wish wash – Stare into space – wish wash – We don't need a single thing if intimacy is the ability to be right now – wish wash – without dragging in the past – wish wash – without trying to dive into the future. Wish wash. Hands on wheel, concentrating, relaxed – wish wash – I wonder if intimacy is 'simply' being so totally open to the vulnerability – wish wash – of not knowing what is right now – wish wash – and just being in it, becoming it; silently – wish wash – Allowing a certain flow, without judging, without wanting it to be any different from what it is – wish wash – without wanting myself to be any different from who I am – wish wash – Seeing that I need nothing – wish wash – I am simply in this world – wish wash – and that in itself is all this moment asks for? – wish wash.

It continues to pelt it down. Glorious.

Just Being

Being
each time
softer

they fell
inaudibly
into silence.

Deep within
the stillness
magic stirred.

I am in the caravan, livid. He is ignoring me again. Familiar feelings sting through my system. I am too far gone to recognise that they are the same as when I was little. Too livid to realise that I have gone into my father complex.

Outside the Curator Cafe I bump into a friend's friend. It turns out that we are both wondering about what to do with our next half hour. I'm waiting to meet Christopher after yet another argument. I'm ready to say sorry, but I'm still judging, still trying to work out what happened and why. Still working out how we got into this emotional accident that we can't get out, as we drown in the aftermath of all the triggered emotions.

The man has a nervous twitch. I am drained from too many emotions. Doesn't help that it's full moon. 'It's a bit silly to blame everything on a full moon…' I say sheepishly.
'But we are mainly water…and the moon can shift so much tide…why not us?' I feel comforted being able to relax into this partial truth. Feeling accepted even in this head floppy state. I feel like my eyes have been doing weightlifting. We meander on through the 'alternative persons' protocol of light conversation with strangers which include the effects of the moon, consciousness and what it means to be alive on this planet floating through space.

'Have you read Gurdjieff?' he asks,
'No,' I shake my head.
'His writings are wonderful, it's about not caring about outcomes, about not judging events, about letting ourselves see that we are simply consciousness, that everything is consciousness, that we are simply a part of its flow.' I feel into my body. It's reminding me. 'We are not even the observer; the observer is part of the whole. We are simply consciousness. We are beings remembering that we are conscious, that consciousness is conscious.'

I actually love these conversations in _____ [4]. I love being able to just dive into metaphysics without constraint with someone who I barely know. I like sharing and hearing their points of view. It's a bit like a T-group, where it's easy to be more intimate, because it's not really real. We don't go into any emotions, or any personal stuff, because we don't know each other; and yet somehow it feels that we are talking about me and Christopher and all this crap that's come between us. Somehow it feels that by talking without introducing interpersonal emotions between ourselves and others we don't have to tread on egg-shells, worried what the other may think we are implying personally…and so strangely this theoretical conversation goes further into this highly-charged emotional situation with Christopher, more so than if I had asked for relationship advice.

The man with the twitch continues. 'We are not our mind. We are not the residuals of memories of what happened. We are not the residuals of pleasures we have experienced. We are just this now.'

It's so nice to hear someone talk my kind of sense. I feel like I am in Safe-landia. Blessedly emotion free, almost thought free. Clear, open. I observe this man talking, the trees in the sunshine, people milling around, cars slowly going around the round-a-bout. I wonder how long can I stay without any mental crap colouring my view of intimacy and stay in this heightened sensitivity with the world. The trick of consciousness, according to Jung is when you ask someone if they are conscious, they instantly become conscious, at least for the duration of the question, and answer a truthful, 'Yes'. Then we tend to unconsciously slip back into our unconscious habits of seeing our minds infused with a past, futures, dreams, desires, fears, schedules, shopping lists – ranting within, rather than what is outside of our minds. It's so easy to confuse our stories with what is actually happening, to confuse our maps with the ever changing territory of reality.

'So, I'm practising,' he confides, 'hmmmm….' his eye twitches, 'it's hard to put it into words – to be present, to not care about the future, or the past, just to be.'
'Like to surrender to a higher consciousness?'
'I don't like religions,' he says, 'I believe, I don't even like the word 'believe'…I am open to the idea of something, but as humans we really don't need to know. It's like as soon as I say, 'I believe in…' I put it in a box, and then I close it and don't let anyone go near it. I need it to stay as I've left it and so then I don't like people talking about it – they could make it look like it needs to change. It's a sealed off box.'
'Dogma!' I'm so into it, I forget that this man and I have not defined what we mean by our terminology, because, well, we've never had a conversation before. Though it doesn't feel like it.
He doesn't answer straight away. Dogma is such a Christian term. 'I guess…' he cedes.

'I see it like,' I press on, trying to define what I've just said, 'taking a photo of a here-now,' I look around, 'here outside Curator cafe, that dog there, the two people on the terrace, this autumn sun miraculously heating the back of my legs through my trousers,' I give a cheekily smile to this Englishman, 'the tree here starting to turn into autumn oranges, you, me, this conversation…and feeling so good that I want it to happen again, exactly as I have taken the photo. Setting it all up…all over again…wanting it to be the same as I remember it in my mind.'

'Like with a sunset?' his eye twitches again – *Is that something repressed trying to get out?* – 'It's so beautiful, and then we want it to be just as beautiful again. Over and over. The same. No clouds, just the perfect sunset, to feel the perfect emotions all over again.'
A laugh bubbles up through my throat. 'But it will never have that first amazement and surprise of it happening,' I feel twinkles of ironic glee in my eye, 'because we would be expecting it!'
'Ha!' We laugh into each other seeing the same funniness, 'Impossible to repeat!'
'Arising and passing away, arising and passing away…'
'Vipassana?'
'Yes.'
He nods in recognition. A dog barks. The sun massages warmth onto my back. He says, 'Yeah, I'm just trying to be in the moment as it is.'

It feels like some higher consciousness (though this stranger would perhaps tell me that's dogma?) created the synchronicity to meet this man and talk to him about consciousness. It has slowed me down, halting me like some kind of psychic policeman from ploughing into confrontation with Christopher. As I relax into non-control the half hour however goes by so quickly that I am now late for my lunch date with him. The man walks me, as briskly as I can push him in tandem, up the high street to Tangerine Cafe where Christopher is probably waiting. Outside it's hard to stop talking. Hard to stop sharing. He reaches into his bag, shows me the book on Gurdjieff that he's reading. I make a mental note of it and instantly forget.

'I don't want to keep seeing the same sunset,' I say, 'but it would be really nice to talk again.'
'Yes,' he says shyly, nervously. And we part our ways.

I never see him again.

But even so, somehow, by just trying to be more present with this man, if only talking through it together and feeling the tingling excitement of simply being and sharing in a non-judgemental space, in a place that is clean and fresh because we have no history together, I feel a connection to him, as if we have been someplace together. Supped from the same source. Something glowing inside feels I have shared the waters of an intimate experience with this stranger.

———

Inside the cafe, Christopher and I sit in silence. I am trying to simply be present. No judgement. No working things out. Just flow. I eat my meal in silence. It is OK. It's not so scary. Eventually I ask, 'How was Plymouth yesterday?' It is my peace offering.
'Yes, good.' It takes him a while to struggle out of his defensive silence. He tells me about the facts and details of his trip. Dry meta-information. He enjoyed himself. We fall back into silence. After a few gulps he offers, 'I don't know how to start.'
'Start what?' I ask hopefully.
'Talking about us.'
'Well,' I say as softly, evenly as I can, 'you could tell me how you feel.'

It soon goes into a warfare of who did what, when, how. I feel attacked. I defend. He sends sling shots of words. We are in the mind. Mind crap. Trying to solve the faulty mind with the faulty mind. 'You don't listen to me, you don't want to hear my version of events, you just tell me…I have no voice.' His words are like a battering ram. I feel our ideas covering over, shielding, from what is really going on.
'Tell me how you felt.'
'You will just attack.'
'If you throw insults at me, I will defend,' I say, something inside, miraculously, keeping my voice calm, 'but if you express your feelings they will be heard and held.'
'So you are the dictator now? You tell me when to express myself?'
I breathe in, sucking in air silently. Pause. Breathe out. 'Just if you want to. If you want, tell me how you feel, how you felt, how it was for you?'

I am getting tired. He feels it. He swallows. I see him quivering inside, he's scared, he plunges in, 'I felt...'

He tells me how he actually feels, from his heart. It is actually all about him. It is totally non-threatening to me. Strangely I am hardly involved. I see him, a human being, struggling with this monster called intimacy, of his fear of his dark inner world being brought out into the light. Fear of rejection by others. Terror of being seen. I too am afraid to be seen as I am. I too am afraid to leave behind the trappings of social approval. As I hear him expressing his truth, my anger dissipates, disappears. My heart softens. I open up again to my true feelings for him and as I do I feel love.

Seeing only what is Not

I

Fir tree
everything but green
I see only
the colours
you cannot absorb,
only what you are not.

II

Lover
I see only
what I can:
through the I glass
into you?

III

It is not you,
I see-through
me.

*Tennis lessons on letting go of the excuses
and accepting ourselves as good enough.*

When Perfection is a damp cloth

She never went to the beach;
she needed the perfect weather
the perfect timing
the perfect mood
to be able to
enjoy it perfectly.

'You look beautiful'. 'You are amazing'. 'You are so intelligent'. If they say those things, and it's easy to say a few easy words, I'll hang on like a little pig on a suckling machine. I'll create fun things to do, cook for them, make presents for them, write them poems, tell them wonderful things about them, ignore and become blind to anything that is not wonderful, and amazing and great. I'll even give them my body though they are not listening to mine. I'll do anything to be reassured that I am good enough. I'll do anything to not be rejected.

Instead:

We are sat at Christopher's table, he has made me a romantic meal. The meat was tough. The energy was soft. I feel myself swirling in love where impossible-to-chew steak is of no import. He leans towards me and takes my hand, his face flickering in the candle light, and says, quite matter-of-factly, 'You are amazing.' I feel myself rising, my ego puffing out, I hold it back. I and me can easily run wildly out of control. 'You said that,' he continues, 'and I am.'

I reel back in the kitchen chair as if I've been hit by a stun gun. Could he seriously, like really, really have said that?

My narcissist radar goes into violet alert. I get scared.

—

'You're A-maze-ing': The Doorway to Narcissism.

How long before they realise it's not true?

How long until they find out I'm just a human?

How long before I turn, in their eyes, into 'Bitch from Hell?'

—

We are lying on the uncomfortable bean bags in my one roomed palace. It is a bright summer afternoon. He declares, amazed at us being together, 'You're perfect.'

I gulp. I know I am not.

This is dangerous territory of inflated ego talk. I want to swim in it, cover myself in the shiny stars of his projection. I want to believe in it, but time brings with it experience: do not accept projections.

'I'm not…' I say as sternly as possible, 'you're going to have to get used to that.'

But still, I can't help but feel titillated with the flattery.

My bad.

———

Another time at the end of a bottle of wine, leaning over his kitchen table he says, his eyes ablaze with wonder, his tongue waxing lyrical, 'You're amazing… really,' with a sort of desperation that smacks of him needing me to believe him, of him needing to believe him, 'you're a genius.'

I just so want to pick up his words and swing that co-dependency round my neck with honours. I smile. I don't respond. That's the best I can do.

I want it to be real.

I don't realise this is the start of his image of me beginning to crack.

When enough is not enough

We lost the glory
of the moment
trying to make it
Glorious.

His accusations are so wild that I cannot take them seriously. He is wildly missing his mark. I am old enough to know who I am and who I am not, and just because I have written about a paedophile, doesn't make me one. I cannot be forcing him into a conventional life, and at the same time haranguing him to live an adventurous life. I cannot one day be the person motivating him to rise in his career, and the next one putting his job and his life and his children in jeopardy.

With his inept reasoning he is skillfully pushing me away out of this bubble of being so happy together.

———

Sadness lingers under my feet like a dark lake just behind the evening mist. I am losing track of where land is.

———

Huge relief sweeps through me as I read[8] about how when 'active avoiders' get frightened enough, nothing is sacred. They will hold back on nothing, dashing to get out of intimacy, and will grab any excuse to flee, such as your values, ethics, hair colour, body size, how you interact with others, how you walk through life, your house, your pet, your family, your religion, your car, your habits, your past, your future, your psyche, your father, your mother, your sisters, your hamster, your choice of fashion, the programs you watch on television, your lack of money, your expenses, your bulging back account, your choice of holiday, your profession, your photo of when you were young, the thing you said on the first date by mistake…the 'fault' that the active avoider is using as their emergency exit is often intrinsic, something that they must have known, without a doubt, when the relationship began. Active avoiders know that you are tall and slim or short or fat before the first kiss or if you have different skin colour, or come from a different country or culture or family mould. The point of the fault finding ad infinitum is not to create solutions but is being used for one definite aim: to create distance in the relationship.

———

I begin to realise that this situation is so bad it is good for me. Christopher with his wild allegations is showing me – nay teaching me! – how to not take on another person's projections of who they think I am.

———

Christopher cannot take intimacy. Cannot take real. It's all OK while he's being super romantic…but he can't hold it up for more than an evening. I think back over the last nine months…we have only spent one whole weekend together. He's always had commitments. Phobia of intimacy. Phobia of being seen for real.

I keep telling myself: it's not personal.

———

Making a short-cut passed the Co-op on the way to tennis I realise that actually I will never be good enough for Christopher – ever. I've entered too many relationships hoping the other will change. I've changed too many times in relationships to try and make it work, trying to mould myself into his version of who he wants me to be…but people don't change. I've waited for years at the bus stop of hope. It never comes. Or hasn't yet. He's going to find fault with all sorts from now on.

———

I will never be good enough for him.

This is not personal.

———

Realisation: this has nothing to do with me.

Result: billowing relief.

———

As I walk across the car park behind the Co-op I realise that when I said to myself sat in the Curator cafe yesterday that Christopher and my Dad are so similar – embarrassing social skills in public, trainspotters, narcissists – I have a choice here: do I still want to be dating my dad energy?

No, actually.

In the sudden, temporary freedom from that inner figure, I gain enough distance for it to dawn open in me: I will never be good enough for my Dad.

It's not personal.

Result: relief. The opened dam(n) pours out enormous streams of billowing relief.

I suddenly realise that *whatever* I do in life, I will never make him be the healthy, engaging, supportive dad that I imagine. It's not possible. I will never feel accepted by him. It is not punishment because I have not been good enough for him. Whatever is inside Christopher when he starts on about how I am ruining his life, is inside him too.

—

It's not personal.

Believe it!

Actually I have done nothing wrong - really. I am OK as a person - really. I am OK as a girlfriend - really. I am an OK daughter…really.

—

I really am good enough.

—

I shift.

—

I feel my life suddenly opening up: I can do what I want to. Sans judgement. Rather than attempting all of the time to be brilliant in order to get somebody's attention (that I will never get), I can just be me (rather than trying to be someone else that won't be accepted either). In knowing that background of non-acceptance will not change whatever I am, wherever I am, whatever I am doing – and that I am powerless to change it – I have the power to chose to be whatever I want to be for *myself*. Really. I am good enough for me. Really truly, honest to god and hope to die.

I don't have to be anything more than I am, right now.

Walking down the pavement I feel my tennis racquet swinging against my back. I've started to walk with a bounce.

—

On the court I forget everything else but the game: that's why I love tennis.

'Sorry!' I shout on nearly every warm up ball. I'm under this false illusion that I would normally never do such imprecise shots. I tut under my breath. 'Normal' in my fantasy world is me being totally on the ball powered by skillful grace.

In the game it's my turn to serve: the shot goes wide. 'I wasn't concentrating,' I say, 'I've really got to get my mind in.' My partner maintains silence. I fuck up the next shot, 'Sorry,' I say projecting my voice over our side of the court, 'my racquet slipped…' My partner maintains silence.

We win the next point. 'Fifteen–Thirty!'

My shot goes into the net. 'Fifteen–Forty!'

'Footing,' I explain, 'my footing,' as if reprimanding myself for such a simple error.

A flash: *you are not accepting yourself as you are. You are making up excuses the whole time.*

First serve. 'OUT!'

I can only do what I can do.

My body relaxes. I serve. I rally without trying to be brilliant. We win the point 'Thirty–Forty'. These excuses have been clouding my concentration. *Just forget what has gone on before. Be just now...* I whisper inside to myself, rallying myself on.

'Deuce!'

'Your van!'

'Game.'

(that really happened).

———

Howard is serving, I'm at the net. The sun is just wonderful on my back. It's a joy to be out. I am trying not to mull over what just happened, I'm trying to have a clear mind and just be on the game.

An image flashes through of me in my life: *me studying psychology all of my life, trying to explain away my behaviour. Trying to explain why I never became the superhero my dad was expecting me to be. Explaining away with all my theories why I am now forty and have no job, or career, or house, or car, or stable partner.*

Through the image I realise I have been living off very clever, intelligent excuses so that I will never have to accept myself as I really am. It's all a ruse: a smoke screen I've created to prevent me from having to see myself: bog standard me. A ruse so that I can keep believing in this super human woman who is amazing and intelligent and wise and will eventually get the recognition and love she deserves from someone (or even just from the world at large) for who I am being.

It is a trick: putting all onus on the outside to give me what I need on my inside.

It is a ruse to not have to love myself.

Going Cold Turkey on Perfectionism

There is no perfect life,
there is no perfect place,
there is no perfect you;

forgive,
accept,
relax.

'Sorry!' A ball hurtles down the side of the court. Should have been mine. I wasn't concentrating on the game. 'I wasn't concentrating…sorry.' Now I mumble to myself, *I don't need to keep making excuses. I am good enough.*

I pass back a ball that's in the net. My brain continues with images and flashes that say: *it's easy to say, holding a psychological map, that it's difficult to go out into the world if your dad is slightly Asperger's, narcissistic or even just socially impaired. It's much easier saying it, than actually trying to go out into the world. It's much easier thinking about why you are not writing than actually just sitting down and writing. Actually doing it! Actually risking it! Much better to say, 'Sorry!' with the idea that normally, under other circumstances, I would have done the perfect shot, or written the perfect book. This world is not ideal. This world is not fair. This world is not a photoshopped magazine. This cover up of 'Sorry!' is a self deceiving code that emits I-am-not-this-who-I-am-now: I-am-much-much-better. Unbelievably better. Unbelievable. 'Sorry!'*

———

Excuses!

———

Accept yourself, as you are!

———

I remember Santiago Rodriguez talking about perfectionism, 'The point is not wasting all your energy on trying to do one test (of life) so super perfectly that you exhaust yourself getting top marks; the idea is to pass well enough to be able to open the next door and have the energy and will to walk through it.' I imagine myself walking through a labyrinth, opening a door, walking through. Once through the door it makes no difference how well you went through it. 'Five out of ten is good enough,' he says. *Five out of ten?* Wow, *Yes!* Five out of ten is good enough if it opens the door to where you want to go.

———

It is Pau's turn to do a presentation in our little Jungian's study group: The Junkies. Us, the geeks who spend our spare time getting together to read text books on psychopathology. 'OCD is something I've been through,' he admits, 'I remember once making a meal for all my family and friends, fifteen people. I did nine different courses. I drew out each plate beforehand so I would know exactly what it would look like. I had all the timings down in a list. I knew exactly when to put something on to boil, while also grilling something else. Afterwards, when it was over, I sat down at the table with everyone. They all said how *rico*, how delicious, it had been. Afterwards when everyone else was relaxed, stomachs full, chatting around the table, I stopped to eat my (cold) food,' he puts brackets around the 'cold' with a tone like a comedian, seeing it's post hoc ridiculousness, 'so I didn't really engage that much - and then they all went. I hadn't really talked to anyone.' He looks around the table at the seven of us, 'It took me years to realise that I was missing the point.'

———

Pau continues, 'With forty percent of the work, you get seventy percent of the results. Double your work effort, to eighty, and you get eighty percent of the results. Go to ninety percent, pushing yourself, exhausting yourself, and the percent rises by increments, you get – let's say – eight-five percent.' I have never ever even considered this. 'It's just not worth trying to be perfect,' he says, 'I mean you can do it, but you lose so much in the rest of your life, it's just not worth it.'

———

I decide I am not going to make any excuses after I play badly. I am just going to stay in it, in the feeling of having lost a point. It's an uncomfortable soup, but it's not *so* awful. I can let myself feel it. I'm going to accept that I will not win every single point, because no-one actually ever does. I'm going to drop all impossible goals. I'm not going to keep excusing myself for being a normal, average, tennis player.

Filters off.

I am just, god-damn-it, going to enjoy playing tennis.

———

Safe mental maps vs. the raw emotions of reality. Where will the ball land?

———

Athena, and her warrior courage, cajoles me into dropping my image of myself.

Nothing happens!

The others have been seeing me all along.

I was only hiding from myself.

———

'I just don't believe that we are here for anything special,' says a beautiful stranger to me as she sips on a G&T. The two of us, strangers, are making forced conversation while our respective friends flirt. Out of the corner of my eye I see my friend lean forward towards the man and blush. I turn away from the emotional spying: 'What is it that you do?' I ask, trying to start up a conversation.

'But when you are anesthetising people,' I say twisting my tongue around the word, 'do you see they are going into 'another world'?' the conversation with this beautiful stranger is getting more interesting.

'They often come around and say, 'Wow that was beautiful.''

I'm not really getting where I was wanting to go: I want to go into the other world with this woman who works on the edge of it every day.

'And you see people die?'

'Yes,' she says, as if it were a dangerous topic that has led her into difficult places with people who can't take it.

'Does that make you live more, being so close to death all of the time?'

'No, not really. I mean, I can only do my best, sometimes in A and E it's impossible to save people. It's my job to be there. Often I'm the last person they see before they die,' I look at her oval face, at her dark almond eyes, feel her serene energy and think that she is really, really well placed to take that role on.

'Wow, that's a powerful place. You are doing such good in the world!'

'I don't think my actions make any difference at all.'

'Wow,' I say again. I'm sort of running out of vocabulary. I'm not used to talking to someone who is so logical.

She is so straight with the world. It is what you see. Filters off. I have all these layers that I put on top. Theories. A Need to Understand. A Need to Feel that I Make a Difference. Espuma. Froth. She looks straight at me, calmly. Takes a sip of her large G&T.

In her serene gaze I panic, how to respond? 'Do you know about holograms?'

___

On the tennis court I suddenly realise that I have been living in a fantasy romance all of my life. The doctor woman who I met in the Barrel House the other night was right. You just get on with life. Just do the job, no filters needed. No need to be anything more. There is no great reason for or against doing it. Just because it is meaningless doesn't mean it's meaningless.

All this extra decoration I've put on top, all this froth on my reality, all these ideas about who I am based on my own self created mental, psychological maps, suddenly seem so infantile. I've become a walking excuse for not being me.

___

What do you do if you pick a hot potato out from a fire and it's burning your fingers?

Drop it.

___

I miss a ball. I say nothing. I feel like an idiot. My face tingles. *what is that anger? Embarrassment? Fear of ridicule? Fear of rejection?* All I know is that my face is tingling and I have just missed. I realise that I can drop all of this complicated psychology that I'm carrying around as a shield of excuses like a hot

313

potato, just drop it without thinking – let it drop unceremoniously to the floor – and accept instead the tingles of my flawed present state, my errors, things that just happen: not winning, not being brilliant. I don't need excuses. I did a crap shot. Take it on the chin. Don't pretend otherwise. It's not that big a deal.

—

'Sorry!' I hear myself over and over again. Reaction. It's a tick. It's going to take a while to get it out of my system.

Attachment

I watch the tree
drop its past
in glorious red leaves;
I try too
but end up
clinging to them
withered and dry.

I don't need to accept Christopher's bad behaviour, just because his mother rejected him twenty-eight years ago. He is treating me mean.

I do not accept meanness.

Not anymore.

I will not explain away why he is not respecting me with the excuse of a well-mapped theory I've complied out of his complicated psychology. Spider webs of complexes.

It's like playing the *Monopoly Game* with someone who refuses to roll the dice.

If he can't do it, he can't do it.

End of story.

—

In the next group of four Tom asks me if I would like to be his partner. I like English tennis, it still has all those antiquated polite mannerisms about it. A lady is propositioned. The gentleman serves. I like Tom. He's good fun. Plays well. He serves first, of course. The first game goes to deuce. Our advantage, deuce, our advantage, deuce. Together we keep battling on. We win a point, 'Van In!' A short lob comes over the net, he rushes in, volleys it, smashes it down the line. It is perfectly on the line. It is a perfect shot. It is our game. I turn around to him in a flash, feeling on fire. We high five, 'Champions!' Big toothy cheeky grins.

Next game, though we are now champs, it also goes to deuce. It also goes backwards and forwards, advantage to you, advantage to us, advantage to you, advantage to us. We are on their advantage. He hits the ball down the line, it is

314

centimetres out.

We turn around slowly to each other, we are miserable losers. We barely look at each other. Heavier steps now.

The games keep going to deuce. So equal it is exciting – and yet we make ourselves feel like losers or champs each game when what's between that great chasm of polar self images is basically the same shot a couple of centimetres either side of the line.

The difference between feeling high as a kite or heavy as lead - is minimal.

Once we eliminate comparison, does it even exist?

———

I think about how easy it is to be turned to stone in petrified fear of failure, when it is not so far from success.

———

I think about life. About how easy it is in a difficult part of a relationship (with myself, or with another) to just brush stroke the whole thing as a complete loser of failed misery. How easy it is to say how wonderful a relationship is when it is going well! How easy it is to forget that they are basically the same, a hairbreadth between an emotion in the tick box and a cross out in the cold.

———

In the big picture, are we all existing in this tiny bandwidth called being human?

———

As I shake hands with the winners it does however shimmer through my mind that those who are better players 'funnily enough' do tend to have better luck down the line.

———

I'm staring out from the top of the toilet wall in the dusty monastery. This is improv. In improv, usually, something happens. Right now it is not, and hasn't been for fifteen interminable minutes. We decided to not even talk to each other before doing our installation, so that we'd have no idea as to the other's plans, so it would be real, sharp, improv. But Nirvan, my improv partner, has managed to disarm all of my props and story line by showing them to the audience. I am caught with nothing.

Words that normally flow so easily out of my mouth seem to have converted into white noise in my head. Empty void. I am retreating to far within. He's just said to me, 'This isn't happening like when we normally talk.' He's a metre away, jammed into the corner of the ceiling and the toilet divider.
'Well....' I look into his eyes, deep panic shuddering through my system, *what to say?* 'it's because,' clammy cold sweat damp all over my body, 'of them'. And nod my head sideways.
'Who?' he asks.

'Them…' my stomach lurches knowing that I am about to turn my head and face my fears. I look at them. Fifty eyes look up to me. Expecting. Wanting something to happen, urging us on onwards and upwards. My head is jammed on the fluorescent light of the ceiling. It cannot get higher than this; or flatter. Every word falls like silent lead, not even crashing: not even that to hold on to in these stormy heights. Nothing to jam against. Thin air.

I meet everyone's eye, gaze for an eternity of seconds into each one. *Am I projecting fear, or do they too feel sick to the stomach too I might chose one of them in a desperate attempt to create something, anything?* I look out from deep within, connecting with nothing but the sweat around me; unsure, vulnerable, wordless, clueless.

I am burning with consciousness of what it is to be me right now. Prickly sweat. Hands the size of bears'. Blank. Breathing is an issue. I sit, silently, allowing myself – because I have no other idea of what to do – to be totally and utterly scrutinised. I just sit there. They are looking at me in this state.

Perched high on that wall as I peer, with my heart in my mouth, down into the crowd I suddenly realise, 'I can deal with this.'

Sat burning on that white, toilet divider wall, faced with zero, being witnessed by so many people being inept, I realise that I am dealing with this that is occurring here-now. It is like a difficult meditation, holding it, being here, observing. Though my body is in a sweaty, clammy, tense state of near collapse, though I feel the gaze of all those eyes boring into my skin, I am staying present. I feel strength in a background awareness: this now is not forever, it will pass. All things arise and pass away. I stare back into all those eyes, swinging my legs inanely. Softly, as realise that inside I am actually quite calm, I feel myself breakthrough. I am being witnessed failing: failing to produce, failing to be witty or wise or stir even a small pot of imagination. Failing with huge amounts of eyes on me. The result? I can take it. And I can take it again, if need be, and worse.

———

After the 'performance' Nirvan and I check in. 'How do you feel?'
'Like a failure.'
'Me too.'
'But I'm OK with that I guess.'
'Me too,' I laugh in the simplicity of it all.
I breathe out.

That is not now. It's over. We can move on. No need to hold onto what is not any longer. In that warm balmy Catalan summer night I stop sweating.

———

The power of it! The power of having stayed emotionally sound through the abject storms of nothingness! Staying firm within my centre faced with so much meaninglessness. I feel a well of courage to do it again. It can't get worse (can it?) and if it does, I know now I can deal with it.

It's only failure.

—

The last game of the day is a mixed again. The other woman is white haired. One of those women who reaching old age wants to be admired and so brings up conversations for us to say how young she looks still. Today she's in a bad mood. I can tell. She's trying to sweep us into her darkness, into her anger over something I have no idea about, nor want to know. I don't go there. She keeps missing her shots. I can feel her tension rising. Half way through she blazes out, 'What kind of game is *this*?!!' Somehow I feel blamed, as if we aren't being good enough opponents, even though we're 2-0 up. 'It's the wind,' I say, 'it's hard to get used to.' *Why I am trying to bail her out? Why I am trying to make it better for **her**?* She continues swinging her bad mood across the net. With each good shot we do, she scowls more. She is barely hiding rage. The three of us, safe in numbers, ignore it.

From the safe distance on the other side of the net, I realise that people who cannot control, nor accept, their own emotions try make others do it for them.

I suddenly realise what bullying is.

—

'It feels like I'm in a battle with a bully,' Christopher says angrily, as he speeds the car down a really narrow country road. I don't like going so fast. Devonian hedgerows blur in the side windows. From the passenger seat I am telling him that I do not want to be badly treated. I am telling him I would like to work through this with him. I am telling him that I do not want to be responsible for him not being able to deal with strong emotions such as this happiness that is surging up between us. I tell him I don't want to be shouted at when he cannot deal with his own feelings.

—

When it is good it is so good. *Why does he not want that to work?* 'You expect me to be someone I am not,' he continues, moaning, foot on the accelerator. *Is that true?* I feel that I am beginning to see and love him as he is; the reality of his foibles and faults and ugly bits. Is he complaining that I'm making him be more real?

Stripped Naked

Mirror, mirror
on the wall
who is the fairest
of them all?

Mirror, mirror on the wall please can I change the question?

How to I return to the ugliness of being human after seeing myself in Love?

Christopher is not perfect. Christopher is not amazing. Christopher is not my shining prince.

I see it.

This is what I have been trying not to see for the last nine months: messy feelings.

I am slowly accepting him as he is. As I see him. Non perfect.

As I begin to see, he is forced to as well. He refuses to admit his feelings.

Instead I am now 'the bitch'.

—

I stumble upon a realisation thanks to the white haired tennis player sending me dagger eyes through her crow's feet because of the perfect shot I've just placed down the tramlines. To my playground glee it zoomed right past her and her racquet. She wants me to feel bad because she couldn't return it. But I don't have to be bullied by her emotions. She turns heel, back to the serving line, it is almost dangerously comical. As she scowls I realise that Christopher does this to me too, but instead of tennis rallies, we play emotional rallies. He too shoots me daggers whenever he cannot manage his emotions.

I realise, as she groans picking up a tennis ball as if a martyr: Christopher is an emotional bully.

—

Dad can't handle his emotions – I've taken that on all my life. I feel bad about not being able to have an intimate relationship with him, about not being able to talk to him about anything that he is not in complete control over, as he monologues about trains, or football, or the weather. I will never get through his castle wall defence. I can only scratch myself on the thorns.

I feel bad that I never made him proud.

—

Her arm is behind my leg left and I'm moving up her body. In my head I imagine myself becoming a human ball, light enough to be held in her arms. I roll out, knees over my head, slowly. I feel like a star bursting. She follows and as our faces meet, she says, 'You're a good dancer.' I presume she's reassuring me because I've told her that dance puts me in my uncomfort zone. I don't feel like a dancer, and less so in this artist residency that turns out to be a dancer's residency. Nevertheless I am shocked at what she says. *Good?*

I slow down, get awkward. *This?* She slowly moves onto my back. I hold her weight, feeling it go down my legs into the earth. It takes a lot of untwisting of inner worlds before I can say, 'Thank you.' *Wow.* A new self image sends trickles of warmth up through my spine. She slips back to the floor. I realise I don't need to be awkward. In this new self identity I roll beside her catching her arm and slowly pull her towards me. 'This week,' I say, staying grounded, 'I've been working on 'good enough'.

'Aha,' she rolls over my stomach. So graceful.

'And not being good enough!'

'Aha!'

'Which is actually, also fine.' I get a flash of being on top of that lavatory wall, sweating. 'Yes!' she says, laughing.

I feel her stomach muscles laughing on top of mine. I'm not doing anything special. I can't do great moves. But I can be here. Be me. And right now, in this human closeness, it really is more than enough: I'm loving it.

—

Time to drop the potato.

A real gift for life

After a long fight
with who she isn't
she re-emerged
with a thread
to weave into the fabric
of the world;
alone with no one to see
she simply
began.

PART VII

Undoing

Deciding to stand up and step out of drowning
in imagined fears of what is happening anyway,
without our control, so to be able to accept that
we are unable to change a blasted thing and
learning to be kind about it.

No sex

Lazy Sunday
sheets twist
our soft warm bodies
into a plait of limbs,
fingers travel
through our valleys;
his breath so close
it tickles my ear.
We whisper a pact
'Let's stay conscious.'
Stroking close
it doesn't take us
where we want to go.
Does not.
The ego cries
feels left behind.

He stands at the door, a man with a brilliant mind, confident in what he is doing. He has gone out into the world and declared his worth, has client waiting lists jam packed for months. I opt for a polite question since he's barely an acquaintance. 'How's your day?' I know he's a acupuncturist. How do days go for people like him who make good money healing others? A pause, narrowly dramatic, '…We nailed the d*v*rce.'

We are in the flat above his, in William's pad. *Have I heard right?* I am treading carefully sat in this beautiful old English building, five centuries old. I laugh at the way he's just come out and said it. He likes that. I find myself looking only at the comforting black beams holding up the ceiling. *How is it between them now?* 'Was it amicable?' I ask eyes travelling to the carpet as I try to draw the line between soft and emotionless matter of fact.
'Two years back we had a divorce party…'
I look up. 'How did that go?'
'We had a massive row.' He looks down.

Strange glimpse into the wilds of this almost stranger's intimacy. Vulnerable silence. I wonder if I should say something, anything to not fall further into it, to try and find a ladder back to the surface. I break the fall, 'Of all aspects in a relationship I think how we leave is the most important,' I look at him, *is this an OK direction to take?* I can't tell. *Should I keep going?* 'Like, yeah sure how we get into it, and how it goes while we're in it are also important, but how we leave is how we remember it.' I look at his hands grasping the edge of the kitchen surface as he leans his body onto it. Not sure where he's at. Nervously I continue bridging the silence. 'We can destroy so much in hasty retreats, rip all those memories to shreds.'

—

Stella's sat on the other side of the cafe table with a cafe con leche. She's come over to my barrio and we're in an over-lit, over-tiled bar on Calle Aribau, inside because it's winter. She has a brilliant mind – emotional rather than academic – coupled with low self esteem: my generation. I feel her sensitive heart that cannot accept herself as she grasps onto reasons for living. She's just flirted with the barista. It makes me want to touch her breasts too. *Wonder what they feel like?*

She wants to fix men, to heal them; they mess with her because she can't see herself, can't see the gorgeous woman that she is. She gives her power away, needing to be validated by someone other than herself. How to get it past those beautiful blonde curls that they need her more than she needs them? Or, to put it more precisely: she really does NOT need them – at all. She's best without abusers. 'It's leaving that's important,' she says, to me, to herself.

She tells me about her friend, who is English. She has a flat in Barceloneta. I imagine those narrow fisherman streets, the cheap fish place, the small rooms; claustrophobia contrasting with knowing you're so close to the open sea. To help pay the rent she got a flatmate in, a Catalana. Over time it became unbearable. *Insorportable.* Stella tells me the story doused in her wonderful wisdom. It was really difficult for the English woman to live with all the little details that came through like weeds sprouting out from the Catalan woman's rotting psyche: tuts, murmuring comments - a sludge of heavy judgement that never seemed to shift from the air.

At ten thirty one night she came into a reunión, a soiree that the English girl was having in her lounge, and spat out to the little group, 'You all have to go now. I go bed. I work tomorrow.' Storms out of the room. Bangs the door. Yet another outburst. Tantrums over split milk. *No lo puedo creer.* In the breath between her story I notice Stella has rings under her eyes. My mother hen wants to know *has she been looking after herself?*

She continues telling me the story: the English woman has had enough, 'I think we should talk.' The Catalana goes berserk, because she knows, consciously or not, what's underneath the sentence. She smells her own weeds. 'You are just a DADDY'S GIRL!!!' she shouts, insides ablaze in yet another paper fire, 'You have this house,' she spits out, 'NOT for your own merit! You go BACK TO ENGLAND!!! Leave us in PEACE!!!!' Stamps her foot, stamps some more. Waits for a reaction.
The English woman says evenly, 'When you are ready, we should talk.'

Next day, the same: tantrum.
'When you are ready,' the English woman says calmly, holding herself and her emotions, 'we should talk.'

On the third day the Catalana comes down the stairs and says, 'I do not think this is work out. I think I must to leave this house.' The Catalana goes, closes the door pointedly, but quietly – a message in itself. The English woman sensing it is coming to an end feels nothing but relief – it is over.

Needy

She tumbles out of herself
her emotions spilling chaotically
out from the overcrowded bus
asking me, an innocent passerby,
to tend to all of them
as if I were not a person
but a vehicle for her
to sponge up the spillage.

We laugh. We like that the English girl wins. Catalans can really get up your pyjama bottoms, especially with us being constantly in the minority. It's just good to get a little boost, to know that we don't always have to be the ones adapting to someone else's culture. I look down into pattern of brown circles around my coffee cup. Cafe con leche time has finished. But we haven't.

'And then there was a time when I was working for a woman child-minding her kids,' says Stella. She's on a roll. I feel the coffee cup. I like feeling its warmth, especially on cool winter evenings. But it's gone cold. *I wonder if we should get something else?* 'She started treating me like shit.' I can imagine: Stella lets people do that. Doesn't stand up for herself. 'I didn't stand up for myself,' she says, I love the honesty between us, 'but we had a contract for me to work till the end of that month – and there was still a week to go.' *Ohh I do love you Stella. What is it that I love about talking with you?* 'If I had gone she would have been in the shit. What to do with little children and no nanny? I stayed – though I'm sure most people would have gone...' She stares as if focusing on a far off point, 'I guess really I should have...' And then as if remembering herself, as if remembering who she is, says, 'I did it for the children.' I feel the tender mix in her between left over feelings of trauma from the nasty woman and a real connection with the children. 'But do you know? She didn't want even to pay me properly!'

'What?'

'Yeah, I know! She did in the end,' and adds on wearily, 'eventually.' She looks out from her story into my eyes, 'What a cow!' she says with flare.

'Yeah!' I agree. 'Cow!' I like being given the chance to be theatrical.

'But it turns out that a couple of years later a friend of mine moved into the same building as the cow.'

'Yeah – cow!' I say, because I liked saying it the first time. We smile, it's only a joke. And it isn't only a joke. This is a safe place for repressed feelings to be un-canned.

She smiles and then says, 'So this building had no lift.'

'Wow! That's quite a coincidence – same building!?' I see a map of all the grid-lines of thousands of buildings in Barcelona.

'Yeah, same building...' And we sit in awe for a millisecond feeling the movements of gods. 'So I'd walk up the escaleras to her flat past 'the cow's' door. But because I'd done what was right, it didn't bother me. I was fine about it, no big heavy rucksack of past memories.'

After a plausible pause, I catch the baristas eye quickly and mouth – *'Dos vinos tintos?'* – while doing an energetic nod and return to Stella. She nods too. 'And of course,' she continues, 'one day I meet her. We bump into each other on the stairs...' There is glee in her eyes.

'And?'

'She looked like she wanted the stairs to swallow her up!'

'God how embarrassing!'

'For her – not for me! I didn't feel I had anything to be ashamed of...'

'Exactly, her nightmare situation! She was banking on never bumping into you

again! On you disappearing into the metropolis.'
'I know! She didn't know what to say – and rightly too…' Her eyebrows arch
into sad glee, '…she really had been a *cow!*'

I gaze into her eyes musing out loud, 'Yeaaaaaah….' I say, half in this world,
half in my imagination, 'if we don't leave a situation well…if we have residual
difficult feelings that we haven't admitted to…if we can't resolve them with that
person, we'll look for an identical situation to bring out those very same
emotions – so we can resolve them with someone else…' This is getting
awkward. I see my patterns. I see her patterns. The boyfriends change, the
situations don't.

We are so engrossed in the story we barely notice the waiter. It is as if we have
paused a film as we silently watch two glasses delicately placed on the table.

It takes a few seconds of silence to regather. 'So,' I say pressing play again, 'I
guess until we learn to leave a difficult situation well, we're stuck in it repeating
on us all over again.'
'Stuck *in* us!' she adds. It is as if we are suddenly in a static world, as if
everything has stopped.

'Cheers!' she says breaking the spell, 'Here's to us coming out well!' We match
Cheshire cat smiles as we clink our drinks. I lose contact with her eyes, as the rim
of my glass full of delicious red wine touches my lips, obscuring my vision.

—

Back in William's 1630 attic, I don't say all of that to him. It just goes through
my memory. It's years back now, I haven't been in Spain for so long, or seen
Stella for five years? More? But all these stories are on my playlist under the
selection, *How We Leave Relationships Is Really Important.* I'm not sure how it
fits in, so I stay quiet, listening into the space. I look down - I listen better
without my eyes. He pushes off the kitchen surface, 'I don't really agree,' he says
like a policeman holding a stiff hand up to stop a car. *Whooa, that's direct!* Heat
rushes to my stony face.

I would never be able to say the same so dryly back to him, this man I barely
know. It feels like he thinks he can say that because he's a man and I'm a
woman: he has no idea who I am and yet he presumes rank. I can take it; I can't
be arsed to argue and I don't want to deal with his feelings if he feels too
'attacked'. With women, or should I say feminines, I feel less need in myself and
in the other to be right – more space opens up to say our own (partial) truths; it
feels more subtle, softer, more heard. With men who I don't know, disagreements
seem more like threats of war. *Are men actually so touchy or is it that I'm just
afraid to stand up to them?* I bite my tongue and take it. It feels claustrophobic.
Does he feel the uncomfortable silence?
'…but I do think it's important,' he looks across at me, still clutching the kitchen
surface, still holding on, 'but how you live a relationship is more important.' He
says it as if it's an undeniable fact.

He's not understood what I'm saying, but I don't want to go into the whole Stella story with the English girl and the other story where she smiles to the cow who is having a nervous attack on the stairs. And I still can't quite remember how it all fits in. But it does somehow. All these experience wire the nerves in our body one way or another.

Suddenly I come out of my mental-scape and remember that he's just 'nailed' a divorce. This is nothing but theory for me, but it's emotional for him. I soften, 'So you say it went well today?' Softer voice. I look at him as if I'm nodding, 'With the divorce?' Hard to know whether to keep talking about it or not.
'Yes.' He seems relieved to be back to where he can dominate.
'Are you friends?'
'Yes. We weren't for a time, but we are now.'

He looks down again. I'm not sure where he is going. So I say to fill in, throwing him a rope, 'I think an end to a relationship doesn't mean a failed relationship,' because I want him to feel OK about himself. I'm saving someone again. *God why do I keep doing that?* Bailing people out from their own difficult emotions, stopping them from feeling them when actually it's just what they need. *Really got to stop it. Got to learn to sit in their silence.* It's uncomfortable. Vulnerable. Might go places I'm not prepared for.

—

Coming down from the miners trail on Sanitas, we've just stopped to admire the view. I'm glad we did, because I had forgotten we were even in mountains, forgotten Boulder below. Forgotten even we were in Colorado. I was in the bubble of our conversation. Woman chat. Full attention inward, picture making. No attention for the outside world. Too many ideas for silence.

'It's so weird…' Carole is a beautiful, tall, blonde woman. Elegant. Graceful. She makes me feel like I'm a gangly teenager gazing up in praise to a goddess. We are talking about her recent breakup, '…he would save the whole world: there was a girl with a drug use problem, his mother with back pain, the ex girlfriend and…' she has forgotten that she is with someone who is not in her head, she pauses, embarrassed at the degree of disclosure. I see in her eye a sort of click where the desire to tell is tipping over the desire to be discreet. I've been there – no point putting up an umbrella once you've got soaked in the rain; once sodden you might as well plunge in. It's similar to the teetering recklessness of the scenario of *should-I-have-a-third-glass-of-wine-or-not?*

She smashes with wonder woman strength out through the membrane of her mental repression, '…he had to get a helicopter out for her.' I had laughed earlier, by mistake, at the wild stories of people he was saving (or was it good that I showed my authentic reaction?) It seemed so extreme the story took on grotesque comic qualities: all because he was too afraid to have a relationship with her – with Carole, this goddess I am walking besides. Meanwhile he tries to show his worth by saving others and leaving her to eat alone. Somehow Carole doesn't get that she can self-validate, that his actions are nothing to do with if she is good enough to be with. I feel her, like I feel myself, wanting to be saved herself. *What from?*

Walking besides her by the pine trees she makes me feel taller and more beautiful – purely by osmosis – but she's sick of being told how beautiful she is, as if the admiring gaze on her beauty is blind to what's underneath. Over time I've learnt not to tell Carole she's stunning even though she's able to knock anyone over just glancing at them.

'One weekend he saved three people, and we didn't eat together once.'

I don't know how to react. Part of me wants to laugh all the tension out. This is just too much. This is horror story land. She still loves him. She wants whatever she got from him at the beginning back. Wants him back. She is in deep grief. I am glad she is out of it, that the relationship is over, that she's not with him. But I can't say that. I just stand there, remembering how in love she was last year, right at the beginning, the way she smiled when she talked about him, how the air their story breathed had such a delicate, exquisite amore.

After a little time I say, 'Just because something has ended doesn't mean it was a failure.'
'Yes!' she says, coming back to the smell of pine, 'my friend said the same: sometimes the most successful relationships are the short ones. Each relationship teaches us something. Long term doesn't mean more successful, not necessarily.'
'Yes!' I say, suddenly on firmer footing.
'But why do we always try for the forever?'

———

'Just because something has ended doesn't mean it was a failure.' The acupuncturist looks up. Under the five hundred year old black rafters he says, 'I agree with you. It is a reflection of society. It is how we deal with death – or don't deal with it.' He is in the doorway now, not sure whether to stay or to go, he's come up looking for his mate, William, not me. 'We don't want anything to change. We can't deal with death.'
'Death of the ego.' I say like a judge. I didn't mean it quite so confidently.
'Yes,' he says, 'as a society we can't accept change or death, and yet everything is changing all of the time.' I feel tingles up my spine that come when a conversation touches something deep, 'We want to keep it as it is. But we can't. We fear change, try to make it look like nothing is changing, but in the background everything's changing all of the time.'
'We are change,' I say. *That was just an easy line* I think to myself. But it's true. We are. But we don't accept it so readily.

———

I remember my bipolar friend. Desperate. Frantic. Desperate to show that he is on top of it all. Desperate to maintain an image to the world that he has it all controlled. All down pat. Life in complete control. Desperately wanting to give off the vibe of polished dogma of, 'This is How It Is.' Wants everything under his own god-like control. Full stop, hit enter. Send. Lineal sequence or parallel sequence. Maps of electrical circuits. Never change. Electricity, ACDC or AC. One can rely on Physics. Press button for up, garage door goes up. Press button for down, garage door goes down. Stick to convention. Stick to what has always worked.

I wonder if he really is happy behind that Kodak smile of the massive metre length photo he has of his family in the kitchen in a sort of reinforcement of happy image? *Can he be?* Meanwhile I know when it was taken he was going through heavy depression. Medicated smile.

Meanwhile his two little children are growing prolifically. Changing, changing, changing – totally out of his control.

——

And that king who orders the waves to stop. What was his name? Canute?

——

Lora, who I lived with in Boulder, CO – is on her morning walk in the Rockies, on the same walk she took me on once, and near the same place where she saw a mountain lion and freaked out and couldn't go back for weeks. We are amazed to be living in the future as she holds her mobile, that she calls a cell, and we see each other through Skype. We haven't spoken for ages. We used to chat every day, downloading the day's images and emotions over the wooden kitchen table without any technology other than our voices and minds.

We shared the magic of our inner worlds together. I thrived on going down into that well with her, going down into Source where Jung says he dipped his hat. Just being there creates bonds of love. It's an intimacy that goes deep into the soul. Most people cannot withstand it. Lora can. I can. We can: our dyslexic brains flying together through images, through spatial awareness, down into our essence. We laughed in glee, hiding behind the moss with the elves and seeing things others don't stop to admire. So few people seem able to float in images nor take delight in flying in loops in the high winds streaming through the skies of intuition: a feat that feels so natural to us as we journey through images of the invisible (only to the eye) – through energy, movements of soul, through creations of consciousness and unconsciousness – forms, shapes, colours all dancing in patterns within patterns. Lora and I can. We labyrinth dance together. That's how come there is so much love between us.

I haven't spoken to her for so, so long. At last we've managed to get ourselves together at the same time on Skype.

Wind whips her hair. She yelps a little as if the wind could blow her over. She is so pure, angel like. She's so transparent that light shines up out of her face. 'Hello!' I feel a smile spreading across my face like a Cheshire cat. I want to hug her. But I can't – so I gaze into my Samsung laptop screen instead. It blurs a little because tears are welling. I hope she can't see, hope she's not got definition. 'Hi!'

Distance is so hard.

'Look at where I am!' she says. There is no need to say. It's where we have been together. We know that's what she's really saying. It is beautiful. It hurts my heart. 'How are you dear?' she asks as if we were around the wooden table. 'Fine. You?'

And we are off! In the first sentence she says the word endeavour. She uses it all the time in her yoga classes. 'Endeavour to feel the flow of breath into your toes.' Lora is into words like 'triggered', 'I feel that…', 'What I hear you saying is…' I like it. Non-Violent Communication. I like to laugh at it and at the same time I feel it's the way forward into more sensitive authentic communication. I've learned a lot from her. She's ten years younger. It makes me feel strange: she's further along on her path than I feel I am, at least professionally. Sometimes I get jealous and angry and project onto her. I did it a lot in the kitchen, because she is really clean and I'm not. And when she wasn't I got really, quite disproportionately angry for apparently no reason. I never talked about it. I knew it was my own crap. When we lie on a bed chatting close, arms draped on each other as we weave another layer on top of our on-going stories, I feel like we are sisters.

She tells me, cell directed to her face, that she is bothered because her mother, who sounds bipolar to me, was being bipolar at the weekend. I'm amazed I can hear so well. There is a lot of wind. She tells me of the big fight between her mum and sister while they were in Kansas. It's so strange to be sat chained to the computer while she is walking in the mountains. I can't hear every word, but I get it all. Lora wasn't there when it happened. Later they both call her separately. Two mirror conversations. 'Can't you see it from this perspective?' she asks to her mom thinking of her sister. 'Can't you see it from this perspective?' she asks her sister thinking of her mom.

I wish I was out walking instead of being in front of my computer, stuck to my desk. I look out of the window. I can see Dartington woods through the rain. 'I get so sick of it all. It feels like because my mother cannot contain her emotions we have to run around frantically trying to contain her emotions for her, holding them all before they blow up.' She breathes out heavily, she's walking fast uphill and feeling. 'It is our family dynamic. It's happened all my life.'

I think of the conversation in William's kitchen with the man who works as an acupuncturist telling me about nailing divorces and changes happening and we not wanting change and doing everything we can to keep things fixed but that change is always happening anyway. I say the whole story to her. I know that she will get it and it will not be a waste of breath.

She stays silent at the end. She knows it's connected. She doesn't get the connection. Not yet…

'So,' I say through the pixels, 'why don't you just give up trying to control her, trying to contain her emotions, trying to control the situation? Cos she just can't contain them. And you can't contain them for her.'

'I know,' she says, we've talked through this before, about only being able to affect our own emotions, no one else's.

'They are happening anyway, whatever you do, or don't do. It's exactly the same result in the end. She can't contain her emotions. She doesn't. They are out there already in all their chaos. It's not your responsibility. You cannot clean up what isn't yours. You aren't in a position to actually change anything about her swirling in her uncontrolled emotions. How you react to it, is just how you react to it, but you're not changing her inability to contain her own emotions. She will always be pumping them out there.'

'A ha?' she says, still following, but not at the end.

I search for a different way to say it, 'It's like life and death and being afraid of things that might happen when they are already happening right now, all of the time, out of our control; things that we are coping with and are used to, but don't notice, like every day we are aging a little, a little closer to death. We don't want to notice, but still we cope with it. We're too afraid to recognise what is happening in front of our noses – as if it would affect our very being in this life, even though it is anyway – and as we become more and more afraid of it happening we try to control that it doesn't, while it does anyway – all around us – regardless of what we do.' I breathe in, watch her hiking easily up hill, 'Like our only choice really is to accept it or not; to accept the swirling of life or not.' It clicks. 'Ohh yes!' she says relief flowing out through a laugh: image – click – in place, 'I've got it!' She laughs again into the wind. 'My mother will always, unless she does a lot of work on herself, be like she is. I can't change that, even if I stress out like a complete crazy nut!' She laughs into her cell, into my room. 'Wow!' she says, 'I feel much better! Like some weight is off. I feel much lighter. Freer!'

Her hair is rippling over her eyes. But I can hear her laugh now into the wind. I miss her. I want to tell her my pain towards Paul and get her perspective on him, her flatmate. I'm about to tell her about how hard it is to adapt to England and how just when I most needed him to support me, to be an anchor for me as I bridge cultures, even if only through pixels over the Atlantic, he writes me a one-liner, 'I'm just taking my space. I have fallen in love. Need time to process.' How it triggers me because it feels just like when I was over there, on a hiking trip with him up near Devil's pass, and sat in his arms on a rock surrounded by thousands of wild mountain flowers I felt myself merging with him, in love, in deep flowing beauty, how I began to believe in what was between us, feeling myself teetering on the edge of fully opening to this love for him, freefalling into believing that this between us could work, dropping my fears and swimming in the bliss of being safe enough to be so vulnerable, and as I gaze into his eyes and tell him I love him, he smashes everything up with his words, pushing me away again with his polyamory bullshit, 'I will always love other women as well you know?' The sting. The impossibility of him safeguarding what is an 'us'. The vertiginous fall all too fast back down to reality.

I'm just gearing up to tell her my story when the line goes dead.

Am I trying to lean on him, across the Atlantic, because I'm too afraid to face this here?

—

I open gmail. No message. Where is he, my Knight in shining armour? I want him to ease this pain I have inside. I want him to tell me that this uncontrollable swirling of life that is dancing between us is fixed, predictable, that we are safe from Time.

—

From: <lora@bouldermassage.com>
To: <julia.butterflypress@gmail.com>

Damn. My cell died. This is how I have been lately; windy and almost out of battery, not enough time and I'm moving so quickly, erratic. I am sorry I didn't get to hear more from you. Glad you got out for a walk with the night.

—

I remember when the line went dead with my bro. How he fell into trying to control my feelings towards him as he imagined me thinking the worst things about him that he worries I do (but don't), while I worried he was thinking that I wasn't a good enough sister. Sometimes, perhaps often, perhaps always, things happen completely independently to what I'm doing. I can't even begin to control them.

—

I remember in Barcelona. I was living with a boyfriend for a year. A relationship where we had both olympically jumped over reality and were feasting on fantasy images. It took me a year of waiting to be impregnated, or rather to realise: we will not get through these arguments of what to call the baby. We are just not suited as a couple. Yes, he will make a great dad. But I don't like being with him. Hard to realise. Hard to let go of images to land in the stark reality. It's nothing really to do with him, or me, just we really aren't suited. End of.

But while we were still arguing, with passion and love, over how to bring up children and what names to give them, the strap to lift or lower the metal venetian blinds had seriously frayed. We had to change it. As he took out the old cord and threaded through the new, it was my job to hold the roll of blinds up to stop them crashing down.

I was stood on a chair, arms stretched out, holding onto the rolled up metal blinds. It was uncomfortable on my outstretched arm muscles. He was taking a long time. Memories of being in the yoga camp and doing 'firm determination' while holding my arms up for twenty-five minutes went streaming through my body.

I'm there holding my arms out, ferociously grabbing the venetian blinds, acutely conscious that I am the only thing between them unravelling and shuttering down to guillotine our fingers. I stand there feeling the pain, arms outstretched, not dropping them. I can't drop them. This is not yoga: this is a matter of safety. I am concentrating on disconnecting my mind reaction to the actual reality of pain. I hold out. Awkward angle this. My fingers feel the pinch. I can't move a muscle, my arms and hands and wrists and elbows are all locked into my shoulders.

My muscles start to burn. My arms screech out *I can't do this much longer.* My voice says straining out of normality to Antonio, 'Hay mucho más?' *How long is it going to be?!!* I feel myself starting to shake.

I just can't do it any longer. 'Antonio!' I shout out dramatically, 'Stand back! I have to let go!!' Feeling the end coming near, I nearly lose control – his fingers still in the mechanism. 'Stand back!' I say agonisingly, gripping onto the very last gram of staying power that I have. 'Ya estoy!' he says, stepping back. 'Ahhhhhhhhhh!' I let go. Step back. Expect to hear the crash.
Nothing happened.

The blind had been sustaining itself.

My colors have u in them

A sentence doesn't cry
when it comes to an end.
So why should we?
My colours now have you in them.

A gift of a conversation with someone who
I never met again about layers of meaning
and getting further within ourselves
to what is Eternal.

That which connects us all

The tree listens
accepts what is
without need
nor expectations
asks us to drop our desires
and enter into
unfolding infinities
to luxuriate
in the soft waves
of simply being.

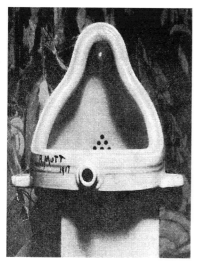

I'm wondering whether to go into Greenlife Health Food Store and check out some clay that is actually shampoo. I'm late, but it'll only take two minutes. 'Hi,' I look around and see a pretty face, beautiful thick black hair, I recognise him from somewhere. 'Hi!' I say probably overcompensating, 'How are you?' I'm gaining time to go through my badly filed internal face recognition system. This is out of context. A blurry image clicks into place. *Got it. The festival of the Day of the Dead.*

'Did you enjoy it the other day?'

'Yes, it was good.'

'Yes,' we both hold back. Silence. Eyes search the other, dart, who are we? He decides I am friend, not foe, 'but afterwards, when I got home, I realised that (did you see that my girlfriend was sat against the wall?)' I nod trying at the same time to look like I'm not nodding, 'I'm we hadn't connected.' Pain flashes across his eyes, he looks down slightly to the right. Pigeons peck around the market square.

———

'I shouldn't say this, I only have her side,' Joseph says dancing that light step he has part way around the kitchen table, 'but it's been rocky for them both. He has a three-year old with another woman and she desperately wants a baby. Wants one bad.'

'..and he doesn't?' I am only half listening while I also mull over such important matters as whether to heat the cast iron pan first. Cast iron pans remind me of Paul. I feel the weight of it. Run my fingers over the concentric circles on the bottom. Comforting somehow.

'No.'

In the silence we both feel it, both feel their stories colliding. I smash an egg, it slides sensually into the bowl.

'She's going to have to get herself a new man,' I hear myself - so dogmatic! I'm a bit shocked. *Is that heartless or just real?*

'I get a bit annoyed sometimes. She's been talking about it, complaining about it for a long time, but sometimes I just want to say to Elizabeth, 'It was you who chose a man who already had a baby who only has enough energy for one.'' I wonder if it's OK to make a noise and start whisking.

'Yea,' I say fork hovering, 'it's hard.'

———

A pigeon flutters. Makes my stomach turn a bit. This guy with the lovely dark hair hasn't said anything but I kinda know his situation even though I have no idea who he is nor what he's actually going through. I've never really met him, but I know a bit about him from what Joseph said in the kitchen a couple of weeks back, so I do have a hunch, and though, or because, we don't actually know each other I am able to launch as if innocently into, 'And do you have a problem with not connecting on a night out?'

He looks at me as if I have brought a message from a far off planet, and furthermore: he understands the alien concept. 'Well…' he looks up to the sky. For a brief moment of time it has stopped raining, 'do I have a problem with that?'

———

I am driving through London, the windscreen wipers are on double-whizz setting, and Paul, who I've recently discovered appears to have no sense of internal direction, is giving me directions from the GPS. My control freak, realising that I am being guided on complicated London roads by a spatially challenged visiting American, goes into overdrive. Through the screeching of the control freak, I'm finding it hard to find the space to trust. Meanwhile inside me is like outside. Teary words, water slashing about the car, 'But it's really not fair – don't you think?' I grip the steering wheel knowing we've got another mile until the next decision between multiple possible directions, 'I mean I did nothing and he has thrown me out of his house, and…' I know that Paul has heard this now many, many times, but I need to keep talking it through, going through the loop until I find a way out…I'm stuck in it. 'It's just not fair!!' Whish, wash – whish, wash – whish, wash. I glance over at the GPS that he has pointing towards himself, I can only see a grey black screen – *is he getting us lost?*

He looks through the rain swept windscreen, 'I went to a Buddhist therapist for years and did couples therapy with Valery. Years of it.'

'Wow…'

'Yeah, so one day I was describing what happens to us, or happened to us: the pattern we were stuck in, this dynamic that was always the same. I would do this, she would do that, I would do this, then she would say that. Game over. I said to the therapist that she always says the same thing, so that it always turns into a non-win situation. I couldn't help it, there was never a pacific way out, it made me feel so angry, and I blurted out, 'It's just not fair!' I was on the edge of rage. And with her sat there beside me, the guy replied really evenly, 'Yes, you are right. Life's not fair. What problem do you have with life not being fair?''

Fuck it. He's right. A light at the end of this spiralling tunnel. *Am I getting out of the cycle?*

Processing.

Processing.

Processing.

———

It was invite only, a practise, for a big arts festival in Wales somewhere. I felt honoured to be in the audience. I got in because the artist is a good friend of Susanne, my new landlady. I expected it to be way too 'modern' for me. I had read the webpage, lying on my bed. I'd got the general idea: a computer programmer has created a program that receives texts sent to the art project by the public, me being one of the public, about anything at all, just random messages, and uses the words within the texts to search twitter for similar content. It then scrambles the twitter message, converts them into voice and then the artist repeats what the computer program has come up with through ear phones, converting it back into 'human'. I send a text in Spanish. Bit of a bastard trick really, but I can't help it.

So though I've read the blurb, sent a text, I have no idea what to expect.

He clears his voice. He's finished the explanation. Are we 'ready?' We all nod. I feel exposed somehow. I wish there was a table or something to hide behind.

He says the first scrambled message.

'hygiene & backslash hashtag horror to safe CAN spread must T5jIjIF2Ia water We You backslash disease quickly https camp avoid provide of dot help dot dot dot colon t dot co backslash items'

I am still in outside mode. Thinking.

'slash Whoops full-stop backslash 3qPrB3mnyh trust hashtag t dot corbert colon Littleprince https backslash'

Just listen Julia, don't be judgemental.

'longread @moiraopain1's power Ooh comma the comedy Moira on hashtag features moodysaydiner full-stop Cart's Read that hashtag her on colon of'

You can't get out anyway now. Just sit, think of it like meditation. This is forced meditation time.

'hashtag Penguin exclamation! bit dot backslash Here's http colon backslash 2iWKAxa hyphen Up Day @pandamoan from Awareness the Happy archives Round full-stop a'

Nothing.

'inverted comma God States continue you America full-stop May you full-stop United Thank to bless of full-stop inverted comma God @PODUS bless the hyphen'

My brain can suddenly make sense at the end. *God sitting at some internet address and blessing the hyphen!* It tickles. I laugh. I wonder what Susanne thinks? She's serious, perhaps an overly serious artist. I wonder if she thinks I've not 'got it' because I laughed? Thank god the woman on the next chair guffawed too. It was just so weird to be in all of this meaninglessness and then to hear a message that grammatically makes sense and yet is still gobbledygook.

'now full-stop be GIVE https But backslash rednoseday had is right backslash amuseBLUOs Txt backslash sent nowhere Pls he Shed t dot com this involved 2get Ed'

I close my eyes again. Breathe in.

'@thecart OVERRATED!I AGREE just IS @emilygather the OWN say WIPE for I ANNA! Can comma being to ARSE @cirrow YOU able Record comma VASTLY YOUR'

His accent is perfect for it. Slightly jolted. Sounds like he's in the Second World War relaying info back to control office. Big Princess Leia headphones add to the image along with his old fashioned cardigan and a big beard. *Can you imagine? All this twitter shit as if it were valuable info back from the frontline of life?*

'& Ben exclamation! when days Mon SilentThinkers Busy finally comma few husband @ITV to with Claire's hashtag we get @morningrise then'

He's actually doing the translation into human voice really fast. Skilled. *What's he hearing?* He's practised a lot, you can tell. He's trained his brain to receive computer communication. *Woah…not sure if I like that or not. Should we be allowing our brains to connect synapses up like a computer?*

'AGAIN! 1 hyphen West THE as duffer's home! and @AndyPack MAN rises BIG corner high 9 colon Ham It's STRIKES 0 heads.'

Actually all of us sat here are letting that through our brains. Through us. Are our brains taking on non human attributes? We are in an open sea of this, letting it go through us. I feel exposed again, my brain doesn't know what to make of any of this.

'Soviet cityzenkane108 Vlad's all me do file underscore talons question mark about lord @underscore like Troll @nothing better to do have'

This is boring. Meaningless.

'staff comma about Great talking Labour hospital hashtag and CarefortheNHS visitors morning Party's patients with campaign with @JLing underscore Barley and friends'

I can make out hints of a political tone.

It's a sea of meaninglessness and once in a while some words join up and my brain can put meaning on top, like it's desperate to, but it's still meaningless… here in this room…all I can really put meaning on is that there is a person desperate to get a political idea out that is, in itself, meaningless.

'someone's hashtag overexposure of hashtag to of Russia complexion hashtag prostitutes In an Could unnaturally hashtag question mark hashtag Asking hashtag for a explain friend. skin urine orange'

Meaninglessness. *Is this life? At the surface of our lives – is this it?*

'Nothing clinching full-stop NationalHuggingDay like hashtag hug a'

Keep feeling your body Julia, ground.

'gigam colon 20,980 android http backslash hashtag game insight imtw backslash dot coins! I've backslash underscore Tribez collected hashtag, androidgames, gold hashtag'

I see the image of all this meaninglessness. People scrambling to make meaning from nothing, linking some words and then wanting to base their whole life on a snippet of meaningless meaning they've managed to put their own meaning to… politics, fashion, whatever wave is sweeping through twitter today, Halloween, or some international disaster or the release of a new film – whatever they've managed to grasp meaning out of in all this meaninglessness.

'backslash 170113 don't hashtag I backslash SEUL hashtag DarlingU know colon less than 3 http backslash c1 dot hashtag dot com backslash baby 1backslash baby 453backslash 35162814520 underscore com underscore 0 dot jpg dot dot dot http'

A sea of meaninglessness, of stem cells, of primordial soup, waves of vague issues sweeping through our collective, and then gone, and then once in a while an eruption of something less random, something that we feel we can predict…

'Times semi-colon hashtag hashtag that fabric prostitutes the comma but staticflickr to resist sure has he is sez hashtag Putin 8c7d3afe4had of London hashtag moral full-stop best Huh question mark 434backslash Russia underscore 798afcdd51 world's'

I don't like this.

'hashtag BestFanArmy NOW hashtag hashtag LittleMonsters hashtag NOWLadyGaga BestFanArmy hashtag iHeartAwards LittleMonsters hashtag iHeartAwards'

Nothing to hold onto. Floating in the nothingness of these words.

'Crotch Makes Girl full-stop full-stop full-stop Sex colon back slash back slash ExistWithLove full-stop Crazy hashtag Moaning net back slash 03de4f137fcc0 Sounds During http freshphotomoments Tattoo full-stop full-stop full-stop'

Ahhhhhhhhhhhhhhhhhh. I want to get out.

Ahhhhhhhhhhhhhhhhhhhhhhhhhhh.

Go into your body, Julia. It's OK, this is not forever.

'day full-stop @ joined and @IpswichST hashtag UK lump national The @Suffolk centreforreform YUP by It's @EmiliaThorny are campaign and @alexiamay'

I don't like it.

'@WSJ it the in who https look exclamation! was @Jerry underscore Styles inspired fPXiPsdSSp backslash t dot co backslash Here's backslash interview my colon'

Breathe.

'colon 1 dot n8pGh6R2Xi Lonely of full-stop t dot co backslash 1 backslash Buffet https backslash'

It's OK.

'nothing HUMAN @Free important do having underscore is help what being & underscore than can There us Please Hub Media in world this more know heart full-stop let a we 2'

I want to leave. Can I leave?

'I'm @David full-stop bragging poo a you about in the to do disabled it Cameron at but hear don't work me toilets you about do question mark'

Just breathe. Feel your feet.

'watching I hashtag weekend Cialis tried hashtag all kept Viagra football full-stop hashtag but commercials getting by interrupted Prostitutes inverted comma Rich Goodly inverted comma e'

You can do this.

'Doritos even to a Sharknado3 Not are Sharknado full-stop hashtag immune'

I'm in my body, watching myself, seeing myself react to this meaninglessness. *Is this our life? Is this how it works?*

'bed Americans hashtag full-stop full-stop full-stop hashtag the made world rest USA of their the must Empire hypen @UN be exclamation! it to hashtag use made? hashtag EU Why full-stop full-stop colon a its policies' hashtag is supply &'

I want out. My brain is being fried. I want to understand something. Anything. *Let my brain unscramble!*

'Join year of and @Twitter comma hashtag biggest KickOffForKids to the at the exclamation! me@BFGFoundation game'

No relief.

'artist was down ticket 1st hyphen racism having accused hashtag black of not White passenger swiftly shut class and hashtag MILKDAY'

When will this be over?

'update you Vine Today's keep lets Camera comma loop exclamation! Twitter making comma Vines the them app & to comma posting they where now'

Just relax. Just relax. It's OK.

'not TravelTuesday a is full-stop hashtag through about below see Tap what to the all is hype full-stop mirage This'

—

I'm on the beach where Agapius and I used to go with the dogs.
Parasporos. We've just had a rather fraught lunch. Its Christmas day and Agapius wouldn't let me do the prawn cocktails how prawn cocktails are made on Christmas day in England, at least in my family, and I've got into a right mess because I want to make an occasion of Christmas day, make it special, put meaning into it, at least make it different from the other days, and Agapius is trying to do that, but his way, which is just a big mess, and he's not listening to me about what a prawn cocktail looks like…I'm just about to blow.

Agapius has never had a western style Christmas. *How can that be so?* He's never even had prawn cocktail before. *Wasn't his mother English?* But actually he can't really use his knife and fork properly so maybe they didn't make things dressy*? What's the point of Christmas if it's just like the random nothingness of the other days?* His mate, who has forgotten its Christmas day, happened to pop round. He's English too. When Agapius put the 'prawn cocktail' on the table, his mate and I looked into each other's eyes. Bonded by tradition, we both knew what we were each thinking. But it's only half a comfort to have English contingent present. Ian is another healer who you wouldn't want to trust out of the therapy session even with a bag of crisps. He only really seems to come around when he needs something.

—

To cool down, we've all decided to go for a walk. I'm just sad, and I'm walking along with Ian who is recently divorced from a twenty-five year relationship because he fell for a young girl who spurned him – typical story. He's coming in and out of the elation of feeling free to live life again coupled with depression over what he's done. But he does have some good stuff to say. He's the type of guy who knows lots of envelops full of wisdom to pass down to others, but it feels as if he's never opened the envelopes himself. It feels as if he just likes the feeling of saying things, knowing things, but his actions are never in line with the content of his envelops - his mind seems disconnected from his heart. However he does often know just the right word or the right phrase to hit the nail on the head.

On this day, Christmas 2011, I remember he was pressing for me to understand. I listen, heart only just quiveringly open. He's says to me, 'It doesn't mean anything that it doesn't mean anything.'

What?

—

Years later, sat here, in this little church hall with the scrambled messages I see this meaninglessness and realise that it really does mean nothing that it is meaningless.

Really.

'not 9 to when like the the person you're 89032 full-stop in hashtag open-bracket look Even full-stop close-bracket smartest @keiranjsmith ways room'

With the realisation, I feel myself falling into a big spacious place inside, hallow, hollow, still. A cathedral or a cave – just big space – and I feel this scrambled-message life of meaninglessness become more distant, as if I am far away behind invisible walls.

How do I react to meaningless? How am I now? Who am I now? What am I now?

This is what it is all about.

Inside, passing beyond all the meaninglessness, behind all of the waves of random social fabrication, what am I?

Where no one looks

I shrug off old ideas
rope bridges across the void
I don't need them anymore.

The trumpeter's ear
jumps on ahead
into greater consciousness
of subtler sound.

Tiny worlds burst open universes.

I float in new meaning
grabbling to understand
observe
create
until this too…

Deep down into the mirrors
the subtle Truth
- resting in perfect silence -
is hidden from no one.

The pigeons have all flown off. I'm getting really late, but I am so enjoying this conversation with this guy about whom I know his private life but can't remember his name. I feel heard - and that to be frank is not so common: I'm drinking it in. We've moved off from *Life-Is-Not-Fair-But-What-Problem-Do-You-Have-With-Life-Not-Being-Fair?* to a theme close to my heart that I'm bleating out to anyone who will listen: 'So,' I say, 'meaninglessness… if we can bear to sit in all this nothingness, is like this perfect place to actually see our own presence… consciousness disconnecting itself from the material, from the ego, from all that meaning created on top of meaninglessness, and if we can go through that random confusion, or maybe underneath it, and simply observe it, we can create a gap between the random confusion of created meaningless-meaning, and, 'who we are'. And if we can do that,' I'm on such a roll I just can't stop, 'A space opens up to see consciousness, and to see how it is in us, by the way it reacts to the meaninglessness… how it is present in us.'

I wonder if he has got me. I wonder if I am talking into thin air again. I look into his eyes. He is staring straight into mine and nods, without nodding. I feel it. I see his Adam's apple swallow.

'Like let's say just for a moment, theoretically, that everything we think is meaningless - even if in the millisecond when the thought occurred it was in perfect accord with what was actually happening, but as time moves on the thought we hold onto is more and more obsolete - then,' I pause, seeing his Adam apple move up and then back down, 'if we don't think, then is everything meaningless?'

'Well, like a dog doesn't 'think', but that doesn't make the dog meaningless does it?'

'Exactly, like if we stop thinking, that doesn't mean we stop having presence.'

I let this delightful concept sink in to me, into him, letting myself feel this delight of simply carving out an idea together.

'Like,' I say, feeling safe enough to walk further into this sea of ideas, exploring life in his soft, intelligent presence; my body is buzzing feeling the tangible excitement of inner adventurers meeting in a rare moment of real togetherness, 'when we don't react to meaninglessness, when we stop trying to find meaning, we stop trying to see ourselves on the outside world, and with all of that energy freed up, we can experience ourselves as we are.' Right now, if I knew him better, I would like to say 'Dar darrrr!!!' But don't. I feel my back straightening though. I don't push out my chest. Not even as a joke.

'But,' he says – I love it! He is still at my side, wanting to keep walking through this! Houston we are still connected! I hold his eyes. 'Is that not just another story for the ego to hold onto?'

Wow…that's a good point. 'Hmmm…' I say, mind whirling. 'Is it?'

———

Amador Vega, in his thin body and grey cardigan is talking to us about the Trinity. Father, son and Holy Ghost. Ghost is such a funny word; I prefer to say Spirit. We are in the non-descript building of the Institut de C.G.Jung in Barcelona. As Amador speaks I see a progression of images: The Father as the

Senex, the solid wisdom of the old, that contains what is. The Holy Ghost comes in, moves everything around and through mother, the material (the fourth element) creates the new form, the new in-form-ation, the new shape in the form of the Son, the Puer. The Puer is the ever youthful, the energetic movement of the new that more closely reflects the form of all that is - the present shape of the ever-birthing of the present. The son strengthens, creates a mould of itself, an image of itself; the image of itself solidifies, grows old, becomes the Senex. The fixed map and the ever-changing reality under the map become more and more disparate, until boom! The Spirit moves in, creating chaos, moving everything around again to create with the ever-changing Mother a new image, a new son, of this here-now reality. A new Puer! The new, birthing image relays new information about the ever-changing reality. The old Senex needs this young Puer to stay alive and be less brittle, less dogmatic. The Senex needs the Puer to connect to the world with this new, improved map of the now. And so on into ad-infinitum.

Birth. Puer. Activity. Growth. Aging. Slowing. Senex. Knowledge. Wisdom. Container. Stability. Security. Internal fixation. World changes. Disconnect. Infirmity. BOOM! New life. Puer.

If we hang onto the fixed images within ourselves, of the world, of our beliefs, of others, of ourselves, we begin to build up walls to keep out the ever-changing, ever more desperate to stay in a world that is still, unchanging, controllable, deathly. In a word: neurosis.

If we don't have a fixed image of the ever-changing reality we can become psychotic, swirling and flying around, groundless, in the constantly changing, chaotic. We would be unable to function. I mean we could drown in all this meaningless. We would go crazy.

———

'**Maybe the ego needs something to hold onto,** some image of itself, so it doesn't go crazy?' There is no way I can describe all that has just gone through my head. I mean I am already late.
'Hmm,' he says 'maybe'. I feel like he looks at me with slight admiration. At least that's the meaning I'm putting on top of the expression in his eyes. It gives me confidence, and though time is ticking I'm going forward with this one. It's just too juicy! Worth being late for. I don't know him, but I'm just going to keep going on this train with him.

'It is only a problem if it becomes dogmatic.' I realise that I am using my own vocabulary here. How can we communicate if I use my own language that only I know? 'So, like dogmatic I mean…I take a photo of you now, as you are now, and it is a perfect representation of how you are now, but when I see you next, I expect you to be the same. Same clothes, same emotions, same place. You know? The adherence to the photo, or the map, rather than the reality, is dogmatic, but the photo itself did have a time place in which it was dead right, in which it represented the Truth.'

I could have said the story of Borges and the King's map, the map that was one to one and rolled over the earth. It was fine for a while. Before the land underneath eroded, changed, and they kept walking on the map. Simulacra and Simulations. Fascinating.
'Hmmmm, yes.'

I know that he is processing, but I'm too excited now to slow down, I'm off on one, tongue uncontrollable, 'And so the ego maybe needs those concepts, ideas, stories about itself, but as long as we don't put any fixed meaning onto them, as long as we see that it is, deep down, meaningless, then it is not dogmatic. As long as we are able to change those images once they are outdated, obsolete.' Is he with me? I think about that prayer that goes something like, 'Give me the strength to change what I can, the knowledge to leave what I cannot, and the wisdom to know the difference.'

He clears his throat. He's back! this man with the beautiful black hair. 'But what I'm hearing,' he says in the typical Non-Violent-Communication talk, 'is that maybe there is more underneath the meaninglessness.'
Yeeeeeeaaaaaahhhhhhhhhhhssssssssssssshhhhhhhhhhhh. It is SO SO SO SO SO SO nice to be heard!!! YeahhhhhhhH!H!!!!H!!H!H!H!H!H!H!H
I beam, waiting for him to say more. He's looking at me. I can't wait. I'm trying to take my turn, give him space. *Has he finished? I can't wait.*

Nothing more...? 'Yes!!!!' I burst in, trying not to sound too excited, 'Only when we accept it is all meaningless can we experience presence! Who we are. That which is within us. That's a deeper sense of meaningfulness, maybe?'
'And then maybe,' he says, his voice meandering, 'we get used to it and add on interpretations of this subtler world with subtler meaning, until we realise...'
'Yes!' I can't keep it in. I nod, eyes shining.
'...that it too is meaningless, and we sink further down into yet a new subtler meaninglessness, seeing ourselves reacting to it, responding to it, seeing ourselves anew in its empty reflection...'
'Like an empty mirror...' I find it so platonically erotic to be so close in our minds.
'Yeah...experiencing our need to see ourselves...'
'Yes! Ever closer to the Truth of who, or actually *what*, we are!'

Mirrors within mirrors

You talk. I talk. She talks.
None of it matters.
Televisions blare out
news to be forgotten.
A flower dies.
You snore.
I worry about the train.
None of it matters.
We argued once

about sex and sacredness
but the memory
caught in cobwebs
has been eaten by time.

Meaningless!
I react to it
and in hearing myself
discover who I am.

The empty mirror.

Faced with this nothingness
I paste on my own meaning
portraying myself
how I am
what I am
where I am.

The meaning is who I am not
and yet I cannot withstand
not knowing.

Anything but nothing, please.

This new meaning holds me up
until it too
- dry, brittle old -
serves no more
and sinks back into the loud gushing
of meaningless meaning.

A flower blooms.
Petals uncurling in
sweet innocence.

In a virgin state
I discover new meaning
my own meaning of
subtler meaninglessness.

The pendulum within
swings ever calmer
ever slower
soft swings
over the impossibly simple
nature of Truth.

We smile at each other, both leaning into it, suspended for a brief moment in time in a still image of our two presences being light and joy and love. We have slipped underneath all our outer meaningless construction. I have slipped under this charming, exciting conversation. I feel him, his presence. I feel me, my presence. Palpable. This is life. This is real living. Silent communication of all that does not need meaning, it is simply self-evident. *Ahhhhhh.* We breathe at the same time. I want to hug him. I want to show love for him. Not sexual. *Maybe.* But I just want to show myself to him. Like a psychic flasher showering love. I would so like him to feel this love I am feeling, inside of me, for him, with him, created by our presences coming together for a brief moment of time. I know that it is not right in society. We must hold ourselves back, because others could be hurt. We could be hurt. Ego bullshit. But we just aren't there yet as a society to allow love to be expressed as it arises – it's crazy. Not yet in our world is it OK to show physical love to strangers, to neighbours, to insignificant others. Sharing can even turn into abuse of power. I just stand there beaming.

'So,' he says 'I've got to go…' I've totally forgotten that I'm late, '…a hug?' *Yes,* I say with my eyes, with my arms, and fall into his embrace. It's a good one. Solid, soft. We fly for a little time in each other's arms. We are breathing together. It's just amazing to breathe with another human being. We pull apart. 'I really enjoyed that,' he says.
'You did?' I say somewhat amazed that someone else would be as excited as I am about what cannot be seen or touched or made money from. I can barely even express it.
'Yes. I did.'
'Me too. A lot.'
'See you around.'
'I hope so.' I can't remember his name. So I don't say it.

We walk off in different directions, I haven't got time to check that clay shampoo thing, even though I'm right outside Greenlife. Now I'm really late. Late and really happy.

Silence

Silence behind the music
moving like the waves
alone we hear it
when free from the world
in the quiet of our hearts
in the nothing
we become
the silence
that holds us all.

Chapter 27: The Eternal is Ephemeral

Hurriedly trying to cover over the fear of death,
desperately unaware that — underneath everything —
love exists eternally.

The Eternal Return

We echo in the depths
forgetting
if we are one or two
now or then;
becoming
closer to what
we have always been:
Timeless.

Unable to sustain it
daily life rushes back in
the clock speeds up;
the Eternal, in a flash,
converts back into memory;
I am stepped back
into my solitary self.

I'm back in Barcelona to clear up my stuff, see old friends and frequent old haunts. I am also feeling how it feels to be myself now that I've been living in England a year. There's an 'International Eye Gazing' event in Plaza del Sol, so I organise a little group to go to it. It's a most marvelous thing to sit staring into another's eyes, into strangers' eyes, into friends' eyes. Nothing to do – all to feel. It really is quite remarkable.

Àngel Priscini turns up. I didn't expect him to. 'I've only got fifteen minutes,' he says, tired. He's just finished working by wyrd coincidence in the next plaza. I haven't seen him for years. In my mind he has been reduced to a story: an ex-boyfriend. 'We lived in Argentina together,' I'll say, as if on rote, 'in a vineyard and olive grove, right by the Andes.' I remember their blue haze. 'We sold chickens in the street.' People laugh. That's the story. That was me 15 years ago.

I don't think I've seen him this time for about three years. When we were both living in the same city we would see each other once or twice a year. Whenever we do we tend to go into a psychic sword fight almost from the beginning. We laugh at each other's masks because we got so close to each other as partners that we know what's real and what's not…we laugh at each other so as to not get close, to not fall into intimacy, to not even go close to where neither of us want to go but could so easily. We stay on the safe level of mask – it's too easy to slip into the past imprinted in our bodies, in our minds, in old habits. It makes no difference how much time has passed between us, it always feels like I've seen him the day before. He's ingrained somehow in who I am.

But today we don't go there – we by-pass the fencing game. Instead I ask his long term partner, stood on the edge of the Plaza del Sol, 'Can I steal him for a little while?'
'Por supuesto,' she says. I know that she knows that I know what he is really like. We smile. It's edgy.
'Will you eye-gaze with me?' I ask him.
I can feel an excitement and a fear. He nods over-confidently. I can tell that he's a bit blindsided. We are going out of our regular comfort zone. We move together through the hundreds of people sat in the plaza gazing into the eyes of the person opposite – friend, lover, stranger – and find a space to put down a thin sarong. We sit crossed legged, touching knees – we have hardly spoken – and gaze into each other's eyes. My brain takes no time to click back into Àngel Priscini. His eyebrows have grey in them, they are more hairy. He has some grey in his hair, but he always did. Maybe a little more? Apart from that, there is no difference. He has a goofy smile on. I don't smile back. I see the muscles in his

cheeks quiver as he lets go, out of mask face. Brave.

Gazing into someone's eyes is like looking into a secret universe. Gazing into his eyes, sat so close, I find myself looking into my own past: I start to remember. I see the image of days we spent under the olive trees, by the grapes, swinging in hammocks; as if re-opening a dusty long forgotten box in the attic of things once loved. Images come spilling out, remembering, remembering, remembering. All those idyllic bar-b-cues under the leafy trees. The Chevrolet. My Fiat 600. The Andes. I remember our comradeship, how we put together the chicken business, making a roaring trade of selling bar-b-qued chickens on the street, how we travelled together through thick and thin. I remember the adventures we hurtled through together.

I remember how united we were: such deep trust. I remember gloriously realising, weeks into our relationship, that I had not been an idiot in believing in him as he walked through the hostel door in Arequipa, covered in dust, after fearing he had abandoned me – how his bus had broken down in the middle of the mountains, what he'd had to do to get to me, Indiana Jones style.

I remember going Che Guevara style down the Rio Madre de Dios river through the Amazon jungle, no map, no guide. Eleven glorious, scary, mind-blowing days with him, Lyndsay and a German on a raft of six logs that the locals had made for us from felled trees; seeing the gold mines and locals working up to their waist in liquid dirt all day, the snake on the path and Àngel trying to jump into the skies to get away; swimming as fast as we could back to the 'safety' of the raft with the call of, 'Crocodile!' The accident in the middle of the river, raft stuck on deathly tree roots and him picking up the machete and saying in the middle of all that danger, 'pass me a banana!' I remember stopping in a village of a half-naked tribe who stared at us from behind banana plants, never having seen whites before.

I remember another trip being stranded on top of a capsized dismantled topper sail in Paraty, Brazil, shouting, 'I NEVER WANT TO SEE YOU AGAIN!' and sitting frostily back to back under the blazing sun stranded in the middle of the sea waiting for someone, anyone, to save us. Lying in bed together, laughing. Laughing so much I wondered if I would be sick.

I remember suddenly so much. I feel Love pouring up through my body, taking me by surprise. It is soft, it is intense - this is how I used to feel for him. I remember the meals around our plastic dinner table, him and me together. It is how I am feeling now. Hot tears spring through my eyes. 'I had forgotten,' I whisper through the tears, breaking the silence. He nods. He reaches for my hands. I see a tear fall from one of his eyes. It is him and me, just like we used to be. Him and me and love. I had covered it up with all those stories that over time had turned to dust. Now, here sat on this Plaza on the other side of the world, I am naked with him. Him with me. It is delicately delicious. I feel alive. I feel as if a part of me, which is not 'I', is dancing with a part of him, which is not 'him'. I feel as if we are giving 'them' space to love. I am floating. It is so beautiful to be with him again, gazing into his eyes, like we did so many pillows ago. So, so beautiful.

We breathe in. He does his funny mouth scrunch that I didn't realise 'til now was his. A smile rainbows between us.

We begin to talk. Soft cloud.

He tells me about his family. I ask him about the passing away of his mother. He tells me how the brothers and sisters have become closer. He tells me about his nephews that were once my 'nephews'. Juanma was four. He taught me how to talk Spanish with phrases such as, 'Goodbye from the hairy pig,' (un saludo del cancho peludo) and, 'witches with moustaches' (brujas con bigotes). He is now nineteen. Tall, slim, handsome doing well in college.

I tell him that I am living in England now, that it is hard, that I have grown up as an adult elsewhere, and fitting back in is challenging. I feel a stranger in my 'own' country. I tell him about my family.

We distance back into the stories of our lives. We move back to the edge of the event to my little group of friends who are watching the mass of eye-gazers. Angel and I take a selfie. We are both shining with happiness.

And he goes.

We were together for about fifteen minutes.

It was enough.

(I honestly couldn't have withstood more.)

—

Seeing Angel that day in the eye-gazing event was one of the most beautiful lessons of my life: despite the years, the ferocious Latino arguments, the terrible breakup, the distance between us, the sporadic communication, despite neither of us wanting to be partners again – our love exists. It breathes, it is. Even if we forget about it.

I feel that once two souls have connected, joined, deep in the well of love, they affect each other for ever. When two chemicals achieve a chemical reaction they change each other forever. When two psyches meet, they hold each other forever. Love, no matter how covered over it may be by ambivalent feelings, by anger, despair, by fear, is Eternal.

I know it because I felt it.

Going to the Depths

They treat the ephemeral
as if it were,
but it is us that are.

I'm in the caravan that I am now living in after breaking up with Christopher, trying to force myself out. It's Friday night. I haven't seen anyone for two days. It's a long bike ride into town but I'm going to do it – even though it's raining. Alexa has invited me to the Sound Art Radio annual party. Her friend is an international artist, who is doing her show here in the township of _____ [4], because she's from here, because these are her friends. It's a fiver to get in. Apparently it is forty if you see it in London, though it wouldn't be in a crummy community hall…

Bike locked up outside the library. I stand outside in the dark. I hesitate. I've got this far, so, breathing in for social protection, I continue onwards, buy a ticket and walk in.

Music is blaring from the radio station DJs. I watch them for a while, alone, feeling a vulnerable, unprotected detachment. They are loving it. I am not: I am wondering why I came. Wine, as in most English gatherings, seems to be the only solution. After an eternity of sonic hell I find Alexa, she too has wine. Good. We chat. It seems we are all in bad moods. I delight in our joint complaining, feeling much less alone.

In the middle of the party the artist is announced. The lights go down. People hush. The solo artist gets out a red electric tea light, walks around with it glowing against her heart. People are watching. She puts it down on the floor. She goes back to her little magic bag. Another red light. Walks around with it. Puts it on the floor. Eventually after four or five of the little lights it's clear she's making a shape. She is slow. Deliberate. She looks down the lines like she's playing snooker while moving with the grace of a lynx. Her back curves deliciously. This beautiful dancer holds us, the audience, in her hands with a soft velvet grace and keeps us there. She is making a perfect triangle. She is calming everyone's mind. Slowly we are becoming entranced by her movements, by the dark light, by the music, by the triangle of red lights.

She takes a long time to make the triangle, so that the last remaining part of my mind asks *What's this all about?* She goes to the table she's set up in the middle of the space. She has sound machines. She begins to mix noises. At first it just sounds like a street digger. Deafening, loud noise. I go onto the edge of shut down without doing so, but after a while I begin to notice that the noises are moving vibrations in me. I can feel when a noise is vibrating my stomach, or when it goes into my toes. It is hypnotising. I feel myself go from a sharp pencil shape into a flat, soft disk of a horizon. Energy has moved out from my sharp mind and is softening, widening - creating a feeling of distant bliss, of nothingness, of simply being.

Do I enter into a trance?

Dark velvet. Red tea lights. Vibrations playing through my body. Empty. Full.

The music slowly recedes back into silence. The artist walks to the door. Stands there for a little time. We are all staring at her. She puts her hands together and says, 'Thank you.' It is then that I remember I am in an artist's show. It is over too soon. It is then that I remember I am Julia and I am sat on an uncomfortable chair pressed up against the radiator for warmth in the Civic Hall. It is then that I remember I am human.

———

The saying goes that a frog thrown into boiling water will instantly jump out, but a frog put into cold water that is gradually warmed, will let itself be boiled.

I've always used this analogy in the negative. But I tonight I've learn it is true in the positive: we were gradually steamed, in that cold Civic Hall, into relaxing into a world that lies below everyday reality. Somehow we were led, Pied Piper style, into someplace else within ourselves.

Child's play

Slowly I return
- a little transformed -
and fall
uncontrollably
back to sleep.

Once the lights blind us back into 'reality', and the Sound Art Radio are back at their positions cranking up the music, Alexa turns to me, glassy eyed and shouts over the music, 'Woah!' She looks slightly dazed, 'It's hard to know where I am! Like I was there, and then suddenly I'm here in the Civic Hall.' I totally get what she's saying. 'It's just so ephemeral.' I nod. I love Alexa. She's a real seeker. Not a magazine cover, but for real, no need to blast it out, doesn't think she's better than anyone else, just experiences purely, wisely. She teaches me so much without knowing she's doing it. 'It's like it wasn't being held 'here'.'
'Yeah,' I say as loudly as I can, the beats continue. 'You know, Christopher used to talk about,' I pause, swallow, it's hard to even really say his name, 'going into the white box…'
'Yeah, like here, suddenly all these lights on, and the DJ's back, and,' she competes with the rhythmic bass, 'it's…god I wish I wasn't so drunk…it's slipping…I can't remember…'
'It's ephemeral,' I repeat, shouting back to her.

———

I return to my bike in the library courtyard to find the gate that I have never noticed is closed, locked, unable to climb over. On the gate there is a sign that I have never seen, that informs the public that the courtyard is locked between 9pm and 9am. I try the back gate. Same.

So I find myself slightly drunk knocking on Alexa's door. Her partner leans his head out of the window. He doesn't recognise me. 'Hi,' I say, trying to sound as if this were all completely normal, 'Is Alexa there?'
'She's in bed…' he says in a voice as if I were in a parallel universe where

355

people knock on your door at 11pm.

'It's just I've got my bike locked up in the library courtyard and can't get home – I wondered if I could bed down here?' I offer as explanation to the head in the window.

'Oh,' he says surprisingly casually, '…OK.'

—

I wake up and instead of having to text Alexa to see if she wants to meet in a cafe somewhere, I just go down into her lounge. 'D'you wanna cuppa tea?'

'I'll make it.'

'Did you sleep OK?'

'Yes, wonderfully.' It's a white lie. I half slept well on top of her son's bunk bed. It wasn't the double to single spacing but the sound of the fish tank all night.

'So,' she says, once I slump temporarily onto the soft sofa. 'What's going on with Christopher?'

'We split.'

She is not surprised. This is not the first time. I tell her what happened – he can't take the feeling of happiness. Feels too dangerous. Can't take real. Wants only fantasy. That he felt abandoned when I went to Spain, even though I podcasted him every day. How he went back into his passive aggressive silence when I needed him to be able to bathe in his house.

'Haven't you got a shower?'

'Not in the caravan, but now I can use the house's shower. It's all OK…' It's actually really great. 'I just realised that given the power of me needing him, he was going to turn it into a power struggle, and I just couldn't deal with it.'

'It's sad.'

'It's really sad,' I agree.

'But deep down we know what we need,' she says softly, firmly.

'Yeaaa…'

'You don't agree?' she looks surprised.

I stare at the coffee table in the middle of the room. 'Well…how to say it? It's like down in that place of knowing, yes, of course, I know, down in the deep still waters everything seems so clear, in that place where we aren't so much 'us',' I tap my body, 'you know? The us that is not who we are in everyday life, but more what we become whatever it is that we are deep down…you know what I mean?'

'Like last night in the show?' she asks,

'Yes!' I look at her, thrilled to be understood.

'Go on…'

'In that ephemeral place, we do know what we need, who we are, where we are going. It seems so obvious…but when we come back to the surface reality, to the material, it's really hard to remember. It slips through my fingers. I can't remember.'

'It's like love!'

'It is love!!!' And suddenly I connect pieces of the puzzle, 'The Eternal is ephemeral!' I gaze into her eyes feeling a shattering sparkle, surprised by the newness. Joy. 'It is the Truth underneath all reality, it is more real that this 'here', and yet 'this' blocks us.' I knock on my head, 'This mortality.'

'Yeah, I think I get yer,' she says slowly, as if dragging herself out of a hangover, 'like when you go deep within and have an insight about life and it makes so much sense, so clean, nice clean lines, obvious, and then you come back out into the messy reality: I doubt if it is true, seems more like an idealistic dream, I doubt if it's even real, if I am capable of achieving what seemed so simple down there!?'

'Yeah,' I say, still tealess, 'once logic kicks in...'

—

'I'm surprised you say you don't know if you really love anyone,' I say daringly, 'I experience you as a loving person.' I sip a thick hot chocolate with Joel in the Tangerine Cafe.

'Ohh,' he says, covering over his reactions, 'I do love my children, that's automatic, but when I have to choose, it takes me into doubt. I get lost in the semantics of it all.'

'Like what?' I ask, feeling too far away on a leather sofa for this private conversation.

'Like what is love, do I love, can I love? I wonder what I am doing things for. What is duty, what is love, what is just trying to have an easier time of it all...?' I can hear him inside, grabbling with himself. His ego commandeering everything he does, twisting his natural expression into a different story.

'But do you feel your presence?' I ask, amazed that this loving man, would not feel his own loving. *Can he even recognise it?*

He looks at me. The poem I've just recited to him is still swirling around in the airs. 'Probably not...'

Suddenly it all makes sense to me. This man, one of the most loving people I have ever met, doubts if he loves - like fish doubting the existence of water. 'I mean,' I repeat, 'I see you as so loving. I see how you love your wife, your children, the people around you... how you conduct your classes... how you make people feel...'

He sits in it. I wonder if he's breaking through into feeling.

'But that's compassion isn't it?'

'Wow,' I remonstrate, smiling to soften the blow, 'you only let yourself be there for milliseconds before you twisted it back out into the logic of semantics!!'

He guffaws, 'You see? As soon as I think, I doubt...'

'But you can't think presence dude, you have to feel presence,' I say and point to my heart.

—

'We need to bring back symbols from those places that seem so ephemeral, but are actually Eternal, just to remember that they exist,' I say as an introduction to the poetry workshop I am facilitating, 'to try and capture what we know and bring it back to the shores of our waking lives.' Even when I'm leading a workshop to dive ephemerally into the eternal realms of the inner worlds, I doubt myself, wondering if I'm just making it up, *is this just a collective fantasy?* 'The poem isn't anything more than a souvenir, it's just a reminder of where we have been inside.'

Between worlds

The lotus rose
and from the mire
through the thorns
white velvet grew.

After the workshop the attendees come up to me with tears in their eyes, thanking me. Their faces have changed, are brighter, more open, flushed. I wonder where they have been. I wonder how. I wonder. I feel so grateful to something unknown.

—

'I know it's not the same,' Alexa says on her sofa, 'but at work I went to my boss and said, 'you know, I do often love my job. I like being with the kids. I like making a difference to them, and helping them with their problems, it's just that it often feels abusive.' I'm not sure I could do what she does. She is a personal assistant to kids who are in a mainstream primary school but who have behavioural issues due to learning disabilities. She gets used, they treat her badly, they get angry at her, they will not talk to her, they will not listen to her, they walk out, do things that are prohibited. They scream in frustration at her. She cannot raise her voice. Hard. Hard work. 'So, I said it to the boss, and she said, 'I know exactly what you mean: I can't help you with that, you will have to decide for yourself if this is something that you can continue doing.''

I get this image of a river of difficulties. The children are not going to change, and if for some miracle they do, they will be replaced by another child with a similar degree of difficulty. The river is not going to get better. The difficulties are not going to suddenly subside. The aspects that make it feel abusive are going to be fairly constant.

'But do you think you're growing as a person through it?'
'Yes, yes I do,' a quiet humility to her voice, 'I'm more patient, I am more compassionate. I've changed a lot through the job.'
'Then I guess the question is, if the problems are never going to change, are they going to help you grow and become more of who you are, helping you find your hidden gifts to bring out into the world, or are they going to drown you, destroy you, bring you down?'

It's that whole Marysas thing again: how much of life's current can each one of us let into our lives so as to heal us in its medicine rather than drowning in its poison?

—

I am complaining about Christopher. 'Men and women are just so different!'

'Tell me about it,' she groans, her voice is deep hangover.

'I mean I try and fool myself that we are all the same, you know?'

'Aha'

'But, like just for a start, we have a spillage of blood, of bad blood maybe. Men don't. Once a month we let it all out, and then we are clean again for a while; meanwhile men don't get that pressure release. It is always there, so they never get to see themselves without it.' I take a sip of my tea.

'It's like inside of Christopher there is that stream of nervous tension, and sometimes it's hidden from you, and sometimes it overflows its banks, but it's always there?' her voice rises at the end into a question. She knows him. She knows the stories between us.

'Hmmmmm, yea, maybe…' I stare into space, holding my cup of tea, 'and I guess,' I say in a far away voice, 'I have to work out, if it's not going to go away, if interacting with it will make me a better person, help me with my growth, give me the impetus to change, or if it will just drown me…' Alexa's eyes are glassy, she leans over to reach for her half warm tea. 'The thing is,' I tell her, 'that underneath there is so much love for him, and him to me, it's just that above, out of the ephemeral, in the stark reality, it's hard to get our psyches to work well together.'

'That's what I'm saying,' she says softly in her comforting Blackpool accent, 'Is it worth it?'

—

Polyamory has helped me grow so much. I've somehow worked through my fear of rejection. *How is that?* I think of all of the times Paul and I split up. How I felt rejected, only for nothing really to have changed. I love him. He loves me. We find it hard to stay together. I think about when Christopher and I, walking down the River Dart one night decided to be monogamous and Paul gracefully, on the other side of the world, stepped away. Months later Paul called to say that he was entering into a new relationship, she wanted to be monogamous. 'Where do we stand?' I hear the vulnerability in his question. I felt his sweet love still there, still present, across from the other side of the world, across from the other side of splitting up, across from the other side of arguments, of things that had gone wrong, of him needing me to be someone else, of me needing him to be someone else, of all that had come between us, 'I left a door open for us,' he says, 'should I close it?'

'Yes,' I say, knowing him. He needs an absolute.

I swim into the stars, feeling this love between us, allowing him to go. I realise it's a similar love for what he has for me. All those times I cried into my pillow feeling so distraught, I realise now how I had never been rejected at all – we had only separated. Through all these joint experiences, respecting each other, allowing the surface to unfold, the bond of love underneath it all holds firm.

—

Careful to keep some froth for the last sip, I sip on the hot chocolate in the 'The Sea Trout' in Staverton. Ganga stays quiet, holding space for me. 'It's sad.' I am on the edge of tears, 'It's the end, and though it feels right, I'm finding it hard to let go.'

'You deserve more,' Ganga says again. It's hard to believe. She's about the fifth person to say so and yet still I cling to denial.

—

We walk out of the pub, along the dark Devon road. It is night, it went dark at four thirty. It is not raining anymore but we both have our damp waterproof coats and trousers on. Ganga says, 'Wow, it's so hard to know: it could be four o'clock or twelve o'clock.'

'And somehow,' I join in, 'it could be any road in the world.'

'Timeless and spaceless…'

We walk in silence for a while, walking through this ubiquitous world, a stem cell world. It feels like we are inside a huge invisible mother cell so full of potential that it could birth us through time and space into absolutely anything, anywhere.

We get to the junction where we have to part. 'So good to see you.'

'Same here.'

'You saved the day for me. I was getting a bit too far into myself all alone in that caravan,' I admit.

'You know where I am,' says her voice in the dark. 'It was lovely to talk. See you soon.' We both have headlamps on. We cannot see each other. If we look straight at each other we'll blind ourselves with the other's light; if we cover our lights with our hands we cannot see each other in the dark. We separate. I am not sure when.

I am walking up the road back into solitude and feel the familiar dread. *Is it the dark? Is it the wet weather?* I am walking quickly as if I need to get back to the safety of the caravan, though actually I have no plans, nothing 'to do'. I am in a tiny road between two high hedgerows. This is a maze. A labyrinth straight out of a book of Borges. No cars. No people. The stars are out shining. I glance up at them and continue at the same pace, slightly out of breath. After a while I notice my teeth grinding. *How long has that being going on?* I pop the gum shield back onto my lower teeth.

—

I think of a brief affair I had with a man called Mark. I was part of a string of ex-girlfriends who all ended up feeling so very similar to me: abused. I remember how he could never, ever spend any time away from either his phone, or his computer: constantly checking mails, messages, texts, consuming YouTube's, films, listening to podcasts. When he didn't have a mobile in his hand he would have his guitar. He was never ever in silence with himself, ever. Not for a minute. He was always plugged in to never have to feel.

I am still walking at a fair pace, pushed on by my fear of not being in the caravan, by my fear of having to endure more solitude, the fear of being disconnected from society. I wonder if I'm doing the same as that awful man, Mark. *Am I giving myself space?* I slow down. I am afraid. The trees seems ominous. I feel so very far away from anyone, anything. *What is in these woods?*

I realise I am walking fast to cover over my feelings. *Who will be there if I get into danger? No-one.* Flashes of images come through me: we, as a human race, become scared if we are not connected to something safe. We need cars to know we can get someplace. We need people close to feel we are safe. We need the mothering of our sibling society to feel we are not in danger. I am walking alone, far, far away from society. I feel afraid.

—

I think of Ian, Agapius's friend in Greece, who after forty-three years of marriage separated from his wife. She beseeched him, '…but what happens if I fall and hurt myself? Who will be there for me?' He replied to her, 'What happens if *I* fall?'

The fear of getting old alone.

—

Being alone, walking up this dark lane, feels like the layers of secure life are being stripped down too close to death. I think of children who need to be close to their mothers else they feel unsafe. I think of adults who need to be close to safety. *Is it really true that eighty percent of tourists do not stray more than half a mile from the car park?* I feel my heart racing, afraid of walking half an hour up the Devon road in the dark. I march on.

—

Suddenly, under the silhouette of a huge winter tree I have a jump of consciousness: this is part of learning how to live – learning to be alone, learning to go through situations without others. I look out, it is actually not cold at all. It is not raining. It is actually really pleasant. I actually do not need to emergency exit at all. In fact – I can relax.

Eternal becoming

Human ideas
become stale
theories, isms
lose their brilliance.
A famous king
now obscure
forgotten.

Nature!
How do you do it?
Always new,
wondrous
moving.
How do you stay
in the Eternal?

I remember a cartoon I saw once. A speech bubble besides a confused character, 'This is it.' So simple, it's alarming. There is no rehearsal for life. This really is it.

Like NOW!

I stop, stand on the road and look up to the stars. The sky is so clear. It is actually quite amazing to think of that light coming through my eyes after travelling millions of light years. I look to the trees. Before as they waved in the shadows they felt ominous like witches about to pounce, but now, having calmed my heart, I allow their beauty to emerge, silhouetted against the night sky, stars shining through the gaps. I breathe it in. I feel closer to myself. This journey home alone can be scary or it can be enjoyable. I make that decision. I, myself.

I realise that I am not in the fabricated mother of society – I am in Mother Nature. I need not feel terrified. This is nature; this is my nature. This is.

—

I wonder if this is how it is to die – to walk alone into the dark?

—

I remember reading about an account of a near death experience. It described a journey through a tunnel, at the end of the tunnel was a light that pulled the soul towards it with a magnetic pull.

The man wrote that we don't have to rush through the journey, rushing into the pull of the light, on the contrary, the tunnel holds so much wonder, so much knowledge, if only we can allow ourselves to experience it. The journey, he said, is so much more nourishing if we have the will power to meander slowly towards the light, in joy and peace, rather than dashing to it in blind panic and fear.

—

I don't know when I leave behind my jacket of fears and enter into the world of slow, but I do. I feel closer to myself, to the earth, to the skies.

—

Meandering home, quite content now, I look up to the stars and laugh at myself sending love up to them, wondering in my parallel mind, if in a million light years (or would it be love years?) they may receive this feeling of joy, of being alive, if they too will laugh benevolently at the relief of my fears being groundless, and smile with me feeling myself immersed in the unfolding beauty, belonging as part of it, as a human being.

—

Walking all on my tod through these lanes, through this marvel of nature, I feel for an ephemeral moment of eternity that I have shed my jackets of fear and have become nothing but light and love, connected to all, even the stars. I am in awe of being so alive.

The Eternal You

'Eternity is within time, not out of it...'
I say as we pack up, amazed how late it is.
Out from his guitar case
he turns to me, face screwed into silly.
I mutter, 'I'm fairly sure,' suddenly
feeling pretty god-damn lame:
I mean, how can anyone 'know' this?

In my frozen stance images flood:
a beloved teacher
vulnerable
standing shy at the front of a lecture hall
talking about 'God,' or 'the Eternal',
as he says,
'Don't look for me outside of time:
I'm not there.'

Then a visiting Argentinean
his dulcet tones declaring,
'Dios es donde vos no sos,'
(God is where you are not).

A flash of lying on the sofa
on Aribau and Mallorca
and the countless times
I've ended up in my heart mind
simply knowing – no faith needed –
that we are but 'channels' of time.

I memory into the times
so at peace I am with the moment
that I forget who is what
and what is where,
unaware even that I am bathing
in a state of blissful surrender
where I forget I am less than this moment,
where I forget I am less than god.

PART VIII

Eternal Becoming

Chapter 28: Moonrise in the World of Slow

Slowing down, worlds open.

The Abundance of Time

On the other side
of centuries
a colossal circular vase
crafted with
bulls and bouquets
dripping milk white
abundance.
So much time they spent
reminding themselves
with their daily objects
of repeated victories
over winter –
beautifying the everyday
to remember the gift
of simply being alive.

Under this same slow sun
their springs too arrived
swimming through time;
relief floods through
honeyed by gratitude
stamped on this lifeless thing.

What would they think of us now
thousands of winters later?
Running, running, running
minds caught not in life, nor seasons
but trapped in machines
- silver rivers of speeding fumes,
rows and rows of single crops,
squares of pixelated life -
as we take the sun for granted
to frantically bulldoze through
our notion of time...?

There is something mystical about being in a field with a moon rise, full moon, blackened trees silhouetted on the horizon, some leafless, their long elegant fingers coming out from the ground. The clouds take on halo qualities as the moonlight reflects on them. Walking through the field at night, alone, with no one around, I feel like the queen of right here where I am. Because right now I am. Water droplets hang onto every strand of grass, glistening under the light of my headlamp, leading me into magical wonder. I move through the mist, awed by the generosity of welcome, allowed into the intimacy of Mother Nature as she beds for the night. Animals seem to accept me as another silent one, connected somehow, because we are.

Why is this surprisingly natural?

Why isn't everyone doing this?

I sink into the ease of it all, awash with sensations of peace and quiet joy seeing new, surprising beauty at every step: the white light of the moon on the top of the trees, the white light of my torch at the bottom. I ease into a closeness, all of us dependent on this same damp air. I see my breath, lit up like bonfire smoke in my headlamp. It is pure heaven to be out here walking through tall grass in the velvety dark, wrapped in the arms of nature.

I hit the road, the drive into Dartington Hall. Tarmac but no cars. Nobody goes there now, not at this time. The same trees. I can hear the river. The walking is easier, faster. I get into a rhythm. I go inside. I begin to associate with the images I am making in my head, going into dreaming, fantasies. It takes me a couple of minutes to realise I am not now Queen of where I am. I realise that I have to remember. I look again for the full moon, but I am not awestruck, not on the road. I do not sense wonder at this tree on my path as the pavement makes a semi circle around it – it is now simply in the way.

I leave and go in again, into my mind, wondering now about this. Is this the difference between being awakened and oblivious? Is this my normal sleep-walking state? We walk on concrete hardness, going fast as to not go slow over our fears. The critic drives the roller, compressing the earth of our psyches so it cannot breathe beneath our feet. Compact sterility. We have to keep trying to remember – it is all too easy to disconnect. We have to set alarms, to wake us from the slumber of being in our minds, trapped prisoners holding all the keys.

Are we so separated from our own true natures that we have to remember to notice our own presence that breathes eternally through us?

I breathe, consciously, it is so easy to do. But it is easier to forget to notice.

The truth hides in the simple: it is where it is more easily overlooked.

In my internal wanderings I forget the trees and the full moon and the white spirited mist that comes out on every breath. I forget even that I am breathing.

I arrive – at last! – at my bike. In the fields I was upset to see the end of my adventure, upset to see the road, upset there was no more walk. On the road I was rushing to get off. I realise that I am still, even on tarmac, alone. Surrounded all around, except underfoot, by nature. I can still feel myself in it, even if I am insulated from connecting to it through my steps. I need the toilet. So beside my bike, I step off the road, jump over the wooden fence and stoop down. Crouched down I peer between the trees.

The river is as beautiful as before, flowing slowly, a powerful silver snake. The banks are pregnant with rainwater. I remember the other day, stood by the river, fifteen minutes or more, watching the reflection of the trees ripple and slowly becoming shocked by its perfect beauty. It is impossible now to repeat that experience, everything is constantly birthing anew: the river, the tree, the reflection, me. Everything is constantly changing its expression of perfect art. If a human could create the art of that reflection in the rippling water, they would be considered a genius. I remember remembering, stood there by the river, to go slowly. Everything changes but I can return to a place of slow that opens up worlds that are constantly weaving their craft of life. With slow comes a deeper awareness, a connection that goes right into worlds that are ready and waiting to open its doors and let us partake of their magic. I pull up my trousers, and instead of rushing back to my bike, to get out of the dark night air, I remember. I stay put and gaze.

As my heart beat slows, I start to hear again the music of nature all around me. As I slow I begin to notice what I notice, realising where I am, that I am part of this deep place within this planet earth. As I slow down I notice just how beautiful the moonlight is on the water, as if I could see through layers of intricate, delicate patterns of beauty. As I slow I begin to feel alive again.

———

In Greece our life drawing teacher, Jennifer, declared that the next class would be in the local museum. Inside I groaned. I had been there months before only to be positively unaware of anything of even vague interest. She explained the 'Slow Art Movement' to us. 'It is like the 'Slow Food Movement' she began, 'not to gobble, but to enjoy'. We were to stand in front of a piece, any piece, within the museum for ten minutes. We're to do it three times.

Which to choose? It took me a while even to be able to stop in front of something. I chose one, it wasn't quite right, I'm not sure why. I stood. No watch. *Does anyone have a watch?* I wanted to know. My logic needed to control something: something inside knew I was shedding off the day and going into some deep cave - I needed security, the torch of at least knowing the time. Yes someone had a watch. I relax. I relinquish control over time - as if I had ever had any control over it! I drag my attention away from the movement of its hands and prepare myself to stare aimlessly.

What is it? What is that drawing on the water vase? What are they doing? I am taken aback in time, wondering why that woman is bent over and that man has – what is that he has is his hand? I move around the vase, there is more. I look. It is kind of interesting. Two women, or men in skirts, offering something to an eagle god. *What are they offering? Has something happened to them? Is it for protection? Giving thanks? Fear?* I imagine myself in their place, but can't, they seem too far away. *What does it mean to them?* There are straight, perfect lines around the vase, *how did they make those lines?*

What time is it? I wonder if we are nearly ten minutes now? *Only four? Only four...god it feels like fifteen. I've seen all of this. What can I do now? Just stare? Really?*

I stare. I stare at the lines and imagine the person who painted them, what 3,000 years ago? Maybe more. His hand, just like my hand, making decoration on a clay pot. Amazing really. And the ink has stayed all that time... *When he was making this line what was he thinking? How did he feel about life?* I read the sign. This was a pot made on Paros - *This very same island! Maybe it was made somewhere I know, somewhere I've been too? Maybe it was made on my street? The artisan must have done the same walks I do along the sea path – 3,000 years ago. What? How?* My mind goes agog.

I begin to slow down. I am feeling this hand, this ghost hand come alive, from so long ago, the artist's hand who worked on this very piece. This piece. I can touch it. This piece right here on Paros. I am separated from that hand, from that artist crafting, from his mind, only now in time...this vase is his production - I feel as if we are connecting through the centuries, our minds, our hands, our bodies. The artist was here on Paros. I am here on Paros. I can feel the movements of his mind; I feel my mind moving around the patterning of the vase enquiring as to his. I begin to feel instead of think.

Ten minutes.

Change.

A tomb stone. The dead man sat before his death with a woman, she is intent on listening to him. *What is he telling her?* I try to feel into what a man 3,500 years ago would feel was the most important thing to say on his gravestone. What will I want to say in my last hours? His choice, the culmination of his life, is written at the bottom in ancient Greek. But I know that those written words can't hold what he's trying to tell her...it's the bend in his waist as he moves towards her with his ideas, something that was really important to him, his last parting gift, the product of his life. I can feel her trying to capture him and his wisdom in the way she leans into him. *Is it his wife? What sort of relationship did they have?* I find myself merging into sensations of what exists between them…sinking into it like a warm bath. I wonder how they considered love, these ancient Greeks. I move around, slowly. I feel the saliva in my throat and swallow. I know that sensation, I am going in…

I touch the edge of the stone, my hands are touching where their hands must have touched. My hands touching where the stonemason cut the stone, where the artisan chiselled them out. *Are they a good likeness? Did she finger his outline for years afterwards as mine is now? Is part of her still held in this stone. How long does a finger touch last?* I am travelling through time, on this island. On my island, my home, on their island, their home. We are neighbours in the corridors of time.

Ten minutes.

I stand in front of a sculpture of a woman. She was on a roof of a fine building. I want to hug her. I want to feel her breasts as they come out from that snake skin that wraps up around her legs. *Is she an Eve?* I want to know why she was chosen to be sculptured. *Was it a temple? Who walked below?* I imagine a colossal building, crowds of hunched people passing below her. *What did they do in the temple?* I imagine myself one of them, being scared by her, or no, maybe, I loved her, she was my guide, my protector, my object of trust. *What did they believe? How did they process this unknowingness of being alive?* I stare in to her eyes, trying to see what she saw. I touch her leg. She is tall. Too tall to even touch her snake belt. I feel myself being drawn into her mystic. I feel myself afraid of her power. Dark power. *Who are you?*

As if an invisible god in the sky I watch the multitudes of people going into the building. *Did they look up and cower? Did she play a part in their lives? Was she adored or feared? Was she venerated, people projecting onto this stone all of their wishes that if they came true, gave this piece of stone, this sculpture of this woman in the snake skin, a power all of her own? Were the people terrified by her? Controlled by her? Was she there to make people enter the building in reverence or to stay away?*

Time has become irrelevant.

I stand in silence inside and just feel.

Awe.

Fear.

Joy.

Another world.

Ten minutes. *Already?*

The whole day afterwards slipped into bliss. I met a friend, felt the love between us. She asked me to go for a drink down by the sea front. I was relaxed enough to accept, to change my plans. We had a wonderful conversation about how we relate to men. I would have missed all of that going too fast. I felt full of poetry after we left, and wrote, wrote, wrote until I was drunk on words and lay on the seafront wall, staring up at Agios Konstantinos and seeing for the first time (how many times have I looked up there?) that there is a clear unfinished triangle, as if the top of the triangle were made of air, of heaven. I feel sublime. I feel wonderfully connected to all that is life, to the world, to the waves that lull me deeper into myself. I am swimming in grace on the shores of the world of slow.

———

And so crouched beside my bicycle, watching the silver snake of the river Dart, I realise that I have slowed down again, this time for the sake of my own nature. I drink in the beauty of the river, feel it. I suddenly have the sensuous access to more pixels in my outer vision, in my inner vision, more details. I open more to receive. I am alive, part of this whole act of Beauty.

I wish I could stay here forever, connected to the wonder of being alive. If only I could always simply be, feeling the breeze, becoming part of the moonrise.

Slow Art

Slowly, seeing through stone
into the mystery between the cracks
we connect to the heart
that created these wonders millenniums ago;
hearts like our own.

A disc thrower
his faint throw intensifying the longer we give him;
our minds becoming as his feet:
slowly unfolding from their bond of stone
to spiral freely out into the movement
of timelessness.

We read the headline, 'Lion eats bull!'
A stone slab in transition of dying
comes alive under our gaze.
We water the dead with our presence
re-creating the god power within.

Blown away by stones
their graceful humility plunges us into awe.
Ohh face long past sculptured I cannot see you
– the Siroccos of time have stolen your fierce lines –
I feel only your soft beauty snaking into a bird
as you dominate the serpent hissing around your belted waist.
You were petrifying once, your black make-up terrifying,
but like Ozymandias
the sands of time have robbed you of your power:
We have lost our fear.
Where can we place it now?

As we breathe in this arcane memory
worn thin through time
it lives on all too faintly
leaving us to grabble with life's mysteries.

What happens to humanity?

Relationships come back to life
the longer we gaze,
the longer we allow ourselves
to deepen into something
impossible to describe.

Chapter 29: Enthusiasm - the Rainbow between Heaven and Earth

Going in and coming out, expressing
the origin of who we all are in our
own unique, original way.

Emanating

Soft light
surrounds you
as I gaze
through my windows
watching
who you are.

Neil, the son of a friend, comes round asking sheepishly for a bag of fertiliser. We both know what he's growing. I like that he is adventurous. We talk about going into that place that Henri Corbin and his studies on Islamic mysticism calls, 'illo tempore'. I am comfortable in this subject, well versed, thanks to the wonderful lectures in the Jung Institute.

'Do you know the difference,' I ask this young adventurer, 'between a genius and a psychotic?' I see his eyes widen on the word genius as if the secret he has told no-one about himself had been publicly revealed coupled with a sudden fear of not knowing the difference between that and loony. He moves his head very slightly.

'They both,' I say, suddenly the elder, 'go to the same place…' I wave my hand in spirals upwards, what else can I do? He nods. He's with me. 'The genius can ground it. They can bring it back down to this surface level of living,' I knock on the solid, wooden table, 'and is able to express it, formulate it, birth it.' I'm not sure if I'm off limits. 'In order to re-create life on earth that is….better.'

I want to talking about bringing heaven down to earth, or go into the matter of V.I.T.R.I.O.L[7] bringing heaven out of earth. But I hang back. He looks at me, a quick dart. It's a big responsibility to talk to teenagers, they have so little filtering system.

'Better!' I say, scoffing at myself, 'What is better? Perhaps I should say, more 'subtle', or, 'harmonious'…' I really don't know if I'm out on a limb here. 'You know?'
He looks up again slowly. 'Like Einstein who moved physics onto a different level…' his voice tapers off into another world.
'Yeah, or a car mechanic I knew in Argentina. I had an old Fiat 600 that was constantly breaking down. I'd go to his garage, and he attended the car with such love. I'd go back to pick up the car and hang out with him, sharing yerba maté – he'd always have some exquisite food of some sort too, snails, or pate he'd made himself – and when I came out of his garage, I'd feel not only had my car been fixed but me too.'

Falling into deeperness

I like being with you.
In your depth,
I feel soft space under me
where I can sink into myself
a little more.

'Poets do that too…' Neil adds.
'Yeah…' I feel a little heat go into my cheeks.

Moving on I say, 'Meanwhile a psychotic stays up there, unable to come back. He can't connect the two realities and is just unable to function on this plane.' I remember a guy I knew in Paros, 'In fact it seems so often that all around them they wreak havoc.'
'What's a psychotic?' he asks bravely.
'Someone whose ego, Jungian ego, not a Buddhist ego…' I look at him. He's not going to admit that he doesn't know. 'You know, like a container?' He nods wisely. 'They can't contain the energy of life going through them and under the pressure the ego container splits, breaks in two,' I put my hands out wide apart, 'then there are two different centres, different 'I's, and these, seeing the 'other' as 'foreign', attack each other.' He looks at me, as if looking into a different world within himself. I can't work out if he considers me some daft old bat, or if he's heard me.
'And,' he says, 'that happens to a lot of people?'

I sense where he's coming from. If you don't pay respect to the world he's about to enter, it can and will destroy. 'It all depends how grounded you are. Like how much of your self-image is stable enough to – under certain conditions – ' I glance into his eyes, checking we're on the same page and find an almost imperceptible nod hidden in the casualness of a straight stare, '…to be confused for a while, to be able to go out of who we are used to identifying as, and be able to fly in the unknown, knowing that we have a safe landing on the return.'

He looks a question at me from his prison of silence. 'You know, so we have a safe landing strip, so to speak, someplace where we can recollect our identity as balanced beings in this ever changing chaos,' I'm not sure if I've overdone it, but I want him to know it's dangerous territory if unprepared, without putting him off from going there; I guess I'm trying to install a proper amount of awe and respect – the camel through the eye of a needle, 'That place within us has to be flexible enough to land any change, to be able to adapt to it, and yet be stable enough to maintain itself as terra firma without falling apart into madness?'

I feel a sort of shudder at the end of a pause of silence, as if he had gone there in his mind and has landed somewhat clumsily back to earth. His face deadpan.

'Yeah,' he says, 'thanks for that…' he holds up the bag of fertiliser and makes a quick exit.

The door closes, softly. He didn't slam it shut in his haste.

He'll be fine.

—

I am giving the 'Journey into Poetry' workshop. We are all sat in a yurt. Fifteen people are looking at me, I am filled with confidence. Words tumble out of my mouth without my thinking them. I am on a roll. 'Consider the word

'Original',' I say, 'not as in 'new,' or 'to stand out from the rest,' but arising from 'Origin'.' I pause to let it sink in a little. I really want them to relax and move away from the tension of trying to be different, so that they can express themselves in their own 'obvious' (to them) creativity and not try and emanate someone else's. Difficult does not mean better. 'Our Origin is a shared heritage that we are all born out of,' I venture, going on out a limb, 'in the same way that we are all made from star dust.'

I look around into each face in the circle. I feel like I am a primary teacher telling a story - I can tell by the velvety drop in silence that they are all with me. 'Origin is endowed to each of us: it is our shared humanity, the source of our birth, of all of our births.' I wave my arms to encompass the world. 'Once we have created a relationship with that which lies deep within us,' I look around the circle, 'once we have followed a pathway to Origin – once we have felt it, experienced it – the way we express it is unique to each of us, in the same way each snowflake's shape is unique.' Almost still faces nod deeply. 'Expressing it, creating with it, is healing…' I shift gear, 'so that's where we are going to go try get to right now, where we are going to swim down to in this guided journey. The poem we write at the end is just the souvenir.'

Creative Freedom

Opening passed
black and white
the infinite
splashes out from within
– reds, oranges, yellows,
greens, purples, indigos –
infusing
with gleeful freedom
into my words and images,
sounds and movements,
liberating me
into feeling
the world
of difference between
'This is the right way'
and
'There is no wrong way.'

After the choir practise I am buzzing. I swim in the sea, immersed in the world, feeling the water running around me, the sun setting. I am in harmony. I am in love. In the absence of a man in my life, I wonder where these feelings of being in love come from.

I don't know, I don't care, I just feel sublime.

The Peace of Letting Go

I swim into the blue
tingling
divine,

alone.

Ears below the surface of sound,
deep within me
someone breathes...

'Like the placebo effect...' I say to Lucien, as I begin to pull down my jeans
to change into more suitable walking trousers, 'Don't worry,' I say, 'I've got
long-johns on underneath.' He laughs, relief and a funny tinge of disappointment.
Not much to see anyway, apart from Marks and Spenser's standard issues greyed
through the wrings of time.

It's weirdly exciting because we don't really know each other. This is the first
time we've met without Christopher. 'What about the placebo effect?' he
continues as if unaffected by my totally unsuitable place for changing attire.
Why didn't I step into the bathroom?
'Well,' I say, stepping into a leg, enjoying him watching, 'people say, 'It's only a
placebo effect', but surely that's the golden medicine? It's proof we have healed
ourselves!'
It feels like he reels back a little against the sideboard. 'Yes! Yes! You're right!'
'It's as if we have tricked ourselves into believing that we can heal – and then we
do!'
He laughs and looks at me as if I were the next prophet. 'Why have I never
thought of that?' and then sort of dances without moving.

I stand, pulling up my thermal padded trousers, stepping into glee. I do love
chatting with Lucien, he is so intelligent, so humble, so sensitive, so vulnerable
on top of a ground rock of deep self-assurance. When I get honest with myself, I
realise that I am flirting with this almost stranger. We are chatting philosophy,
which turns me on, and yet it is completely safe, because he's married, and he's a
good man.

'My dad told me about this janitor in the hospital who had to go in for an
operation...' I begin. Lucien looks at me, as if he could listen to stories all day
long. We are both slightly high on the excitement of expectation, him for where I
am going in this labyrinth, me for where he may take me onto, 'he couldn't sleep
in the night, but of course, he knew all the nurses because he worked with them.
So he calls out to the night nurse, 'Jackie, will you give me a sleeping pill?' But
she says, 'I can't Joe, it's against protocol.'
'Oh come on Jackie, I can't sleep!'
She looks at him, and lets out a long breath as if deciding what to do. 'OK then,'
and she hands over a little pill.

Next morning he says to her, 'Wow, what were those sleeping pills? I haven't slept better in years!'

'They were aspirin!''

We laugh. It is so nice to laugh together, feeling our minds dance through ideas. There is an uncomfortable silence which I fill with, 'All we need to do is believe we can heal, or that 'something' will heal us,' and start to look for my hiking socks.

'Like the brain relaxes enough,' says Lucien across the room to me, 'to let the endocrine system kick in and secrete hormones; and so balance the body with its present conditions - so that the inside mirrors the outside... it's like we stop blocking our own health!' I love how he takes ideas further.

'What's the endocrine system?' I ask pretending that I'm used to getting ready to go out as someone watches me.

'The system of glands through our body that secrete into the bloodstream all of the hormones and stuff that we need to be healthy and function well...'

I look at him, leaning against the sideboard still in my lovely, new pad. I feel so at home here. So good here. I feel so good with him here too, though it's a bit weird because without Christopher around, we barely know each other. I just know that we both yearn for sensitive, intelligent conversations, like an oasis in a modern desert of thoughtlessness. 'It's like a phrase in Argentinean – I like it because it rhymes – 'Dios es donde vos no sos!' which means, 'God is where you are not.' He looks at me. The god word is always so triggering...I hasten to add, 'Like when we remove ourselves, our egos, our sense of individual self, we can experience the divine within us...'

'The healing capacity?'

'Exactly!' I love it how he so easily connects concepts. 'We open up, let go, surrender into our innate wisdom, instead of becoming infirm. 'Ferme' like in French,'

'To close?'

'Yeah, so 'Infirm' is to be enclosed within: controlling, not allowing anything to come in. Not allowing life to change us.' He smiles, he likes it. It's so nice to say these things and someone appreciate it as much as I do. So satisfying. In fact it is so pleasurable that I feel sensations rippling through me, healing my loneliness.

'So healing is getting in contact with our own source of mending ourselves, our own self capacity to heal?'

'I guess...' I suddenly get a sense that the day is not forever, winter days in England are short. 'We should be getting going, I've got the picnic ready and flasks of hot tea.' But I've not got my boots on or the flasks in my bag. My mind is going in one direction and my body in another. I hang in the space pulled between directions: shoes, flasks. Lucien looks at me in a strange way. I can't work it out. *Is he itching to get away?* My feminine side though has a completely different take. I put my boots on at lightning speed.

———

Flicking through Facebook I read some quotes from Confucius, born 500 BCE. Just 500 years BEFORE Jesus Christ! I think of all of the wise people we have the richness to get to know about, the books that have been passed down to us throughout so many different ages, so many different cultures. It makes a pattern in my head, like a map with dots all over it. I feel like I am seeing the world from space at night, all the street lamps shining like stars in the darkness. Each wise person shining out their light. I feel the comfort of 'seeing' people emanating all over our collective psychic landscape their sculptured wisdom connecting us all. My heart is gladdened imagining all these people, hundreds, thousands of saints and Sufis, aborigines and maestros, shepherds and scholars, mechanics and midwives shining out the treasures they've collected from the depths, from the heights, from within, from without. I am awed by the myriads of unique lights emitting the experience of connection with Origin, Source, from where we are all from. So many wonderful people. So why do we get so stuck on Jesus Christ? Could it not be that he is simply one more of them, one more street lamp shining out brightly on the map of deep human wisdom?

Suddenly I see that map of the globe obliterated, all the darkness streaming in, as we are forced to look at only one point of light emanating out of Israel. Fixing our attention on a single part of the immensity of the whole, we make Jesus into a false idol. It suddenly seems as if we are afraid to acknowledge anything but Jesus! How absurd that millions of people are trying to concentrate themselves into this one single point of light particular and unique to Jesus, ignoring their own rich tapestry of life, modelling themselves on his expression of what we all are, while ignoring our own unique expression of the same, shared Origin. The Origin from where we were all birthed wherever we were on the globe.

I feel the encroachment of so many mental illnesses, of having closed down life, stuck within the confines of a restricted inner life. Whole congregations trying to grab onto one thing, one single thing, as if there were no other thing that existed in the world. Our minds plummeting into creating the feeling of scarcity as we wish for time to stop, desperate for space to stop spinning, trying to recreate a single life again that kneaded over the centuries has been turned into dogma.

Two-thousand years later as we spin out further away from 'that' time, we have at our backs a history of fighting and killing, of desperately attempting to reduce the world to what we think we should experience, what we have been told Jesus Christ would like for us.

I respect the true message of Jesus Christ, whoever that may have been, as a much deeper experience than I may have had, or may ever have, combined miraculously with a pristine expression of the Eternal, of Source, a perfect expression of Origin, (as he called it: from 'God the Father'). So precious and valuable, especially in its day, and somehow it still moves people's hearts though it was created in a different society, a different time, with different constraints. Jesus expressed the Eternal. But there are other people too who have experienced 'God the Father.' I have (though an absolute beginner and nowhere near to the same degree). And though JC didn't surf the internet, never ate a frozen meal and had to cope with a lot of illiteracy and a penal system that ready accepted public humiliation, capital punishment and thought nothing of nailing wrists to crosses,

I can use his experience to help me see my own though a different lens. But surely, Jesus' experience is not more alive in me, than my own? Why would I give my power away to an idol?

Which feels like blasphemy and sounds horrible, conceited, arrogant, even decades after surviving Catholic schools, where it was drummed into us that Jesus Christ was the only son of the Father. The only One.

But let's distinguish between 'Jesus who was a man' and 'The Christ State'. We all have our different ideas about Jesus as a man, and how will we ever know? The Christ State, at least to me, is a state of being in deep connection with Self, with Source, with 'God the Father'. It is, for me, the western equivalent of the Buddha State, as Siddhartha says, 'There have been many Buddhas before me and will be many Buddhas in the future,' and goes on to teach us, 'All living beings have the Buddha nature and can become Buddhas.' And so, it makes sense that he would teach us the way to Buddhahood, something that we can all, to varying degrees, taste. The Christ State lives on, because it is in each of us. We can all potentially, consciously connect to Origin.

Let's say Jesus is gone; and yes, of course his spirit is still amongst our collective consciousness, else I would have to do an introduction on who Jesus is, but, admit it die-hards, his physical body is dead. So let's say that he has affected the shape of our collective consciousness. I'll go with that. But he is NOT THE ONLY ONE. We all affect the collective. To different degrees. There are sages and wise, loving spiritual people who also have deeply affected the collective. Thousands of them. Millions of us also each making tiny little dots on the map, adding our little fairy light to the tree of life.

I feel painful sadness mixed with fury wondering about whole generations of wisdom decimated, ignored, unheard, as we silenced, or even killed, sages who were not Jesus Christ pushed on by the belief that the only real word has already been spoken, lost in the waves of time.

—

What is Love?

—

I invite two girlfriends around for dinner. We are lounging around the table, just finished bowlfuls of spinach curry. Delicious. The candles are flickering and we are doing that women's thing where instead of needing to actually say anything in a lineal, conclusive way, we are meandering through ideas, laughing at the way the conversation turns, enjoying the absurd, feeling the sensitive, processing life together in such a womanly way that it is deeply nourishing.

Introvert Ganga launches into a story, 'There was a girl in a camp that I was facilitating,' she looks at us over the candles, 'I was playing the ukulele, I'm not so good at it. There were only six of them, all between seven and eleven. I felt like we were all equals around the fire. One of the girls wanted to tell a story, but she kept forgetting important bits.' Her eyes are dark and penetrative that somehow pick up reflections of any existing light anywhere close, 'But she didn't care. Her friend kept having to add in details for her. To remind her. But she just wanted to tell a story. She really got into it. She enjoyed it so much, she got so much pleasure out of it, that I really enjoyed her telling the story...' Ganga sighs happily, remembering, and adds, 'And she wasn't bothered at all if it was perfect or not.' She pauses. I imagine her sat around the fire with the kids, all of them caught up in the togetherness of the story. 'It was actually really beautiful.'

We sit there imagining our versions of the little girl, fully immersed in the feelings of the sketchy story, a story that maybe doesn't even make much sense, enjoying being bathed in her joy, in her excitement of whatever it is that is motivating her to tell with such enthusiasm.

We stir out of our joint silence. 'Yea...' says Kirsten softly, 'I guess it was because she was sharing emotions rather than the actual story itself. I guess the story was just a by-product really.'

—

Enthusiasm. Etymology. 'En Theos'. To be 'In God.' Divine inspiration.

Enthusiasm

Find what temple
empties you out
into the world of stars.

'Olé!' shouts Mercè after I've read her the poem. I smile, lapping it up. It feels like I am eating sunshine. 'Olé!' she likes it, 'Me gusta!' I feel my eyes sparkling.

—

In the South of Spain, when it was the home of the Moors, there would be dancing in the evening. They would watch the same dancers dance the same dance, but some nights a dancer moved within the same movements into a greater depth of aliveness, into a finer level of grace, their movements becoming so harmonious that the dancer would be danced, the dancer would become the dance. It moved the hearts of those watching, filling the whole atmosphere with something lighter, brighter, more expansive. The Arabs, enchanted, shouted out, 'Allah! Allah!': God is presenting itself through the movements of this human, shining through their skin. The human has become more like God for the sake of God, and God has become more human for the sake of human.

'Olé!' they call out in Spanish, its Arabic roots long forgotten, cheering on bullfighters and goal scorers. They jump up, arms outstretched to the sky, floating for a little moment of eternity in a collective glow.

—

Taking a break from writing, I watch a YouTube. It is an outdoor city music festival somewhere. There are at least 50,000 people sat on lawns or are they wide avenues? Big screens relay what is happening to the onlookers far away. On the stage there is a formal orchestra playing. Then a man from South America joins them. His eyes sparkle in the sheer joy of being on that stage, revelling in the experience. He doesn't seem one bit nervous, quite the opposite.

He starts to play his concertina, accompanied by the orchestra, as if his musical instrument were a woman he has long loved and is being allowed to touch for the first time. He, so present to the moment, is sparkling with joy. He looks at the conductor as if he were in love with him. He looks at the audience, a big sea of faces, as if he were the most privileged, luckiest man alive. He looks full of gratitude for being alive, right here, right now. He is simply brimming over, revelling in his feelings unabashedly. He is allowing people to see that he is LAPPING IT UP. His genius is in being vulnerable in front of thousands of people sharing this, a dream come true. He is simply loving it. No question about it. He doesn't care about anything else in the whole world: he is so present, his eyes shine, his body makes subtle sublime movements as he adores the connection to the conductor, as he wallows splendidly in the support from the orchestra, as he accepts the adoration from the crowd.

I feel my eyes welling, and somehow, without any reason, I am crying.

The camera pans around the crowd, so many people crying, wiping their eyes, crying, weeping. *Why?* Is it that the old man on the accordion expressing to his heart's delight contrasts all too sharply what most of us are constantly holding back? What has triggered this emotional outpouring of my own, and the crowd's, as we feel all that joy and love and delight of adoring and being adored? What is this flowing out of me, and the tears through the crowd, as he glows his light out so unabashedly? The music is secondary, it's the backdrop. The shine of his soul in the flame of his eyes has reminded my system that it is safe to relax, to open up, to be able to release into his beauty, into all that he's expressing from so deep down, expressing this that is within all of us.

As I immerse into him, I feel myself floating in a pool of cool, clear, pristine feelings, forgotten and so well-known. I feel part of a brittle me, harangued by daily modern living, breaking and falling away. I sob in relief. It is humanity. It is the joy of being alive. I feel as if I am in the audience itself and we are all remembering again, whatever it is within him reconnecting us to our emotions, as he holds us in his own. I am crying with release. I am releasing the trauma of being in hard places, as he embraces me in this, his soft, innocent beauty.

—

Simon has come around to give me a Hakomi session. We did a couple of classes together. He is on the point of qualifying to be a registered practitioner. I trust him. He is my friend; I know his strengths and his foibles and I know he can contain. I've seen him in action with others lots of times. We talk a little on the sofa. 'Shall we start?' he asks.

I tell him about my fear of being with others, of feeling vulnerable that he was coming round coupled with feeling overwhelm of being invited to an afternoon tea date with a girlfriend. I tell him it makes me feel insecure, that I find it hard to feel safe. I can feel myself, as I talk with Simon, entering into a wound of mine, of being afraid to be intimate with people, friends, others.

'Can you feel it?'

'Yes, I can feel it now.'

'How does it feel?' I feel the urge to cry out. 'It seems like you have an urge to cry?'

'Yes…' I choke back the tears.

'Allow yourself to feel whatever it is. All emotions are accepted and welcomed.'

Tears start to pour down my face. We sit there. I feel what it feels like to have tears pouring. Flashes from secondary school run through my mind. The woods. The playing fields. My Form room. The common room. The corridors. People I have long forgotten. I am on the edge of overwhelm. 'I feel so tired suddenly, drained, exhausted.' My observer inside knows this is good, we are getting close to where the ego does not want to go. This is resistance with cow's bells on it. Energy is seeping out of me. I cry, 'I feel like curling up under my duvet and hiding away from the world.'

'Do you want to just do that?'

I pause. *Do I?* 'OK,' I say dubiously, it feels as if I should be forcing myself to go out into the world, rather than curling up to die. 'We could go to my bed, it would be more comfortable?'

'I was thinking that, because you mentioned wanting to be under the duvet.'

He sits on the bed and I lie underneath two duvets. I feel myself speed out of myself. Dark lines, as if grooves on a vinyl, but straight parallel lines, pull me diagonally down into the stars. I feel myself zoomed into my safe place. I release, imploding. I am floating in space, high above planet earth. I feel safe. At last.

Strangely Simon says, 'I'm going to do the probe again, feel what you feel after these words, 'Julia, you are safe.'

Yes I know. I know. It is because I am not on the planet earth, if only just for this miraculous now. It feels like a gulp of air, after drowning in earthly fears and anxieties. It's break-time. I am at complete ease. I am floating. Safe. It feels as if I am 'resetting' myself after being harangued by daily modern living. A blessed release from it all. I am away from all that.

I stay here, breathing it in. Floating in wonderful, velvet darkness. Careless. Safe. Caressed. I feel myself go to a familiar place where I feel supported, loved, surrounded by loving presences.

'What's happening?' Simon asks. I can't answer. I am in a place of no words. No words come. Part of me, the good girl, wants to reassure him but I am too far away to reconnect with logic, too far gone to connect to Simon sat on my bed in a different world from here. I stay quiet. I cannot form an answer.

I am where I come from. I stay in the wordless space, being filled with love, quietly being nourished. It is so good to be here. I feel presences with me, my peeps. *Ahhhhh,* reconnection. Loving support.

My head suddenly goes very dizzy. 'Simon,' I manage to word out loud, warning, 'I'm on the edge of dissociating…' And suddenly from nowhere something racks through my body, I double up in the bed. I scream softly. Something is riding up through my body, leaving it: a surge of sensations that I can only sense, not feel, running up through my body, out through my mouth. I scream again, this time louder. Each scream is progressively louder. Inside I am calmly observing. Enjoying even. Scream.

'Are you OK?' Simon asks, worried I could be dissociating, re-traumatising myself in the wound.

I cannot answer at first. Another scream hurtles through, this time it's really loud. My protector says to me *It's OK, it is safe, no one will hear, go for it!*

Scream.

'Are you ok?' Simon repeats.

I cannot answer.

'I'm here,' he reassures. I feel myself pulled back slightly from totally letting go.

'I'm OK,' my observer manages to send a message back to him as if from the front line.

I let loose into a hurtling scream.

The screams get louder.

A sudden shift: I feel myself falling back to the material plane, inside I feel a tangible bump, as if I have fallen from a great distance, from a world of unconditional light and love into the body of a baby. I feel the difference between the expansive place I was and the sudden constraints of a material place where solids exist and therefore shadows. I feel the anxiety of my 'new' parents. I feel myself screaming in the gap between unconditional love and human love. I feel claustrophobic, cut off, my peeps a long, long, long way away. Separated here, surrounded by strangers. Inside this new body I am very alone.

I lie in bed, in my bed, with Simon sat beside me, his hand on my head and hip.

My breathing slowly regulates. I breathe a long breath out and open my eyes. I feel him gazing at me. I cannot meet his gaze. I am at peace while also being racked with embarrassment, vulnerable in the face of having been witnessed in one of my most private spheres.

'How are you?' he asks. I feel like a new born coming into the glare of airport lighting after being on a long distance plane.
'As if I've been in a different world, floating in space.'

'And how do you feel?'
'Embarrassed.'
'Why?'
My words come slowly. 'Sharing my innermost world. My reasoning isn't really very logical.'
'From a certain perspective,' the reassurance is in his voice. I feel as if he gets it. I feel as if he is not judging me at all.
'And the screaming?' I say quietly.
'I was worried, until you said you were OK.'
I am staring into space. Still not able to meet his eyes.
'It's so embarrassing to be so intimate. Why is it so hard?'
'Look at me...do you feel safe?'
I look into his gaze. 'Yes,' I say unhesitatingly, and the moment I say it, I don't. I start to feel panicky. My chest gets heavy again. *What does he want? What will happen if we connect? Will he need from me? Will he take from me?* I gaze into his eyes, fearful thoughts whirling through my mind. We continue to gaze into each other's eyes for a while. It is beautiful and agonising at the same time. All the while emotions flow up and out: fear, terror, gratitude, enjoyment, more gratitude, amazement of being in this tender, intimate place with another, of Simon showing up, of it being safe, feeling unsafe, feeling safe...the heaviness in the chest easing.

I am still gazing into the universe behind Simon's eyes.
'What's going on for you?'
I am jolted back. Words! A wonderful defence against being in that wild place of intimacy. Blessed release from this silent tension of complete vulnerability. We are back on safe ground. Logic kicks back in, trying to work out what I have just experienced, rather than having to experience directly. I drop my gaze. 'Why is intimacy so scary?'
'I guess it is because it is when we are truly seen.'
'And why would that be so scary?'
'I guess when we are seen, we are scared of being judged,' Simon pauses.
'Judging is such a big part of being human.' We both laugh, wishing it not true.
'We are not meant to be alone, disconnected. We are built to be social beings and because of that we form ideas of ourselves based on other people's vision of us, of their judgements...especially as a baby, the judgements of the world and of our parents really do form us deeply.'
'We're so malleable,' I say from my pillow.

We fall into silence. I remember falling just now into the body of a baby, feeling so much terror and existential panic of being separated from 'where I come from', from 'my peeps'.
'Woo, that was a really strong experience.'
'I was worried.'
'Yeah, I could feel you, especially when I'd said I was on the edge of dissociating, but I didn't, I walked the knife edge between dissociating and 'coming back'. I was fine. I was calm inside observing.'
'Wow.'

'It felt like a release, like a psychic zit. As if a massive chunk of energy were detaching from me, energy that I had identified with, but wasn't mine anymore.' We lapse back into silence again.

'What is intimacy?' I ask, as if by Simon being the therapist he should know. I love being in the role of therapeutee of asking like a child and I know Simon answers so well. Reassuring.
'I guess this…' his eyes sweep where we are. 'I don't know, but this… I don't have words.'

I feel the pillow against my head. I stay quiet hoping something will come through him. I'm wondering if he'll say sensations…that is what I'm feeling right now, lying here, sensations bubbling through, eternally birthing, never the same.
'Like this…you know?' he repeats.
I feel into the now, I feel, or see, a sort of white misty cloud forming between us…is he talking about that? I stay as quiet as possible trying to pick up on what he's perceiving. It feels like we are bird spotting…sitting in intense silence, concentrating, breathing together, wondering if anything will fly out of the woods. 'Presence. Present. Our presence. Lots of spiritual books talk about it, the Present and Presence.'
I nod as if I am being told a bed time story. This is so nice.
'Allowing Spirit.'
'What do you mean by Spirit?'
'I don't know, I feel it. I don't know how to put it into words. It's formless.'

I feel the room slightly edged in white cloud. The duvet feels slightly lighter, the air brighter, more expansive. I remember the idea that I had a couple of weeks back that Love is a verb not a noun, it is the merging of presences, of two people being conscious and being aware of the other and allowing each of those rivers to run together for a while. 'Like my presence and your presence; merging presences?'
'Yeah and being seen. When we are present, we see ourselves in the other.'

I think of Roberto in Barcelona. I have an image of a single cell dividing, and then him saying, 'Each cell recognised themselves in the other and Love was experienced for the first time.'

'In my cosmo-vision,' I say, head on the pillow, coming further and further out from 'that' place, slowly back into the room, 'like you say it feels that Spirit is formless…and the Soul is what gives it form.' It's hard to talk. 'It's the container, the memory of everything gone before,' I say slowly, softly. 'Soul is the same material as Spirit, but sort of sedimentary: layers of Spirit, like cooled lava, forming on top of each other, slower, more 'material'…'
Simon nods, as if this were perfectly obvious.
'So,' the pillow rubs the corner of my lips as I speak, 'I guess we separate from the one formless Spirit, like a drop from a bursting rain cloud, into form, into our own shape, in order to look back and be able to see it?'

Protection and Destruction

I paste myself
with words
trying to separate
me from myself
to see through
the mirror to
where the I is not.

'Because the Presence that we become aware of is,' I say dreamily, 'what we are all made of. If we were just Spirit, we would have no way to see ourselves.' Simon nods.

'Like just now, I felt as if Spirit were surging up through me and bashing out an old piece of dried up formation that my soul no longer needs to hold, so that the form of the soul can become closer to Spirit.' My mind adds on, in silence, *so that the Soul can come closer to being able to hold, or contain, in a more pristine form.* It's a new theory that is ruminating around my soul about how we don't need to become anything, get anywhere, nor get 'better', only to practise holding what 'is'. But I can't explain it all. I don't have the energy, or the time and now is not the place.

'Wow...' he says with his blue eyes. He is not afraid to maintain a gaze between us. I stay swimming in it. Practising holding.

'And somehow,' I say eventually, dropping my gaze again, getting back to the thread as if time had not passed, 'when we truly see each other we see the Presence in the other, the Spirit, which is Universal, and we see ourselves more truly. Because that is what we all are: Presence. But seeing ourselves as One our ego lashes out, gets scared, because it wants to see itself as separate, wants to see its own image of itself – as different – and the mirror image from the other person destroys part of that false ego idol. But... without the ego, we would never be able to separate to be able to see ourselves: so we need it.'

'Yeah,' says Simon, 'Yeah,' he nods, 'Wow that's the irony. It's beautiful and also really annoying...' We look into each other's eyes again and laugh, giggling like little children.

Emanation

A shaft of light through a window

a smile
a word
a belief...

Walking through the supermarket

a smile
a word
a belief...

As we love

our smiles
our words
our beliefs...

Whole worlds
transformed
simply by being.

Discovering presence
in myriads of sparkles.

Angelic winds

I sit in a warm bath
of gentle souls,
feeling the soft velvet
of love soaked words
carry us down
feather-like to
where we each end
to become
a temple to One.
As my muscles relax
opening
I sense others too
softly breathing
into this space.
Intoxication in the air
I glide on angelic winds
unsure as to who
is leading who.

'I like to meditate on dying, I imagine myself on the death bed,' Alicia says in her dark haired, olive skinned Spanish.

I find myself sat on a bench, on a finger of land between two waterways, listening to the dulcet shapes of Spanish words as sparks of miraculous sun, sparkle in the English autumn. 'I want to look back over my life and feel it was a good one, that it was worth it. I want to feel I expressed myself as my soul needed.' Her words are flamenco dancers accompanied by twirls of her wrists drawing the words out from space.

I listen to her. I have been where she is describing. I have felt that unquenchable thirst to be satisfied with life, a desire to lie peacefully fulfilled at the end of my life. I want the person who I will be when about to pass onto the other side, to be satisfied with what I am doing now, satisfied with how I am architecturing my life. I want that someone about to pass through, who is not me in this now but is me in the future, to look down from a greater height and be satisfied with my existence. It is an existence I can only connect to here, now, blinded ironically by my very existence in it, blinded by what it is to be alive, to exist, in this present, in this mind, in this body as my cells work industrially under my skin changing, changing, changing. Do I ever see the wood of my existence or am I blinded by the trees in an ever arising need to stay alive?

'I'm not sure if what I am doing I want to continue with,' she continues, 'I like what I do. I enjoy teaching dancing, massaging, I enjoy it all…but there is an element of routine to it all. When I was a little kid I always wanted to write…'

I hear her yearning. I hear her attachment. I hear how we, she, or I – I don't know who – you? – block ourselves from being with ourselves right here, right now, with this desire to be happy with ourselves in the future, for what we have done, for what we are doing now; yearning to not be where we are now, to not feel ourselves now, to not feel the misery of the uphill slog of trying to be, nor the responsibility of having to constantly choose our life, burdened with the onslaught of responsibility to make our lives as higher an expression of ourselves that we can muster.

I know how it feels, because I've played chess. I always lose. I am just desperate to get to checkmate, to know who wins, to review the battle. I want to be back in my place of stability knowing who won and why and how. I want to be able to look back and analyse the movements, to know the outcome. I always lose chess,

I barely ever enjoy the game, find myself unable to drop into the joy of process, of the journey. I stress, bash on ahead, wanting to know the end.

The sun shining up the estuary really is beautiful. I am half listening, half in my own world, wondering why no-one seems to want to be with our own presence here now, without knowing tomorrows. I wonder why we have this incessant need to be something, to have done something, to have something to show. I wonder if I am fooling myself, into accepting myself in this state of not having achieved anything of any merit in the external world for far, far too long.

I am still tingling from the poetry workshop yesterday. We read the words of mystics that touched us on that edge where we become divine for the sake of the Divine and the Divine becomes Human for the sake of Human. That place where Rilke says to enter we must leave everything behind, even our name, like a child leaves behind a broken toy. The whole day was exquisitely sublime. We, the workshop, dropped into that place, our psyches delivered on the feathered words of Sufis and Saints describing their inner worlds, their connections, their love of god, their god of Love. I can dance in all that heavenly space. Flow freely. I can weave my own magic in those realms. I feel myself a giant going into those wondrously intimate places, infinitely smaller than the material world, infinitely more expansive than a Universe. I exalt flying in the glory of existence.

But it doesn't pay the bills.

What will my soul think as it dies about how I am being now?

And again I hear myself blocking myself from my essence, comparing myself on some external merit, comparing myself with another possible me that is outside of me, outside of this space, time. I find myself praising a life unlived more than my life lived. Will the dying me on the bed even remember how I lived? Me, here, today, sat on this bench, as the slanted autumn sun sparkles Iris on the waves? Will the me on dying be bothered about the me now, more than its own pressing situation, as it prepares to go into death?

'I sometimes see it,' she says laughing at the simplicity of it, 'as if we were born into [she says a name of a big car] or a Volvo or a mini. But we are all on a journey not matter what.'

I think of India and how my parents have just been there with the Institute of Mechanic Engineers, how they were whizzed in hire cars from one place to the next, 'We barely had time to swim in the wonderful swimming pools,' Dad complained, showing off. 'Ohh the colours of the markets!' Mum said.

At the tender age of twenty-one I travelled around the world with Chrispy, a childhood friend. We dragged our heavy rucksacks through India, catching the smells on long, slow buses as men spat out of the windows in front, to sometimes receive a splash of it through the windows further back. We managed to see as much as they did, but in three times the amount of time. Where my parents had swimming pools, we had wash areas that looked like animal feeds.

I had my journey there. They had their journey there. They don't compare. Not better or worse. Just different.

'We each have this car,' she continues, out of the corner of my eye I see the exotic movement of her wrists and arms floating down the side of her body, 'they are all different, but we are all essentially having the same experience, we are all alive in this world.'

I know what she's getting at. Images fly through my echoing mind of the world being just one, A-pollo, the absence of the multiple, one single union of all; and the world of Dionysus being millions of different worlds, as many worlds as people, as many worlds as there are living sentient beings. One pure white light splitting into spectrums of infinite colours. I imagine my car – what type of car do I have? – and remember, 'I don't have a car.'

'Me neither!'

'I've only ever owned one once,' I say remembering my blue love in Argentina, 'a Fiat 600.' I remember pouring water on the characteristically overheated engine located in the boot at the back. 'I think some of us are born on a bicycle.'

'Yes!' she says chuckling, 'and others maybe bare footed!'

I imagine the joy of bare feet on fresh cool grass as it tickles slightly between the toes. I smile feeling in my imagination the delight.

'We are all breathing,' she says mesmerised as much and I by the water in the estuary. 'A man with bare feet is still just as alive as a man in a big car.'

I imagine a 4x4 driving up over the mountain, having a great time, feeling the power in each of the four wheels. I imagine a posh sports car that is light and delicate and needs a good road surface to whoosh through membranes of speed barriers. I imagine clapped out Fiat 600s that can't go very far.

Is it better to experience a lot, running quickly over the surface, or to go into the detail of the small that slowly sinks into its depth like dew into grass?

I remember the lines from the poetry workshop,

'See it as large, and a millet-grain cheats us of the universe:
See it as small, and the world can hide in a pinpoint.' [9]

The grain of corn, holographically, holds all the secrets of the world. It contains all that is everything, all that we are made of too. It is all in the grain of corn! It contains all of the world. But we can also lose the world staring at a grain of corn, at a tiny detail in our lives, obsessing over microscopic details. In vain attempts to absolutely control this tiny thing, we can miss the big picture. But at the same time we can look so much to the big picture, to the universal, that we miss out on the details within each individual, the tiny that is unique, unrepeatable.

Star dust.

The River Dart continues, miraculously, to sparkle. To exist. It is not the same river it was only moments ago. Seconds ago. Milliseconds ago. It is constantly flowing. This water is not the water from before. That sparkle is ephemeral. I come back to 'earth', to the 'matter', to the details of our conversation. 'We are all experiencing being alive. Going fast and far is no 'better' than not going so far and instead feeling the joy of grass between the toes.' *Details or big picture? Which is better? Neither.* 'I guess it is all simply experience of what is, as we experience it?'

'Yes,' she says, turning around to look at me, 'we are all breathing. We all breathe. No matter where or how we are.'

Which is better? Who is better? It suddenly appears such a ridiculous question. It is like asking if an orange is better than a turbine harvester? Is a leaf better than a ewe? Is a banana better than a wooden table?

'We are alive. We are who we are.' I murmur, 'We can only experience as we are,' I say half to myself, still spellbound by the dance of the sun on the water, still feeling the presence of my legs, of my body, of my arms. I'm practising to stay conscious of my body.

'Yes!' she says, 'I see it too like a tree. If you have a seed of an oak tree, you will only get an oak tree. You will never get an apple tree. And the seed of an apple tree will only give a tree with the fruit of apples, not oranges…'

I look up, at the dock buildings, converted into nice apartments. It's so nice to sit here with this woman, mixing in our words into this shared silence '…we are born as we are born,' she says quietly, contentedly.

I like listening to people who have thought about things. On the surface it seems incredibly simple, but underneath there is a whole world of movement, like soils that seem still on the surface and yet underneath is being churned by worms and insects, is being fertilised by mould, earth that is breathing air and receiving water, finding nutrients from the fire of the sun in the interplay with plant and tree roots. On the surface, still, simple. So easy to overlook the simple.

In the mesmerisation of the sparkles, this kind silence peppered with words, the warm sun on my skin, I am sinking into slow, into opening to the horizontal, into peaceful surrender. In my mind I am imagining trees that are in their glory, tall and magnificent. I imagine trees that have miraculously grown high up on mountains, smaller, wiry with sparser, smaller fruit. She looks at me again, nodding me back into the conversation. 'I guess,' not really knowing what I'm about to say, 'if you have a message inside, a gift, this thing that is unique to just us that only we are born with, then there are many ways to express it, maybe through dance or through writing, or through massage, or through being an accountant, or driving a big lorry.' I am showered in images of possibilities 'Blades of Grass' style: even the lorry driver me. 'It is being in contact with the gift and finding a way to express it that allows it to be in its glory - but I wonder how important the conduit of the expression is?' I wonder if *how* we express what we are is anywhere near as important as *what* we express.

'Hmm,' she hums, 'I sometimes ask little children, 'Why do you have blonde hair?' They look at me funnily, confused, 'I was just born like this,' and they scrunch up their little noses as if it were a silly question. But it's a deep question. Why are we as we are?'

I remember being about seven and going to my mum's friend's daughter's house. We had to pretend we were friends, but we didn't know each other; we just pretended that we did. It was easier that way. As 'Aunty' Veronica showed mum around the house, Claire showed me her toys. She didn't have any action men, or Hungry Hippos, or guns to shoot down empty baked bean cans. She had this head. Plastic.
'What's it for?' I asked, totally confused. *What can you do with a head?*
'It's for practising hair and makeup.' *What?* This did not clear things up for me. Not at all.
'It's not got a lot of hair.'
'I know,' she says her words embroidered with equal measures of faint sadness, faint embarrassment, 'I cut it, but it didn't grow back. I thought it would.'
Boring. I stand back. I don't really want to touch it. It makes me feel like nails being scraped down a black board. I've suddenly got more saliva in my mouth. We made it work though, maybe in her desperation, and to my delight, she asked, 'Do you want to go outside and make mud pies?' She pretended we were in the kitchen, I pretended they were bombs.

Who made it that I wanted to climb trees, that I hated having my hair combed, who decided that I would just love school, love playing the tuba, love Mr Fredrick my music tutor? Who made it that I would hate the two handed piano and cry? Who decided that I would be good at football and tennis and swimming but plead at the age of four to not do ballet anymore? Who decided that I would never want to wear a skirt even when I was three?

Who decided that my cousin would love playing with his mum's make up, would spend hours brushing his hair and would regularly have gaping holes in his hair from swinging the hair scissors wildly, blindly round the back of his head? Who decided that he would love being in the kitchen learning from his Mum to cook, while I loved learning how to wallpaper with my Dad?

Who decided that I would not like cheese, or honey, or tuna? And spread my margarine as thin as possible. Who made it that I really didn't care too much for dessert, while my cousin loved anything sweet, spread his margarine disgustingly thickly, and stole cheese from the fridge? Who decided I would be tall and skinny, and my cousin tall and plump? Sorry, I mean big boned.

Who decides what we will love?

Who decides what we will *will*?

Why do you have blonde hair little girl?

Oak tree, what did you decide?

I think it was Schopenhauer who said, 'Man can do what he wants, but he cannot will what he wills for.'

Can we be anything other than the seed planted in the soils of our psyche? Can we be happy trying to be something we are not? Why cannot we just accept ourselves as we are, right now, in this present moment? I notice the sun continuing to shine, the trees waving to the wind, the air streaming into my lungs and out again now slightly warmer.

I wonder why I find it so hard to accept the 'normal' that is me. The 'unique' that is me. Why do I try so hard to be something more, something else? I come out of my wandering mind, back to the sparkle, back to my new Spanish friend. It feels we have been sat like this, on this bench, together for long, sparkle filled years. 'Funny isn't it,' I muse, 'how hard it is to accept ourselves? Funny how we often don't even plant the seed we were given, or allow it to express its essence, to give its fruit. Why?'
'I think that we get all caught up in the ideas of fame, of wealth, of a happiness that we think we can achieve if only we were, or had, something else.' We nod together and after a long pause she continues, her words laced with humour, 'We want big cars.'
I laugh. 'Big cars even when we are not made for them!'
'Yes.'

Cars. Money. Fame.

Big fractal blocks without any details. Nothing subtle. Nothing unique.

'Yet we can only be the seed we possess.'
'What is your seed?' I ask, daringly. *Am I being too personal?*
'I don't know. I'm thinking I might retreat over the winter, go back to Spain, to think about who I am. Connect to myself again. I feel myself in a routine, and happy, but I want to feel who it is that I am, so I know what I want to do with my life.'

We breathe together.

'I guess we can plant the seed in so many ways, in so many places. There are lots of nourishing ways to do it. We just really have to have the courage to plant it,' my words feel like soft butter.
'Yes, but to do that first we must feel who we actually are.'
I breathe in, getting ready for my spiel, 'We are all containers of Spirit.' Alicia has been on the path, she's been in and out of meditation centres, I'm sure she'll be ok with it. I surge on ahead, 'It is our individual soul, that shapes the Universal Spirit into our unique likeness,' I pause, breathing in the joy of walking through my secret garden and being given this rare gift of being able to open it up for another, 'in a kind of dance where the Spirit too shapes our Soul into a closer likeness to what they have both emanated from,' I can't describe the images: black backdrop, ephemeral channels, connections, Indra's web, marble glass connectors reflecting all but themselves, flows of Spirit ever birthing through the web, consciousness forming, shaping. The image shifts, *maybe I can describe this better?*

'Volcanoes hold shape, like Soul does, molten material flows out through them, like Spirit does, creating a new shape to the Volcano, a new form, giving it new in-formation…' I don't know how to express it all. I try a different tact, 'The Soul contains Spirit, and yet the Spirit moulds the shape of the Soul…I guess until between them they have achieved 'that which is above is the same as that which is below'. So they are mirrors of each other, one the flow from the Source, the other the manifestation, or recreation, of Source.' I can see it all so clearly in my mind's eye. *How to put this into words?* 'You know? Those precious moments when we become All and All becomes us?' She nods ever so lightly, as if a bird's wing nestled gently in an uprising thermal. 'Those moments when we find ourselves – like slipping into a warm bath – in deep stillness and suddenly become a moment of Eternity…?' I sigh into the image in my head and it gently drops me down into a deeper level of inner peace. I have no idea if I've managed to express what I have inside. 'Well,' I surrender, 'that's what I believe.'

There is a deep silence between us. She is listening. The sun is sparkling. *I can do this, just go simple,* 'My mum says that soul is how we make people feel. I think she banged the nail on the head.' I see her nod gently, 'We each convert Spirit into how we see the world. The purer we are in our expression, the closer it is to the divine, to the seed that we were given, that which we are…' I love swimming down here. I feel her open still, holding space to go on, '…and that we create, we re-create the world closer to the Truth of what It is.' I feel myself, my soul, expanding out into the material world, encompassing and allowing in the estuary, the buildings, the birds soaring in the skies, the seagulls fighting on the sparkling water, this bench, me and this beautiful woman beside me. 'I'm not sure if it really matters in what way we actually express it, what materials we use, but simply that we do.' I look down the sun drenched river, 'We were born with this quality of being, with this gift.'
She pauses, letting it in and then asks, 'But how to find out what our soul is?'

We are going in spirals deeper and deeper, round and around fractals, going smaller, more detailed, going further into the matter – into Matter – deeper into the mother of things. Mother and Matter. Same roots. Now we have removed the cars, the fame, the money – and yet we have the same question.

How to remove the clouds from the sky. How to break through our mind that covers over that which waits to shine out? I make a stab in the dark, 'Could an answer be found through the connection to our bodies? I mean our bodies know when they experience pleasure. Could it be so simple?'

The truth lies in the simple. It is the perfect hiding place. We overlook it. It's too simple.

'I guess it has to do with how we love.'
'Yes and how we love ourselves.' *Should I share?* This is my deep secret, this is my world deep down. I'm not sure how to tell her through words. I pause, waiting for my body to tell me. *Should I?* It relaxes, opens up. OK. *Now?* My knees separate a little. OK. I feel my openness. I feel brave. 'The other day I was walking through the woods,' I wave my arms to the upstream of the river, 'you

know in Dartington?'

'Si.'

'I was alone. I haven't had bodily contact with another human in so, so long. I so wanted a hug, so I looked for a tree instead,' I feel my cheeks tingling, 'in a huddle of trees I wrapped my arms around the thick trunk of sycamore. I let myself drop into it, pretending it was a man, a lover.' *Why am I exposing myself so?* 'It was so nice.'

I look across to her. She nods gently. I feel her holding me softly in this strange vulnerability. 'I felt so full, so embraced. So alive!' I am between worlds, the sparkles of the water, the dark evening wrapped in the woods, 'It was a white river of sparks flowing like honey through my body, or my mind, or both. I felt like I was being hugged by a romantic partner. I felt like I feel when I hug deeply after sex, or how I feel actually in any really deep, long, relaxed hugs with men or women who I feel comfortable enough to open up with. I really went into it. It was a beautiful peaceful feeling, of being loved, of being protected, of simply being. It was so nourishing. I felt alive. I felt this is what I miss.' I smile softly, my eyes have gone soft boiled egged. I breathe in and out, relishing the memory.

'I was really in there, lapping up this embrace, lapping up what I had been so longing for. When eventually I slowly opened my eyes I realised – remembered – that I am hugging a tree; not a human. I mean trees have their own kind of energy – that deep peace of growing through all manner of time, of storms, of heat, of moving around obstacles, that gives that feeling that everything is always OK, as they slowly grow through no matter what.' I feel myself reconnected to the peace of the woods, remembering the sycamore and that wonderful flow of pleasure: peaceful, stable love. I am drinking it in.

'But what really got me was that this felt like all of the hugs I have. Of course they all have a slightly different taste, but they all have this sparkly, white nourishing feeling; with men, or at the end of yoga workshops, or with really good friends.' I pause, feeling myself coming out of the woods, 'And I suddenly realised, THIS IS ME. This is my presence.' I feel it again, me, flowing through my insides. I feel me hugging the tree there, while feeling me sat on this park bench here. 'But at the same time it is not me. It wasn't me 'me',' my hands point inwards to my chest, 'It was apart from me, or maybe,' I look out struggling for words, 'further in than me – it doesn't have words – it doesn't speak in words. More than being 'me' it feels as if it's me standing in the river of emotions, bathing in it. It is deeply me. It isn't me. You know what I mean?'

She smiles. Nods. We both breathe in. Both breathe out.

Deep enjoyment emanates out of being so present to the air in my nose, my lungs and out again returning to the world. Such a deep privilege to be sat here breathing together. I feel heard enough to continue. 'I think that is my presence. That is who I am. It is there that I connect to Presence that is not me.' She puts her hand on my arm. So nice to feel her. We sit in companionable silence. Breathing it in. It is so nice to just sit; feel; sense; just be. So beautiful to be present with someone else being present. So rare.

Eventually she breaks the silence, 'I wonder if we all feel the same inside or different? If our presence is one Presence? If we all feel it differently or the same?' I think about the word original and how we are all so desperate to be different, when the word 'original' comes from the same root as 'origin'. That place of one-ness, that ground of shared humanity. Apollo. The place where we are all the same. 'I don't know. I guess it all depends on how deeply we connect to it,' I say, 'I guess the deeper we go into it, the more deeply personal we express ourselves, the more Universal it becomes.' I laugh, 'You know the irony of it all?!' She laughs with me. Sometimes life seems so simple. A cosmic joke. The air is fresh around us. Sparkles. New friendship with this beautiful stranger. I feel a peace inside of my heart. Do I feel love for her - *so soon?* - or do I feel love *with* her now? And then it comes to me, 'I think that's what we need to be doing: to keep trying to stay in contact with that presence.' *Wow, so simple - so hard to do!* 'Then it doesn't really matter where we are, or what we are doing, it just flows out of us, expressing itself in our every action.'
'Spirit flowing through our Soul!'
'Yes!' It is so nice to be heard! She understood…! 'As we feel into each action, as we become conscious of all that we are doing, the action itself becomes impregnated with who we are. We express ourselves. Like we express orange juice from an orange!'

I'm on a roll. I feel her hand on my arm still, put my hand on her hand. 'And as we seek that sinking into ourselves, into the joy, the peace of being, the expansion of being, we will naturally find what we like to do to express it. The message we have inside, the seed, the presence, can be delivered to others through so many means…different professions, different creative expressions, hobbies, chats, nature connections…whatever it is that gives us pleasure…the message will resemble what we are; and how we do it – if we do what we do with love, with pleasure, with what we are, this message we were born with inside, will flow out of us loud and clear…'

I feel slightly high. I remove my hand. I'm still remembering to feel my legs and my arms, still trying to remember that I am on a bench by the sparkly waters. I have images of psyches diving into the oneness of Origin, of Source, and coming back out into our individual selves and expressing this that unites us all in our own unique way; each of us being unique separate beings, each of us having our own unique expression of what is it to be alive.

'So getting back to what you said at the beginning,' I continue, 'I don't know if it's important when we are lying on our death bed, to think – *Did we express our seed throughout our lives?* – but rather, to concentrate on being present in the here-now, to practise the art of living our lives, connecting to ourselves, to our own presence within, to what is here-now.' Image after image flows through my mind. I see myself on my death bed, 'Perhaps it is as simple as when we die to be with ourselves, to have the ability to bathe in our presence – then and there – rather than wondering about past experiences in our lives and what would have happened if we had done something differently – which ironically would take us out the present moment of dying! I wonder if I'll even be interested on my death bed in this dilemma of what to be in life now, when this now,' I knock the bench with my knuckles, 'is not that now, the 'now' when I pass away.' I've confused the matter, 'I mean, as I drift into death, I would like to be able to be with myself. I would like to be so familiar with my presence that I can totally be with just myself, in that moment, in my presence, in Presence. I would like to feel calm enough to make that transition in absolute peace of being.'

'Ahh, yes,' she takes her hand off my arm and hugs herself, 'and I guess we practise that through our lives, in what we do, in how we do it, in staying present to ourselves.'
'I wonder if it even makes any difference what we did in the past? It's not *what* we do but *how* we do it.'
'Yes,' she adds, 'not what we do, but how we do it: soaking in our us-ness.'
'Though a tree does grow best where it is nourished, I guess.'
She turns around to me and says, 'Which is love. Love nourishes.' I see her irises sparkle, 'How can we love ourselves more?'

I think of a poem from yesterday, I've got it in my bag still. I rumble around, leaning slightly, looking at her, while my hand searches, 'Can I read you a poem? It's from the workshop I was telling you about.'
'I'd love you to.'
I locate the paper. Pull it out without ripping it against the corner of the zip of my bag and rifle through the pages. 'Here it is. It's by Rabia of Basri. She was born in 717 CE. Amazing…it feels like a message through time. Through space and time. It feels like it's been written today about today.'
'Yes. Go on. Do.' She settles back onto the bench, as if awaiting a great joy.
'It's called, 'Die before you Die'' I pause. I like dramatic. I clear my throat a little and read the poem.

Ironic, but one of the most intimate acts
of our body is
death.
So beautiful appeared my death – knowing who then I would
kiss,
I died a thousand times before I died.

'Die before you die,' said the Prophet Muhammad.

Have wings that feared ever
touched the sun?

I was born when all I once
feared – I could
love.

After the last line of the poem the words dance, hovering their echoes in the soft silence, building bridges between us. We both breathe in as if imprinting the poem in our lungs.

'That's beautiful,' she says in a far away voice, gazing into the distance. *I wonder what she is seeing inside?*

I breathe out, drop my hands with the paper onto my knees. Life is so good!

The birds are floating aimlessly in the skies. The river has changed yet again. The sparkles sparkle million of miles across from the sun itself…

'Yes!' I say suddenly stunned by an idea, 'Maybe when we are lying on our death bed, disconnecting from our past, and with no future, at least in this body, we go so into the present moment, so into our presence, that we actually totally hear our own message, loud and clear, our own seed coming to life before our eyes, and…and…' I say intoxicated with the newness of what is coming out from my lips, 'being able to be with ourselves in the way that we love – in our own unique way! – in the way that our reactions to life have (in)formed our soul how to love!' I feel a laugh spilling out in air ripplets from my nose, 'We may discover that this, our message, in the end was only really meant for ourselves!' Alicia laughs, 'Can you imagine?'

It makes everything so simple, all our actions meaningless, all our actions vehicles of our own learning about who we are, how we do things. I am stunned by the idea. Our whole lives learning to listen to ourselves, learning to love ourselves, learning to be present to all that we do, to become closer to ourselves – so that at the end, when we have the final vision of who, or even what, we are, we will be able to see it, hear it, sense it, taste[10] it loud and clear: so we can become fully present to it. So we can fully slip through into who we are.

I feel exhausted. We sit there for some time leaning back on the bench, staring out. Gazing. Feeling our presence. I scan through the sensations in my body. I can feel my legs wanting to move. I want oxygen into my muscles. As I do, Alicia turns to me, looks me deeply in the eyes, as if nodding, and we both stand, ready to move on away from the sparkling waters, to continue in our respective 'cars', each with our own seed, and walk back into town.

In my arms

I know about love
the way a field knows about light
the way a tree grows
through the twists and turns of time;
I know about hugging trees tight
like after our love making
yielding to this presence
inside of me, but not me.

Chapter 31: Will you Marry this Moment?

Realising all is good enough
as it is,
as we are.

The Poppy

She stands out
so very alone,
so very red
amid the other flowers
daring to be herself.

My friend, a heart brother, recently dragged himself through the dark valley again. Heroin. He went through deep, sharp psyche pain, going down, grovelling in the sharp caves of broken humanity - and had the strength to come back up. His journey is something that will not really be understood by anyone who is not really sensitive. He is. I am. That's how we get each other, support each other. I admire him. Taking the route of fallen angel, going into the depths, and returning, is not for the faint hearted. I don't dare. I don't know that I would come out of the other side. That's why I respect him.

'It's about accepting what is,' he says. 'This program, you know?'
'The twelve-step?'
'Yeah,' he nods. In that nod I feel the strength of support from his fellow recoverers, 'it's helped me see that something really does exist, something more than us, something...'
'What?'
'I don't know, something that exists outside of us, and inside of us, something bigger than us.' I look at him, this fine, beautiful man, chiselled with memories of looking for something that is not here, that doesn't exist outside of idealism. I feel a surge of love for him, of wanting to hug him, to tell the little boy inside that everything really is OK. 'Without that belief,' he continues, 'without discovering 'god', I couldn't have got through the recovery. It's the silver lining, the gift after going through all of this, all of this horrendous trip back from Hell.' He fingers his black key-ring: five years clean.

———

And then a cosmic joke. Just after getting his five year clean key-ring, he falls again. Just once. But that just once is so fucking dangerous. Reading his message I feel my throat constrict, the tears well in my eyes. I want to scream out, to run to wherever he is. To hold him. I feel the panic of the void; feel the terror of freefalling back into chaotic realms of pain. I am impotent to help him in any other way than being here for him. But, I reason, he is able to write the message, able to use the computer, able to create logical sequential sentences in the world of the living. I breathe in, relief flooding up through the dropping tears: he is out of death, out from down there, out from Hades, the place of abject terror and absolute rejection. Out from the place of black nothingness.

I float between images of him. Clutching to the realisation that he's managed to dredge himself out. Brave soul. Fallen angel. How did he claw his way out from that devouring vortex? I feel proud for him. I feel deeply honoured that he trusts me enough to tell me, the only person outside his support group. Sweet gratitude runs through my drying tears for him sharing with me, for connecting in such vulnerability. Pain. Terror. Relief. He is out the other side. I write back trying not to think, to just let the words come out by themselves:

i am constantly amazed by this life...that as we face the fears that stab at our hearts...that petrify and break us...as we actually look at them and move through them....once on the other side they really don't exist...they are nothing....

i cannot grasp it.

it is counter-intuitive....

we are ruled by things that don't exist....and ignore beauty and peace that does....

how is that?

—

I like hanging out with South Americans. There is this feeling where you can just express yourself, your emotions, just as they are…there is less judgement going on, more comprehension. I feel safer in the comradeship of knowing that we are all connected through this thing called life, with all of its roller coaster of emotions. Humanity is not pushed away. Grief, pain, sadness are not brushed under the carpet; joy, alegría, the good life when it comes along, are celebrated so much more freely than with my European friends, fuelled by the knowledge that they don't last forever. There is an acceptance of where each person is right now. It is not necessary to maintain a perfect image. Everything, to me, seems more excepted, however you are, joyful or full of angry woe – it's fine. Held. Not given too much attention and not ignored.

I'm walking up the dull grey English street with Mauricio; Mauricio who is all colour, who has and expresses emotions, who doesn't need to keep up an image of being on top of it all. The Brits treat him as if he were *loco,* he comes at things from a completely different angle, with history, and culture and…and feelings. I love being with him. It's easy to be me in his presence. Strangely I am not attracted to him sexually, which opens up so much space between us to explore, to investigate, to enjoy. I'm complaining about being single and lonely, while he complains about not having his own space being a father of three and a husband. As I walk alongside him I feel seen, heard. I gasp into this life-jacket that he offers with his kind heart in the high seas of angst.

'I feel so afraid!' I say into his heart field, 'Why should I be so afraid of what is already happening? Single. No man even on the horizon. And it's fine, and yet I make all these stories up – like as if being alone were a failure – about being petrified of being rejected and being alone and having no one to support me.' 'But you are doing it now already…you are alone,' I look up at him and realise that my worst fears have come true – and they are not so bad: there is light at the end of the tunnel. 'You are here in this street,' he continues giving mouth-to-mouth to my dying hope, 'breathing! Your body has been fed, you've slept, you're alive!' He puts his hand on my shoulder, '…and you have a friend here,' he points to his heart.

—

What am I so afraid of? Why I am so afraid this moment will not be forever? Or that it will be? Why am I afraid that outside of this moment I will not cope, will be heart-broken, or heart-filled, or hurt, or given more joy than I can cope with only to kamikaze fall back to stony ground? Why am I so petrified of being destitute, overwhelmed, dragging myself through future days of pain, when there is so little reason for the scenarios in my head to become real, if any? Why am I even afraid? What twists me inside to try and control this thing – this thing called life – that I have no idea about? Instead of trusting life, I cling to my stories that hang grey dog-eared curtains between me and what is it to just be right now? I even forget about accepting what is right here as I flail, olympically oblivious to anything but my own mind.

To me from Paul:

You
stranger and familiar
never seen except
in this moment.

'This moment? What does it mean?' I ask Mauricio. It is starting to drizzle – again. 'Why am I so afraid to be in this moment. Am I seeking something more?' It feels almost like an insult to say that to someone who is in this moment with me. He gets it though. Soft understanding.
'Si,' he says kindly, 'like why are we so afraid that it may not last forever and at the same time so afraid that this might be all there is?'
'Why are we always trying to control everything?'
'Exacto!'

—

I am sweating from every conceivable pore. We've travelled across the globe to be in a dance workshop in Thailand. *Is this what we are meant to be doing?* A worry brings me out of the experience of dancing. *Is this good enough?* I try to return to the non-thinking state, allowing my body to move of its own accord. *Relax Julia relax, you know you can do this.* I open my eyes and look out at all the other bodies, they are moving so gracefully. I see a woman move in a way I want to try. Feel embarrassed. *Can I just copy? Is that OK? Will she mind? Will she even notice?* It's pretty hot. I'm in my sports bra and Thai shorts. The windows and doors are all open. The bamboo roof does little against the blare of the sun. A slight breeze clings to my humidity. It's so hot that I wonder if this is healthy.

Just dance! I say to myself. *Relax!* The outside world is so on the edge of being alarming that under the compressing tension I feel all of my inner emotions amplified into volcanic firework displays of fear of dehydration mixed with peaks of pleasure, fear, embarrassment, grace. *Is this OK?* I swirl in the middle of my exploding innerscape. From the corner of the room the guru guy shouts on the top of his voice, his voice shattering into my core, 'STOP TRYING TO BE

OK!' For a few brief seconds my internal world goes into still silence, receptive, listening. 'STOP TRYING TO BE OK!' he repeats into the cave of my being 'YOU ALREADY ARE OK!!!!!'

Instead of being

Trying so hard
to be good enough
she stopped
being it.

Paul and I were in the Rockies, walking along the Hessie Trail. It could not have been more perfect. The weather was glorious. Sunny, but not too hot because we were so high up. It was butterfly mating season, which only occurs a few weeks of the year. Hundreds and hundreds of butterflies fluttered all over the place, crisscrossing in our paths. The sun was shining into a warm balmy breeze. Thousands of flowers were blooming, spraying colours, making the land look like a bedcover. We stopped for a break. Silence. Wonderful to breathe in this pristine, clean air. The love between us was palpable. I lean into his chest, as we take a break and sit on top of a rock in the middle of paradise. I turn around to him and drenched in a feeling of absolute and utter love whisper, 'I love you soo much!' I am flowing, joyfully, the world entirely ours, the gods creating everything for us to simply be in love with. I am even aware that I feel unshackled from any fears. It is me and him, and I feel nothing but love, beauty, peace.
'Me too you…' he replies.
'This is just so wonderful…thank you…thank you…' and I kiss him, tenderly, softly…I am floating in heaven. I am floating in his kiss, in his arms.

After a little time he gently pushes me away, up and out of eternity. I stare into his eyes, love struck. He cannot cope, 'You know that I still have feelings for others?'
He crushes me. This polyamory crap looms in the distance like a raincloud. The balloon is burst. I fall heavily to the ground still full of colour, full of flowers, but suddenly they don't feel as if they are there for us at all, they just are. This is not a scenery of love, it is just nature doing its thing.

We don't talk for two hours.

The next day, body intact but heart still sore, we are walking up the High Lonesome Trail up to Devil's Pass. It's exciting to be at 11,775 feet (3590 m). In between tiny steps up the steep path I am stressing about 'us'. The blow up from yesterday is still resonating inside my sore heart. *Will we be together? Will we have to separate? Will we have to deal with visas? Will we have to marry?* It seems like a joke. If we are forced to marry to be able stay together in the same country the stress will more than probably break us up. *And all these feelings he has for others? Are they real? Are they a defence mechanism?* He's consistently used it over and over again to stop intimacy rising up too closely between us; the countless women that he has fallen in love with flash through my mind. *Don't go there Julia.*

I stop to look at the panoramic view. Stood there on top of the world I breathe out, long and deep, trying to get my breath back. *Whenever we get truly intimate he pulls back quickly, overwhelmed.* My heart is racing. But I can't get around the fact that I feel deep love for him. I want to be with him. I look down to where he is climbing. I feel tender love just watching the way his body moves; so graceful. I love being with him, except when he's pushing me away. *How would I live without him? How can I live with him?* And there and then, stood almost on the very top of the Continental Divide a poem flutters into my mind:

An end to the funeral garb age

Will you marry
this moment
'til death do you part?

'I do. I am.'

The moment dies.

Will you be a widow forever?

I've just 'performed' the funeral garb age poem to Mauricio stood in the middle of the street in our raincoats. 'It's a play on words you know? Garb, means clothing, and garbage is how the Americans say 'rubbish'.'
'Ha! Nice!'
'Yeah…' I drink in his smile, rehydrating the desert within, 'you know over the last couple years I've said that poem in poetry slams in the States, in Spain, in England…' I say to Mauricio, 'People seem to get it, they're moved by it.'
'Ahhh because it is hermoso: this moment, right now…here…' he waves his hand around the dull, grey street, like a ballet dancer. Watching the trail of his hand makes me slow down to look properly. As I look with more awareness; I suddenly realise how pretty it is. I had been completely in my head. 'It is not going to change,' he says, 'only we can change.'

I stand there, hearing the drizzle pitter-patter on my hood, seeing how the street shines in its wetness. I watch as what I was seeing as dull grey, comes into life and begins to sparkle. Brave rays of sun have gotten through ephemeral clouds and are shining on the smooth slabs of concrete. 'But, change…' he says, pressing one finger against his cheek as he moves the word around in his mind, 'I guess the real journey is 'changing' in the sense of relaxing into being rather than having to become something else.'

Suddenly everything seems so simple again. I am in me, gathering silence, hearing me breathe, able to look out through clear inner skies. I think of

Cinderella – watching how as I begin to look around with a renewed openness of heart, my surroundings begin to shine out their hidden beauties. As I allow myself to see the beauty of black tarmac sparkle in rainwater, I feel myself being brought out of a psychic cramp; as I see Beauty blossoming all around me, I begin to connect more with the beauty within me. As I recognise it without, it gives me space to also recognise it within. I am coming out of hard, grey intolerance, softening into my gifts: acceptance, observance, patience.

The journey: relaxing into being

All that we want
we already are:
trust,
relax
be.

Going slower into the cracks, into the portals of this reality, here-now, I feel rays of hope shine out through me, softening my angst of life. It feels like watching Easter flowers burst out into a new, fresh, ever changing world. Suddenly the wisdom of a dearly loved lecturer springs into my mind. He said it is our duty to Spirit to admire It, to appreciate It, to give space for Its beauty to emanate. 'How much can you allow of this moment in?' Mauricio says standing on the shining pavement, 'Can you allow yourself to feel you are good enough for it? Can you allow the moment itself to be good enough?'

I look around, his words help me leave my grey fears behind if only for this very moment and I realise in a magical sort of relief, as a softness enters my heart, that actually, everything really is OK. Really it is. I feel so alive stood on the sparkling pavement, soft grey turning into silver, rays of brave sunlight captured in the glass of shop windows. I hear him, and stood there in the drizzle, a space opens. I suddenly notice where I am and bask in the privacy of the sweet silence of this normally so public place realising how wonderful it is that people have stayed indoors away from the weather.

I turn to him and realise what deep friendship I have with this man. I accept it by recognising it. I appreciate it. I notice it. I am not looking for anything else right now. For this heady moment stretching into me, I don't need anything else other than what is. This right here, this right now, standing in the soft drizzle, looking bravely into the eyes of another human being as we meet in this thing called being alive.

It is enough, really; it is really, really enough. He is. I am. It is.

I let myself feel.

I let it enter into me.

I let myself free.

Good enough

And suddenly
I realise:
I need not be more.

THE END

THE BEGINNING

About the Author

Julia Robinson has spent her life out of the box, hitchhiking around the world, floating down the Amazon in a self-made raft, selling roasted chickens in Argentina, working at an orphanage in Nepal, studying Jungian psychology in Catalonia, going to art school in Greece, writing and dancing in Colorado. Now back in her native England, she expresses the breadth of her experience in her poetry and writings. She has written this book around her poems, to give them context and accessibility.

She presently lives in Totnes, Devon and is gently, slowly, allowing a new adventure to enter into her heart. Who knows where it will lead...?

If you would like to read more poems, blogs and whirling words by Julia, or alternatively if you would like to contact and share your ideas, opinions or spotting of a glaring error, please go to:

www.on-intimacy.com

List of Illustrations

Front cover

THE POINT OF NO RETURN, with kind and inspiringly open permission from the artist Tatyana Druz. She states, 'My camera is the way to share what I see, and not what should be seen.'

Back cover

AUTHOR IN HER HOME ON PAROS, photograph copyright John D.C. Masters, all rights reserved, 2013.

18+ sign designed by Freepik from Flaticon.

Chapter Illustrations

1. THE FOOL (1909) Pamela Coleman Smith, Tarot Card from Rider-Waite tarot deck. Not under copyright.

2. FLAMMARION ENGRAVING (1888). Unknown Artist. 'A medieval missionary tells that he has found the point where heaven and Earth meet...' Public Domain. Recoloured by Heikenwaelder Hugo (CC BY-SA 2.5)

3. VIBRATION. Unknown Artist. CC0 Public Domain sourced from pixabay.com.

4. UNTITLED PHOTO by Valeria Boltneva. CC0 Public Domain sourced from pexels.com

5. THE SLEEP OF THE BELOVED XXXVIII by Paul Maria Schneggenburger. With wonderfully kind courtesy from The Galerie Johannes Faber

6. MLLE URQUHART (1880s). Unknown photographer. Public Domain.

7. BIRD IN CAGE. CC0 Public Domain sourced from pexels.com

8. DONUT BOKEH: IMAGE DETAIL OF POINT LIGHT SOURCES PROVIDED BY A CATADIPOTRIC LENS (2007) by Jean-Jacques Milan. Permission granted under the GNU Free Documentation License, Version 1.2 and the Creative Commons Attribution-Share Alike 3.0 Unported license.

9. KISSING THE FROG. Alexas Fotos. CC0 Public Domain sourced from pexels.com

10. ALTEREGO (ca 1920) by Erzsébet Korb. Public Domain. Wikimedia Commons.

11. CINDERELLA Public Domain. CC0 Public Domain sourced from Pixabay.com

12. SLEEPING BEAUTY (1899), by Henry Meynell Rheam. Public Domain sourced from Wikimedia Commons.

13. THE FLIGHT OF ICARUS (between 1635 and 1637) by Jacob Peter Gowy. Public Domain sourced from Wikimedia Commons

14. SUN CORONA MAGNIFICENT CME (CORONAL MASS EJECTION) (August 31, 2012). NASA. National Space Science Data Center. Creative Commons Attribution 2.0 Generic.

15. ECHO AND NARCISSUS (1903) by John William Waterhouse. Public Domain sourced from Wikimedia Commons.

16. DEATH AND LIFE (1910/15) by Gustav Klimt. Public Domain sourced from Wikimedia Commons.

17. TEBO INTIMACY, drawing by Noella Roos. Creative Commons Attribution-Share Alike 3.0 Unported license.

A CRACK INTO: Untitled Photo, Sebastian Boguszewicz via Unsplash, CC0, Public Domain.

18. WALKING AT THE EDGE OF THE END OF THE WORLD, by estarsid, licensed under the Creative Commons.

19. TAKO TO AMA (1813) an erotic ukiyo-e by the Japanese artist Hokusai. Public Domain, sourced from Wikimedia Commons.

20. LIONS ON THE MASAI MARA HAVING SEX (2013) by Christopher Michel. Sourced from Wikimedia Commons, Creative Commons Attribution 2.0 Generic license.

21. REPLICATION (MODEL: LUDMILA), photograph by Tatyana Druz. With doubly generous permission from Tatyana Druz.

22. STAIRCASE SPIRAL ARCHITECTURE CC0 Public Domain sourced from pixabay.com.

NOT QUITE A CHAPTER AT ALL: PORTRAIT OF JULIA, by John Winks, with permission of artist.

23. DANDELION SEEDS FLOATING by Piccolo Namek. Creative Commons Attribution-Share Alike 3.0 Unported license.

24. LUNA (1870) by Edward Burne Jones. Wikimedia Commons. Public Domain.

25. OPHELIA (DETAIL) (c. 1851) by John Everett Millais. Public Domain sourced from Wikimedia Commons.

26. FOUNTAINE (1917) The original Fountain by Marcel Duchamp photographed by Alfred Stieglitz at the 291 (Art Gallery) after the 1917 Society of Independent

Artists exhibit. Public Domain sourced from Wikimedia Commons.

27. ANDROMEDA GALAXY IN ULTRAVIOLET (21 Feb 2008). Courtesy of SOHO/GALEX consortium. SOHO is a project of international cooperation between ESA and NASA.

28. FUNERARY STELE OF THRASEA AND EUANDRIA Marble. (ca. 375-350 BC). Antikensammlung Berlin, 738. Photo taken by Marcus Cyron. Multi-license with GFDL and Creative Commons sourced from Wikimedia Commons.

29. RITA HAYWORTH AND JACK COLE (1945). Life magazine, Volume 18, Number 7 (page 110). Promotional still from the film Tonight and Every Night. Public Domain sourced from Wikimedia Commons.

30. THE ALCHEMICAL TREE OF LIFE STANDING UNDER THE INFLUENCE OF THE HEAVENS, 'AVRE POTABILIS PREPARATI' (17th Century) by Wolfgang Killian. Public Domain.

31. MIRRORING, PUDDLE, BLACK AND WHITE, RAIN, CC0 Public domain sourced from Pixabay.com

AUTHOR personal photograph 2012.

CC0 is the **Creative Commons License**

Footnotes

1 Thomas Merton's translation of Chuang Tzu's poem, 'In the End is My Beginning.' 250 BCE.

2 'Remember' in Spanish is 'recordar': 'Re'–again, 'Cor'–heart. To pass through the heart again.

3 I wanted a verb from oblivion. There isn't one, so I made it up.

4 Names omitted for privacy

5 Pre-Menstrual Tension (known in some countries as Pre-Menstrual Syndrome PMS)

6 When I get home I look up Trevon on the internet. It's true: he is actually world famous. Surely that's good enough?

7 V.I.T.R.I.O.L: *Visita Interiora Terrae Rectificando Invenies Occultum Lapidem* "Visit the Interior of the Earth and Rectifying (Purifying) you will Find the Hidden Stone." (The 'Hidden Stone' is what the Alchemists said instead of 'The Christ State' in order not to be persecuted.)

8 He's Scared, She's Scared: Understanding the Hidden Fears That Sabotage Your Relationships by Stephen Carter and Julia Sokol, 1997.

9 Li Shang-Yin (812?–858), written on a monastery wall.

10 Spanish etymology of Sabio (wise person) is rooted in both Saber (to know) and Saber (to taste). Sage, savant and savoury all have the same root in English.

24106366R00243

Printed in Great Britain
by Amazon